# YSEC Yearbook of Socio-Economic Constitutions

Volume 2021

The broad theme of the series revolves around the constitutional frameworks for economic activities and their interaction with the social sphere. It is this very interaction this Yearbook strives to focus on. At the same time, it is this focus which distinguishes it from other formats in the field. The reference to "constitutions" mirrors the Yearbook's ambition to contribute to a better understanding of those legal rules which provide the very foundations for our economic and social well-being within a community governed by a constitution, irrespective of whether on the local, national, regional, or global level. The Yearbook aims to, first and foremost, provide a forum for doctrinal legal treatment of the questions that various socio-economic constitutions are faced with in today's globalized context, while at the same time remain open to neighbouring disciplines to the extent that they inform the doctrinal treatment. For further information please visit https://www.ysec-yearbook.eu/.

Steffen Hindelang • Andreas Moberg
Editors

# YSEC Yearbook of Socio-Economic Constitutions 2021

## Triangulating Freedom of Speech

Springer

*Editors*
Steffen Hindelang
Uppsala University
Uppsala, Sweden

Andreas Moberg
University of Gothenburg
Gothenburg, Sweden

ISSN 2662-7124 ISSN 2662-7132 (electronic)
YSEC Yearbook of Socio-Economic Constitutions
ISBN 978-3-031-08513-0 ISBN 978-3-031-08514-7 (eBook)
https://doi.org/10.1007/978-3-031-08514-7



This Springer imprint is published by the registered company Springer Nature Switzerland AG
The registered company address is: Gewerbestrasse 11, 6330 Cham, Switzerland

# Preface

The book is the second volume of the Yearbook on Socio-Economic Constitutions. The series was launched with the ambition initiate, inspire and distribute research that highlight and analyse legal questions that arise when rules within constitutional frameworks for economic activities on local, national, regional and global levels interact with the social sphere.

Each volume of the yearbook covers a specific theme, chosen by the editors in close cooperation with the editorial board. The current issue addresses constitutional legal challenges to the freedom of speech associated with the technology shifts we keep experiencing in today's networked world. The contributors answered an open call, and the most suitable selections were chosen by the editors and the editorial board. The series also includes contributions on more general questions within the general field of socio-economic constitutional law, as well as book reviews of recent publications in the field.

In our work to achieve and maintain the highest standards possible of the research published in the series, we are very grateful to be assisted by a large number of esteemed colleagues. It is a well-known fact, sometimes not sufficiently acknowledged, that the publication of high-quality research is a collective process which would be impossible to conclude without the help of the research community. When ensuring the quality of the contributions to this volume, the editors have relied on the skill and expertise of a number of peer reviewers. We are very grateful for the work put in by (in alphabetical order) Dr. Helene Andersson, Prof. Javier Barnés, Dr. Vladimir Bastidas, Dr. Graham Butler, Dr. Adam Cygan, Prof. Diogo Feyo, Prof. Eduardo Gamero Casado, Dr Letizia lo Giacco, Prof. Xavier Groussot, Max Hjärtström, Prof. Anna Jonsson-Cornell, Prof. Anna-Sara Lind, Prof. Dr. Jörn Lüdemann, Prof Jónatas Machado, Dr. Radu Mares, Prof. Gregor Noll, Dr. Julian Nowag, Prof. Katrin Nyman-Metcalf, Dr. Juan-Pablo Pérez-León-Acevedo, Dr. Kristoffer Schollin, Prof. Mårten Schultz, Prof. Dr. Stephanie Schiedermair and Prof. Dr. Dominik Steiger. Thank you!

Uppsala, Sweden — Steffen Hindelang
Gothenburg, Sweden — Andreas Moberg

# Contents

# Introduction

**Steffen Hindelang and Andreas Moberg**

## Contents



In today's networked world, technology shifts happen faster than most people even realize. Some of these shifts have made us all potentially powerful: media powerful. We used to sit in silence in front of newspapers and TV screens and the world was explained to us by the few "who always knew what was right and wrong." Today, thanks to the Internet, social media, and Web 2.0, we can not only share our own thoughts with everyone in a more self-determined way, but we can also take part in public debate and even co-organize it ourselves. Of course, the Internet is not *the* counter-draft to the communication (power) structures of the past. Gains in communicative self-determination are threatened due to algorithmization, platformization, and value extraction from self-created private markets in data capitalism. However, there is arguably more *potential* for self-determination in the technology relating to the Internet, social media, and Web 2.0 when it comes to mass communication by individuals than there has ever been before with "old media."

The empowerment of the individual challenges the old "grand speakers" who are suddenly detecting "fake news," echo chambers, and filter bubbles everywhere on the Internet. Internet-based communication allegedly hinders us from the "one truth"; as if newspaper hoaxes, propaganda, and narrow-mindedness were an invention of the Internet. The current heated debate about "fake news," copyright, and "upload filters" shows that we are unsure of how to deal with the newer and more

S. Hindelang (✉)
Uppsala University, Uppsala, Sweden
e-mail: mail@steffenhindelang.de

A. Moberg
University of Gothenburg, Gothenburg, Sweden
e-mail: andreas.moberg@law.gu.se

 
S. Hindelang, A. Moberg (eds.), *YSEC Yearbook of Socio-Economic Constitutions 2021*, YSEC Yearbook of Socio-Economic Constitutions (2022) 2021: 1–4,
https://doi.org/10.1007/16495_2022_43, Published online: 27 May 2022

complex phenomena of Internet-based speech. In no small part is this because an important benchmark—our constitutional compass—is still strongly rooted in the past. Constitutions change at a significantly lower speed than technology. Societal changes pull constitutional changes; but what about normative content control?

Already there are demands for "old-times clarity": truth filters on social media platforms, horrendous sums of liability for platforms that encourage (over-)thorough cleaning up and, if some had their way, ideally an "Internet truth advisory board." However, it is equally true that private individuals "regulate": they decide what is found on the Internet and who may post on a platform. Accounting for all interests at play and to strike a "fair" balance avoiding both a public or private care curate by over- or under regulation is a complex matter. The authors of this volume do not only provide reflections in their highly topical contributions, but also suggest their understanding of what accounts to a "fair balance" within the larger frame of freedom of speech in a digital age.

## 1 Constitutional Challenges Protecting the Freedom of Speech After the Technology Shift

The first three chapters in this volume tackle questions related to constitutional challenges caused by technology shift as such. In the first chapter, Francisco Ballaguer Callejón identifies a shift in how information and data is handled online. He conceptualizes the role of large technology companies as "the new mediators," controlling and constraining access to data and information online, which allows them to reconfigure the public sphere in democratic systems. Control of freedom of speech online can be turned into a marketable product. The chapter engages in various ways that law could be used to moderate the impact of the "new mediators" on a shared social perception of reality. In the second chapter, Anna Aurora Wennäkoski explores how the technology shift has turned, regulating the protection of freedom of speech into a regional or even global matter, and how constitutional theory is sometimes found lacking when trying to keep up. In her article, she analyzes attempts to control and protect the freedom of speech via regulation of the digital sphere at the EU level, and finds that the matters may well require common efforts at the level of constitutional law to ensure the sustainable protection of the freedom of speech. In the final chapter of the first subsection of the volume, Kári Hólmar Ragnarsson analyzes how the freedom of expression has been dealt with in three recent constitutional reform processes. According to Ragnarsson, the potential problems associated with Internet speech have been severely overlooked and, thus, been neglected while positive aspects of the same notion were granted constitutional protection. The chapter shows how the complex situation, also addressed by Wennäkoski, where constitutional protection of a global phenomenon is treated within the traditional paradigm of the sovereign nation state led the constitutional reformers to shun an opportunity to reinvent the protection of the freedom of speech.

## 2 Regulating Freedom of Speech After the Technology Shift

The four chapters in this part explore selected features of technology that pose challenges to the current conceptualizations of the freedom of speech. In the first of these, Katja de Vries analyses the legal context of "speaking machines." By posing the question "can machine learning (ML) be a source of speech that is protected by the right to freedom of expression in Article 10 ECHR?" Katja de Vries pushes the limits of our current conceptual legal framework. De Vries takes the starting point that there is no good reason why ideas generated by non-humans are less important to protect since they could equally well contribute to free exchange of ideas as speech and ideas generated by humans. In her chapter,[1] Katja de Vries presents two "normative grey zones for freedom of expression" of "speaking machines"—ML-generated child pornography and ML-generated fake news—to discuss the complicated balancing act required in case protection were also to be given to non-human utterances.

In the second chapter of the second section, Sten Schaumburg-Müller highlights that the obligations following from case law from the European Court of Human Rights on how to balance the freedom of expression and the protection of private life is difficult to apply directly to the companies who run online platforms, since the international conventions bind states, and not private entities. Turning to alternative norm systems, Schaumburg-Müller analyzes the potential impact of the United Nations Guiding Principles to Business and Human Rights, particularly in the context of Facebook. As the platform has established an Oversight Board and committed to the UN Guiding Principles, Schaumburg-Müller considers what consequences, if any, such an approach will have for the protection private life and the freedom of expression in the digital era.

The third chapter of this section is written by Berdien B.E. van der Donk and it is about freedom of speech in relation to online platforms, such as Facebook. Van der Donk does not take the mainstream approach discussing the corporation's responsibility in relation to what the users say or do. Instead, it puts its focus on the rights of the platform owners to set the rules, the so-called house rules it wants to enforce vis-à-vis its users. In her chapter, she discusses to what extent the freedom to conduct a business and the right to property are available as legal protection for these actors against interference with a possible right to draft their own house rules. The chapter provides an in-depth analysis of the Court of Justice of the European Union's caselaw interpreting Articles 16 and 17 of the European Convention on Human Rights in relation to the legal position of platforms and suggests an answer to the

[1] Editors' note: we guarantee that the chapter is written by Katja de Vries and not by GPT-3.

question of whether and in which way the contractual freedom of platforms may be restricted.

In the fourth and final chapter of the second subsection of the volume, Dmitry Kurnosov returns to the Roman poet Juvenal's question "*quis custodiet ipsos custodes*?" In Kurnosov's version, the gate keepers are the private actors controlling the digital infrastructure, which means that they de facto control many people's possibility to practice freedom of expression. In an approach similar to the one applied by van der Donk in the previous chapter, Kurnosov places the major platforms in a position between government and the individual, where they seem to have been given a specific role. This is perhaps especially so in the particular case of political election campaigns, which is the focus of Kurnosov's chapter. He points out that the on-going trend of securitization of elections has led to the major platforms developing election related policies, and that these standards may or may not comply with internationally recognized standards of free elections.

## 3 Indirect Regulation for the Protection of the Freedom of Speech

The volume's third part consists of two chapters focusing on how technology shifts have created some sort of spill-over effects that pose new challenges in legal fields not regularly associated with freedom of speech. In the first of these chapters, Jan Polański investigates the potential of antitrust law to enhance the possibilities to protect freedom of speech. As Polański shows in his chapter, the historical links between antitrust and political values are strong, especially when studied in a comparative political perspective. With examples from the US political history, the chapter argues that the links between antitrust regulation and freedom of speech is closer than most would assume. In his chapter, Polański applies a comparative approach, where the regulatory frameworks of antitrust and freedom of speech in the USA are compared with the legal context in the EU. He arrives at a pragmatic proposal on the potential use of EU competition law for the specific purpose of protecting freedom of speech.

In the final chapter of both the section and the volume, Ondřej Svoboda explores how the regulation of export control may or may not contribute to the societal interests of protecting freedom of speech and the right to privacy. Svoboda argues that the technological advancements that present the opportunity to almost effortlessly express ideas on a global scale also provide surveillance opportunities that were previously only thought of in dystopian science fiction novels. In the chapter, Svoboda carries out an analysis of existing regulation of trade in surveillance equipment on both the global level and the regional (EU) level and uses it as a backdrop to discuss current efforts to regulate the use of such equipment in the light of individual rights protection.

# Part I
# Constitutional Challenges Protecting the Freedom of Speech After the Technology Shift

# The Impact of the New Mediators of the Digital Age on Freedom of Speech

**Francisco Balaguer Callejón**

## Contents



**Abstract** New technologies have had an impact that is both positive and negative on freedom of speech, constitutional rights and democratic processes. It was positive in the early stages of the development of the Internet and particularly in the early stages of Web 2.0, when the Internet was designed in a more participative and cooperative manner. In recent years, nevertheless, hierarchical processes of information and data organisation have appeared through large technological companies that monopolise the distribution of information and opinion and which are the new mediators between users and the public sphere. Freedom of speech is currently constrained by these mediators, namely large technological companies that control the communicative processes. This paper analyses the role that these new mediators are developing, taking into account their impact on freedom of speech and on the configuration of the public sphere in democratic systems.

Two elements stand out among the new mediators: the dialectic of freedom of speech is shifting from the public to the private sphere and from the state to the global sphere. These are two elements that together help fuel the power of the new mediators and weaken the state's capacity for regulation and control. But in the ecosystems developed by technology companies, the new mediators exercise a

F. Balaguer Callejón (✉)
Department of Constitutional Law, University of Granada, Granada, Spain
e-mail: balaguer@ugr.es

 
S. Hindelang, A. Moberg (eds.), *YSEC Yearbook of Socio-Economic Constitutions 2021*, YSEC Yearbook of Socio-Economic Constitutions (2022) 2021: 7–32,
https://doi.org/10.1007/16495_2021_32, Published online: 10 April 2022

power that is not strictly private since they occupy and monopolise a public sphere. In the environment created by the new mediators, freedom of expression becomes a mere commercial product, so that information and opinion are transformed into ephemeral merchandise organised through the algorithms of Internet applications, which decide their impact on and their incidence in the public sphere.

These algorithms have been created with an economic purpose and promote fake news and radicalisation to attract the attention of the public and thus generate greater profit. The new mediators, by promoting fake news in democratic contexts (without trying to impose a specific narrative, as in dictatorial ones), generate a destructive tension about reality. Instead of contributing like the traditional media does to the social construction of reality or as in dictatorships to the reconstruction of reality based on the interests of the dominant oligarchy, they are causing the "destruction" of reality, that is, of a shared social perception of reality.

Among the many measures that can be adopted, those related to competition law stand out, with institutional measures through regulators that may avert an even greater concentration of power. However, rather than restrictions, it is openness that is desirable—open technology that puts an end to the closed-off, hierarchical nature of applications. Telephone communication, for example, is open and allows mobile phone operators to operate, making global communication possible, and the same is true for e-mail servers. Communication applications that are currently closed-off (WhatsApp and Telegram, for example) should also be open, intercommunicable and managed by a plurality of operators.

## 1 Introduction

The 2016 US presidential elections would be the starting point for an in-depth review of the role of social networks and technology companies in communication processes and the organisation of the public sphere. The Cambridge Analytica scandal was also to be a decisive factor in revealing the line of continuity between previous processes (such as the Brexit referendum in the United Kingdom) and subsequent ones (like the presidential elections in Brazil). It is a line of continuity involving the activity of large technological companies, essentially Facebook, through its applications.[1]

[1]Cf. Balaguer Callejón (2019): https://www.ugr.es/~redce/REDCE32/articulos/04_F_BALAGUER.htm.

Italian version: Francisco Balaguer Callejón, "Social network, società tecnologiche e democrazia" *Nomos | Le attualità nel diritto*, n. 3, 2019: http://www.nomos-leattualitaneldiritto.it/wp-content/uploads/2020/02/Callejon-3-2019-ver.pdf Portuguese version: Francisco Balaguer Callejón, "Redes sociais, companhias tecnológicas e democracia", *Revista Estudos Institucionais*, v. 6, n. 2, maio/ago. 2020: https://www.estudosinstitucionais.com/REI/article/view/485.

The presidency of Donald Trump has brought about a great many studies carried out in recent years because the trauma did not end with the presidential election but lasted for 4 years and led to another traumatic event: the assault on the Capitol and the outgoing president's threat to the very heart of democracy and the United States Constitution. A threat that it was possible to avert thanks to the powerful identification with the Constitution held by electoral officials (including those in states governed by the Republican Party), the courts (even the Supreme Court, despite its conservative majority), large corporations and even—at least publicly—the technology companies themselves.

It is too early to assess the true extent of the impact that the assault on the Capitol has had on the future of American politics. In the academic sphere, however, it will again foster studies on these issues since the danger of democratic involution is still present, as evidenced by the fact that conspiracy theories have penetrated so deeply among many Republican voters and most of their representatives. The assault on the Capitol has not been the end of the road for this Dantesque development in the United States' politics, nor has the technology companies' attitude been clear enough to ensure there will be no new threats to democracy and the Constitution. As we shall see below, the example of Facebook is clear: although it prevented Trump from using its applications, with its algorithms, it effectively helped to spread the Trumpist stances that led to the assault on the Capitol.[2]

This shows us the two facets of the new mediators of the digital age when it comes to freedom of speech. On the one hand, there is their ability to restrict freedom of speech to the point that they can prevent the President of the United States himself—the highest political authority of the nation where their head offices are based (even though it was the outgoing president who up until then had been allowed to use the same type of discourse based on fake news, alternative realities, insults to rivals, threats, etc.[3])—from using their apps. On the other hand, there is the capacity of these mediators, instead of contributing to democratic debate and the expression of pluralism, to generate an environment in which freedom of speech becomes something quite different—an instrument for aggression and radicalisation, which can end up being turned into concrete political actions, be it votes in an election or an assault on democratic institutions.

Both facets imply an extraordinary, unprecedented ability to shape the narrative of reality. In democratic countries, the traditional media try to influence the prevailing narrative by contributing to the social *construction of reality*. In dictatorial regimes, one can speak of a *reconstruction of reality* tailored to the interests of the dictator or the dominant oligarchy. However, in the new communication context of democratic countries, of which Trumpism has provided a paradigmatic example, it is evolving towards the *destruction of reality*, that is, of a shared social perception of

---

[2] See Sect. 5.

[3] Accumulating no less than 30,573 false or misleading claims in his 4 years in office, according to the verification work carried out by the Washington Post.

Cf. https://www.youtube.com/watch?v=Jq5kLbR79Pg, 24 January 2021.

reality. Pressured by a business model based on the permanent use of their applications, forcing them to constantly attract the public's attention, the new mediators create algorithms that organise the communication processes within their applications, with a very destructive impact on the public sphere.

From the point of view of democracy and constitutional values, this is not creative destruction, contrary to what some authors claim.[4] There is no creativity whatsoever because the new mediators do not have the least interest in democracy as such (not even to destroy it, granted) since their aims are essentially economic, attempting to gain the greatest possible profit. Nor is there, a priori, any specific interest in promoting a concrete political alternative in their general activity. Their applications are not designed for ideological reasons to censor discourses expressed by different political trends in the democratic countries where they are present. If they indirectly favour populism with their algorithms or directly encourage it in electoral processes, it is not because the new mediators have a political interest in a specific option; rather, it is simply a reflection of their economic interest. It is the search for economic profit that leads them to promote the tension and radicalisation that are at the root of the growth of populism or that has made them favour these options in some countries' electoral processes.

The political gridlock that has been brought about in countries where these populist options have triumphed also favours them and enables them to obtain greater revenue, but it cannot be said that this has been a conscious political choice. Naturally, when politics is gridlocked, the possibilities of government control diminish, which also favours them. This is something that perhaps they were able to intuit before the United States presidential elections in 2016, but there were certainly other factors, essentially economic ones, that led them to go for the Trumpist option and not a prior assessment of their possible political interests.

In any case, the new mediators' promotion of Trumpism (despite their eventual veto of the outgoing Trump) clearly shows their scant respect for constitutional and democratic principles in their applications' environment. As Shoshana Zuboff points out, some tech companies like Facebook have helped weaken the foundations of tolerant coexistence, which were grounded in a shared common sense based on trust in norms.[5]

Technology companies have built a business model that places them in a paradoxical situation: on the one hand, they try to project a clean image to the public that is consistent with constitutional and democratic values. In this way, they try to counteract the poor image generated by their irresponsible behaviour in other areas, especially interference in politics, most notably by Facebook. However, on the other

---

[4]Nielsen and Fletcher (2020).

[5]"Society renews itself as common sense evolves. This requires trustworthy, transparent, respectful institutions of social discourse, especially when we disagree. Instead, we are saddled with the opposite, nearly 20 years into a world dominated by a political-economic institution that operates as a chaos machine for hire, in which norm violation is key to revenue" Shoshana Zuboff "The Coup We Are Not Talking About", *The New York Times*, 29 January 2021, p. 8: https://www.nytimes.com/2021/01/29/opinion/sunday/facebook-surveillance-society-technology.html.

hand, they do not want to give up the use of algorithms that allow them to obtain higher revenues, despite the serious social problems they are causing.

With the health crisis, we have seen the same thing: these companies' policy as regards their image projects the idea of collaborating to prevent the spread of fake news and conspiracy theories that harm the fight against the pandemic.[6] However, the pre-existing structural problems have to do with the business model they have built and with the design of their algorithms. For this reason, the one-off measures they take, either to prevent excessive damage to their public image or because they truly wish to avoid the most serious consequences of their intervention in communication processes, do not go to the heart of the problems.[7]

This paradoxical situation inevitably affects freedom of speech because it generates an environment in which fake news and alternative realities get promoted since they favour this business model. It is a question not of inefficient control or moral incapability to differentiate falsehoods from truth but of specific interest in promoting falsehoods. They do not do so out of a specific political motivation (as in dictatorial systems) to impose a specific narrative. This "destruction" of reality has nothing to do with the imposition of an "alternative reality", just as the "destruction" of politics has nothing to do with an alternative political proposal.

We could say that what the new mediators of the digital era are promoting is essentially instability and insecurity. Fake news coexists and competes with real news but does not replace it in favour of a concrete narrative that imposes itself in the public sphere. The "alternative reality" coexists with the "real" reality, but in a democratic context it does not replace it. Both narratives compete, and occasionally one of them may impose itself on the other in a public debate or in the convictions of the governing majorities that take shape. However, an interest in distorting reality, transforming it and generating narratives that favour a specific political option is significantly different from an absolute disinterest in reality or any type of narrative and its possible usefulness in favour of a political option.

[6] "Medical disinformation spread on social media, with false claims about the origins and spread of the virus and quack cures to address it gaining significant audiences. The platforms responded with dramatic and unprecedented measures: aggressive filtering of content deemed problematic, promotion of content from respected (particularly governmental) sources, and dedicated portions of their websites to assist in providing accurate information and assisting in logistics related to the pandemic response. In many respects, it seemed like the platforms had found a path to redemption from the backlash of 2016", Persily and Tucker (2020), pp. XV–XVI.

[7] The concern about disinformation in health matters promoted by social networks is great. At the European level, for example, the *Communication from the Commission to the European Parliament, the European Council and the Council on additional COVID-19 response measures* says: "Every effort should be made to ensure that targeted communication reaches segments of the population that are most vulnerable and those most likely to spread the disease through social interaction. It needs to be clear, consistent and up-to date. Special attention needs to be paid to social media monitoring and response. Vaccination is a specific area where public authorities need to step up their actions to tackle misinformation as a main cause of hesitancy and coordinate on disinformation response", *Communication from the Commission to the European Parliament, the European Council and the Council on additional COVID-19 response measures*, 28 October 2020, pp. 5–6.

We can see this difference between the old mediators and the new ones of the digital age. The traditional media constructed narratives that could be attributed, to a greater or lesser extent, to political tendencies, though not necessarily to partisan options. Thus, they participated in the social construction of reality. The new mediators, however, do not build narratives but rather open up the platforms to all possible narratives, even though they privilege (through their algorithms) those that promote fake news and alternative realities. They do not reflect the reality of the societies in which they act, nor do they operate as representative platforms for freedom of speech. On the contrary, by promoting falsified news and alternative realities, they generate tension regarding reality itself, which has great destructive potential.

This paper analyses the impact of these new mediators of the digital age on freedom of speech. It should be noted that it is an analysis that will follow an essentially constitutional approach. It is necessary to note this because, in recent years, many studies have been carried out on technological companies, their impact on the public sphere and their relationship with democracy and constitutional rights, in particular regarding freedom of speech. In such a complex reality involving a large number of variables, all contributions that can shed light through different disciplines must be considered in the analysis. This is not a normative reality that can be analysed only from legal and constitutional perspectives.

But the constitutional perspective has its own requirements that must be considered, unlike those of other disciplines. For example, a sociological approach can address issues related to this topic from the point of view of the effectiveness of disinformation campaigns.[8] This approach is useful for sociology but not so for constitutional law because the attempt to interfere in an electoral process by manipulating it is against the law, regardless of whether or not it achieves its result.

The same is true when matters related to the impairment of democracy are approached from the point of view of a prior "minimalist" conception of the meaning of democracy.[9] However respectable such an approach may be for other fields of study, in a constitutional study one cannot set out from a minimalist conception of democracy, nor can one assume the idea that the process itself is not relevant to the outcome. Democracy is a process, and the cleanliness of democratic processes cannot be contingent upon its outcome.

Constitutional analysis is related to norms, principles and values that serve as control parameters. Functional analysis in other disciplines may be based on different criteria, however. For example, a specific provision for the internal control of a

---

[8]Cf. Hwang (2020), pp. 257 and seq. As indicated by this author, regardless of whether they are effective, these campaigns pose threats to the health of democratic processes and can accelerate the erosion of trust in institutions that are essential to preserving democracy, among other negative effects.

[9]For instance, Rasmus Kleis Nielsen and Richard Fletcher, "a fairly minimal conception of democracy as liberal, representative, and based on relatively diverse and inclusive elite competition that offers a basic structure for making and implementing political decisions but no guarantee that these decisions will be *good* ones". Nielsen and Fletcher (2020), p. 156.

private company may be seen as a positive step within that functional analysis compared to a previous situation of lack of control. For constitutional analysis, the logic is different because private internal control (for example, Facebook's "supreme court") cannot replace independent public control. Its private nature is the very essence of the problem posed at the constitutional level. Moreover, constitutional analysis must consider the nature of the processes and not only the outcomes.

It is the absence of normative points of reference that also makes it difficult for other disciplines to understand the critical nature of legal-constitutional studies. A constitutional study can only balance out such criticism to a certain extent because the assessment it makes must always take into account the existence of previous parameters that have to do with essential values such as democracy or fundamental rights. The impact on these values cannot be balanced out by measures that may be positive for other disciplines but that do not affect the essence of the constitutional problems that arise and do not represent a real way of solving these problems.

This is not to say that the differences between constitutional systems should not be recognised, and particularly the differences between the concept of freedom of speech and the evaluation of the role of the new mediators in the United States and Europe. But these differences are not an obstacle to a specific constitutional approach to the matter because the rules of cleanliness in electoral processes, compliance with constitutional norms and respect for fundamental rights are all similar.

The data we use are the same in different disciplines, but the approach is different. For sociology, the actual impact of certain practices is more relevant than their legal or constitutional legitimacy. For economics, competition has different implications than it does for constitutional law. For us, its effect on the economy is not so important, but we must take into account the consequences that competition may have on freedom of speech and pluralism so that the incorporation of these data is instrumental as regards the purpose of our research.

## 2 The Context of Freedom of Speech in the Digital Society

Web 2.0 generated great expectations of democratic participation via the Internet, which manifested itself in an expansion of the public sphere and communication processes into the virtual realm. The network was then able to play a significant role in defending just causes worldwide and even in fostering processes of democratic transformation of authoritarian regimes. However, its evolution over recent years has been very negative. Communication and participation channels have been concentrated in a monopolistic way into the hands of a few global companies[10] with an

[10] Jason Furman and others (2019), p. 11: "The largest digital companies have made extensive use of mergers, as their market shares have grown. Acquisitions have included buying businesses that could have become competitors to the acquiring company (for example Facebook's acquisition of

economic interest focusing on two areas: advertising[11] and the accumulation of users' personal data, which are subsequently used as merchandise.[12] To favour their business model, these companies promote ever-increasing user activity in their applications, which forces them to design them with the aim of attracting and keeping their attention. In terms of freedom of speech, this commercial orientation leads them to design their algorithms to promote the most aggressive discourses, based on falsified news. Of course, this does not mean that these companies do not also make positive contributions to the construction of a common public sphere, or that they all act in the same way. But the trends in recent years have been very negative, especially in some specific cases, generating great social and political concerns.

In the context of analogical communication, the news used to occupy an essential place. This was especially true with the written press, where readers' motivation focused precisely on the news, which captured their attention, and the advertising market was also oriented in this direction. As Nielsen and Fletcher point out, this situation is undergoing a major transformation with the new Internet platforms, where the news occupies a very minor role compared to other services offered, such as messaging, searches, social media, etc. It is these platforms that are monopolising the resources of the advertising market[13] by offering personalised advertising on a large scale via the extraction of user data.[14]

---

Instagram), businesses that have given a platform a strong position in a related market (for example Google's acquisition of DoubleClick, the advertising technology business), and data-driven businesses in related markets which may cement the acquirer's strong position in both markets (Google/YouTube, Facebook/WhatsApp)".

https://assets.publishing.service.gov.uk/government/uploads/system/uploads/attachment_data/file/785547/unlocking_digital_competition_furman_review_web.pdf.

[11] While Facebook bought Instagram for 1,000 million dollars in 2012, in 2014 it paid no less than 19,000 million dollars for WhatsApp without the latter company, according to *The Economist,* despite the enormous price that Facebook has paid for it, generate income. Although the text does not pronounce the possible reasons, it seems clear that the economic motivation, not being in advertising, must be based on some other interest for Facebook, and it is not difficult to imagine what that interest is. Cf. "Dismembering Big Tech", *The Economist*, Oct. 24th, 2019 edition: https://www.economist.com/business/2019/10/24/dismembering-big-tech.

[12] Cf. House of Commons, Digital, Culture, Media and Sport Committee, DCMS. *Disinformation and 'fake news': Final Report*, Published on 18 February 2019 by authority of the House of Commons, pp. 26 and seq.

https://publications.parliament.uk/pa/cm201719/cmselect/cmcumeds/1791/1791.pdf.

[13] "In the United States alone, from 2008 to 2017, newspapers lost more than $20 billion in print advertising, close to half of total industry revenues, and cut newsroom employment by 45%", Nielsen and Fletcher (2020), p. 145.

[14] Cf. Nielsen and Fletcher (2020), pp. 143 y ss. For these authors, "This is an epochal shift on how news is distributed and curated. Direct discovery has been a defining feature of the mass media environment in the twentieth century, but the twenty-first-century digital media environment is increasingly defined by algorithmically based forms of personalization, as people rely on products and services like search engines and social media that do not create content but help users discover content", Ibídem, p. 150.

From that perspective, for the new mediators, news and freedom of speech as such are nothing more than data within their business model. Unlike traditional mediators, which draft part of the news themselves and produce a significant amount of the information they transmit, these new mediators use the news prepared by traditional media like any other content processed by their algorithms. For them, it is data they give to the users of their services, just like any other services they give: a recommendation to purchase a product, an image, a video, a comment or a rating through "likes".

This also partly explains why, as Shoshana Zuboff points out, these companies are not particularly interested in the truth or facts, because for them truth and lies are equivalent: it is simply data they consume voraciously: "asking a surveillance extractor to reject content is like asking a coal-mining operation to discard containers of coal because it's too dirty".[15]

But neither can it be said that this disinterest manifests itself in a "neutral" stance regarding freedom of speech or fake news. In fact, their algorithms boost lies and content that can generate greater debate and interest among the public. Indeed, technology companies are the new mediators of the communication processes, and this function of mediation is carried out by means of artificial intelligence through algorithms essentially aimed at increasing their profits and not at favouring the public, democratic participation of citizens in these processes. Therefore, disregard for the truth has a lot to do with their business model, and it is difficult to change this without altering that business model.

An additional problem that arises in today's digital society is that traditional media[16] tend to mimic the new mediators to compete with them and thus gain better options in the advertising market. This is an approach that will not allow the balance with the new mediators to be rebuilt if we consider that these media cannot handle the volume of data that technology companies have at their disposal, nor can they process it to build user profiles with the same precision. It is also a destructive approach because it transforms media that have traditionally taken care of information and opinion in a more serious, meticulous way by making them introduce more and more frivolous and superficial content.

The consideration of information and opinion as a commercial product is not exclusive to the new mediators. Traditional media have also been working in a commercial context in accordance with certain ideological orientations, seeking to connect with a similar public for the precise aim of obtaining an echo or at least generating an impact on that public. The new mediators, however, restrict themselves to distributing information or opinion in accordance with the allocation processes carried out by their algorithms. Freedom of speech no longer has any substantial meaning because opinion is just another product within an ecosystem

[15] Zuboff (2021), p. 4.

[16] Which are currently experiencing a deep crisis, Cf. *The Cairncross Review. A sustainable future for journalism*, 12 February 2019.

driven by algorithms according to the new mediators' economic interests and business model.

In short, the current context of freedom of speech has undergone a problematic transformation from the constitutional point of view because it has turned this right into a mere commercial product that can be economically evaluated in terms of its results yet has nothing to do with forming the plural public opinions typical of a democratic system. This transformation is related to the surge of new mediators that are taking up practically the entire space for information and opinion, displacing traditional media. It is true that there are also positive aspects that can be pointed out from different perspectives, including the constitutional one, but the technological platforms have broken up the balance of the early days of Web 2.0, when there were no closed-off, hierarchical applications within veritable ecosystems but only an open system based on html language, which made it possible to exercise freedom of speech without constraints arising from the internal workings of applications via algorithms.

Although the idea of participation has placed the new communication systems in juxtaposition to the traditional media since the development of Web 2.0, the truth is that the new systems not only offer less real participation but also make it possible for technology companies to penetrate further into users' opinions. Thus, instead of promoting citizens' expression of free opinions, what these platforms have ended up doing is inducing that opinion via a hierarchical system of algorithms that direct targeted content with the capacity to influence users' conscience and decisively modulate their opinion.

The case of the blogger Hossein Derakhshan, who had about 20,000 followers when he was arrested in Iran and sentenced to several years in prison in 2008, is well known. When he was released from prison in 2014, everything had changed with the development of social networks, so he turned to Facebook with a post that got only three "likes". The reason for this impressive decrease from 20,000 to three people who followed his messages is explained by Derakhshan himself: the HTML language on which blogs were based used to be decentralised and open, unlike the Internet applications developed by technology companies: "...we have gone from a non-linear form of communication—with nodes, networks and links—to a linear, centralised and hierarchical one".[17]

Therefore, direct participation as in the early days of Web 2.0 is no longer possible because there are necessary mediators such as big technology companies that control the communication processes. Another example, which is more recent, is the blog of the Former President Donald J. Trump called "From the Desk of Donald J. Trump", which was created as an alternative to Facebook and Twitter since he was banned from both platforms. The blog lasted less than a month because the site was getting little traffic. As Trump had 88 million followers on Twitter, 32 million on

[17] Cf. Derakhshan (2015): https://verne.elpais.com/verne/2015/08/21/articulo/1440144333_222956.html.

Facebook and 24 million on Instagram, the blog reached only around 200,000 interactions.[18]

The new mediators thus have a greater ability than traditional media to influence the formation of public opinion. However, their influence is not limited to the specific content they transmit but is also related to the way in which they transmit that content, generating a change in cultural patterns that is highly relevant from the perspective of freedom of speech. Communication processes in the digital context have been designed by the new mediators with their own characteristics, which have a special impact on shaping freedom of speech.

These are non-specialised processes that are not specifically aimed at posting or receiving social and political information or opinions. On the contrary, on the platforms, the personal sphere is inevitably mixed with posting or receiving informative content, which makes it an informal process in which the language and attitudes of the participants are manifested with greater spontaneity and less reflection or preparation.

These processes are carried out with the speed typical of communication processes through the Internet, i.e. in real time. This immediacy not only enhances their informality but also helps generate attitudes and cultural and political patterns in which the perception of time changes substantially. Political processes have ended up being contaminated by this perception of time, contributing to the fact that politics is also shaped by excessive dynamism in which agendas and issues are pressured by the communication processes taking place in social networks and Internet applications.

This acceleration of historical time has come about with the third globalisation and technological development we are experiencing in the twenty-first century. The communication processes reflect and enhance it further. The outcome is a loss of value for freedom of speech, not only because of the proliferation of opinions and information generated every day on a global scale but also because of its ephemeral nature in the digital communication context. From a constitutional point of view, not only does the exercise of freedom of speech as an individual right suffer but also its contribution to the formation of free and informed public opinion.

## 3 Tech Companies as New Mediators in Communication Processes

The context of freedom of speech has undergone radical changes with the social transformations and evolution of mass media over the last 200 years. The most relevant changes have occurred in the last 20 years, in the twenty-first century, and

[18] Cf. Zadrozny (2021). In nbcnews.com: https://www.nbcnews.com/tech/tech-news/trumps-blog-isnt-lighting-internet-rcna890.

are generating new cultural patterns and new paradigms that force us to rethink the dogmatic categories that had been built up around this fundamental right.

It is now a context clearly dominated by the new mediators, the big technology companies, which have become global agents with the capacity to shape communication processes in the state and intervene in the organisation of public debate, political agendas and even electoral processes, empowering certain political parties, movements or candidates over others. Two elements stand out among the new mediators: the dialectic of freedom of speech is shifting from the public to the private sphere and from the state to the global sphere. These are two elements that together help fuel the power of the new mediators and weaken the state's capacity for regulation and control.

The tension surrounding freedom of speech is shifting to the private sphere because the new mediators are private companies. However, due to the way in which communication processes have been shaped in the digital era, these companies have occupied much of the public sphere, providing services via a monopoly or oligopoly. This makes it necessary to rethink the categories of public and private in relation to the exercise of freedom of speech. The dialectic of freedom of information and opinion no longer manifests itself in the tension between the media and the public power that could restrict that freedom. On the contrary, the occupation of the public communication space by the new mediators through private channels gives them a broad decision-making capacity over freedom of speech.[19] The tension surrounding freedom of speech in communication processes is now being formed around the new mediators and cannot be assessed from the exclusive perspective of private law. This is a clear example of how the constitutional analysis encounters problems of principle that cannot be resolved from a functional perspective (for example, through the internal control carried out by the new mediators with instruments of private law).

Unlike traditional media, which essentially offered information to the public through a static procedure in which each individual had the ability to select his or her own information sources, digital platforms have some characteristics that have proven to be problematic, not least because they feed on and reinforce each other:

- Firstly, the platforms generate an ecosystem in which users can occupy much of their time, sometimes not only for leisure but also for work, due to the variety of services that these platforms offer: communication systems through voice or e-mail, entertainment through audiovisual content, information through search systems, virtual work through a connection between different users, etc.

[19] "National constitutions and human rights laws protect internet users from *state* interference with their legal exercise of speech rights, but platforms are generally free to ban any speech they want; and, because Community Guidelines are privately defined and enforced, platforms' decisions are generally not subject to review by courts", Keller and Leerssen (2020), p. 226. Moreover, as indicated by Josu De Miguel "Los prestadores de servicios no están en condiciones de ponderar derechos y bienes jurídicos adecuadamente, porque se rigen por las reglas de mercado", De Miguel (2016), p. 159.

- The platforms do not simply offer all these services; they offer them at no cost to the user. In return, they extract data from all the activity carried out on the Internet by these users, which they then make profitable through advertising and which they also use to personalise the services they offer.
- Among these services, there is also the distribution of news (also personalised), which will now no longer be actively selected by users but will be provided to them according to their search and reading histories in the same way as other services provided to them by the platforms, thus contributing to the so-called bubble effect.[20]

The monopolistic conditions in which the new mediators operate and the way in which they order and distribute information and opinion through algorithms mean that the ecosystem they have created ends up creating a kind of plural monism, paradoxical as the expression may seem, in which the lack of communication between different world views is ever greater. It is a pluralism of monist stances that do not recognise the others and assert themselves as the only possible ones. Such a lack of communication is not a new phenomenon; radical division has been constant in recent times in some political systems before the development of social networks and Internet applications. This is therefore not something that can be attributed exclusively to the new mediators. However, not only are the new mediators not helping to mitigate it, but they are aggravating it very intensely.

As far as information is concerned, an active, direct search for information also used to lead to selective procedures aimed at reinforcing one's own stances.[21] However, there is a fundamental difference between one process and the other: whereas in the active, direct search by users there is a conscious attitude, in the case of information distributed by platforms, its reception is passive and subject to being shaped beforehand through algorithms by these platforms. The process of separating users from social complexity and plurality is induced and controlled by the platforms, sometimes through advertising techniques or subliminal propaganda.

The ecosystem in which millions of people live who use these platforms and applications in a massive way on a daily basis is still articulated on the basis of private law through individual contracts.[22] However, the technology companies with which they enter into a contract exercise a power that is not strictly private in that they occupy and monopolise the public sphere. Hence, as some authors point out, the powers they exercise are similar to governmental powers and are increasingly taking on a shape resembling a public power but with no democratic legitimacy.[23]

[20] Cf. Pariser (2011).

[21] Cf. Nielsen and Fletcher (2020), p. 151.

[22] Cf. Balaguer Callejón (2021a).

[23] "Facebook exercises government-like powers, even though it is not a government; it is a private, for-profit company largely controlled by a single individual, whose primary objective is not necessarily to serve the public interest of his political community. Facebook can try to acquire the trappings of a government, like its own internal Supreme Court or its own currency, but these

Indeed, if one were to compare any of these tech companies, such as Facebook, to previous organisations known to date, one would have to compare them to an authoritarian state in terms of the way the company delivers its services. In the Facebook environment, people who use its applications (Facebook, Instagram and WhatsApp) do not just receive news. They also communicate with other people by sending and receiving messages of different kinds; they can upload their photos and videos or their comments, whether personal or commercial; they receive commercial information about products they can buy; and they can connect with other people to hold meetings and attend or participate in conferences. Much of their life takes place through Facebook applications in a virtual context that also has a physical projection. This part of their life is conditioned and governed to a large extent by the algorithms created and used by Facebook, a company whose power to shape them corresponds to its founder and CEO.

All this activity is governed by a private contract with the conditions established by the technology company, which also has the power to decide whether to allow these people to use its applications. This decision is subject to an internal control body created by the company itself, which must apply the code of conduct approved by the company itself and whose members have also been freely appointed by the company itself. There is no transparency, no control and no accountability. There is a very important contrast between the power that this company accumulates in the public sphere through its applications and the control to which it is subjected as regards breaches of fundamental rights it may cause or the effects on electoral and democratic processes that it can generate.

These authoritarian conditions are getting stronger, increasing the power of the company to the extent that its activities are shifting from the state to the global level. The new mediators operate in global environments with hundreds of millions of users who also form global communities, albeit segmented into national environments. In a sense, these companies are like the old colonial companies, with a capacity to intervene in the politics and public sphere of many territories in which, unlike in other historical times, they no longer need to have a physical presence to exercise power and influence.[24]

One key issue is undoubtedly that of competition. The new context of freedom of speech raises the problem that the monopoly of the most widespread social media, supported by computers and a hierarchical organisation through algorithms, essentially affects the shape of political pluralism and pluralist democracy. This means that freedom of speech no longer contributes to forming a plural public opinion, precisely because of the control exercised over it by social networks and Internet applications under monopolistic conditions.

Those who do not have a democratic structure cannot contribute to democratic development, and the same applies to pluralism: monopolistic conditions cannot

---

efforts in the end do not make its behavior more democratically legitimate", Fukuyama and Grotto (2020), p. 210.

[24] Cf. Balaguer Callejón (2021b).

contribute to the development of pluralism. Free competition is to the economy what biodiversity is to nature and pluralism is to politics. We cannot have democracy without pluralism or pluralism without competition. The new mediators are affecting two essential pillars of the democratic system: pluralism at the political level and competition at the economic level.

Furthermore, there is no doubt that they are also affecting the capacity for technological innovation, making it difficult to develop new environments that can compete with the current ones. To solve these problems, institutional measures can be taken through regulators to make the further concentration of power more difficult. However, rather than restriction, it is openness that is desirable: an open technology that puts an end to the closed-off, hierarchical nature of applications. Telephone communication, for example, is open and allows all mobile phone operators to operate, making global communication possible, and the same is true for e-mail servers. Communication applications that are currently closed-off (WhatsApp or Telegram, for example) should also be open, intercommunicable and managed by a plurality of operators.

## 4 Narratives Based on False Facts or Alternative Realities

Among the many elements of tension that are being articulated around freedom of speech, the tension between freedom of opinion and freedom of information, between the news and assessment of the news, between facts and their meaning, between reality and narrative is all particularly relevant. Freedom of speech rests on freedom of information because it is linked to what human beings know about life, society, politics and the world in general. This knowledge is fed by information, which is what gives us a picture of reality. Information, however truthful it may be, is not reality but part of the social construction of reality.

The tension between freedom of opinion and freedom of information derives from the fact that the social construction of reality is a collective one, so that it is not possible to perceive facts without attribution of meaning conditioned by social and cultural contexts. This attribution of meaning is inevitable and conditions our concept of what we consider to be true, both in terms of facts and in terms of representations, ideas and world views.

For many millions of Americans, a fact as objective and incontrovertible as the outcome of an electoral process governed by pre-established rules with reliable instruments for monitoring has led to an outcome that is very different from reality. For them, the fact is that Joe Biden did not win the election but stole it from Donald Trump. Such a gross distortion of the facts is not new, but its reach and impact require a prior intention to construct a specific narrative and impose it on the public sphere.

The construction of narratives based on false facts is something that has occurred frequently in history. Indeed, like Umberto Eco, one can talk of a "force of the false" (as opposed to the force of truth), which, whether through intentional lies or genuine mistakes, has been the driving force behind many historical events.[25] Before the development of the social networks, we have seen examples of these narratives, as in the case of the war in Iraq. Much of American society was certain that the reason for that war was that the Iraqi leaders had manufactured weapons of mass destruction. It later emerged that this motive had been "fabricated" and did not correspond to reality.[26]

Even so, although disinformation generated through fake news is nothing new in history, what is new is the social networks' capacity to turn fake news into mainstream trends in democratic contexts, occupying a fundamental part of the public sphere.[27]

What is also new is the fact that this news is transmitted in an environment of privacy and even intimacy (for example, via WhatsApp), which makes it extraordinarily effective because it eliminates the distance from the sender of the message. The new mediators hide this mediating function from the users, unlike traditional media, since they carry it out within a complex ecosystem in which the news or information occupies a marginal role.

From a constitutional point of view, fake news is destroying the public sphere and altering the structural conditions for democratic processes. It favours fragmentation, radicalisation and access to power for populist movements with little respect for democratic rules.

To understand the destructive potential of fake news, we can draw on a metaphor that comes from an Arabic proverb in which truth was a mirror that fell from the sky and when it hit the earth it shattered into many pieces. Hence, each person has only a piece of the truth, a fragment of that broken mirror. Truth is not, therefore, something that can be known individually as a whole but the result of collective construction. To know the truth, we must put each of these pieces together.

This metaphor explains the meaning of pluralist democracy. It helps us see the need to consider the truths of others not as something to be excluded but as something necessary in order to know the truth in its entirety and build together a common truth based on transaction, consensus and compromise, which are fundamental elements of constitutional democracy.

[25] Cf. Eco (2003), pp. 292 and seq. For U. Eco, "il riconoscere che la nostra storia è stata mossa da molit racconti che ora riconosciamo come falsi deve renderci attenti, capaci di rimettere continuamente in questione gli stessi racconti che ora teniamo per veri, poiché il criterio della saggezza della comunità si fonda sulla vigilanza continua nei confronti della fallibilità del nostro sapere", p. 322.

[26] Some additional examples prior to the accelerated expansion of social networks: "President Obama was not born in Kenya. President Bush did not have advance notice of the September 11 attacks. The predictions of astrology have neither scientific basis nor the capacity to forecast the future. AIDS was not created by white physicians and multinational pharmaceutical companies in order to reduce the size of the African and African American populations. The Holocaust is not a myth fabricated by Zionists and their supporters." Schauer (2010), p. 897.

[27] Cf. Pitruzzella (2017).

However, in a world increasingly controlled by tech companies through social networks and Internet applications, it is these companies that now have the ability to decide which pieces of the mirror and which fragments of the truth will be present (and not) in public debates through their algorithms. Not only that, but they can also help fake news or post-truth (i.e. distorted fragments) to have a significant impact on the public sphere.

Given the monopolistic or oligopolistic conditions in which these companies operate in communication processes, Holmes' doctrine stating that the free marketplace of ideas should make it possible for the truth to impose itself seems impracticable under current conditions, if it ever made sense.[28] With the way communication processes have developed in the digital world, the new mediators have brought about an increasing fragmentation and radicalisation of the public sphere, in which different social sectors live in veritable bubbles that ignore and deny the truth of others in a continuous process of reaffirmation of their own convictions.[29]

The free marketplace of ideas was reflected in the 1980s in the United States in the criticism of media regulation, considering it unnecessary because the market itself would best serve the public interest.[30] It is a formulation that ended up generating a more pro-monopoly mentality in the traditional media insofar as it hindered the government from taking antitrust actions. Public action would have to focus on consumer welfare in terms of price and quality.[31] The result was to be a

---

[28] As indicates by F. Schauer: "Once we fathom the full scope of factors other than the truth of a proposition that might determine which propositions individuals or groups will accept and which they will reject—the charisma, authority, or persuasiveness of the speaker; the consistency between the proposition and the prior beliefs of the hearer; the consistency between the proposition and what the hearer believes that other hearers believe; the frequency with which the proposition is uttered; the extent to which the proposition is communicated with photographs and other visual or aural embellishments; the extent to which the proposition will make the reader or listener feel good or happy for content independent reasons; and almost countless others—we can see that placing faith in the superiority of truth over all of these other attributes of a proposition in explaining acceptance and rejection requires a substantial degree of faith in pervasive human rationality and an almost willful disregard of the masses of scientific and marketing research to the contrary", Schauer (2010), p. 909.

[29] Cf. Pariser (2011).

[30] "This pro-market revolution in economic thought had major implications for media regulation. In the early days of the FCC, there was a presumption that the government was a guardian of public interest and that commercial interests on their own would not necessarily produce positive outcomes in terms of either efficiency or democratic control – hence the "public interest" mandate in the 1934 Communications Act (...) By the 1980s, however, this view had changed to one that held that largely unregulated media markets would best serve public interest and that state regulation did not serve a neutral "public interest" but was politically driven.", Fukuyama and Grotto (2020), p. 211.

[31] "The pro-market revolution of the 1980s had consequences for the other form of possible state intervention: antitrust. Led by Robert Bork, Aaron Director, George Stigler, and others, a number of conservative legal scholars and economists began arguing for a much narrower understanding of the grounds on which the government could launch antitrust actions. Bork argued that the original Sherman Act envisioned only one standard for public concern, which was consumer welfare as measured by prices and/or quality.", Fukuyama and Grotto (2020), p. 212.

much less interventionist attitude,[32] which, not surprisingly, has subsequently been maintained, thereby helping consolidate monopolies of large technology companies.

As monopolies, their impact on the freedom of opinion is decisive since, as Fukuyama and Grotto rightly point out, "because the market for social media is less competitive, a decision to remove certain content is much more consequential than the decision of, say, *USA Today* not to carry it".[33] Their impact on freedom of information is equally decisive because the monopolistic conditions in which these companies operate foster the effectiveness of narratives based on false facts or alternative realities. From this perspective, they are problematic for freedom of information and the construction of a free and plural society that enables the conditions required for constitutional democracy.

## 5 Configuration of the Algorithms by the New Mediators

The new mediators promote extreme positions not because those positions coincide with their managers' ideology but because the instability they arouse favours their business model, which is based on advertising and therefore on the repeated use of the networks by users in order to sell more advertising. The more attention they attract, the more money they make. In addition to this motivation, there is a second equally important one: that of gridlocking politics to prevent their activities from being checked by the public authorities, which is why they empower populist movements.

Is a different arrangement possible for the social networks? Clearly it is, at least from the information we have, particularly from Facebook. According to the *Wall Street Journal*, the company commissioned an internal report to determine whether it would be technically possible to change the algorithms it uses and thus avoid this radicalisation of the public sphere. The conclusion was that it was perfectly feasible but that the consequence would be a loss of revenue for Facebook, so the company's decision was to not change the algorithms, continuing to generate the same problems in the public sphere.[34]

A concrete example of how it has continued to do so is the recent US presidential elections. Despite the neutral attitude maintained by Facebook by not favouring either of the two candidates or using the electoral manipulation techniques it used in

[32]"In contrast to its European counterparts, then, the United States by the early twenty-first century had taken a much more relaxed position than its European counterparts toward the regulation of legacy media. This was driven both by the explosion of bandwidth provided by cable and internet technology and by an ideological shift toward greater distrust of government regulation. The Europeans, facing similar pressures, have themselves backed away from pervasive state control over legacy media and permitted greater market competition, though their public broadcasters remain powerful players in many European countries", Fukuyama and Grotto (2020), p. 213.

[33]*Ibídem*, p. 215.

[34]Cf. Horwitz and Seetharaman (2020).

the United States in 2016 and has used in other countries, the truth is that it has generally continued to boost the most extremist discourses. This could be seen after the 2020 election, when Trump refused to recognise the election result and incited a coup attempt to prevent the elected candidate from becoming president.

Here, Facebook was clearly anti-Trump in relation to this attempt to reverse the election result and was thus able to appear to the public as a company committed to democracy and constitutional values. At the same time, however, its algorithms continued to boost the massive public presence of Trumpist stances, favouring discourses that questioned the election result and urging followers to "stop the steal" that Trump claimed had taken place in the election. In the investigation carried out by the *New York Times*, people whose activity had previously had hardly any echo on Facebook began to have thousands of followers when they started disseminating statements related to Trumpist stances, thanks to Facebook's algorithms.[35]

This attitude on the part of Facebook, on the one hand helping to fan the flames through the design of its algorithms and on the other appearing publicly as the one trying to extinguish them by adopting measures against the arsonist, shows us that this company continues to move in a very ambiguous way in its apparent commitment to American democratic and constitutional values. If this is its behaviour in its own country, it is likely that this commitment is even weaker in others and that its activities of interference in the public sphere and electoral processes will possibly continue outside the United States in future.[36]

## 6 Freedom of Speech in the Different Communicative Contexts: Political, Economic and Technological

Technology and economy have defined and continue to define the context of communication processes and freedom of speech. Technology affects the organisation of these processes, which in turn can stimulate technological[37] and economic development. However, from a constitutional point of view, these processes no longer work on the side of constitutional principles and values, as they historically did in the modern world until the twenty-first century.[38]

[35] Cf. Thompson and Warzel (2021).

[36] Cf. Nielsen (2020).

[37] "Media and technology have always had a deeply intimate, symbiotic relationship. Advances in communications technology inevitably impact the development, distribution, and consumption of media. At the same time, consumer demand for content and new media experiences can in turn drive the market for new communications technology", Fukuyama and Grotto (2020), p. 206.

[38] Cf. Balaguer Callejón (2020). Portuguese version: "Constituição, democracia e globalização. a legitimidade da Constituição frente à crise econômica e às redes sociais", in Angelo Viglianisi Ferraro Francisco Balaguer Callejón, Ricardo Maurício Freire Soares, Flávia Sulz Campos Machado (Organizadores), *Racionalidade, Direito e Cidadania*, Studio, Salvador, 2021.

On the contrary, it is now possible to see the deterioration of constitutions and politics when faced with the economy and technology, the great legitimising factors of the twenty-first century that are now moving along their own paths, detached from the idea of progress and freedom that has historically been linked to constitutionalism. This deterioration has much to do with the conditions of globalisation and its negative impact on the state, which logically extends to the state's constitution.[39]

Whatever can be placed outside the state and into the global sphere has been externalised, such as the "economic constitution" itself, which is now inoperative in most constitutional systems. What cannot be located outside the state is being progressively disabled, preventing the state and politics from being able to work properly or control global economic factors and technological agents.

These processes, driven by globalisation, call democratic and constitutional systems into question. All the phenomena of deterioration of freedom of speech that we have mentioned in this paper are fundamentally related to political processes in democratic contexts. They are the manifestation of a democratic regression that affects constitutional structures and fundamental rights.

It is significant, from this perspective, that this chaos-generating machine that social networks have become and the impetus they have given to populism in the United States, Brazil and other democratic countries have been limited to political circuits and have not affected economic traffic. If, however, we were to apply the proliferation of fake news and the growth of post-truth and alternative facts to the economic or technological spheres, an economic collapse would be inevitable.

As it is shaping up, freedom of speech in the political sphere does not seem to have any limits, while in the economic and technological spheres such limits do exist in such a way that legal certainty and trust in the rules are still generally respected. There is no "destruction" of reality, nor are narratives allowed that could endanger large corporations, their economic performance or their capacity for technological innovation.

We can also draw a parallel here with the interpretation that has been made of the First Amendment in the United States with respect to the limits of freedom of speech, insofar as some regulation of commercial advertising has been admitted so that it would not be protected by the First Amendment, unlike political propaganda and, in general, political debates. The fact that commercial advertising is not protected by the First Amendment with regard to false statements and factual falsity contained therein is evidence that in this area there is control over factual falsehood. This does not occur in the political area, however, since freedom of speech is specially

[39] Cf. Balaguer Callejón (2018a): http://www.ugr.es/~redce/REDCE30/articulos/02_F_BALAGUER.htm Italian version: "Le due grandi crisi del costituzionalismo di fronte alla globalizzazione nel XXI secolo", en *Passato, presente e futuro del costituzionalismo e dell'Europa*, a cura di F. Lanchester, CEDAM, 2019, pp. 59–82. Portuguese version: Balaguer Callejón (2018b): https://portalperiodicos.unoesc.edu.br/espacojuridico/article/view/20205.

protected in this area in accordance with the interpretation made of the First Amendment.[40]

It is true that the absence of protection of the political sphere in the United States with respect to factual falsehood is something that existed even before the development of social networks, stemming from that extensive interpretation of the First Amendment and the idea that the marketplace of ideas could correct falsehoods by itself and make the truth prevail.[41] This idea is certainly very favourable to those who have a greater capacity and influence to impose their own narrative, regardless of whether that narrative is based on real facts or not. This was the case in medieval duels to establish the truth, in which the most skilful or the most powerful also won.

Let us imagine for a moment that Donald Trump's false claims in his 4 years in office, which according to the *Washington Post* came to 30,573,[42] had been devoted to generating instability in the economic and technological spheres, massively defaming large US corporations, spreading false news about the Wall Street stock market or generating alternative realities about the functioning of the US economy. Now the inevitable question is: why politics and not the economy? Why has the level of American politics been allowed to fall to levels unimaginable a few years ago without the economy or technology being subjected to the same attacks or destructive activity of the same magnitude?

If social networks and technological agencies have left the economic and technological spheres untouched, it is equally possible that they could have prevented the deterioration of politics and democracy, which has occurred not due to freedom of speech being exercised but due to the specific design that the new mediators have created for communication processes in digital environments. As this paper has argued, technology companies are not responsible for all the shortcomings identified. Some of them were already established to a greater or lesser extent in the public sphere. However, the truth is that these companies have not corrected the negative

[40] As indicated by Frederick Schauer: "although the existing doctrine is moderately clear with respect to the permissibility of restricting false or misleading advertising of securities or commercial products, the issue is different when we turn to questions of factual falsity in political debate", Schauer (2010), p. 913.

[41] For Frederick Schauer, one of the issues that have to do with communication processes and that is outside the First Amendment is a factual falsehood: "One of these questions is that of the increasing acceptance of patent factual falsity, and it is a question whose economic, psychological, sociological, cultural, scientific, political, and policy dimensions are far more important than the legal and constitutional ones. This may disappoint some lawyers and constitutionalists, but when they discover that the First Amendment, they so properly cherish has done little to prevent the problem of widespread factual falsity, they may come to realize as well that the same First Amendment can also do very little to solve it. Just as neither the law nor the Constitution can be the cure to all of the policy problems of our day, neither can the First Amendment be the cure for all of the communications and informational problems of our day. Far more than First Amendment freedoms have created a society in which truth seems to matter so little, and far more than First Amendment freedoms will be necessary to do anything about it." *Ibídem*, p. 919.

[42] V. *supra*, footnote 3.

trends but have rather contributed to their development, generating new problems related to the ecosystems of digital environments governed by algorithms.

## 7 Conclusions

To understand the impact of the new mediators of the digital age, we must first explain the conditions under which freedom of speech is exercised in the communication processes that these new mediators have developed. They are hierarchical processes in a closed-off environment of Internet applications where algorithms designed by the new mediators control the entire process, determining how messages are received, who receives them, what impact they will have in the public sphere, how far they can go in terms of content and what internal control systems will solve any conflicts that may arise.

The new mediators are running veritable ecosystems in which freedom of speech is exercised within a personal context that breaks down the users' barriers, making them more receptive to the information they receive. The environment is a dynamic, informal one that is generating new cultural and political patterns that affect freedom of speech. In this context, news and opinions of political and constitutional importance count for very little compared to the other activities (entertainment, work, personal communication, etc.) that take place within the applications and which make up a genuine digital life occupying much of the users' time.

Moreover, the communication processes of our time reflect the acceleration of the historical period we are going through, boosted by technological development and the organisation of new communication environments. The result is a loss of value for freedom of speech, not only due to the proliferation of opinions and information generated every day on a global scale but also because of their ephemeral nature in the digital communication context. From a constitutional point of view, it is not only the exercise of freedom of speech as an individual right that is suffering but also its contribution to the formation of free and informed public opinion.

In the ecosystems developed by technology companies, the new mediators exercise a power that is not strictly private in that they occupy and monopolise a public sphere. In this communicative environment, it is a sovereign power comparable to that of authoritarian states over their subjects. On the one hand, they can restrict freedom of speech to the point of expelling users. On the other, they generate an environment in which freedom of speech, instead of contributing to democratic debate and the articulation of pluralism, becomes an instrument for social division and radicalisation, generating a kind of plural monism in which isolation between the various views of the world is growing. It is a pluralism of monist stances that do not recognise other views but assert themselves as the only possible viewpoints.

They thus develop an extraordinary, historically unprecedented capacity to shape the narrative of reality. In democratic countries, the traditional media try to influence the prevailing narrative by contributing to the social *construction of reality*. In dictatorial regimes, one can speak of a *reconstruction of reality* tailored to the interests of the dictator or the dominant oligarchy. But in the new communication context of democratic countries, with Trumpism as a paradigmatic example, there is an evolution towards the *destruction of reality*, that is, of a shared social perception of reality.

The traditional media used to construct narratives that could more or less be associated with political tendencies, though not necessarily with partisan options. They thus participated in the social construction of reality. The new media, however, do not construct narratives but open their platforms up to all possible narratives. However, they do so with their algorithms prioritising those that promote false news and alternative realities because they can thus get more attention from the public and hence more advertising revenue. They do not reflect the reality of the societies in which they operate, nor do they operate as representative platforms for freedom of speech. On the contrary, by promoting fake news and alternative realities, they create tension about reality itself, which has great destructive potential.

What the new mediators of the digital age are promoting is essentially instability and insecurity. Fake news coexists and competes with real news but does not replace it in favour of a concrete narrative imposing itself in the public sphere. The "alternative reality" coexists with the "real" reality but does not replace it. Both narratives compete, and occasionally one of them may prevail over the other in a public debate or in the convictions of the governing majorities that are formed. But having an interest in distorting reality, transforming it and generating narratives in favour of a specific political option is significantly different from having an absolute disinterest in reality or any type of narrative and its possible usefulness in favour of a political option.

For the new mediators, news and freedom of speech as such are nothing more than data within their business model. Freedom of speech no longer has any substantial meaning because information and opinion are just another product within an ecosystem driven by algorithms. It is an environment in which fake news and alternative realities are promoted because they favour their business model.

It is not a matter of inefficient control or a moral inability to differentiate falsehood from truth but of specific interest in promoting falsehoods. They do not do so in line with a specific political motivation (as happens in dictatorial systems) to impose a specific narrative. "Destruction" of reality does not necessarily go hand in hand with the imposition of an "alternative reality" in the same way that the "destruction" of politics need not go hand in hand with an alternative political formulation.

In short, the current context of freedom of speech presents many problems from a constitutional point of view that have to do with the surge of new mediators that are occupying practically the entire space for information and opinion, displacing traditional media. Of course, there are also positive aspects that can be pointed out from different perspectives, including the constitutional one. But the technological platforms have broken up the balance that existed in the early days of Web 2.0, when there were no hierarchical applications within closed-off ecosystems but rather an open system based on HTML language that made it possible to exercise freedom of speech without constraints arising from the applications' internal organisation by means of algorithms.

Although the idea of participation in the new communication systems has been seen as a contrast compared to traditional media since the development of Web 2.0, the truth is that the new systems not only offer less real participation but also make it possible for technology companies to penetrate further into the users' opinions. Thus, instead of making it possible for citizens to freely express their opinion, what these platforms have ended up doing is to drive that opinion with a hierarchical system of algorithms that channel content individually with the capacity to influence the users' conscience and decisively modulate their opinion.

It is significant that the new mediators have limited themselves to intervening in political circuits and have not directly affected economic traffic. If we were to apply the proliferation of fake news and the development of post-truth and "alternative facts" to the economic or technological sphere, an economic collapse would be inevitable. However, while freedom of expression as it is taking shape in the political sphere seems to have no limits whatsoever, in the economic and technological sphere, legal certainty and trust in the rules are still generally respected. There is no "destruction" of reality, nor are narratives that could endanger large corporations, their economic performance or their capacity for technological innovation allowed.

One essential issue as regards the communication environments developed by the new mediators and their effect on freedom of speech is competition. Those that do not have a democratic structure cannot contribute to democratic development, and the same can be said of pluralism: monopolistic conditions cannot help develop pluralism. Free competition is to the economy what biodiversity is to nature and pluralism to politics. We cannot have democracy without pluralism nor pluralism without competition. Technological companies are affecting two of the essential pillars of the democratic system: pluralism in the political sphere and competition in the economic sphere.

There is no doubt that they are also affecting the capacity for technological innovation, hindering the development of new environments that can compete with the current ones. To solve these problems, institutional measures can be taken through regulators to make the further concentration of power more difficult. However, rather than restrictions, it is openness that is desirable—open technology that puts an end to the closed-off, hierarchical nature of applications. Telephone communication, for example, is open and allows mobile phone operators to operate, making global communication possible, and the same is true for e-mail servers. Communication applications that are currently closed-off (WhatsApp and Telegram, for example) should also be open, intercommunicable and managed by a plurality of operators.

## References

Balaguer Callejón F (2018a) Las dos grandes crisis del constitucionalismo frente a la globalización en el Siglo XXI. Revista de Derecho Constitucional Europeo, n. 30

Balaguer Callejón F (2018b) As duas grandes crises do constitucionalismo diante da globalização no século XXI. Espaço Jurídico J Law 19(3)

Balaguer Callejón F (2019) Redes sociales, compañías tecnológicas y democracia. Revista de Derecho Constitucional Europeo, n. 32

Balaguer Callejón F (2020) Constitution, démocratie et mondialisation. La légitimité de la Constitution face à la crise économique et aux réseaux sociaux. In: Mélanges en l'honneur du Professeur Dominique Rousseau. Constitution, justice, démocratie. L.G.D.J, Paris

Balaguer Callejón F (2021a) La constitución del algoritmo. In Gomes ACN, Albergaria B, Canotilho MR (Coord) Direito Constitucional: diálogos em homenagem ao 80° aniversário de J. J. Gomes Canotilho. Fórum, Belo Horizonte

Balaguer Callejón F (2021b) Inteligencia artificial, democracia y derechos. In: Filho WSG, Santaella L, Kaufmn D, Cantarini P (eds) Direito e Inteligência Artificial: Fundamentos -vol 1. Lumen Juris, Rio de Janeiro

Cairncross F and others (2019) The Cairncross Review. A sustainable future for journalism

De Miguel J (2016) Las transformaciones del derecho de la información en el contexto del ciberperiodismo. Revista de Estudios Políticos, 173

Derakhshan H (2015) Soy bloguero y pasé seis años preso en Irán. Así veo internet ahora. El País, 23 August 2015

Eco U (2003) La forza del falso, in the compilation of the same Author, Sulla Letteratura. Tascabili Bompiani, Milano

Fukuyama F, Grotto A (2020) Comparative media regulation in the United States and Europe. In: Persily N, Tucker JA (eds) Social media and democracy. Cambridge University Press

Furman J and others (2019) Unlocking digital competition. Report of the Digital Competition Expert Panel

Horwitz J, Seetharaman D (2020) Facebook executives shut down efforts to make the site less divisive. Wall Street Journal, 26 May 2020

House of Commons, Digital, Culture, Media and Sport Committee, DCMS (2019) Disinformation and 'fake news': Final Report, Published on 18 February 2019 by authority of the House of Common

Hwang T (2020) Dealing with disinformation: evaluating the case for Amendment of Section 230 of the communications decency act. In: Persily N, Tucker JA (eds) Social media and democracy. Cambridge University Press

Keller D, Leerssen P (2020) Facts and where to find them: empirical research on internet platforms and content moderation. In: Persily N, Tucker JA (eds) Social media and democracy. Cambridge University Press

Nielsen RK (2020) Las plataformas tienen que decidir si todos sus usuarios globales son iguales". El País, 10 November 2020

Nielsen RK, Fletcher R (2020) Democratic creative destruction? The effect of a changing media landscape on democracy. In: Persily N, Tucker JA (eds) Social media and democracy. Cambridge University Press

Pariser E (2011) The Filter Bubble. What the internet is hiding from you. Penguin Books

Persily N, Tucker JA (2020) Preface. In: Persily N, Tucker JA (eds) Social media and democracy. Cambridge University Press

Pitruzzella G (2017) La libertà di informazione nell'era di Internet. In: Pitruzzella G, Pollicino O, Quintarelli S (eds) Parole e potere: Libertà d'espressione, hate speech e fake news. Italian Edition, Egea

Schauer F (2010) Facts and the first amendment. UCLA Law Rev 57(4)
Thompson SA, Warzel Ch (2021) How Facebook incubated the insurrection. Right-wing influencers embraced extremist views and Facebook rewarded them. The New York Times, 14 January 2021
Zadrozny B (2021) Trump's blog isn't lighting up the internet. In nbcnewscom, May 11, 2021
Zuboff S (2021) The coup we are not talking about. The New York Times, 29 January

**Francisco Balaguer Callejón** Professor of Constitutional Law, University of Granada, Spain; Jean Monnet Professor ad personam of European Constitutional Law and Globalization; Director of the Journal Revista de Derecho Constitucional Europeo; Visiting Professor in the USA, France, Italy and Portugal. Dr. H.C. in Brazil.

Author of more than 500 publications in 12 countries: Spain, France, Mexico, Italy, Peru, Portugal, Brazil, Belgium, Holland, Germany, United Kingdom and Switzerland.

More than 500 lectures, courses and seminars given in German, English, Italian, French, Portuguese and Spanish in 12 countries: Belgium, Brazil, France, Germany, Italy, Mexico, Peru, Portugal, Spain, Hungary, Switzerland and the United Kingdom.

Member of editorial boards and committees of 60 journals of constitutional law and comparative law, as well as editorial councils in eight countries: Italy (25), Brazil (15), Spain (14), Mexico (2), Peru (1), Portugal (1), Malta (1) and Russia (1).

Research interest areas: constitutional law, European law, globalisation, sources of law, fundamental rights, digital society, new technologies, populism, democracy, federalism and regionalism, economic crisis and health crisis.

# The Freedom to Conduct a Business as a Counterargument to Limit Platform Users' Freedom of Expression

**Berdien B. E. van der Donk**

## Contents



**Abstract** This chapter focuses on platforms' protection against (unjustified) interference with the free drafting of house rules, viewed through the lens of European fundamental rights protection. It discusses the difference in the protection of two fundamental rights in the European Charter of Fundamental Rights: article 16's freedom to conduct a business and article 17's right to property. The articles' subject of protection ('the essence of the right') will be mapped by analyzing the Court of Justice of the European Union (CJEU) case law between, respectively, 1974 and 1979 until 2020, and the outcome of this analysis will be applied to the process of running a platform. It will show that article 16, rather than article 17, covers platforms' house rule drafting. However, it is unlikely that restrictive measures will interfere with the essence of article 16. Measures limiting house rule drafting can therefore be justifiable.

To be justifiable, the measures must live up to the principle of proportionality. Therefore, subsequently, the question arises whether potential measures live up to this principle. To prevent a purely normative way of answering that question—due

B. B. E. van der Donk (✉)
Centre for Private Governance (CEPRI), University of Copenhagen, Copenhagen, Denmark
e-mail: berdien.vanderdonk@jur.ku.dk



S. Hindelang, A. Moberg (eds.), *YSEC Yearbook of Socio-Economic Constitutions 2021*, YSEC Yearbook of Socio-Economic Constitutions (2022) 2021: 33–58,
https://doi.org/10.1007/16495_2021_33, Published online: 12 March 2022

to the fact that a standardized test does not exist—the unfairness test of the Unfair Contract Terms Directive will be used as an interpretational guide. It is concluded that measures limiting a platform's contractual freedom can, and most likely will, be justifiable to protect platform users' freedom of expression. That opens the door for future legislation.

Outside the direct realm of platforms, this chapter demonstrates that the freedom to conduct a business has been reduced to an empty shell, or rather a shell that has never been inhabited. Apart from the situation where an undertaking would be able to demonstrate that a proposed measure would mean the end of the business, the freedom to conduct a business does not provide any effective protection.

## 1 House Rules: The Ability to Draft and Enforce Them All

On 11 August 2020, Facebook increased the scope of its rules on hate speech. From this date forward, it became explicitly prohibited to upload to the social media platform content containing harmful stereotypes. In Facebook's definition, such harmful stereotypes include anti-Semitic claims relating to Jewish people controlling the world and content that includes any form of blackfacing.[1] Across the Atlantic Ocean, 8800 km from Facebook's headquarters in Menlo Park, this amendment to Facebook's Community Guidelines had immediate consequences in the Netherlands. Due to the amendment, sharing content portraying the original version[2] of the national tradition of *Sinterklaas* and his helper, Black Pete (*Zwarte Piet* in Dutch), fell within the scope of the new restriction on blackfacing, and consequently Facebook began to remove content related to Black Pete from their platform.[3]

The Dutch tradition of Sinterklaas has been thoroughly discussed in the Netherlands during the last decade, both in and outside politics, and has two main groups leading the debate: those requesting to respect the tradition as is and those against the tradition and demanding change. Despite years of (political) discussion, the Dutch government has not taken active steps to ban the depiction of Black Pete. When asked, the Dutch prime minister stressed that the Dutch government does not take a stance on anything related to 'folk culture' and urges that a decision to ban Black

[1] Facebook Community Guidelines, August 2020 Policy Rationale (III: Objectionable Content), available at: https://www.facebook.com/communitystandards/recentupdates/hate_speech/ (accessed 3 February 2021).

[2] In the last years the tradition has been subjected to change, though not consequently. Different "Petes" have emerged, such as colourful and cookie ones.

[3] The decision to remove content was upheld by the Facebook Oversight Board, see Case decision 2021-002-FB-UA (Black Pete).

Pete must come from society itself.[4] One might well wonder whether a social media platform's decision to ban the content in question qualifies as a change 'from society itself'. Those against the tradition see Facebook's alteration to the Community Guidelines as a welcome recognition of the values they fight for.[5] Those in favour of maintaining the original tradition feel muzzled as they have seen their Facebook pages getting blocked and their personal profiles receiving multiple warnings. To avoid the suspension of their profiles, they have moved their protest 'underground'.[6]

It seems problematic that a national debate on whether or not a country's tradition is harmful and should be restricted is concluded by a private company. It seems more problematic that a private company with its headquarters 8800 km away from the dispute is implementing its own norms and values into Community Guidelines that affect 2.7 billion users. The debate on Black Pete in the Netherlands took off because a small number of people disagreed with the status quo and challenged it. In case people with opinions that differ from the majority would have had their accounts blocked and/or permanently suspended, the current progress in the debate would have never taken off.

The discussion is not limited to hate-speech-related content. Take for example euthanasia, a controversial practice worldwide, which is legal in some jurisdictions and criminalized as murder in others. In September 2020, French pro-euthanasia activist Alain Cocq wished to stream his personal suffering on Facebook. In his eyes, his suffering was caused by a lack of access to active euthanasia in France. and streaming this suffering would therefore contribute to the discussion on legalizing euthanasia. Facebook prohibited and blocked his live streaming. According to Facebook, allowing Cocq to stream his death would go against its Community Guidelines, which prohibit portrayals of suicide. It did not matter that Cocq's actions constituted a political protest: a distinction between suicide and euthanasia does not exist in the Community Guidelines. Despite the fact that there is no consensus on the legality of euthanasia worldwide, Facebook regulated the matter privately and consequently applies a unified rule to its 2.7 billion users worldwide. One could wonder how that decision would have turned out if identical content was streamed by a Dutch, Swiss, Canadian or Colombian national—all countries where active euthanasia is legal. In fact, the Dutch public broadcaster actively engages in

[4] See Het Parool, 'Mark Rutte: "Zwarte Piet: dat lossen we op"', 6 June 2020, available at: https://www.parool.nl/nederland/mark-rutte-zwarte-piet-dat-lossen-we-op~b0396703/ (accessed 27 April 2021) (translation by the author).

[5] See, for example, the post by Jeffrey Afriyie, one of the founders of the campaign 'Kick out Zwarte Piet' in his Facebook post of 11 August 2020, available at: https://www.facebook.com/jklrebel/posts/3445187648827371 (accessed 27 April 2021), stating that Facebook has endorsed their opinion on the discriminative nature of blackface.

[6] See, for example, Trouw, Grootste Pro-Zwarte Pietpagina's verdwijnen van Facebook, 4 September 2020, available at: https://www.trouw.nl/binnenland/grootste-pro-zwarte-pietpagina-s-verdwijnen-van-facebook~b0a2d3b3/?referrer=https%3A%2F%2Fwww.google.com%2F (accessed 27 April 2021), describing that due to the biggest 'pro-black Pete pages' being removed from Facebook, organizers are reaching out to other platforms to get their message across.

producing content that shows how euthanasia is being carried out, which content is freely available through the national public channel.[7]

There is a general consensus that the dissemination of illegal content on the Internet must be put to a halt, but how about the opposite scenario? What if house rules on online platforms restrict the access to content that is perfectly legal, at least in certain jurisdictions in the world? Has the time come for increased restrictions on the freedom to draft house rules? Well, that depends on the scope of protection the platform enjoys to freely draft such house rules. Usually, these dilemmas are viewed and assessed from the point of view of the users: they are limited to expressing themselves and imparting information. This chapter takes the opposite approach. As these platforms are run by private companies, consequently an often brought-up argument against restricting their contractual freedom is that these companies should be able to decide what they want and when and how they want it as users could just use another service.[8]

Therefore, the focus of this chapter lies with platforms' protection from (unjustified) interference with the free drafting of house rules, as viewed through the lens of European fundamental rights protection, in order to assess whether such a private company argument can hold its ground. To do so, the author will start by discussing two relevant fundamental rights in the European Charter of Fundamental Rights (the 'Charter'), namely the freedom to conduct a business in article 16 and the right to property in article 17. The first part of this chapter focuses on the difference between these two rights and assesses which right protects which platform actions. It starts with an overview of the discussion on the (necessity of a) differentiation between these two rights. Subsequently, the articles' subject of protection ('the essence of the right') will be mapped by analyzing the CJEU's case law between, respectively, 1974 and 1979 until 2020. Limitations that restrict the essence of either articles 16 or 17 are per default not permissible. The outcome of the analysis will be applied to the process of running a platform.

It will show that a platform, based on article 16, will be able to oppose restrictions interfering with its contractual freedom. However, it is unlikely that such a restriction will interfere with the essence of the freedom. Therefore, the author continues by assessing to what extent article 16 would protect a platform from non-essential interference. Even if it does not affect the essence of the freedom, a measure is unjustifiable if it does not live up to the principle of proportionality in article 52 of the Charter. The scope of article 16 will be based on the justifications invoked before the CJEU. As part of this assessment, the question as to whether less restrictive measures exist must be answered. To prevent a purely normative way of answering that question and due to the fact that a standardized test does not exist,

[7] Such content is freely available to all Dutch residents, see, for example, the documentary 'Levenseindekliniek' (Life-end clinic), 2Doc (Season 3, episode 31), available at: https://www.npostart.nl/2doc/15-02-2016/VPWON_1248719 (accessed 27 April 2021).

[8] As shown by recent developments in Dutch case law, see infra.

interpretational guidance will be sought in a European directive with a similar purpose: the Unfair Contract Terms Directive.

Finally, the author will conclude that measures limiting a platform's contractual freedom are justifiable. However, concluding that restrictive measures are compatible with the fundamental rights of the Charter does not necessarily mean that this would effectively and sufficiently solve the problem discussed. To address this, a few concluding remarks are made regarding the necessity to reach a consensus on the qualification of platforms.

## 2 Picking Sides: Differentiating Between Articles 16 and 17

In three recent decisions of the District Court of Amsterdam in the Netherlands, the Court concluded that the right to property grants a platform the right to freely decide on the content of the user terms applicable to its service, even when such rules would impede the freedom of expression of the users of said service.[9] However, when viewed through the eyes of the platform, the Charter contains two articles of relevance to protect the platform against such unjustified limitations of house rule drafting. Apart from the right to property in article 17, the Charter also provides the platform with the freedom to conduct a business in article 16.[10] If the platform's infrastructure qualifies as property, forcing entry to it could be a restriction of the right to property. Therefore, obliging a platform to provide access to content it does not wish to provide access to potentially limits the protection under this right. Opposingly, one could also argue that it is a limitation of the free choice of the platform on how to conduct its business when it cannot freely decide which restrictions it wants to include in its user terms.

When considering the textual interpretation of these rights, one could wonder whether it is necessary to distinguish the freedom to conduct a business from the right to property at all. Their area of application (property and business) seems, at least partially, to be overlapping, and the CJEU frequently mentions them in

[9] See, most recently, Rechtbank Amsterdam (BLCKBX/Google) (2021) ECLI:NL:RBAMS:2021:4308. Previously, the Court reached similar conclusions in Rechtbank Amsterdam (Café Weltschmerz/YouTube) (2020) ECLI:NL:RBAMS:2020:4435; and Rechtbank Amsterdam (Smart Exit/Facebook) (2020) ECLI:NL:RBAMS:2020:4966. See, for a discussion of the latter two in English, van der Donk (2022).

[10] The possibility for the platform to invoke the protection of the right to freedom of expression and information has been left out of the discussion of this chapter in order to shift the focus and attention to the other applicable freedoms in the Charter, in line with the recent developments in Dutch case law. In the United States, the equivalent (but broader scoped) First Amendment protection has developed in one of the most applied counterarguments to limit the user terms of online platforms. However, the two articles differ in their scope and application; see, for a discussion, Heller and van Hoboken (2019).

conjugation without differentiating between either article.[11] So why distinguish the two? Does it matter to qualify a measure as a restriction of the freedom to conduct a business or the right to property?

Whilst the rights may have (seemingly) overlapping areas of application, the freedoms have developed independently in European case law prior to their codification in the Charter. Due to this difference in origin and the provisions in the Charter on limitations, the qualification of whether a restriction limits either article 16 or article 17 has legal consequences, and therefore distinguishing the two has consequences for the protection that a platform can derive from it. However, distinguishing the two is easier said than done.

## *2.1 Discussion on the (Necessity of a) Differentiation*

In the 1974 case *Nold v. Commission*, the CJEU expressly recognized the right to free pursuit of business activity as a distinctive freedom.[12] This freedom is one of the sub-freedoms of article 16's freedom to conduct a business. Despite this explicit recognition by the CJEU, a discussion emerged on the necessity to separate the freedom to conduct a business from the right to property. This overview will start with a summary of the arguments against a distinction, and those in favour follow afterwards.

### 2.1.1 Arguments Against a Distinction Between Article 16 and Article 17

Firstly, it has been argued that the recognition of the freedom to conduct a business as an independent right has proven not to have any practical legal relevance. On the purpose of article 16, Oliver argues, for example, that the right has never had any substantive meaning in any disputes, which he links to the close relationship between the freedom to conduct a business and the right to property.[13] It has similarly been argued that the right to property does not provide any effective protection, and as such this close, intertwined relationship means that the freedom to conduct a business does not add any independent value.

On the right to property, Groussot et al. argue that claims based on this right have a very low success rate as article 1 of the Protocol and the corresponding case law of the European Court of Human Rights (ECtHR) accept very broad justifications for

---

[11] See, for example, *Case C-200/96 (Metronome Musik)* (CJEU), §21; *Case C-265/87 (Schräder)* (1989) ECLI:EU:C:1989:303 (CJEU), §15; *Case C-210/03 (Swedish Match)* (2004) ECLI:EU:C:2004:802 (CJEU), §72.

[12] *Case C-4/73 (Nold v Commission)* (1974) ECR 491, ECLI:EU:C:1974:51 (CJEU), §12.

[13] Oliver (2013), p. 281.

the limitations to the right to property.[14] Or formulated differently, the claim that a certain (state) measure is unfair because it forms a limitation to the party's right to property is rarely followed by the ECtHR. Advocate General Cruz-Villalón hints in that same direction regarding article 16 in his opinion on the case *Mark Alemo-Herron*, where he states that '(...) to date the case-law has not, in fact, provided a full and useful definition of this freedom'.[15] He continues: 'The judgments in which the Court has had occasion to rule in this area have gone no further than either referring to the right to property or simply citing the provisions of Article 16 of the Charter.' In line therewith, Groussot et al. state that 'the enshrinement into the Charter of the freedom to conduct business is more housekeeping rather than the extension of an already existing right',[16] hinting at the fact that article 16 is a mere codification of prior case law of the CJEU rather than an independent right with its own scope of protection. Adding thereto, article 16 of the Charter is, to say the least, compact in writing, and a grammatical interpretation does not provide any substantive clarity, and neither do the preparatory works.[17] When article 16 lacks a 'full and useful definition' and is merely used in conjunction with or at least interpreted in a close relationship to the right to property, then why have two different articles in the Charter? If the scope of these two articles was to be interpreted identically, the need to codify article 16 seems unnecessary.

Secondly, the legal basis for the inclusion of an independent freedom to conduct a business seems shaky. According to the explanation relating to the Charter, the freedom provided for in article 16 contains three sub-freedoms: the freedom to exercise an economic or commercial activity, the freedom of contract and the right to free competition.[18] Interestingly, this distinction is not reflected as such in the constitutions of the Member States. According to a 2015 analysis by the European Union Agency for Fundamental Rights, the freedom of economic activity is present in 21 out of the 27 Member States of the European Union.[19] The others, the freedom of contract and the right to free competition, are included in respectively one and

---

[14] Groussot et al. (2014) <https://papers.ssrn.com/abstract=2428181> accessed 10 November 2020, p. 5.

[15] *Opinion of AG Cruz-Villalón to Case C-426/11 (Alemo-Herron and Others)* (CJEU), §49.

[16] Groussot et al. (2014), p. 4.

[17] See *Opinion of AG Cruz-Villalón (Alemo-Herron and Others)* (n 9), "*However, despite the fact that the freedom to conduct a business derives from these three sources, to date the case-law has not, in fact, provided a full and useful definition of this freedom*"; Groussot et al. (2014); and FRA European Agency for Fundamental Rights, 'Freedom to Conduct a Business: Exploring the Dimensions of a Fundamental Right' <https://primarysources.brillonline.com/browse/human-rights-documents-online/freedom-to-conduct-a-business-exploring-the-dimensions-of-a-fundamental-right;hrdhrd99922015012> accessed 27 April 2021, p. 9.

[18] See European Commission, 'Explanations Relating to the Charter of Fundamental Rights' (2007), on article 16. This has been confirmed in *Case C-283/11 (Sky Österreich)* (2013) ECLI:EU:C:2013:28 (CJEU), §42: "*The protection afforded by Article 16 of the Charter covers the freedom to exercise an economic or commercial activity, the freedom of contract and free competition (..)*".

[19] FRA - European Union Agency for Fundamental Rights (2015).

11 Member States.[20] It seems therefore that at least two aspects of the freedom to conduct a business do not follow from the majority of the constitutional norms of the Member States to which the CJEU refers and on which case law on article 16 has been explicitly based.[21] The lack of a constitutional basis has led Everson and Gonçalves to conclude that the inclusion of the freedom in the Charter is controversial.[22] They argue that the freedom to conduct a business is deducted from the periphery of the constitutional rights to property and work rather than based on the Member States' constitutions themselves.

Furthermore, Everson and Gonçalves interestingly conclude that this deduction of the freedom to conduct a business from the periphery of the right to property by the CJEU is contrary to the line set out by the European Court of Human Rights (ECtHR). In *Marckx v Belgium*, the ECtHR limits the applicable scope of the right to property to existing possessions only, rather than creating a 'right to acquire possessions'.[23] Contrarily, the CJEU has distilled the freedom to conduct a business from the right to work and the right to property, which seems to include a right at least similar to the right to acquire possessions. Thereon, Everson and Gonçalves conclude that the historical case law of the CJEU 'appears to broaden the scope of an existential sphere of subjective economic freedom for the individual European, in order to include within it a performative or entrepreneurial economic role'.[24]

### 2.1.2 Arguments in Favour of a Distinction Between Article 16 and Article 17

Despite the controversy, it follows from this conclusion that the scope of protection of the freedom to conduct a business seems broader than the scope of protection of the right to property. The arguments in favour of a distinction between article 16 and article 17 are in line with this conclusion.

The main argument to differentiate article 16 from article 17 revolves around the potential different protection of the respective articles. The different nature of article 16's protection as compared to article 17's has been pointed out by several. Everson and Gonçalves argue that the freedom to conduct a business can be viewed in two

---

[20] For the interpretation of the scope of article 16, this matters due to article 52 (4) of the Charter, which prescribes that fundamental rights which result from the constitutional traditions of the Member States, shall respect those traditions when interpreting the rights and freedoms in the Charter.

[21] However, Everson and Gonçalves argue that a connection could be made to article 6 of the International Covenant on Economic, Social and Cultural Rights and the corresponding right in article 1(2) of the European Social Charter. See Everson and Correia Gonçalves (2014), 16.11. In addition, the freedom of contract is included in the legislation on private law in several Member States.

[22] Everson and Correia Gonçalves (2014), 16.01, p. 438.

[23] Marckx v Belgium, §50, and ibid, 16.11.

[24] ibid, 16.12.

ways. Firstly, the freedom could be seen as a 'normal' fundamental right that protects, 'at its settled core, the existential status of the individual European, or her economic opportunity within the "marketplace"'.[25] Referring to article 16's 'performative character', they state that '(...)rights of freedom to conclude a contract, or to initiate economic activity, the freedom to conduct a business, in its broader performative character, is one which also recognises the existence and impact of an "entrepreneurial" element within human affairs. It thus may also imply a far deeper, and constitutionally secured, commitment to the maintenance of a specified form of political economy, or a distinct form of economic and social organisation.'[26]

Advocate General Cruz-Villalón, after concluding that the freedom to conduct a business is basically a toothless bulldog, adds another point of perspective to the debate corresponding to Everson and Gonçalves' second aim of the freedom's protection. He states that 'on the other hand, although the freedom to conduct a business is closely linked to the fundamental right to property (...) it protects different legal situations. If the right to property operates in the sphere of tangible and intangible assets, the freedom to conduct a business protects economic initiative and the ability to participate in a market, rather than the actual profit, seen in financial terms, that is earned in that market.' Thus, rather than protecting tangible and intangible assets like the right to property, Cruz-Villalón concludes that the freedom to conduct a business covers a socio-economic aspect, namely economic initiative and the ability to participate in the market. That hints in a direction of a deeper, political construction, where entrepreneurial activity in itself is protected, as pointed out by Everson and Gonçalves.

This double dimension of the freedom to conduct a business has subsequently been pointed out by the European Union Agency for Fundamental Rights. When describing the 'essence of the freedom to conduct a business', it refers, firstly, to the individual protection for citizens to pursue their aspirations and expressions whilst, secondly, pointing to the freedom's promotion of entrepreneurship and innovation to guarantee a sustainable social and economic development.[27] This distinction is in line with the strict interpretation of the right to property, followed by the ECtHR. In line with the ECtHR's case law, as pointed out above, the right to property does not include a right to acquire possessions. It merely protects the (in)tangible possessions owned. By including article 16 in the Charter, it has expanded the scope of protection from the sole protection of possessions (article 17) to a broader economic right to participate in the market (article 16).

[25] ibid, 16.04.

[26] ibid, 16.01.

[27] FRA - European Union Agency for Fundamental Rights (2015), p. 7.

## 2.2 Telling the Two Rights Apart

As an apparent difference in subject matter exists, it is necessary to determine which one provides the most potential for platforms to oppose restrictive measures. To do so, a need to assess what is covered by respectively article 16 and article 17 is needed. However, a textual interpretation of either one of these articles does not provide any substantive clarification on the material scope. So where to look for a definition?

As article 17 corresponds to article 1 of the Protocol to the ECHR, article 52(3) of the Charter applies, which dictates that an article in the Charter with an equivalent article in the ECHR may not provide lesser protection than the protection offered by the ECHR. As a consequence, limitations to article 17 may not reduce the scope of protection beyond what would be allowed under article P1-1 ECHR. Contrarily, a broader scope of protection is permissible. Therefore, to determine to what extent the right to property could be limited, the case law of both the CJEU and the ECtHR has to be taken into consideration, though since the ECHR only provides minimum protection, the case law of the CJEU will be relied on primarily to define the material scope. A corresponding right in the ECHR does not exist for article 16, and therefore article 52(3) does not apply. Consequently, solely the case law of the CJEU defines and interprets the material scope of the article.

To subsequently use the definitions of the freedom to conduct a business and the right to property to decide to what extent a platform is protected against state interference with the drafting of user terms, the focus lies in defining the 'essence' of these two fundamental rights. The essence (also referred to by the CJEU as 'the very substance of the right') of a fundamental right is the 'core' of the right, protected against any interference. A restriction of the essence of a fundamental right cannot be justified.[28] In order to define the essence of the freedom from a legal technical perspective, it is necessary to differentiate between (1) measures that restrict that very essence of the freedom and (11) measures that affect that same freedom but do not restrict its essence. Whilst the latter can be justifiable, the first constitutes an unjustified interference by nature and must be omitted. To determine the essence of a freedom, one can look at the limitations that were found to be restricting the very essence of the right, because to restrict this essence, one must first define the essence. In the second category, it subsequently matters whether these measures are justifiable or infringing.[29] If the measure does not affect the right in any way, the party cannot claim protection under the freedom to conduct a business.

---

[28] See, for a thorough analysis of the need to take the essence into consideration, Lenaerts (2019), p. 779.

[29] See also *Opinion of AG Stix-Hackl to Joined Cases C-184/02 & C-223/02 (Spain and Finland v Parliament and Council)* (CJEU), §112, where she refers to the same differentiation as the 'first step' in the process of examining a potential infringement of the freedom to conduct a business.

### 2.2.1 The Material Scope of the 'Freedom to Conduct a Business' in Article 16

As the basis for article 16 is the prior case law of the CJEU,[30] the issued decisions of the Court on the freedom to conduct a business and the sub-freedoms included therein are analyzed. The starting point for the two sub-freedoms,[31] the freedom to exercise an economic or commercial activity and the freedom of contract, is the year when they were recognized as a general principle for the first time. This is respectively 1974 and 1979.[32]

#### 2.2.1.1 The Essence of the Freedom to Exercise an Economic Activity

The case *Nold v. Commission* is generally acknowledged as the first recognition of the freedom to exercise an economic activity.[33] According to the analysis of the case law of the CJEU from the first recognition in 1974, the essence of this sub-freedom can be summarized as the protection of the continuation of economic activity. That means that a measure can limit the way the economic activity is carried out as long as it does not prevent the absolute end of the economic activity.

The Court concluded, for example in *Germany v. Council*, that a measure restricting the number of bananas to be imported into the Union was compliant with the freedom.[34] The measure did not prevent the import of bananas per se; it merely regulated the amount. The same conclusion follows from *Deutsches Weintor* (labelling restrictions on alcoholic products does not prevent an undertaking from selling alcohol) and *Spain & Finland v. Commission & Council* (regulating the work time of truck drivers does not prevent people from driving a truck in general).[35] As summarized by AG Stix-Hackl in her opinion on the latter decision, the measure was 'concerned only with how such a freedom is to be exercised; it does not jeopardize the very existence of that freedom'.[36] In 2017, this same rationale has been endorsed by the CJEU once again. It concluded in two cases that subjecting undertakings to an obligation to be contactable by consumers when concluding distance and

---

[30] See European Commission (2007).

[31] The freedom to conduct a business recognizes the right to free competition as a third sub-freedom. The right to free competition is omitted in this analysis, as its application does not influence the drafting of house rules.

[32] *Nold v. Commission* (n 10); *Case C-151/78 (Sukkerfabrikken)* (1979) ECLI:EU:C:1979:4 (CJEU).

[33] See, for example, European Commission (2007), on article 16; Groussot et al. (2014), p. 2; Oliver (2013), p. 283.

[34] *Case C-280/93 (Germany/Council)* (CJEU), §87.

[35] *Joined Cases C-184/02 & C-223/02 (Spain and Finland/Parliament and Council)* (CJEU), §54; *Case C-544/10 (Deutsches Weintor)* (2012) ECLI:EU:C:2012:526 (CJEU), §57.

[36] *Opinion of AG Stix-Hackl to Joined Cases C-184/02 & C-223/02 (Spain and Finland/Parliament and Council)* (CJEU), §115.

off-premises contracts was necessary in the light of consumer protection. Those obligations are compatible with the freedom to conduct a business as long as the measures only prescribe how the freedom is to be exercised ('be contactable') and do not prescribe the precise nature of the communication.[37]

Additionally, the CJEU clarified that claims of reduced profitability are by any means unopposable under article 16's protection. The CJEU's interpretation is clear: the uncertainty related to the profitability of an undertaking is inextricably linked to economic activity, and therefore one cannot claim to be protected from such uncertainty.[38]

Concluding, the essence of the freedom to exercise an economic activity can be summarized as the protection of the continuation of the economic activity. A measure fully prohibiting the sale of bananas, a measure creating an obstacle for truck drivers to drive or requiring costly measures without providing undertakings with the free choice of application of their resources does not respect the essence of the freedom. Such measures infringe the essence of the freedom to conduct a business protected in article 16 of the Charter, and an undertaking could oppose such a measure with a reference to the protection it enjoys under this freedom. Opposingly, it can be concluded that a measure does not interfere with the essence of the freedom to exercise an economic activity when the measure solely regulates how the core business should be carried out. They can, for example, regulate that alcoholic beverages may not be labelled and marketed with health claims, prescribe how many bananas can be sold, specify when and how often one can drive a truck and require that an undertaking should implement a filtering system (of their choice).[39]

#### 2.2.1.2 The Essence of the Freedom of Contract

The second sub-freedom of article 16, the freedom of contract, was first mentioned in the 1979 case *Sukkerfabrikken Nykøbing*.[40] According to the subsequent case law, the freedom of contract consists of two elements: the freedom to decide whom to do business with and the freedom to determine the price of a service.[41] In *Alemo-Herron*, the CJEU provided a general clarification on the scope of protection provided by the freedom of contract: 'the transferee must be able to assert its interests effectively in a contractual process to which it is party and to negotiate

---

[37] *Case C-430/17 (Walbusch Walter Busch)* (2019) ECLI:EU:C:2019:47 (CJEU), §35; *Case C-649/17 (Verbraucherzentrale Bundesverband/Amazon EU)* (2019) ECLI:EU:C:2019:576 (CJEU), §46.

[38] Ibid, §14.

[39] On the filtering obligation, see *Case C-360/10 (Sabam/Netlog)* (2012) ECLI:EU:C:2012:85 (CJEU).

[40] *Case C-151/78 (Sukkerfabrikken)* (1979) ECLI:EU:C:1979:4 (CJEU).

[41] See *Case C-90/90 (Neu)* (1991) ECLI:EU:C:1991:303 (CJEU), §13; and *Case C-437/04 (Commission/Belgium)* (2007) ECLI:EU:C:2007:178 (CJEU), §51. These two sub elements were later confirmed in *Case C-283/11 (Sky Österreich)* (2013) ECLI:EU:C:2013:28 (CJEU), §43.

the aspects (...) with a view to its future economic activity'.[42] In *Werhof*, it adds thereto that 'in particular, parties are free to enter into obligations with each other'.[43] In *Sky Österreich*, the CJEU confirms explicitly that the freedom to determine the price of a service is part of the scope of protection of the freedom of contract.

However, based on the CJEU's prior conclusions in both *Werhof* and *STEB*, one can argue that the 'freedom to determine the price of a service' should be extended to include the freedom to decide on any terms of the contract, not just the price, as long as the terms comply with the mandatory rules of public policy. In *Werhof*, the CJEU concludes more broadly that the freedom of contract encompasses 'a freedom of the parties to arrange their own affairs'.[44] In *STEB*, the CJEU extends this view: 'In that regard, it should be noted that the contracting parties are at liberty—subject to the mandatory rules of public policy—to define the terms of their legal relationship'[45] That raises the suggestion that the scope of the freedom of content extends to the entire content of the agreement, rather than solely protecting the freedom to set the price. That seems to furthermore be better in line with the CJEU's argumentation in *Alemo-Herron*, concluding that a party must be able to effectively take part in the negotiation process.

However, like the freedom to exercise an economic activity, the freedom to decide on the terms of the contract can be subject to a measure prescribing a framework. A party can be obliged to update the terms of the contract regularly; for example, could a measure impose an obligation to 'cost orient prices and to adjust those prices on an annual basis'?[46] Such a measure does not affect the very essence of the freedom of contract as it does not dictate the price, nor does it prevent the service to be carried out. The CJEU concludes in *Polkomtel* that the very essence of the freedom of contract is not affected as the discussed measure solely implements a framework. This line of reasoning equals the argumentation in *AGET Iraklis*.[47] That would mean that a measure, in line with the practice set out above regarding the freedom to exercise an economic activity, can prescribe *how* the contractual terms should be negotiated but not *which* terms should be included—apart from those explicitly prescribed by law (mandatory rules of public policy).

For online platforms, that would mean that a platform is not allowed to deviate from mandatory rules but has the right to decide freely on the remaining terms. As child pornography is illegal by law, the platform, even if it would, cannot agree with the user that such content will anyhow be legal on the platform. However, if something is not explicitly made illegal by law (euthanasia content in the Netherlands), the platform can restrict that content in their user terms.

---

[42] *Case C-426/11 (Alemo-Herron and Others)* (2013) ECLI:EU:C:2013:521 (CJEU), §33.

[43] *Case C-499/04 (Werhof/Freeway Traffic Systems)* (2006) ECLI:EU:C:2006:168 (CJEU), §23.

[44] ibid.

[45] *Case C-277/05 (STEB)* (2007) ECLI:EU:C:2007:440 (CJEU), §28.

[46] *Case C-277/16 (Polkomtel)* (2017) ECLI:EU:C:2017:989 (CJEU), §52.

[47] *Case C-201/15 (AGET Iraklis)* (2016) ECLI:EU:C:2016:972 (CJEU).

One can deduct from these cases that a measure making it impossible for an undertaking to effectively assert its interests through contracting, for example a restriction of all possibilities to participate in the negotiation of the terms of a contract, would limit the very essence of the freedom of contract. Unfortunately, a clear definition of what should fall within the scope of 'effectively asserting its interests' and 'to negotiate aspects that affect its future economic activity' is lacking. It seems therefore hard for an undertaking to challenge a measure restricting the freedom of contract, as seen by the CJEU's decision in *Sky Österreich*, where a discussion on the essence of the right was omitted by both the Advocate General and the CJEU. It follows from the case that measures solely prescribing a framework or the requirements for the entering into a contract, limiting the possible contract parties or the terms of a contract, are not per se limiting the very essence of the freedom and could therefore be justifiable under article 52 (1) of the Charter. In addition, this case shows that a party can be obliged to enter into a contract if subsequently given the opportunity to participate in the negotiation process.

Furthermore, the content of the contractual terms itself does not constitute the essence of the freedom of contract. Only within the borders of the law are the parties at liberty to define the terms. That leaves broad discretion to the authorities to limit the freedom to decide on the terms of the contract.

### 2.2.2 The Essence of the 'Right to Property' in Article 17

According to the wording of article 17, lawfully acquired possessions, including intellectual property, are protected against unjust interference. However, the exact definition of 'possession' cannot be deducted from a textual interpretation of either article 17 or article P1-1 ECHR. Defining 'possession' or 'property' is therefore left to the CJEU and the ECtHR.[48]

From the ECtHR's case law, it follows that a 'possession' must represent an economic value in order to fall within the scope of the article.[49] These possessions do not necessarily have to consist of material goods.[50] The material scope is further limited to existing possessions, as mentioned above. Article P1-1 does not guarantee a right to acquire possessions, nor does the article protect any future income. The CJEU confirms this line set out by the ECtHR in *Inuit Tapiriit Kanatami and Others v Commission*.[51] Like the freedom to conduct a business, the right to property does

[48] Praduroux (2019), p. 172.

[49] *Parrillo v Italy* (ECtHR), §215. In Parrillo v Italy, the ECtHR found that "having regard to the economic and pecuniary scope of that Article, human embryos cannot be reduced to "possessions" within the meaning of that provision."

[50] ibid, §211.

[51] *Case C-398/13P (Inuit Tapiriit Kanatami and Others/Commission)* (2015) ECLI:EU:C:2015:535 (CJEU), §60.

not protect the mere profitability and very existence of a business.[52] In that same line, the CJEU found in *Standley and Others* that a restriction imposing an (indirect) economic burden did not impair the substance of the right to property as such restrictions merely regulate the exercise of the right to property.[53] A similar conclusion was reached in *Booker Aquaculture*, where the CJEU did not find an impairment of the essence of fishermen's right to property.[54] In the case, the fishermen were obliged to kill and dispose of infected fish. As these infected fish did not have any commercial value and the risk of a disease outbreak is inherent to the fishing industry, the Court reasoned that a measure requiring the disposal of infected fish did not impair the very essence of the right. Likewise, a prohibition to plant new vines was found not to be a restriction of the use of one's property, despite the fact that it restricts the peaceful enjoyment hereof (the vineyard), as the opposite scenario (not restricting the planting of new vines) would have had a similarly negative effect, contributing solely to 'a continuous overproduction'.[55] This was later confirmed by the CJEU in relation to measures aiming at decreasing milk surpluses, as the property could still be used for different purposes than producing milk.[56] Furthermore, the CJEU concluded in *Generics (UK) and Others* that the essence of the right to property is not impaired if it is not practically impossible for the undertaking to continue to produce and develop its products (in this case medicines).[57]

In *Plovdiv*, the CJEU reached the conclusion that the confiscation of a third party's possessions, which were used to commit an offence of which the third party was unaware (in good faith), constitutes a restriction of the essence of the right to property.[58] To stay with the banana examples used above, that would mean the confiscation of an undertaking's bananas because their shipping boxes were being used to smuggle cocaine. When the undertaking was in good faith and thus unaware of the smuggling, confiscating property restricts the very essence of the right to property.

In conclusion, the right to property provides protection against unjust interference with previously acquired possessions (caught fish) or the further exploitation of previously acquired possessions (milking of possessed cows, planting vines in a possessed vineyard). It does not provide any protection for the acquisition of future possessions, nor does it protect the profitability of the exploitation of possessions.

---

[52] *Case C-258/81 (Mettallurgiki Halyps/Commission)* (1982) ECLI:EU:C:1982:422 (CJEU), §13.

[53] *Case C-293/97 (Standley and Others)* (1999) ECLI:EU:C:1999:215 (CJEU), §§55-56. Farmers claimed that their right to property was infringed by imposing the economic burden of reducing the nitrate concentrations in water sources on their farmlands.

[54] *Case C-20/00 (Booker Aquaculture)* (2003) ECLI:EU:C:2003:397 (CJEU), §86.

[55] *Case C-44/79 (Hauer/Land Rheinland-Pfalz)* (CJEU), §19 and §29-30.

[56] *Case C-177/90 (Kühn)* (1992) ECLI:EU:C:1992:2 (CJEU), §17.

[57] *Case C-368/96 (Generics (UK) and Others)* (1998) ECLI:EU:C:1998:583 (CJEU), §85.

[58] *Case C-393/19 (Plovdiv)* (2021) ECLI:EU:C:2021:8 (CJEU), §55.

### 2.2.3 Conclusion on the Differences Between Property and Conducting a Business

At first glance, the main difference between the right to property on the one hand and the freedom to conduct a business on the other hand seems to be the subject matter: property versus the use of that property. Whereas the right to property covers the protection of acquired possessions with an economic value, the freedom to conduct a business covers the continuation of economic activity. For example, a restriction limiting the number of cows (possessed property) to be milked falls within the right to property. A restriction limiting the acquisition of cows (prospective property) falls within the scope of the freedom to conduct a business. In the latter case, the measure does not affect an already present economic value as prospective cows are not yet owned by the company.

The analysis confirms that the right to property does not extend its protection to the acquisition of property. When comparing the two banana examples, the freedom to conduct a business protects the continuation of the selling of bananas, whereas the right to property protects the bananas themselves. Furthermore, article 16 protects against the interference with acquiring possessions (such as quantitative limitations restricting the acquisition of bananas), whereas article 17 protects against the interference with the exploitation of existing possessions.

## 3 Running a Platform: Property or Conducting a Business?

So, on which article could a platform potentially best base an opposition? Should the platform's infrastructure, or the content shared thereon, be qualified a(n) (in)tangible asset, and is it interfering with that property covered under article 17, or is it rather the freedom to define how to apply, use and care for one's (prospective) tangible and intangible assets, covered by the freedom to conduct a business, that applies to the drafting of house rules? Is providing access to information shared by other users equivalent to the sale of bananas or, rather, to the bananas themselves?

As a principal note, like the banana company, a platform may rely on both article 16 and article 17 in different situations. It can invoke, for example, article 16 to cover the business aspects (running the platform) and article 17 to cover the (in)tangible assets (technical infrastructure, intellectual property). The answer as to which to apply to the posed dilemma depends on the qualification of the platform and the information created in the process. When the information created by (the users of) the platform is seen as a possession, then obliging a platform to include other types of information (read: acquire possessions) is not covered by the right to property as such an obligation does not interfere with the platform's previously acquired possessions. It obliges the platform to increase the number of possessions, rather than interfering with the possessions already owned. Additionally, one could wonder and discuss whether the content, created by the platform's users, can be considered possessions of the platform at all.[59]

It seems more logical that such an obligation would interfere with the intended scope of protection of the freedom to conduct a business. When a state obliges the platform to acquire possessions, the platform is limited in the way it wants to conduct its business—namely, to deny access to certain types of content it does not wish to host. Similarly, the owner of the banana company might not want to import pineapples as a side business. In addition, the freedom of contract, a sub-freedom of the freedom to conduct a business, provides both parties with protection against unjust state interference in the contracting process. House rules cover the relationship between the platform and its users in a contractual way. Based on the CJEU's decision in *STEB*—contracting parties are at liberty to define the terms of their legal relationship, subject to mandatory rules of public policy—the freedom of contract provides the platform and the user the possibility to agree on anything within the borders of the law. As long as there is no prohibition to moderate content not qualified illegal by law, the platform is free to exclude legal content through its user terms.

Based on these arguments, it seems most likely that the platform will be able to oppose a state measure obliging the inclusion of legal content on the basis of the freedom to conduct a business in article 16 rather than the right to property in article 17. It follows subsequently from the analysis on the freedom to conduct a business that it is allowed for a state to regulate the way a business is carried out. However, the examples following from the case law only cover those circumstances where the state *limited* a company's economic activity (selling fewer bananas, marketing prohibition on tobacco and alcohol products), not *increasing* the economic activity. Could a company be obliged at all to include something as part of their business against their will? From the previous paragraph, it is clear that a measure may not, in effect, make it impossible to continue the economic activity. That means that a restriction of the free drafting of house rules may not constitute the end of the platform. However, the risk that a platform would not be able to continue to provide its service if it must provide access to legal content on its platform seems, to say the least, exaggerated and is most likely non-existing. Such a requirement to host could of course be negatively formulated as a prohibition to moderate content that is not addressed by laws, as similarly, the banana company is prohibited to add harmful pesticides to its bananas.

That does not mean that any limitation that does not cause the platform's bankruptcy is allowed. As touched upon above, limitations that impair the essence of a right are per default inadmissible, though also when a measure does not impair the very essence, it can still be unjustifiable. To provide a full overview of the way platforms can rely on the protection provided for in article 16, the next paragraph

---

[59] For the discussion on the application, this discussion can be omitted here. If the content is a possession, then acquiring more falls outside the scope of article 17. If the content created by users cannot be seen as a possession of the platform, article 17 would not apply either.

assesses the proportionality assessment for limitations to the freedom to conduct a business in the CJEU's case law. This provides an overview of situations where the restriction does not impair the essence of the freedom to conduct a business but anyhow posed an unjustifiable limitation of article 16.

# 4 Defining the Scope: A Closer Look at the Freedom to Conduct a Business

In his opinion in *Nold v. Commission*, Advocate-General Trabucchi states that limitations negatively affecting one undertaking's business can be of significantly bigger interest for society as a whole and can therewith be justifiable. In his words, limitations might, in fact, be beneficial to 'well-ordered economic, commercial and productive activities, in the interests not only of producers, but also of consumers, by means of a reduction in distribution costs (. . .)'.[60] That point of view corresponds to article 52(1) of the Charter, which allows the limitation of a fundamental right when such a limitation is in accordance with the principle of proportionality. To live up to this principle, a limitation may only be made if it is necessary and genuinely meets an objective of general interest or is needed to protect the rights and freedoms of others. A measure thus always has to pass the necessity test and either fulfil an objective of general interest or protect the rights and freedoms of others. If not, the restriction in the measure is not justifiable and infringes the fundamental right protected.

## *4.1 General Interest and/or Protecting the Rights and Freedoms of Others*

There is no limited list as to which objectives of general interest could be used to justify a national measure limiting fundamental rights. In relation to measures limiting the freedom to conduct a business, the CJEU has approved the following as an objective in the general interest: public safety and public health,[61] such as the prevention of epizootic diseases;[62] the fight against terrorism[63] and road safety;[64]

---

[60] *Opinion of AG Trabucchi to Case C-4/73 (Nold v Commission)* (CJEU), p. 514.

[61] *Case C-376/98 (Germany/Parliament)* (2000) ECLI:EU:C:2000:544 (CJEU); *Deutsches Weintor* (n 36); *Case C-157/14 (Neptune Distribution)* (2015) ECLI:EU:C:2015:823 (CJEU); *Swedish Match* (n 12).

[62] *Case C-101/12 (Schaible)* (2013) ECLI:EU:C:2013:661 (CJEU).

[63] *Case C-402/05 P (Kadi & Al Barakaat Int Foundation)* (2008) ECLI:EU:C:2008:461 (CJEU).

[64] *Spain and Finland v Parliament and Council* (n 36).

preventing tax evasion;[65] harmonizing legal protection;[66] cultural development;[67] securing a free internal market,[68] including securing the free movement of goods[69] and services;[70] the protection of workers;[71] and ensuring common policies such as an agricultural policy[72] and a common fisheries policy.[73]

The objective of the measure limiting the freedom to conduct a business can also be rooted in a need to protect the rights and freedoms of others. For the issue at stake in this chapter, one can conclude in short that limiting the free drafting of house rules to secure the freedom of expression and freedom to impart information of the users, safeguarded in article 11 of the Charter, would constitute a legitimate aim. In *Sky Österreich*, the CJEU emphasizes this, stating that the protection of the fundamental freedom in article 11 of the Charter 'undoubtedly constitutes a legitimate aim in the general interest' as this freedom is of significant importance in a democratic and pluralistic society. It concludes that 'the European Union legislature was entitled to adopt rules (. . .) which limit the freedom to conduct a business, and to give priority, in the necessary balancing of the rights and interests at issue, to public access to information over contractual freedom'.[74]

## 4.2 *The Measure Must Be Necessary*

When a measure either serves an objective of general interest or is aimed at protecting the rights and freedoms of others, it subsequently needs to pass the threshold of necessity. To test whether a measure is necessary, the Gebhard test can be applied. To pass the Gebhard test, a measure must be necessary, suitable for the attainment of the objective pursued, and it must not go beyond what is necessary in order to attain that objective.[75] A measure is in general not necessary if a less intrusive measure exists that is capable of achieving the same objective or goal.[76]

65 *Case C-534/16 (BB Construct)* (2017) ECLI:EU:C:2017:820 (CJEU).

66 *Metronome Musik* (n 25), §22.

67 ibid, §23.

68 FRA - European Union Agency for Fundamental Rights (n 15), see p. 24, where they refer to the prior authorization of mergers, prohibiting the abuse of a dominant position, and certain forms of agreements under competition law. See also the case law discussed.

69 *Case C-112/00 (Schmidberger)* (2003) ECLI:EU:C:2003:333 (CJEU).

70 *Case C-36/02 (Omega)* (2004) ECLI:EU:C:2004:614 (CJEU).

71 *AGET Iraklis* (n 48).

72 *Association Kokopelli* (n 25), §43.

73 *Case C-540/16 (Spika and Others)* (2018) ECLI:EU:C:2018:565 (CJEU).

74 Ibid, §66.

75 *Case C-55/94 (Gebhard)* (1995) ECLI:EU:C:1995:411 (CJEU), §37, where the CJEU mentioned the necessity-test for the first time.

76 See, for a further discussion on the Gebhard test, also Reich (2014), p. 157.

From the case law, one can firstly conclude that a measure is deemed disproportional when the measure is manifestly disproportionate to achieve the aim.[77] That means that when a less restrictive measure is not capable of achieving the objective, a more restrictive measure is justifiable. The suitability of a measure to attain the objective pursued was the point of discussion in *Spain & Finland v. Commission & Council*, where the objective pursued was road safety (minimizing the risk of traffic accidents). The proposed measure limited the number of hours that truck drivers were allowed to drive, and in addition, it limited the truck drivers' freedom to allocate time to administrative work. It was argued by Spain and Finland that less restrictive measures were available, namely better enforcement of driving hours. If truck drivers would stick to the number of driving hours, the objective of road safety could also be achieved. Spain & Finland argued therefore that the restriction did not need to cover the allocation of time for administrative work, which in their eyes posed an unjustifiable restriction on the truck drivers' freedom to conduct their business. Opposingly, the Parliament and the Commission argued that it was necessary to regulate the administrative hours as these hours contribute to the overall fatigue level of the truck drivers. As it was this overall fatigue level of the truck drivers that posed a threat to road safety, a more severe measure was needed. The CJEU agreed with the latter argument and found that the measure limiting the number of hours that truck drivers can spend on either driving or administration was necessary to attain the objective pursued. The less restrictive measure (only regulating the driving hours) was incapable of sufficiently achieving the objective pursued.

Later, the CJEU confirmed that this doctrine does not only apply when the less restrictive measure is not capable of achieving the aim at all. Also when the less restrictive measure is not as effective in achieving the goal, a stricter measure can be justifiable.[78] That does not mean that a measure needs to be a hundred percent effective in order to pass the test: when a measure proves ineffective for a small portion but serves to attain the objective on a general level, the measure can be proportionate.[79] Furthermore, despite the fact that a measure poses substantial adverse consequences for a certain (small) group of traders, it could still be effective in achieving the overall aim. In these situations, the overall interest of all the traders

[77] *Schräder* (n 9), §22; *Case C-44/94 (The Queen/Minister of Agriculture, Fisheries and Food)* (CJEU), §58; *Association Kokopelli* (n 67), §39.

[78] *Swedish Match* (n 25), §56; *Association Kokopelli* (n 25), §52; *Sky Österreich* (n 11), §55.

[79] See *Schaible* (n 25), §41, where the CJEU rules that the simple fact that some of the animal ear-tags might get lost, that does not demonstrate in itself that the system of ear-tags as a whole is unsuitable to prevent the outbreak of epizootic diseases amongst these animals. Schaible argued that around 5% of the tags used would be destroyed in the process. The CJEU concludes: *"As regards the allegations concerning the technical flaws of the identification system, even if the percentage of the means of electronic identification attached to animals which are lost or become defective can reach the level indicated by Mr Schaible, such malfunctions cannot, in themselves, demonstrate that the system concerned is, as a whole, unsuitable."* Similar reasoning can be found in *UPC-Telekabel* (n 25), §63.

in the market,[80] or the (long-term) effects on the Community market as a whole,[81] must be taken into consideration rather than the interest of the smaller, negatively affected group. Therefore, a measure can withstand the test if there are no available alternatives that would preserve the interest of the parties or the Community to a greater extent, despite the fact that these alternatives might be effective in achieving the objective and are less intrusive for a specific group of traders.[82]

In solely one case included in the scope of this assessment, the CJEU deemed a measure that limited the freedom to conduct a business disproportionate. In *BB Construct*, a Slovak company was subject to a tax guarantee with a maximum of 500,000 euros. The CJEU concluded that '(...) the provision of a guarantee—having regard to the fact that it is for a significant amount—would deprive, without justification, the company concerned of its resources from the moment of its creation and would prevent it from developing its economic activities, that guarantee is a manifestly disproportionate interference with the freedom to conduct a business'.[83] The CJEU found the tax guarantee disproportionate because it would prevent the company from developing any economic activity. One could similarly argue that such a restriction would limit the very essence of the freedom to conduct a business (the continuation of economic activity) as the measure made it impossible for the company to carry out any business at all and was therefore never to be subjected to the Gebhard test.

## 4.3 Limitations to House Rule Drafting

For limitations to house rule drafting, that means the following. Firstly, as shown before, a measure limiting the essence of the freedom to conduct a business is unjustifiable. However, as also pointed out above, the risk that a measure covering the content of house rules would make it impossible to continue the economic activity of the platform can be disregarded. Therefore, unjustifiable measures that would restrict the essence of article 16 do not seem to exist.

Secondly, moving on to limitations that might be justifiable, one should consider whether a proposed restriction might be manifestly disproportionate to achieve the aim. In the case of restricting access to legal content, the aim to be achieved would most likely be the protection of the rights and freedoms of others, more precisely the protection of the platform users' freedom of expression and information protected in article 11 of the Charter. Limiting the freedom of contract in a way that prohibits platforms to exclude legal content does not seem manifestly disproportionate for the protection of the freedoms of expression and information of its users. Following the

[80] Ibid, §40.
[81] *Zuckerfabrik* (n 25), §76.
[82] *Metronome Musik* (n 25), §26.
[83] *BB Construct* (n 25), §41.

CJEU case law, if the restriction can potentially achieve the aim, despite the fact that there are other measures available, the chosen restriction passes this test. The threshold for the requirement seems low: as pointed out above, referring to the CJEU's decision in *Sky Österreich*, the European Union legislator may favour providing access to information over the freedom of contract.

Thirdly, one should consider whether a less restrictive, evenly effective measure is available. To do so, the proposed measure should be assessed. Exactly how restrictive would a measure limiting platforms' possibility to block access to certain types of content be, and what kind of other measures would be available that potentially would be less restrictive? To prevent a purely normative way of answering that question and due to the fact that a standardized test does not exist, interpretational guidance will be sought in a European Directive with the same purpose: the Unfair Contract Terms Directive (UCTD).[84] As the name indicates, the UCTD prohibits unfair contract terms, which is a more general limitation of the parties' liberty to freely draft user terms and therewith a less restrictive, existing measure. If the unfairness test of the UCTD would sufficiently achieve the aim, the necessity for a stricter regulation vanishes. If it does not sufficiently achieve the aim, new measures should at least pass the threshold of the UCTD's unfairness test.

### 4.3.1 Comparing Restrictiveness: The Unfairness Test of the UCTD

According to article 3 (1) of the UCTD, a contractual term is unfair if it causes a significant imbalance in the parties' rights and obligations arising under the contract—to the detriment of the consumer—and is contrary to the requirement of good faith. The UCTD contains indicative, non-exhaustive lists of unfair terms (the black and grey lists). These lists neither cover, specifically, the exclusion of legal content nor, more generally, the limitation of fundamental rights protection.[85] Therefore, the assessment depends on the 'general' unfairness test. The assessment can, according to the Commission's guidance, be boiled down to two elements: the good faith assessment and the assessment of significant imbalance.[86] To assess the requirements of good faith, the national court must assess whether the supplier could reasonably assume that the consumer would have accepted the contract term in a similar way if he was given the chance to negotiate it individually.[87] The outcome hereof depends strictly on the circumstances of the case. In general, it seems impossible to define whether the average consumer would have created a Facebook

---

[84] Council Directive (EEC) 93/13 of 5 April 1993 on unfair terms in consumer contracts [OJ L 95].

[85] See, for a discussion on the necessity to extend the black and grey lists to better suit online services, Loos and Luzak (2021) Accessed 26 February 2021.

[86] This is however not undisputed. Advocate General Hogan suggests in C-34/18 (*Ottília Lovasné Tóth*) that good faith should not be treated as a separate requirement. See Commission notice of 27 September 2019 (n 12), §3.4.1. and the references in footnote 215.

[87] Ibid, §3.4.1. and the case law cited.

account and agreed to its Community Guidelines if he or she had been explicitly aware that Black Pete or euthanasia content could be removed in the future, especially since online platforms regularly update their user terms and change the application of specific terms, which might have been decisive for the user to be present on the platform.

Moreover, the national court must assess in what position the consumer would have been if the questioned contract term would not have existed. This analysis 'will enable the national court to evaluate whether and to what extent the contract term places the consumer in a legal situation less favourable than under the otherwise applicable contract law'.[88] The imbalance is significant if the impairment of the consumer's legal situation is sufficiently serious. As the good-faith assessment does not provide any clarity, the outcome of the unfairness test in the UCTD depends on this part of the assessment.

That means that the outcome depends on whether the consumer, without the restriction in the platform's user terms, would have been able to share the content freely. Thus, would the consumer be better off without the contractual term? Unfortunately, a clear-cut answer to that question does not exist as it depends on the societal view of online platforms, making the analysis highly normative in nature.

In the offline, physical world, anything is *allowed* unless explicitly *forbidden*. One could enter a park, a bar and a supermarket unless physically or legally 'fenced off'. A person can freely express himself or herself unless restricted by laws—in the broadest sense of the word. The status quo in the online world, and especially on online platforms, is the exact opposite. The technical infrastructure is controlled by user terms, and thus by default anything is *forbidden* unless it is explicitly *allowed* in the user terms or by the technical infrastructure created by the platform. Opposed to a park or a bar, one cannot simply physically walk onto a platform. When online platforms are viewed as an extension of the offline world, the status quo without any contractual term would allow a user to share anything that is not illegal. Opposingly, if these Community Guidelines are purely viewed as a private service agreement between two parties, then anything that is not explicitly agreed upon is not part of the agreement. In that case, a user is not allowed to share anything that is not explicitly laid down in the agreement. Under the first view, a user term excluding legal content would cause a significant imbalance in the rights and obligations of the parties to the detriment of the consumer because without this contractual term, the consumer would be allowed to post legal content. That would mean that, as a result of the unfairness test, user terms excluding legal content are unfair. In the second view, the exact opposite is true.

Therefore, in order to reach a conclusion on the unfairness of the disputed contract terms, the debate on how to qualify a platform must first be resolved. The worldwide character of online platforms makes reaching a consensus on this issue problematic. Views of online platforms are society bound, and therefore legislators in general, and the European legislator specifically, should dare to develop their own

---

[88] Ibid., §3.4.2.

stance in this debate, ruling out the arguments in the debate that originated elsewhere. For example, the outcome of the debate on the legal qualification of online platforms should differ depending on whether it serves a society where people generally trust the government over private companies, as compared to a society where private companies are trusted over the government. Despite the fact that the legal qualification of online platforms is debated thoroughly,[89] a conclusion remains to be made.

### 4.3.2 Is a Less Restrictive Alternative Available?

The last conclusion remaining to be answered in this chapter is whether a less restrictive alternative exists as opposed to a restriction of the platforms' contractual freedom. It seems that a less restrictive alternative, such as the unfairness test in the UCTD—which is also a restriction of the platforms' contractual freedom—is not able to achieve the sought aim in a similarly effective way and that a system without any restrictions would lead to a significant imbalance on the users' side. Such a significant imbalance does not seem to correspond to the sought aim (protecting the users' right under article 11 of the Charter), nor does it live up to the aim sought by the UCTD itself (consumer protection).

As shown above, neither the good faith test nor the assessment of significant imbalance would be able to make up for the weaker position of the consumer when entering into an agreement that contains terms that have not been individually negotiated. There is little doubt as to whether the consumer is in a weaker position as opposed to the online platform: the only choice the consumer has in relation to the user terms that apply on the platform is whether to accept or reject them. Individual negotiation is not a part of the procedure, nor is there a possibility to reject certain clauses the consumer does not agree with. It is all or nothing. Moreover, due to the way online platforms currently operate, switching from one to another is equally burdensome for the consumer.

The consumer could bring a case before a national court to have the contractual term assessed for unfairness. He or she can hope that the circumstances of the case will point in the direction of unfairness, though that does not provide a sustainable, general solution and does not seem to fully take into consideration the weaker position of the consumer. It is undesirable that a consumer must first sue a platform with significantly better resources in order to have an idea of whether a contractual term is unfair. Especially in a time where the importance of being present on these platforms increases, proper and effective protection for consumers is highly needed.

[89] See, for a comprehensive discussion on the different views, Suzor (2018).

## 5 Concluding Remarks: Restrictions Are Permissible, But Will They Solve the Problem?

Based on all the above, there is room for the European Union legislator to adopt rules (further) limiting platforms' contractual freedom. The scope of the Charter's right to property does not provide protection against interference with the free drafting of house rules on a platform. The scope of article 16's protection includes a platform's contractual freedom, though a successful opposition based on the protection provided by the freedom to conduct a business seems unlikely. Firstly, the essence of the freedom to conduct a business solely covers the 'continuation of the economic activity', which essence will not be affected by a measure prohibiting user terms to exclude legal content. Secondly, such a measure will most likely pass the Gebhard test and thus be deemed justifiable. The number of legitimate aims that can be invoked to limit the freedom to conduct a business is endless, and based on the CJEU's ruling in *Sky Österreich*, the legislator will be allowed to favour the users' freedom of expression and information in article 11 of the Charter over the platforms' contractual freedom. Restricting the moderation of content to those types of content that are covered by legislation would therefore be justifiable.

However, concluding that limiting the user terms would be compatible with the fundamental rights of the Charter does not necessarily mean that this would effectively and sufficiently solve the problem as the cause of the problem seems to be rooted in the fact that there is (still) no consensus on the qualification of platforms. Therefore, a decision should be taken on what platforms actually are and how they relate to the offline world around us. Do they represent an online version of a public park, a bar or restaurant, a festival with entry tickets, a broadcaster or perhaps something completely new? When we know how platforms relate to the world around us, it is possible to determine whether these platforms should follow the 'allowed, unless explicitly forbidden' theory. If that theory would apply, a measure prohibiting the exclusion of legal content is a logical step to take.

Outside the direct realm of platforms, this chapter has also shown that the freedom to conduct a business has been reduced to an empty shell, or rather a shell that has never been inhabited. Apart from the situation where an undertaking would be able to demonstrate that a proposed measure would mean the absolute end of the economic activity, the freedom to conduct a business will not provide any effective protection.

## References

European Agency for Fundamental Rights (2015) Freedom to Conduct a Business: Exploring the Dimensions of a Fundamental Right

European Commission (2007) Explanations Relating to the Charter of Fundamental Rights

Everson M, Correia Gonçalves R (2014) Article 16', The EU Charter of Fundamental Rights: A Commentary. Hart

Groussot X, Petursson GT, Pierce J (2014) Weak Right, Strong Court – The Freedom to Conduct Business and the EU Charter of Fundamental Rights. Social Science Research Network Scholarly Paper ID 2428181

Heller B, van Hoboken J (2019) Freedom of Expression: A Comparative Summary of United States and European Law. https://www.ivir.nl/publicaties/download/TWG_Freedom_of_Expression.pdf

Lenaerts K (2019) Limits on limitations: the essence of Fundamental Rights in the EU. Germ Law J 20:779

Loos M, Luzak J (2021) Update the Unfair Contract Terms Directive for Digital Services. https://www.europarl.europa.eu/RegData/etudes/STUD/2021/676006/IPOL_STU(2021)676006_EN.pdf

Oliver P (2013) What purpose does Article 16 of the charter serve?', General principles of EU law and European private law. Kluwer Law International

Praduroux S (2019) Property and expropriation: two concepts revisited in the light of the case law of the European Court of Human Rights and the European Court of Justice. Eur Prop Law J 8:172

Reich N (2014) General principles of EU civil law. Intersentia

Suzor N (2018) Digital constitutionalism: using the rule of law to evaluate the legitimacy of Governance by platforms. Social Media + Society, 4

van der Donk BBE (2022) Should critique on governmental policy regarding Covid-19 Be tolerated on online platforms? An analysis of recent case-law in the Netherlands. J Human Rights Pract (forthcoming)

**Berdien van der Donk** is a PhD fellow at the Centre for Private Governance (CEPRI), University of Copenhagen, Denmark; a lecturer in EU Internet Law at Copenhagen Business School; and a legal analyst for trademark and domain name cases at Clarivate's Darts-IP. She obtained an LL.M. from the University of Copenhagen and Leiden University (the Netherlands).

Her main research interests involve platforms and their user terms, intellectual property and fundamental rights law. Her latest research focuses on the invalidity of clauses in user terms limiting access to information on social media platforms in a way that goes beyond what is prescribed by law and unravelling a potential discrepancy between the use of user terms by social media platforms as opposed to the use of user terms by non-platform actors in the Member States of the European Union.

# Internet Platforms and Freedom of Expression in Constitution-Making

**Kári Hólmar Ragnarsson**

## Contents



**Abstract** Internet speech provides opportunities for democratic discourse but has also proven to cause harm to democracy by elevating disinformation, harassment, and extremism. Regulating power in the digital world challenges traditional understandings of freedom of expression and might require a legal response at the constitutional level. This article explores how Internet speech and freedom of expression have been addressed in three constitutional reform processes commenced after the 2008 financial crisis in Iceland, Ireland, and Norway. In all cases the novel or emerging problems involving Internet speech, and particularly the power of Internet platforms, were missed by constitutional reformers while positive aspects of Internet speech were embraced and granted constitutional protection. The experiences highlight, among other things, the importance of timing of constitutional reform: Reformers necessarily focus mostly on problems of the past but the timing of a "constitutional moment" may not be optimal to address what will become pressing

K. H. Ragnarsson (✉)
Faculty of Law, University of Iceland, Reykjavík, Iceland
e-mail: khr@hi.is



S. Hindelang, A. Moberg (eds.), *YSEC Yearbook of Socio-Economic Constitutions 2021*, YSEC Yearbook of Socio-Economic Constitutions (2022) 2021: 59–90,
https://doi.org/10.1007/16495_2021_37, Published online: 10 April 2022

problems. Reformers are constrained, or perceive themselves to be constrained, by international law and traditional constitutional law doctrine where the state is the principal risk for fundamental rights. The power of private entities, including Internet platforms, goes unaddressed, and the global scale of Internet speech, far beyond the territorial jurisdiction of constitutional law, presents various complexities.

## 1 Introduction

Democracy is built on freedom of expression. Without a check provided by criticism from the public and the press government accountability is next to impossible.[1] The free exchange of ideas and conflicting views of the good are at the core of self-government and, for its proponents, are crucial to the functioning of deliberative democracy.[2] The deep relationship between democracy and freedom of expression is ingrained in the protection of fundamental rights in Europe. The ECtHR has held that "freedom of expression constitutes one of the essential foundations of [democratic] society, one of the basic conditions for its progress and for the development of every man."[3] Imparting and receiving factually accurate information on matters of general interest enjoys uncontested protection. Freedom of expression, furthermore, protects ideas that "offend, shock or disturb. . .Such are the demands of that pluralism, tolerance and broadmindedness without which there is no 'democratic society'."[4]

However, Internet speech complicates this picture. Disinformation, anonymous harassment, echo chambers, cultivation of extremism, and the power of global Internet platforms, such as Facebook and Twitter, are just a few of the issues causing strain on our understanding of meaningful freedom of expression.[5] A canvassing of experts by Pew Research in 2020 revealed that around half of the experts consider that technology will mostly weaken democracy and even the optimistic half often expressed some concerns.[6] The novel problems may call for an update of constitutional approaches.

This article explores how recent efforts of constitutional reform in Europe have treated freedom of expression and Internet speech. From these efforts we take lessons on the potential and limits of constitutional reform as a method to address new societal problems more generally.

---

[1] For an exploration of democracy as the foundation of freedom of expression see Schauer (1983).

[2] E.g. Fishkin and Mansbridge (2017).

[3] ECtHR: *Handyside v. the United Kingdom*, no. 5493/72, § 49, Series A-24.

[4] Id.

[5] See Sect. 2 below.

[6] Anderson and Rainie (2020).

In the aftermath of the 2008 financial crisis several countries looked to constitutional reform as a response to perceived failures of existing institutional structures.[7] The article considers the experience of Iceland, Norway and Ireland, which embarked on different paths of constitutional reform. The article particularly asks how the drafters of reform proposals in the three countries viewed the benefits and risks of Internet speech, the role of Internet platforms, whether ideas of freedom of speech were reconsidered in light of the rapidly changing context, and what the reformers believed constitutional change could accomplish. All three cases involved changes to freedom of expression protections: Ireland saw the repeal of blasphemy as a constitutionally mandated criminal offence. Norway's constitution was amended to include an updated bill of rights, highly influenced by international human rights law, but a recent bespoke provision of freedom of expression was left intact. In Iceland's unsuccessful "crowdsourced" constitutional reform, social media was regarded as an entirely positive (and integral) factor to the constitutional reform process itself and democracy more generally. The reform proposal included constitutional protections of access to the Internet and information technologies, but with surprisingly limited transformational aspiration.

Our review of these efforts of constitutional reform will, in part, involve a search for traces of "digital constitutionalism" that "seeks to articulate and realize appropriate standards of legitimacy for governance in the digital age."[8] If constitutionalism generally "focuses on power exercised by the state and is not well adapted to ensuring that the decisions of private actors are legitimately made,"[9] digital constitutionalism involves a focus on power on the Internet, seeking to limit "abuses of power in a complex system that includes many different governments, businesses, and civil society organizations."[10] In our modern era the "primary challenge involves not only the role of public actors in regulating the digital environment but also, more importantly, the 'talent of constitutional law' to react against the threats to fundamental rights and the rise of private powers, whose nature is much more global than local."[11] Digital constitutionalism involves a conscious effort to regulate power, most often using traditional tools of constitutional democracy, particularly including law, public institutions and fundamental rights. To be clear, digital constitutionalism does not require a capital-C constitution, but our context is that of constitution-making and therefore we are asking if actually existing constitutionalism has gone digital.

After setting the scene by summarising central issues concerning constitutional freedom of expression and Internet speech (Sect. 2), the article explores the three cases of Iceland, Ireland and Norway (Sect. 3), briefly describing the different reform

[7] See generally e.g. Contiades (2013).

[8] Suzor, 2018, p. 2. See generally Celeste (2019), Redeker et al. (2018), De Gregorio (2021).

[9] Suzor (2020), p. 2.

[10] Suzor (2020), p. 1.

[11] De Gregorio (2021), p. 2.

processes and focusing on the treatment of freedom of expression and the Internet. It then provides analysis and draws lessons more generally on constitutional reform (Sect. 4) and offers a short conclusion (Sect. 5).

The key take-aways include that conventional understandings of constitutional doctrine, including state action / horizontal effect as well as the inherently territorial scope of constitutions in a hyper-globalised world of information sharing, storage and creation present significant hurdles to any constitutional reforms intended to address the complex problems of Internet speech. We further argue that while constitution-level changes may, at least potentially, be necessary or appropriate considering the scope of the issue, timeframes for reforms are problematic. Constitutional drafters are constrained by a lack of clairvoyance; demonstrated best in the Icelandic case where the problems with social media were unforeseen. Drafters focus on tackling the (perceived) problems of the past—Ireland's blasphemy laws, Iceland's failed political institutions, Norway's arguably outdated rights provisions—counting on general principles modelled on international or comparative law to evolve through practice to react to new problems. These general principles, however, may introduce (perceived) constraints on the institutional alternatives open to constitutional drafters, preventing them from developing new solutions.

## 2 Internet Platforms and Constitutional Freedom of Expression

Internet speech has at least two significant characteristics: First, low cost. Practically anyone can participate in public discourse on a global scale, rather than acting simply as passive observer as was the case traditionally.[12] Second, transnational corporations operating Internet platforms perform important roles and wield significant power but have been subject to limited constraints.[13]

Traditional freedom of expression doctrine in Europe extends, of course, to the Internet, whose importance has been frequently noted, for example by the ECtHR:

> [T]he Internet has now become one of the principal means by which individuals exercise their right to freedom to receive and impart information and ideas, providing as it does essential tools for participation in activities and discussions concerning political issues and issues of general interest. ... User-generated expressive activity on the Internet provides an unprecedented platform for the exercise of freedom of expression ...[14]

[12] E.g. Benkler (2006), p. 212, Massaro and Norton (2021), pp. 1634–1635, Wu (2018), p. 554.

[13] E.g. De Gregorio (2021), p. 1.

[14] ECtHR: *Cengiz and Others v. Turkey,* no. 48226/10, §§ 49 and 52, 1 December 2015.

The ECtHR has considered, for example, government restrictions on accessing the Internet or specific websites,[15] various questions on the liability of intermediaries, hosting services, etc.,[16] and a criminal conviction for Internet obscenity by the UK of a French national, based in the UK but operating a US-based company,[17] under the freedom of expression clause in Article 10 of the ECHR. This provides some indication of the kind of issues faced by national courts around Europe eventually, in some instances, making their way to the supranational level. Analogies and contrasts between Internet platforms and traditional forms of communication are a noticeable theme in the ECtHR's case-law when the Court seeks to find the best fit between existing doctrine and new technologies: In a case concerning the liability of Internet platforms allowing third-party comments, the ECtHR observed that the Court's frequent references to "the essential role which the press plays in a democratic society" must, in a modern society, be read as "encompass[ing] the electronic media including the Internet."[18] In the very same case the Court also struggled with the more unique features of Internet speech, particularly the potential chilling effects of imposing liability for third-party comments.[19] The Court has held, in a case not involving the Internet, that freedom of expression "does not bestow any freedom of forum for the exercise of that right," rejecting, except possibly in extreme cases, the existence of a positive obligation for States to regulate private property rights so as to ensure access of others for the purposes of expression.[20] Internet speech depends on the intermediary role of private companies. There may be no alternative to relying on these private Internet platforms to use "essential tools" of the Internet, which plays an "important role" in public discourse.[21] The Council of Europe has emphasised the "public service value" of the Internet and the "legitimate expectation" that affordable and reliable Internet access is provided without discrimination of any kind.[22] Internet access is not formally viewed as a human right on the international level, but is frequently described as a condition for freedom of expression.[23]

The rise of Internet speech, particularly social media, has presented a range of novel problems from the point of view of freedom of expression: In the Internet age we do not only see "old school" restrictions on freedom of expression—such as

---

[15] ECtHR: *Ahmet Yıldırım v. Turkey*, no. 3111/10, 18 December 2012, ECtHR: *Akdeniz v. Turkey*, no. 20877/10 (dec.), 11 March 2014, ECtHR: *Vladimir Kharitonov v. Russia,* no 10795/14, 23 June 2020.

[16] ECtHR: *Delfi AS v. Estonia* [GC], no. 64569/09, 6 June 2015.

[17] ECtHR: *Perrin v. the United Kingdom*, no. 5446/03 (dec.), 18 October 2005.

[18] ECtHR: *Magyar Tartalomszolgáltatók Egyesülete and Index.hu Zrt v. Hungary*, no. 22947/13, § 87, 2 February 2016.

[19] Id, § 86.

[20] ECtHR: *Appleby and Others v. the United Kingdom*, no. 44306/98, § 44, ECHR 2003-VI.

[21] ECtHR: *Cengiz and Others v. Turkey*, no. 48226/10, § 49, 1 December 2015.

[22] Council of Europe (2014).

[23] UN Special Rapporteur on the promotion and protection of the right to freedom of opinion and expression (2011).

criminal or civil sanctions on publishers or speakers—but "new school" restrictions, where expression is regulated by control over the infrastructure of the Internet.[24] Such "new school" techniques, even when essentially involving the familiar theme of government infringement on individual rights, are harder to fit within existing freedom of expression doctrine. Even more problematic for existing legal standards is the vast authority exercised by the Internet platforms themselves. The debate on the role of platforms such as Facebook and Twitter as modern public squares—while simultaneously being squarely private, for-profit companies—and the related questions of platform liability and content moderation rages on.[25] Facebook now has its own supreme court (the Oversight Board) applying international human rights law almost as if the Internet platform had ratified international treaties.[26] None of this is made simpler by the fact that most content moderation decisions, i.e. the decisions of Internet platforms to remove user content, are made by algorithms, not people.[27] The truly global character of Internet speech, and regulation thereof, adds yet another layer of difficulty and has been highlighted by decisions of the CJEU, allowing worldwide removal of material considered illegal by a domestic court in a single EU country.[28]

Tim Wu's influential analysis of the novel character of modern Internet speech is based on the observation that "it is no longer speech itself that is scarce, but the attention of listeners."[29] Threats to freedom of expression, and with it the resiliency of democracy, in this context focus on listeners, for example by "flooding" listeners with fake information, or going after speakers by "unleashing 'troll armies'" or similar tactics. These threats arise in the context of an "attention industry," where listener's attention is commodified and re-sold by Internet platforms, and alongside the development of the "filter bubble," where listener content is tailored to pre-existing preferences and which is difficult for new information to pierce.[30] In this environment, power is wielded by both public and private actors by weaponising speech; "deploy[ing] speedy, cheap, and abundant speech to control others' speech, to mislead and manipulate listeners, and to undermine meaningful public discourse."[31]

These problems have led some to argue that our conception of freedom of expression, or at least existing legal doctrine, must change.[32] In Wu's formulation:

---

[24] Balkin (2014).

[25] E.g. Douek (2021).

[26] Hofverberg (2021).

[27] Massaro and Norton (2016), Kaminski et al. (2017).

[28] CJEU: CJEU, Case C-18/18, Eva Glawischnig-Piesczek v. Facebook Ireland Limited, ECLI:EU:C:2019:821.

[29] Wu (2018), p. 548.

[30] Wu (2018), pp. 555–556.

[31] Massaro and Norton (2021).

[32] But see Tushnet (2021) (arguing that in fact the U.S. First Amendment doctrine as it stands is flexible enough to accommodate all the suggested responses).

"What we need most is a reconceptualisation of what it means, in our times, to protect and promote a healthy political speech environment."[33] On the global level, advocates of "digital constitutionalism" have proposed various versions of Internet bills of rights, seeking to respond to some of the problems posed by Internet speech.[34]

In constitutional reform, however, we have not seen a trend towards solutions to the novel problems involving Internet speech. The most notable constitutional trend involving the Internet is the emergence of provisions constitutionalising access to the Internet. The Constitutions of Mexico, Sudan and Georgia declare access to the Internet as a constitutional right.[35] Greece's Constitution, after a pre-crisis 2008 amendment, protects the "the right to participate in the Information Society" and declares that facilitating access to "electronically transmitted information" is a state obligation.[36] Ecuador's 2008 Constitution guarantees as a right "universal access to information technologies and communication" and prescribes that media systems shall facilitate rights to communication, information, and freedom of expression and strengthen public participation.[37] What is the value of such constitutional protection? In 2017 it was reported that 58.3% of Ecuadorians use the Internet, which is a comparatively decent amount of Internet access,[38] but more generally we might have a problem with constitutional rights being effective only 58% of the time. Incidentally, Ecuador also provides a leading example of the kind of novel speech suppression technique highlighted by Tim Wu: In 2015 Ecuador's president Rafael Correa marshalled a troll army to harass his online critics.[39] After leaving office, Facebook blocked Correa's page for violating terms of service.[40] This is all to say that Ecuador's constitutional right to Internet access has little to say about the complicated scenarios arising from Internet speech.

With this context in mind, we turn next to our three cases of constitutional reform efforts.

[33] Wu (2018), p. 568.

[34] Redeker et al. (2018).

[35] Constitution of Mexico 1917 (rev. 2015), Constitution of Sudan (2019), Constitution of Georgia 1995 (rev. 2018).

[36] Constitution of Greece.

[37] Constitution of Ecuador 2008 (rev. 2021), Articles 16.2 and 384.

[38] Freedom House (2019) Freedom House gives the country the score of 4/6 in the relevant category.

[39] The Guardian (2015).

[40] The Associated Press (2019).

# 3 Constitution-Making and Internet Platforms

## 3.1 *Post-2008 Constitutional Reform: Case Selection and Methodology*

The Global Financial Crisis amounted to the deepest financial crash since the Great Depression and its effects were felt in the economic sphere for more than a decade (or until the effects became difficult to separate from the next crisis: COVID-19). According to the IMF a vast majority of 24 economies hit by the crisis of 2008 remained below their pre-crisis output trends in 2018.[41] The crisis also had profound effects on politics[42] and on constitutional law in various jurisdictions.[43]

Crises frequently play a decisive role in constitution-making.[44] We look to evidence of the Global Financial Crisis as a "constitutional moment."[45] Indeed, some sort of constitutional shifts took place in a range of countries after 2008, even if some did not involve formal amendments (Greece)[46] and in others the link to the crisis is perhaps less direct (Hungary).[47] Looking at Europe, three processes of attempted constitutional reform in the years following the 2008 crisis stand out: Iceland (2010–2012 and beyond), Ireland (2012–2014) and Norway (2011–2014). These involve formal textual changes in comparatively well-functioning democracies, at least in the sense that recent debates on democratic backsliding[48] do not apply, and in each case addressing potential reform of some aspects of freedom of expression provisions.[49]

The review will focus on official reports and records of deliberations of the relevant institutions, with specific attention to freedom of expression and the Internet. This review of the original sources is backed up by secondary literature.

---

[41] IMF (2018), p. 74.

[42] E.g. Funke et al. (2016) (finding that polarisation in politics and the vote share of far-right parties increases after financial crises) and Tooze (2018), pp. 564–599 (tracing the connection from the 2008 financial crisis to the election of Donald Trump as US president).

[43] E.g. Contiades (2013).

[44] Elster (1995), Ackerman (2015).

[45] Ackerman (1991), p. 5. But see e.g. Sajó (2005), p. 243 (noting that "the vast majority" of constitutions does not originate in such moments).

[46] Contiades (2013).

[47] Id.

[48] See Democratic Decay & Renewal (2021).

[49] In the process of case-selection, we reviewed the freedom of expression clauses of all the European constitutions coded in the Constitute database (https://www.constituteproject.org/) and reviewed in full all European constitutions amended after 2008, with a view of identifying specific clauses on Internet speech. We are therefore confident that no essential case is left out of the sample of three. Georgia warrants special attention as its Constitution, amended in 2018, guarantees Internet access. However, serious concerns have been expressed as to the democratic qualities of the amendment process, warranting its exclusion from this study, see Venice Commission (2017).

## 3.2 Iceland

Iceland entered the crisis with a banking sector roughly 14 times the country's GDP[50] and left with a crushed economy and a public debt surge of 80% of GDP, although the banks were largely allowed to collapse.[51] Street demonstrations and political turmoil led to, among other things, a left-leaning coalition government taking power in 2009. A part of the public's dissatisfaction was aimed at the structure of political institutions and an ambitious, although continuously contested and ultimately unsuccessful, effort was made to reform the country's 1944 constitution.[52]

The Icelandic process, starting in 2010, has been the focus of scholarly attention internationally, primarily from the point of view of public participation and the use of new technologies to that end.[53] The principal elements of the process involved a National Forum of randomly selected participants in a roundtable setting, and a subsequent formation of a Constitutional Council of 25 individuals tasked with preparing proposals for amendments. The Council consisted of individuals initially elected by voters to serve on a constituent assembly. However, in January 2011 the Icelandic Supreme Court invalidated the elections due to legal-technical irregularities (without any suggestion that the outcome of the elections was affected).[54] Following the Supreme Court's decision the members of the Council were appointed by a Parliamentary resolution. Importantly, the members were not politicians and there was a strong sentiment that constitutional reform should be removed from the realm of ordinary politics.

The Constitutional Council decided to exceed its suggested mandate and compose an entirely new constitution which was eventually delivered to parliament in July 2011.[55] Little progress was made on the proposals until October 2012 when a consultative referendum was held on certain questions relating to the constitutional reform process. A clear majority of voters approved, inter alia, that the Constitutional Council's proposals should form the basis of a new constitution. Yet, no vote took place in parliament on the proposed constitutional bill and no government since—parliamentary elections took place in 2013, 2016, 2017 and 2021—has supported the "new constitution," as the Council's proposals are usually referred to, opting instead to explore piecemeal amendments through the ordinary political process, all of which have been unsuccessful. Significant support of the new constitution among civil society groups and the public has, however, remained. For example, in 2020 a

---

[50] Bibler (2010).

[51] Oddsson and Mathiesen (2008), p. 1.

[52] See Árnason and Dupré (2021) for accounts in English from many of the central actors in the story.

[53] E.g. Tushnet (2016), Elster (2016), Meuwese (2013), Landemore (2014).

[54] Supreme Court of Iceland: Ákvörðun Hæstaréttar vegna kosningar til stjórnlagaþings [Decision of the Supreme Court Regarding Elections to the Constitutional Assembly] 25 January 2011.

[55] Stjórnlagaráð [Constitutional Council] (2011a).

petition for the ratification of the new constitution was backed by the verified signatures of some 17% of registered voters.

International attention to the Icelandic process often focuses on the catchphrase "crowdsourced constitution."[56] While surely an overstatement, the phrase highlights the importance of digital tools and public participation in the process. As described by Gylfason and Meuwese, mainly three categories of digital tools were used: (1) social media, as the Council interacted intensively with those interested in the process, both domestically (mostly through Facebook) and internationally (mostly through Twitter); (2) online video streaming of the Council's plenary sessions; and (3) the Council's website, which included various interactive features, the option to post comments (some 3,600 comments were received in a country of roughly 360,000 people), and where a "work-in-progress" version of the draft bill was posted and updated regularly.[57] The relationship with tech was even more intricate as leading employees at Icelandic tech companies had personal interest in constitutional reform and were heavily involved in designing systems and procedures in the runup to the Council's work. In the aftermath of the reform process, the language of tech has been frequently employed, specifically by using the analogy of updating Iceland's operating system, including in this version by a member of Parliament: "We are finally updating, jumping from Windows 95 to Linux."[58] Digital tools and tech metaphors were perhaps appropriate as already in 2010 some 95% of Icelanders were Internet users and a staggering 70% used social media.[59]

As to the substance of the Constitutional Council's proposals, the bill of rights tracks—at least in broad terms—international human rights law and many modern constitutions in terms of the rights included and their formulation. Where the Council sought to include "new" rights, these were usually based on examples from other jurisdictions.

As to freedom of expression, the Council's draft includes a provision largely mirroring Article 10 ECHR/Article 19 ICCPR but adds a separate related provision on the right to information, mostly focused on information and documents in the possession of public institutions, and two brief provisions on, respectively, freedom of the media and freedom of culture and academia. In the present context, however, we will focus on a proposed third paragraph of the provision on freedom of expression:

> The public authorities shall guarantee the conditions for an open and informed discourse. The access to the Internet and information technology shall not be limited unless by a court verdict and subject to the same conditions as apply to the limits of the expression of opinion.[60]

---

[56] E.g. Lessig (2016).

[57] Gylfason and Meuwese (2017).

[58] Gunnarsson (2019).

[59] Hagstofa Íslands (2010).

[60] Stjórnlagaráð [Constitutional Council] (2011a).

The first sentence of the provision is essentially a direct borrowing from a 2004 amendment to the Norwegian Constitution (see below), an idea introduced by one of the legal experts appearing before the Council's human rights subcommittee.[61] The idea was originally not framed as involving the Internet at all, but rather public broadcasting and financial support and regulation of media, and the relevant expert indeed considered the invocation of Internet access in the context of the provision to be questionable.[62]

The Council's explanatory memorandum accompanying its final draft states that the government's role includes ensuring access to the Internet. However, the intention was to prevent the State from limiting Internet access and the provision should not be understood as introducing an obligation to ensure a high-speed Internet connection for all.[63] The Council's explanations emphasise the importance of the Internet for human rights and democracy. As to the limitation clause of the second sentence of the provision, the only example mentioned in the explanatory memorandum is the situation of a prisoner convicted or suspected of computer crime or Internet harassment.[64]

In plenary sessions, members of the Constitutional Council discussed proposals for including access to the Internet in the freedom of expression provision at some length. Most agreed that Internet access was indeed necessary to foster a modern democratic society,[65] while some noted that the inclusion of the word "Internet" might be problematic as it might be overridden by newer technology in the future (comparing it to the hypothetical inclusion of the fax machine).[66] Significant discussion took place on whether positive obligations were to be placed on the state to ensure access to high-speed Internet, including to geographically remote locations.[67] The prevailing view, however, was that the emphasis in the provision should be on negative obligations.[68] The records do not indicate which sort of limitations would be prevented by the provision, although one member of the Council referred to "censorship of the Internet" as "one of the major threats to democracy in the world."[69]

---

[61] Þórhallsson (2011a).

[62] Þórhallsson (2011b).

[63] Stjórnlagaráð [Constitutional Council] (2011a), p. 54.

[64] Id.

[65] Stjórnlagaráð [Constitutional Council] (2011b), p. 387 (Mr. Vilhjálmur Þorsteinsson), p. 394 (Ms. Katrín Oddsdóttir).

[66] Stjórnlagaráð [Constitutional Council] (2011b), p. 388 (Mr. Þorkell Helgason), pp. 390–391 (Mr. Erlingur Sigurðarson), p. 483 (Mr. Ómar Ragnarsson).

[67] Stjórnlagaráð [Constitutional Council] (2011b), pp. 388, 402, 551.

[68] This emphasis on negative obligations is sometimes lost in discussions about the Council's proposals. For example, the main Wikipedia entry on "The 2010–2013 Icelandic constitutional reform 'lists' obliging the state to provide Internet access to all citizens" as among the important proposals of the Council, see Wikipedia (2021).

[69] Stjórnlagaráð [Constitutional Council] (2011b), p. 394 (Ms. Katrín Oddsdóttir).

The more or less uniform assumption of the Council was that more Internet speech and more unfiltered access to such speech would result in more democracy. Getting government out of Internet speech was therefore generally seen as a worthy goal. Drafters had followed the importance of social media in the Arab Spring of 2010–2012, which at the time still appeared as modest success stories, and the attempts of governments in, for example, Tunisia and Egypt to block Internet access.[70] What we now view as clear examples of the perils of Internet speech for democracy—the 2016 US elections and associated and subsequent analysis of disinformation, fake news, echo chambers, etc.[71]—were still several years away, or at least not generally understood. Closer to home, information technology played an important part in the Icelandic Constitutional reform process.

After receiving convincing support in the October 2012 referendum, the Council's proposals were reviewed by a legal expert group and subsequently presented as a formal constitutional bill in Parliament (the Althingi). The legal experts made various tweaks to the draft. This included removing the sentence on access to the Internet and information technology. According to the legal experts, there was no added value in mentioning these specific methods of communicating ideas, as any limitations would in any event need to fulfil requirements of necessity and proportionality under the general freedom of expression clause. The additional requirement of a preceding court order to allow limitations on access to the Internet was not, in the legal experts' view, reasonable. The only example noted by the Constitutional Council was that of prisoners being barred from accessing the Internet, but the legal experts took the view that procedural fairness and legality would be sufficiently ensured in that situation without this specific clause.[72]

Subsequently, various standing committees of parliament considered the bill and proposed amendments. The Constitutional and Oversight Committee proposed the reinsertion of the Council's language on access to the Internet and information technology as a part of the freedom of expression clause in this formulation:

> The law shall guarantee the conditions for an open and informed discourse. The access to the Internet and information technology shall not be limited unless under the conditions set out in Article 29 [a general limitation clause, requiring legality and proportionality].[73]

The Committee's opinion explained that this clause declares access to the Internet as a human right, but attaches only negative obligations from the State, not a duty to provide Internet access in fact. The Committee emphasised the importance of the Internet for democratic discourse and its vulnerability for censorship, as well as the vast potential for citizens to use the Internet to claim rights, justice and accountability.[74] The Committee stated that the provision would prevent government actions

[70] For an assessment of the Arab Spring some 10 years later see Feldman (2020).

[71] See generally e.g. Perisly and Tucker (2020).

[72] Althingi (2012a), p. 72.

[73] Althingi (2012b).

[74] Althingi (2012c), on Article 16.

that prohibit certain individuals or groups from accessing the Internet, information technology or other media to express their opinions, while noting that prisoners' access may still be limited, if prescribed by law. In the Committee's separate discussion on information freedom, as a part of the freedom of expression, the Committee noted that the right to receive, gather and distribute information entails, among other things, freedom of access to available information databases, including the Internet.[75]

To reiterate, the constitutional bill, including the Parliamentary Committee's amendments, never reached the floor of parliament for a vote. The bill has been proposed on later occasions by opposition members of parliament, but not been put to a full vote.

Two themes clearly stand out from the Icelandic experience (putting aside the eventual fate of the proposals): An entirely positive view of the impact of Internet speech for democracy and a very cautiously drafted proposal on access to the Internet. The proposal may have been so cautiously drafted as to render the clause redundant. Neither the Constitutional Council nor the Parliamentary Committee was prepared to prescribe positive obligations for the State to provide Internet access. Actions of the State limiting access to the Internet would have been caught by the provision, but, as per the view taken by the legal expert group, it is difficult to see how the proportionality analysis of such limitations would be any different than regarding other limitations on freedom of expression. The sense of the drafters (or at least the lowest common denominator of consensus) seems to have been: The Internet is important in the context of freedom of expression, hence it should be mentioned in the Constitution. The details of what the clause should "do" were much fuzzier, unaided by the fact that the written explanatory notes, and the records of discussions in the Constitutional Council, are highly abstract, lacking concrete examples of problems that the proposal was intended to tackle or prevent.

## 3.3 *Ireland*

Facing the collapse of a banking sector five times the size of the economy,[76] in the aftermath 2008 Ireland quickly transitioned from an aggressively neoliberal growth strategy of emphasising a deregulated, low-tax financial sector—the "Celtic Tiger" years—to be the second country, after Greece, to undergo a troika-led bailout. Significant political shifts followed, including a collapse of the coalition government in 2011 and a historic defeat of the traditionally largest party, Fianna Fáil in the elections that followed. At least three of the major political parties included proposals for constitutional reform in their election platforms and the new coalition government set out to establish a "Constitutional Convention" to consider reforms of

[75] Id.

[76] Lenihan and Honohan (2010).

several aspects of the Irish constitution.[77] In 2012 the Convention was set up as a 100-member body composed of a specifically selected chairman, Tom Arnold, 66 randomly selected citizens, several members appointed by political parties in Northern Ireland and the remaining members selected from the Irish legislature. The Convention was instructed to consider the following constitutional issues: (i) reducing the Presidential term of office; (ii) reducing the voting age to 17; (iii) reviewing the electoral system; (iv) giving citizens resident outside the State the right to vote in Presidential elections; (v) considering same-sex marriage; (vi) amending the clause on the role of women in the home and encouraging greater participation of women in public life; (vii) increasing the participation of women in politics; (viii) removing the offence of blasphemy from the Constitution.[78] For each issue, the Convention delivered a recommendation and the government was to provide a response to each recommendation. In several cases the recommendations led to constitutional amendments. Eventually, the Convention went beyond its original mandate to adopt some 38 recommendations.[79]

Significant features of the Irish Convention were the random selection of citizen members and emphasis on deliberation, placing it in a new-ish category of constitutional convention; a "mini public."[80] The process was initially mostly met with either indifference or criticism, including directed at the inclusion of politicians as members and the limited authority of the Convention.[81] With the benefit of some hindsight, academic evaluation of the process is split. By some it is treated as a modest success story, resulting in significant changes to the Constitution based on meaningful citizen involvement.[82] Others argue that the experience has been "oversold," and claims of representative or deliberative legitimacy are highly flawed with respect to composition, agenda, expertise and evidence.[83]

One of the issues considered by the Convention concerned freedom of expression specifically: whether to remove the offence of blasphemy from the Irish Constitution. The choice of this topic appears to have been somewhat unexpected; the Chairman of the Convention explained that it "was not an issue that would have been foremost in most people's minds. Indeed, many would not have been aware that such a clause existed in the Constitution."[84] Less charitably, some constitutional experts considered the idea of identifying blasphemy as a major constitutional issue

[77]Farrell et al. (2017), p. 121.

[78]Dáil Éireann (2012).

[79]Blokker (2017), p. 46.

[80]Farrell et al. (2017), p. 120.

[81]Farrell et al. (2017), pp. 124–130.

[82]Blokker (2017), p. 51, Farrell et al. (2017), p. 131 (claiming that "As a process, the Irish Constitutional Convention was a great success," while the assessment is less clear in terms of outcomes.) See also Suteu (2015) (highlighting both positive and negative aspects).

[83]Carolan (2015).

[84]The Convention on the Constitution (2014).

to be "a joke."[85] Since 1855 there had been only one attempted (private) prosecution, which failed, and the legislative definition of blasphemy in the Defamation Act 2009 had never been tested in court.[86] Indeed the 2009 law was enacted largely based on a constitutional obligation and despite the view expressed by a parliamentary committee that there should be no constitutional prohibition of blasphemy in a "modern Constitution."[87]

The Convention's consideration of the issue took place over a weekend in November 2013. Before the session, public comments were received through the Convention's website. Some 94 comments about blasphemy were received. A review of these comments reveals that a substantial majority were in favour of removing the provision on blasphemy, and a significant number tied the issue to the broader question of the relationship between religion and the State. None of the public comments discussed blasphemy in the context of social media and the role of Internet platforms, with the exception that two NGOs highlighted instances in other countries where individuals have been prosecuted for blasphemy based on Tweets, Facebook posts or blog posts.[88]

Having considered the public comments, as well as hearing from legal experts and civil society groups on both sides of the issue, a clear majority of the Convention (61%) took the position that the offence of blasphemy should be removed from the Constitution.[89]

After limited progress on the issue following the Convention's recommendation, blasphemy was brought to the public's attention in 2017 when comedian Stephen Fry came under criminal investigation for statements made in a TV interview in 2015.[90] The investigation was subsequently dropped. In 2018 the Irish legislature held a referendum to repeal the constitutional provision. The proposal passed by 64.85% of votes cast, with 43.8% of voters turning out, and the 37th Amendment to the Constitution was signed into law in November 2018.[91]

Expression on social media certainly was a part of the background of the amendment. While many, including the authors of a 2008 legislative committee report, had considered the blasphemy provision a "dead letter,"[92] those who campaigned for its repeal highlighted instances where individuals have been punished for blasphemy in other jurisdictions for Internet speech. Thus, civil society groups highlighted the case of an Indonesian man who was arrested for a Facebook

---

[85] O'Mahony (2012), cited in Carolan (2015), p 739.

[86] The Convention on the Constitution (2014).

[87] House of the Oireachtas (2008), p. 69.

[88] Public Submissions to the Convention on the Constitution (2014).

[89] The Convention on the Constitution (2014).

[90] Fry's statements included: "The god that created this universe, if it was created by a god, is quite clearly a maniac, utter maniac, totally selfish."

[91] Referendum Commission (2019).

[92] House of the Oireachtas (2008), p. 73.

post and a poet jailed in Saudi Arabia for a tweet.[93] Importantly for these civil society groups, the Irish blasphemy law had been used by proponents of such laws at the international level as a Western example of recent legislation.[94] While perhaps a dead letter domestically, the Irish law thus served a different role in the international sphere.

Even while social media was in this way important for the issue being addressed by the Convention, the fact that expression took place on Internet platforms played only a limited role. Bloggers and users of Twitter and Facebook enjoyed the lower costs associated with distribution of expression on Internet platforms but threats to their freedom came from the traditional threat to individual rights: an overreaching State. There was no discussion of any role or responsibility of Internet platforms themselves. As to the responsibilities of the State concerning the policing of speech, a majority of the members of the Convention favoured legislation to prohibit incitement to religious hatred.[95] It was not the Convention's task to assess how such legislation would be framed or enforced in the world of global Internet platforms.

The Constitutional reform questions considered by the Convention were framed against the legal background–as explained to the Convention by legal experts–of a particular Irish historical development and, perhaps more importantly in the modern era, the ECHR's test of justifications for restrictions of the freedom of expression under Article 10 ECHR. The Irish reform was thus nestled within European human rights law, with its (more or less) settled methodology of analysis, which was not designed in the context of Internet platforms.

The Irish experience highlights (1) the interplay between international law and domestic constitutional law, both as import and export. On the export side, we saw the importance of invoking best/worst practice for global constitutionalism[96] when the Irish law was held up by the proponents of blasphemy laws elsewhere. On the import side, analysis of Irish constitutional law and the options open to constitutional reformers was highly dependent on the ECHR.

(2) Reformers were largely considering an abstract, even theoretical, issue since the blasphemy laws had not been enforced. Rather than seeking to address new and thorny contemporary problems of freedom of expression, the Convention was tasked with a legacy issue, where the outcome appears to have been foreseeable. As an exercise of deliberative democracy, it was mostly that: an exercise.

(3) The focus of the Convention, as well as the public comments and civil society groups, was on the traditional elements of blasphemy laws, addressing the classic and important questions of religion and the State, but not necessarily in the modern context of Internet speech.

---

[93] Humanist Association of Ireland (2014) and Atheist Ireland (2014).

[94] Id.

[95] The Convention on the Constitution (2014).

[96] See generally Dixon and Landau (2021).

## 3.4 Norway

Norway's 1814 Constitution is considered the second-oldest working constitution in the world, after the Constitution of the United States, although it has been subject to various amendments. In 2014 the Constitution's provisions on constitutional rights were significantly amended and placed in a separate chapter. These amounted to the most drastic changes to the document since 1814. Unlike for Ireland and Iceland, the 2008 financial crisis did not play a major role in the background of the 2014 Norwegian reform. This is perhaps unsurprising as the effects of the crisis in Norway were comparatively mild. The main purpose of the reform was to mark the 200-year anniversary of the document by modernising its human rights provisions. New rights were not being created, but certain rights explicitly protected in international law, and incorporated through a 1999 statutory human rights act,[97] were now elevated and clarified as an integral part of the Constitution.[98] The amendment process was markedly different from those of Ireland and Iceland in that it followed the traditional parliamentary process without innovations in terms of public involvement. After an unfruitful debate had taken place within legal circles for decades, the bicentennial anniversary of the Constitution served as the catalyst for reform.[99] Parliament formed a Human Rights Committee in 2009 with the mandate to strengthen the position of human rights in the constitutional order, with broad political support, composed of members of parliament, one law professor and one Supreme Court Justice.[100] Anine Kierulf notes that the process does not fit well within the categories established in the literature on constitution-making as the catalyst for change was neither an external crisis, nor the ordinary political process, but rather the perceived deadline of the bicentennial anniversary.[101] Kierulf also points out that the Human Rights Committee conducted "no broad engagement of or interaction with the general public or the legal or political community."[102] The constitutional reform attracted limited attention in the 2013 parliamentary elections although public discourse picked up in 2014.[103] The process and outcome were determined through the ordinary channels of politics, including party-line voting.

The 2014 reform added, or reformulated, several civil and political rights to the Constitution, including the right to free and secret elections, personal liberty, fair trial, equality before the law, and privacy. Economic, social and cultural rights proved more contentious; provisions on education, work and a healthy environment were passed, while the right to health and a right to participate in cultural activities

97 Act No. 30/1999, Lov om styrking av. menneskerettighetenes stilling i norsk rett (Menneskerettsloven).

98 Bårdsen (2016), p. 4.

99 Kierulf (2018), p. 239.

100 Id, p. 240.

101 Id, pp. 239–240.

102 Id, p. 240.

103 Id, pp. 242–243.

failed to pass. The formulation of these provisions largely tracks international legal instruments.[104]

No proposal was made for amendments to the freedom of expression clause in Article 100 of the Norwegian Constitution, which was significantly amended in 2004.[105] The 2011 Human Rights Committee report notes that Article 100 is formulated differently than Article 10 of the ECHR, however, the ECHR has been frequently applied by the Courts.[106] The Committee considered the possibility of amending the freedom of expression provision, particularly by bringing the text closer to the ECHR and ensuring consistency as to permitted limitations of constitutional rights.[107] In the end, however, the Committee did not propose any changes to Article 100 of the Constitution, noting that changes to the 2004 language were not required by international law and any proposed changes might add uncertainty to the meaning of the clause, as well as reopening a complicated debate in the parliament.[108]

The 2011 report includes a discussion of the 2004 amendment on freedom of expression, its application in practice, similar clauses in comparative and international law, and possibilities of amendments but makes no reference to changes in the context of freedom of expression may have changed, even in the short period since 2004 (in fact, as discussed below, the 2004 language was mostly drafted in 1999).[109] Internet speech is not mentioned and the Committee's discussion is mostly limited to rather abstract and legal-technical issues, which aligns with the mandate to ensure consistency with Norway's international obligations.

The 2004 rehaul of the freedom of expression clause in Article 100 of the Norwegian Constitution was also based on the findings of a committee report, in that case the Committee on Freedom of Expression, appointed in 1996, whose final 1999 report set out the basis for the 2004 amendment.[110] This committee's 16 members included seven professors from five different disciplines and the 1999 report is a 300-page deep exploration of freedom of expression. The 2004 amendment passed by parliament is very close to the committee's recommendation. The 1999 report discusses the freedom of information in various contexts and includes an interesting analysis of the new information society, which holds up remarkably well.[111] The committee contemplated, among other things, how the Internet would transform the way in which ideas are transmitted and distributed away from the one-way format of

[104]Constitution of the Kingdom of Norway 1814 (rev. 2020), Chapter E (human rights).

[105]Kunngjøring av Grunnlovsbestemmelse om endring av Grunnloven § 100, FOR-2004-10-29-1402.

[106]Menneskerettighetsutvalget [Human Rights Committee] (2011), p. 160.

[107]Id, pp. 161–163.

[108]Id.

[109]Id, pp. 159–163.

[110]NOU (1999).

[111]Id, pp. 70–72.

traditional media towards more interactivity.[112] For the committee, the Internet seemed an overall positive development for freedom of expression by facilitating freedom of information, i.e. making possible previously unimaginable quantities of information exchanges.[113] "So far," the committee wrote in its 1999 report, the conditions of freedom of expression seemed to be improved by the Internet.[114] However, the committee also foresaw problems with Internet speech including its chaotic nature, especially in terms of volume and quality of information (including "gal informasjon," i.e. disinformation).[115]

For present purposes two issues stand out from the 1999 report and 2004 amendment.

First, one of the more apparent departures of Article 100 of the Norwegian Constitution from the formulation of freedom of expression in international law is the inclusion of three fundamental justifications for the existence of freedom of expression:

> No one may be held liable in law for having imparted or received information, ideas or messages unless this can be justified in relation to the grounds for freedom of expression, which are **the seeking of truth, the promotion of democracy and the individual's freedom to form opinions.**[116]

The problems commonly associated with modern Internet speech, particularly social media, are of course closely related to the three grounds identified in the Norwegian Constitution. Truth seeking is jeopardised by disinformation; while capable of promoting democracy, Internet speech may also have disrupting effects on the functioning of democracy; and the development of the individual opinions in the age of the Internet is impacted by "echo chambers" and other polarising characteristics of social media.

Second, the sixth and final paragraph of Article 100 as amended in 2004 sets out what is commonly referred to as the "infrastructure requirement":

> The authorities of the state shall create conditions that facilitate open and enlightened public discourse.

As noted in Sect. 3.2 above, this was important inspiration for the Icelandic Constitutional Council's proposal on Internet access. The language was proposed in the 1999 Freedom of Expression Committee report to capture the idea that the State is responsible for the "public space" and should actively ensure that individuals and groups can in fact enjoy freedom of expression.[117] The clause is thus intended to place positive obligations on the State to facilitate speech by ensuring the

---

[112] Id, p. 70.

[113] Id, p. 71.

[114] Id, p. 72.

[115] Id, p. 71.

[116] Constitution of the Kingdom of Norway 1814 (rev. 2020), Article 100, para. 2, sentence 1. (Emphasis added).

[117] NOU (1999), p 249.

functioning of the necessary infrastructure. Examples mentioned by the committee include institutional arrangements and financing of education, libraries, art and culture, support provided to publishers, regulation of and direct and indirect support of the media, as well as more broadly issues surrounding taxation (particularly VAT) and financial aid schemes.[118] If one of the three central identified processes of freedom of expression—the search for truth, promotion of democracy, and individual development—is not functioning as intended, the infrastructure requirement may require the State to take positive action.[119] Importantly, however, the intention does not seem to have been to create a justiciable individual right, but rather to issue a directive to the legislature.[120]

The Norwegian Government appointed a new Freedom of Information Committee in 2020, mandated to present an official report (the same format as the 1999 report) in 2022.[121] The central mandate of this new committee is to "review the social, technological, legal and economic frameworks for freedom of expression in today's society."[122] The committee includes academics, activists, journalists and artists. Modern complications surrounding Internet speech and platforms are front and centre in the explanation of the background of the appointment of the committee, including: the role of platforms as the new gatekeepers, Internet hate speech, cancel culture, global reach of platforms, online harassment, disinformation, and the use of algorithms and artificial intelligence. Constitutional amendments are not listed among the measures to be considered by the committee to strengthen public discourse (but are not expressly excluded either). Starkly different than the previous committees discussed above, the progress of the 2020 committee can be followed online, it has convened various open meetings and invites input from the public.[123]

## 4 Analysis/Lessons Learned

### *4.1 Digital Constitutionalism, or Lack Thereof*

A recent analysis of "digital constitutionalism" in the EU identifies three phases in development of regulation of the information society: (1) "Digital liberalism," characterised by optimism towards new technology and an emphasis on liberty. (2) "Judicial activism," characterised by the leading role of the Court of Justice, using and developing existing rules to protect fundamental rights, as these are understood by the Court, against new threats in the digital age. (3) "Digital

[118] Id, pp. 88 and 249–250.
[119] Id, p. 249.
[120] Id, p. 250.
[121] Ministry of Culture (2020).
[122] Id.
[123] Ytringsfrihetskommisjonen (2021).

constitutionalism," characterised by "the injection of democratic values in the information society."[124]

Our three constitutional reform processes fall within the paradigm of digital liberalism: This is clearest in the case of Iceland where Internet access and Internet speech were viewed almost entirely as a positive force and the risks identified were those of too much government involvement. The Internet and social media were the foundation of a reinvigorated democracy in the eyes of the Icelandic Constitutional Council. Similarly, the Norwegian drafters were mostly optimistic of the potential of the Internet for democratic deliberation, although, curiously in light of the timing, the 1999 Norwegian report on freedom of expression put its finger squarely on some of the important risks of Internet speech. In Ireland the problem of blasphemy was admittedly highly abstract, but the concrete cases presented to the Constitutional Convention were mostly about convictions in other countries for blasphemous Internet speech. So, again, the aim was to free Internet users from state oppression.

Digital constitutionalism focuses on regulating power on the Internet, considering its monumental importance, and injecting democratic values into the digital space. The picture of power relations in the mind of our constitutional reformers was somewhat simplistic considering what we know today. More Internet speech does not always equal more democracy. Power is wielded not only by governments through regulation or force, but also through government leaders' and supporters' speech, by Internet platforms through gatekeeping and attention selling, by troll armies and organisers of harassment campaigns, and even—at least it sometimes seems—by black-box algorithms or artificial intelligence.

Digital constitutionalism in constitution-making would need to engage with these power relations, figure out which principles to enshrine in constitutional text and which subjects to delegate to ordinary politics. The task goes way beyond introducing the kind of "right to access to the Internet" provisions that currently represent the leading examples of treating the Internet with the same level of seriousness in constitutional text as it has obtained in our daily lives.

## 4.2 The Power of Private Intermediaries

Central to projects on digital constitutionalism, and discussions on power on the Internet more generally, is the role of Internet platforms and other intermediaries. They are sometimes described as performing quasi-public functions—the metaphors include modern town squares or public utilities such as water and electricity.[125] Yet, from the point of view of constitutional law, these companies, the people behind the corporate veil, as well as their customers, are primarily rights holders. Facebook and Twitter are, in this setting, much more like a private owner of building deciding for

[124] De Gregorio (2021).

[125] Ghosh (2019).

themselves who may enter and who must leave, rather than an operator of water utilities. This picture may be changing, however, towards increased recognition of the platform's quasi-public role; in 2018 Jack Dorsey, Twitter's CEO, said that Twitter's rules on content moderation would be rooted in "human rights law"[126] and Facebook has established its quasi-independent Oversight Board to review the company's conduct based on human rights law almost like a court would review administrative action.[127]

Constitutional reformers in Norway, Iceland and Ireland did not contemplate the role of Internet platforms as they considered possible reforms of freedom of expression provisions. The obvious reason is timing; the problems surrounding Internet platforms simply had not materialised in the eyes of the public.

However, the impact of business on human rights more generally was certainly an acknowledged issue at the time. The Icelandic Constitutional Council was so concerned about private power that it proposed a far-reaching provision on full direct horizontal effects of its proposed provisions on fundamental rights.[128] This idea was met with scepticism by the group of legal experts that reviewed the proposals[129] and was amended during the 2012 parliamentary process so as to only include indirect horizontal effects, including a dedicated provision on the obligation of the state to protect people from human rights abuses at the hands of private individuals.[130] The 2011 preparatory report for the 2014 Norwegian reform states that in a modern democracy it is likely true that more abuses of human rights are committed by private entities than public authorities.[131] The Norwegian reformers, however, did not propose a specific provision on the effects of the Constitution on legal relationships between private parties, while stating that there already was established case law on indirect horizontal effects.[132] The Irish Constitution has been interpreted by the Courts as including direct horizontal effects in the sense of allowing private entities to claim damages from other private entities for violations of human rights.[133] This, in fact, was an important inspiration for the Icelandic Constitutional Council's proposals of direct horizontal effects.[134]

Internet platforms are not only private but transnational entities. Constitutions, on the other hand, are traditionally fundamentally territorial in scope. The possibility of extra-territoriality of constitutional law is one of the thorny issues that has been highlighted in cases of Internet speech. In Sect. 2 we noted the case of Eva Glawischnig-Piesczek, who obtained a judgment from the Austrian Courts (with

[126] Cited in Douek (2021), p. 765.

[127] Hofverberg (2021). We should stress the inclusion of the word "almost" in this sentence.

[128] Stjórnlagaráð [Constitutional Council] (2011a), pp. 46–48.

[129] Sérfræðingahópur (2012), p. 7.

[130] Althingi (2012b, c).

[131] Menneskerettighetsutvalget [Human Rights Committee] (2011), p. 46.

[132] Id.

[133] Gardbaum (2003).

[134] Althingi (2012a), p. 43.

input from the CJEU) ordering the worldwide removal of certain defamatory statements about Ms. Glawischnig-Piesczek.[135] Among the interesting aspects of the case is that the statements in question (including calling a politician a "miese Volksverräterin" (lousy traitor) and "korrupten Trampel" (corrupt bumpkin)) would surely be protected speech in other jurisdictions.

Horizontal effects and extraterritoriality are among the least explored and most complicated aspects of constitutional rights. They may become, however, among the most important with respect to Internet platforms. Constitutional reformers intending to engage with the power of Internet platforms are in some sense working against two traditional benchmarks of constitutional rights—state-centrism and territorial limitations. Only a handful of genuine alternative practices are well understood, and these entrenched features of constitutional law may act as significant hurdles for developing novel understandings of freedom of expression in the privatised and globalised world of Internet speech.

## 4.3 *The Impact of International and Comparative Law*

Human rights law, particularly the ECHR and the practice of the ECtHR, were integral to the three reform processes. In Norway, the express purpose of the 2014 reform was to bring human rights home and mirror international law. In Ireland, the freedom of expression doctrine developed by the ECtHR was thoroughly presented to the Constitutional Convention by legal experts, essentially framing the drafting choices available.[136] In Iceland, explanatory notes accompanying the proposed freedom of expression clause referred to the ECHR, case law from the ECtHR as well as the ICCPR and other UN instruments, although stating that while modelled on the ECHR, the proposal also contained novel aspects.[137]

As intended, the ECHR thus created a floor for national protection of fundamental rights,[138] and the reformers seemed strongly committed to the project of international protection of human rights. The more interesting question is whether international law placed constraints on reformers. A clear example of such constraints appears to be the impact of the Venice Commission of the Council of Europe on the Icelandic process, as the Commission's somewhat critical opinion of the Constitutional Council proposals, based on the Commission's view of international best practice,[139] proved an important tool for opponents of the process. In Jon Elster's

[135] CJEU: CJEU, Case C-18/18, Eva Glawischnig-Piesczek v. Facebook Ireland Limited, ECLI:EU:C:2019:821.

[136] The Convention on the Constitution (2014) (setting out as annexes presentations from legal experts).

[137] Althingi (2012c).

[138] ECHR, Article 53.

[139] Venice Commission (2012).

framework of "upstream," "midstream" and "downstream" constraints on constitution-making, the formal "downstream" constraints on constitutional reformers in Iceland were the required ratification of Parliament and a referendum.[140] We can, however, also think about conformity with international law as a constraint, either as a "downstream" constraint, as we can imagine a highly negative review from a body such as the Venice Commission leading to the failure of the process. Or we might think of international law functioning as a "midstream" constraint on constitutional reformers, as during the process they must ensure that their proposals conform to international law.

We might also think of international law functioning as a different kind of constraint, more difficult to assess or quantify. Constitutional reformers may be constrained by the sense that international law offers only a handful of options, determining largely what a bill of rights could or should look like. Yes, there are some choices to be made (level of protection for socio-economic rights, as was debated in Norway's 2014 reform is one example) but the choices are somewhat determined by international law. "Determined" here does not refer to legal determinacy—as international lawyers know, the law develops rapidly even if some of the treaties are decades old—but to the perceived determinacy of the options available, thus placing limits on the institutional imagination of constitutional reformers.

Aside from international law, comparisons with domestic law of other jurisdictions were also an important aspect of all three reform processes. Norway's reformers included in their report a comparison with constitutions in the other Nordic countries as well as Germany, France, USA, South Africa and Switzerland.[141] In Iceland, we saw how the "infrastructure requirement" of the freedom expression clause was borrowed from Norway and then expanded on, and the Council's ideas on direct horizontal effects were modelled on South Africa and Ireland. The Council's proposals more generally refer to some 27 different foreign constitutions, with Sweden and Finland scoring the highest number of references.[142] There was less emphasis on comparisons with other constitutions in the output of the Irish Constitutional Council, although the Council was presented with an overview of blasphemy laws across European states.[143] As noted above, however, one of the factors relevant to Ireland was to prevent the Irish Constitution from being used in "abusive constitutional borrowing,"[144] i.e. used by other states to justify oppressive practice.

If a study of comparative and international materials is important for constitutional reformers, how does this fit with the emerging view[145] that it is important for the public to participate in the drafting of constitutional design? A question surely

[140] Elster (2016).

[141] NOU (1999), pp. 197–238, Menneskerettighetsutvalget [Human Rights Committee] (2011), pp. 34–39.

[142] Helgadóttir (2014).

[143] The Convention on the Constitution (2014).

[144] Dixon and Landau (2021).

[145] See e.g. Choudhry and Tushnet (2020), Democratic Constitutional Design (2021).

worthy of further study and closely related to questions of expertise in constitution-making, since the members of the public depend on expert advice.[146] At this point we only note that in the case of Ireland the selection and influence of experts has been subject to critique.[147] In Iceland, for better or for worse, experts had significant influence, for example as the Constitutional Council's subcommittees welcomed experts as guests and commissioned their written opinions while not inviting civil society groups or other interest groups to present their views. Yet, the Icelandic proposals have been criticised heavily for lack of expertise.[148] Even as regards the isolated issue of access to the Internet, which has been a focus of this article, we saw the Council struggle with international material as the Council overstated the views of UN bodies.[149] Constitutional reformers inevitably face the risks that all comparativists face, including a general lack of breadth resulting in a narrow sample, lack of depth resulting in underappreciation of details and local circumstances, and "cherry picking" resulting in, among other things, overstating the determinacy of the direction of development of comparative law. Although these, and other, risks are always present non-expert constitutional reformers may be more vulnerable to them.

## *4.4 Time*

Perhaps the most important factor in our stories of constitutional reform is timing. To the extent constitutional reform is driven by crises or "constitutional moments"—a category in which we would place Iceland, Ireland and even, tentatively, the 2014 Norwegian reform, although the trigger of reform was the Constitution's undramatic bicentennial—the timing is not necessarily perfect. Constitution-making driven by crisis is not limited to reactions to the crisis ("fixing what went wrong") as evidenced by both Ireland and Iceland. A crisis acts as trigger but does not demarcate the extent of reform. More simply put, using the Icelandic timeline as an example: 2021 might be a better year for reconsidering the constitutional treatment of Internet speech as compared to 2011, but the timing of the constitutional moment did not align.

Constitutional reformers are constrained by a lack of clairvoyance. The problems of the future are unforeseeable and therefore unforeseen. Although new constitutions are often "portrayed as platforms for launching new futures," the unavoidable truth is that reformers know only the past.[150] In some cases an overemphasis on the

[146] On that topic see e.g. Tushnet (2008).

[147] Carolan (2015).

[148] See Elster (2016), p. 197.

[149] Stjórnlagaráð [Constitutional Council] (2011a), p. 54 (attributing the view that access to the Internet has been "defined as a human right" to the UNHCHR, while, in fact the cited report of a UN Special Rapporteur on freedom of expression does not go so far, although certainly highlighting the importance of access to the Internet for rights enjoyment, see UN Special Rapporteur on the promotion and protection of the right to freedom of opinion and expression (2011).

[150] Scheppele (2008), p. 1379.

problems of the past means that risks are underestimated. For its critics, this is the case of the Weimar Constitution, whose extensive emergency powers contributed to Hitler's dictatorship.[151] In our case studies, a focus on the past is certainly a characteristic of the Irish experience in addressing blasphemy,[152] Iceland's institutional reform after the financial crisis, and, at least partly, of the Norwegian 2014 reform which was focused on aligning the Constitution with international instruments such as the ECHR and ICCPR. These, in turn, are more than 50 years old treaties, although of course the Norwegian reformers were looking at international law as currently practiced, not just the treaty text.

In other cases, reformers clearly seek to construct a framework capable of enduring and of addressing future problems as they arise.[153] We might possibly place the 2004 Norwegian reform of the freedom of expression in this context. The background 1999 report on freedom of expression explores the fundamental justifications of the right[154] and the resulting Article 100 of the Norwegian Constitution incorporates that depth by proclaiming that any restrictions of freedom of expression must be in line with "the seeking of truth, the promotion of democracy and the individual's freedom to form opinions."[155] The idea, thus, is that by entrenching not only fundamental rights but their timeless moral justifications, the Constitution will be more successful in adapting to new contexts. And as mentioned previously, these justifications fit quite well with some of the pertinent issues in modern Internet speech. The problem, perhaps obviously, is that the underlying moral justifications are indeterminate and possibly in conflict with each other, but, such is the nature of much of constitutional law.[156] The practical consequences of introducing indeterminate principles in constitutions may include empowering courts, as they will have the final word on interpretation.

In Iceland, the deliberations of the members of the Constitutional Council shed interesting light on expected endurance of the proposals. Various members of the Council expressed concerns about the use of the word "Internet," as they feared that it would stand as an obsolete relic of the past as the new constitution might survive current technologies.[157] This worry seems rather unreasonable because the average age of constitutions is said to be around 19 years.[158]

---

[151] E.g. Skach (2005).

[152] To be clear, the Irish Convention also addressed very contemporary problems, including abortion and same-sex marriage.

[153] On the endurance of constitutions generally see Elkins et al. (2009).

[154] NOU (1999).

[155] Constitution of the Kingdom of Norway 1814 (rev. 2020), Article 100.

[156] For one version of a broad indeterminacy thesis associated with critical legal studies see Tushnet (1996).

[157] Stjórnlagaráð [Constitutional Council] (2011b), p. 388 (Mr. Þorkell Helgason), pp. 390–391 (Mr. Erlingur Sigurðarson), p. 483 (Mr. Ómar Ragnarsson).

[158] Elkins et al. (2009).

A lack of ability to address future problems with specificity is, at the very least, understandable and perhaps unavoidable.[159] Another side of the problem is that entrenching solutions to present-day problems might render it more difficult to react to future ones. For example, at least some members of the Icelandic Constitutional Council saw "censorship" of the Internet as a serious threat while they also advocated for strong direct horizontal effects of constitutional rights.[160] Taking constitutional provisions based on those ideas seriously might affect content moderation by Internet platforms and/or government regulatory powers. Of course, courts or other constitutional interpreters might find a workaround, but the hypothetical highlights the possibility of unintended consequences[161] of constitutional reform, largely because of timing and, thus, the state of knowledge.

These arguments about time in constitution-making recall, of course, the classic argument between Thomas Jefferson and James Madison around the drafting of the U.S. Constitution. Famously, Jefferson argued that the dead should not govern the living and thus each generation should write its own constitution.[162] Madison countered, and his position eventually prevailed in practice, with an argument in favour of entrenchment and stability.[163] One of Madison's points involves crisis, as he was concerned that constitutional overhaul outside the context of crisis would be overly affected with day-to-day politics and self-interest. On the other hand, post-crisis constitution-making has its own risks, including an overemphasis on the immediate past and a lack of rational consideration of alternative arrangements.[164]

When faced with criticism of the details of the proposals, advocates for the new constitution of Iceland have sometimes argued that any such small flaws can be fixed through amendment after adoption of the full text.[165] This raises a final point of view of time in constitution-making. One that accepts that the perfect must not be the enemy of the good and emphasises the foundational legitimacy of the "constitutional moment" in which the constitution was born, rather than its details. For proponents such a point of view the questions would become, first, whether the foreseen flaws are too much to bear, even in the short term; second, whether openness to frequent amendment has too high a cost ("wiki-constitutionalism")[166]; and third, whether flaws and fixes could realistically be agreed and implemented once the constitutional moment fades and ordinary politics resumes. Can we really get there from here?

---

[159] See generally Scheppele (2008).

[160] Stjórnlagaráð [Constitutional Council] (2011b), p. 394 (Ms. Katrín Oddsdóttir).

[161] The classic analysis of "unintended consequences," including their sources, is Merton (1936).

[162] Jefferson (1789).

[163] E.g. the Federalist Papers: No. 49 (1788).

[164] Elkins et al. (2009), p. 18.

[165] Fontaine (2020), interviewing activist/lawyer Helga Baldvins Bjargardóttir ("Of course, it's not perfect. It's supposed to be a living instrument.").

[166] Lansberg-Rodriguez (2010). Incidentally, the neologism "wiki-constitutionalism" has no relationship to the kind of crowdsourcing associated with Wikipedia but describes the tendency of constant rewriting of constitutions practiced in some states, especially in Latin America.

## 5 Conclusion

The novel problems of Internet speech place strain on legal protections of freedom of expression. Addressing these issues at the foundational level through constitutional reform is, putting it mildly, complicated. The recent experiences of Iceland, Ireland, and Norway highlight how constitutional reformers lack tools to address the power of private intermediaries such as the Internet platforms that significantly impact our daily lives. Horizontal effects of fundamental rights remain underexplored and seem risky in the eyes of experts as well as the politicians needed to ratify constitutional amendments. Reformers look to international and comparative law for inspiration, but the available blueprints are flawed or non-existent. In turn, overreliance on international and comparative law empowers experts in an age where value is increasingly placed on public participation in constitution-making. All these complications arise in a context where the timing of constitutional reform is driven by external factors, often crises. Reformers are necessarily focused on solving past problems and optimistic towards a new future. Problems of the future remain unforeseen, and the constitutional moment may not be duplicatable once such problems materialise. Pushing towards digital constitutionalism in actually existing constitutionalism through constitutional reform will require significant work.

## References

Ackerman B (1991) We the people: foundations. Belknap Press, Cambridge

Ackerman B (2015) Three paths to constitutionalism – and the crisis of the European Union. Br J Polit Sci 45(3):705–714

Althingi (2012a) Frumvarp til stjórnarskipunarlaga um stjórnarskrá lýðveldisins Íslands. Submitted to the 141st legislative session 2012–2013, document 510, https://www.althingi.is/altext/141/s/pdf/0510.pdf

Althingi (2012b) Frumvarp til stjórnarskipunarlaga um stjórnarskrá lýðveldisins Íslands. Ákvæði frumvarpsins með fyrirhuguðum breytingum. [Consolidated final version of the 2012 constitutional bill] https://www.stjornarradid.is/media/forsaetisraduneyti-media/media/stjornarskra/Frumvarp_til_stjornarskipunarlaga_lokagerd.pdf

Althingi (2012c) Framhaldsnefndarálit um frumvarp til stjórnarskipunarlaga um stjórnarskrá lýðveldisins Íslands. Frá meiri hluta stjórnskipunar- og eftirlitsnefndar [Constitutional and Oversight Committee's majority opinion on the 2012 constitutional bill]. Submitted to the 141st legislative session 2012–2013, document 1111, https://www.althingi.is/altext/141/s/1111.html

Anderson and Rainie (2020) Concerns about democracy in the digital age. Pew Research Center, 21 February 2020. https://www.pewresearch.org/internet/2020/02/21/concerns-about-democracy-in-the-digital-age/

Árnason ÁÞ, Dupré C (eds) (2021) Icelandic constitutional reform: people, processes, politics. Routledge, New York

Atheist Ireland (2014) Submission from Atheist Ireland to Constitutional Convention on Removing the Offence of Blasphemy, http://www.constitutionalconvention.ie/AttachmentDownload.ashx?aid=3700a009-d7f3-e211-a5a0-005056a32ee4

Balkin J (2014) Old-school/new-school speech regulation. Harv Law Rev 127(8):2296–2342

Bårdsen A (2016) Guardians of human rights in Norway: challenging mandates in a new era. Address to the Centre on Law and Social Transformation in collaboration with Bergen Resource Center, Litteraturhuset Bergen 11 May 2016, https://www.domstol.no/globalassets/upload/hret/artikler-og-foredrag/guardians-of-human-rights%2D%2D-11052016.pdf
Benkler Y (2006) The wealth of networks: how social production transforms markets and freedom. Yale University Press, New Haven
Bibler J (2010) Hversu stórt var fall íslensku bankanna á heimsmælikvarda? FME [ICELANDIC FINANCIAL SERVICES AUTHORITY], 12 March 2010, http://www.fme.is/media/frettir/12.03.2010.Hlutfoll-JEB.pdf [https://perma.cc/L7J9-LSPC]
Blokker P (2017) Constitutional reform in Europe and recourse to the people. In: Contiades S, Fotiado A (eds) Participatory constitutional change: the people as amenders of the constitution. Routledge, New York
Carolan E (2015) Ireland's constitutional convention: behind the hype about citizen-led constitutional change. Int J Const Law 13(3):733–748
Celeste E (2019) Digital constitutionalism: a new systematic theorisation. Int Rev Law Comput Technol 33(1):76–99
Choudhry S, Tushnet M (2020) Participatory constitution-making: introduction. Int J Const Law 18(1):173–178
Constitution of Ecuador 2008 (rev. 2021). https://www.constituteproject.org/constitution/Ecuador_2021?lang=en
Constitution of Greece as revised by the parliamentary resolution of May 27th 2008 of the VIIIth Revisionary Parliament., https://www.hellenicparliament.gr/UserFiles/f3c70a23-7696-49db-9148-f24dce6a27c8/001-156%20aggliko.pdf
Constitution of Mexico 1917 (rev. 2015), Eng transl, https://www.constituteproject.org/constitution/Mexico_2015?lang=en,
Constitution of Sudan 2019, Eng transl., https://www.constituteproject.org/constitution/Sudan_2019?lang=en,
Constitution of Georgia 1995 (rev. 2018), Eng transl, https://www.constituteproject.org/constitution/Georgia_2018?lang=en,
Constitution of the Kingdom of Norway 1814 (rev. 2020). https://lovdata.no/dokument/NLE/lov/1814-05-17?q=grunnloven
Contiades X (ed) (2013) Constitutions in the global financial crisis: a comparative analysis. Ashgate, Surrey
Council of Europe (2014) Recommendation CM/Rec(2014)6 of the Committee of Ministers to member States on a Guide to human rights for Internet users
Dáil Éireann (2012) Resolution calling a Convention on the Constitution, http://www.constitutionalconvention.ie/Documents/Terms_of_Reference.pdf
De Gregorio G (2021) The rise of digital constitutionalism in the European Union. Int J Const Law. https://doi.org/10.1093/icon/moab001
Democratic Constitutional Design (2021), http://stjornarskra.hi.is/en/about/
Democratic Decay & Renewal (2021), https://www.democratic-decay.org/
Director, IMF, 15 November 2008
Dixon R, Landau D (2021) Abusive constitutional borrowing. Oxford University Press, Oxford
Douek E (2021) Governing online speech: from "posts-as-trumps" to proportionality and probability. Columbia Law Rev 121(3):759–833
Elkins Z, Ginsburg T, Melton J (2009) The endurance of national constitutions. Cambridge University Press, Cambridge
Elster J (1995) Forces and mechanisms in the constitution-making process. Duke Law J 45(2):364–396
Elster J (2016) Icelandic constitution-making in comparative perspective. In: Ingimundarson V et al (eds) Iceland's financial crisis: the politics of blame, protest, and reconstruction. Routledge, New York, pp 187–202

Farrell D, Harris C, Suiter J (2017) Bringing people into the heart of constitutional design. The Irish constitutional convention of 2012–14. In: Contiades S, Fotiado A (eds) Participatory constitutional change: the people as amenders of the constitution. Routledge, New York
Feldman N (2020) Arab winter: a tragedy. Princeton University Press, Princeton
Fishkin JS, Mansbridge J (2017) Introduction. Dædalus 146(3):6
Fontaine AS (2020) Where is the new constitution? – a nation still waits for Iceland 2.0. Reykjavik Grapevine, 9 November 2020. https://grapevine.is/mag/feature/2020/11/09/where-is-the-new-constitution/
Freedom House (2019) Freedom on the Net 2019. Ecuador. https://freedomhouse.org/country/ecuador/freedom-net/2019#:~:text=Ecuador's%20Constitution%20guarantees%20%E2%80%9Cuniversal%20access,of%20expression%20(Article%20384)
Funke M, Schularick M, Trebesch C (2016) Going to extremes: politics after financial crises, 1870–2014. Eur Econ Rev 88(C):227–260
Gardbaum S (2003) The "horizontal effect" of constitutional rights. Mich Law Rev 102(3):387–459
Ghosh D (2019) Don't break up Facebook — treat it like a utility. Harv Bus Rev, 30 May 2019, https://hbr.org/2019/05/dont-break-up-facebook-treat-it-like-a-utility
Gunnarsson BL (2019) Speech at Althing 24 October 2019, transcript. https://www.althingi.is/skodalid.php?lthing=150&lidur=lid20191024T134250
Gylfason T, Meuwese A (2017) Digital tools and the derailment of Iceland's new constitution. In: Prins C et al (eds) Digital democracy in a globalized world. Edward Elgar Publishing, Cheltenham, pp 249–274
Hagstofa Íslands (2010) Notkun heimila og einstaklinga á tölvum og neti 2010. https://hagstofa.is/utgafur/utgafa/visindi-og-taekni/notkun-heimila-og-einstaklinga-a-tolvum-og-neti-2010/
Helgadóttir R (2014) Lessons Concerning Constitutional Borrowing from the Icelandic Draft Constitution 2011. In: The IXth World Congress of Constitutional Law: "Constitutional Challenges: Global and Local" Oslo 16–20 June 2014. https://www.jus.uio.no/english/research/news-and-events/events/conferences/2014/wccl-cmdc/wccl/papers/workshop5.html
Hofverberg E (2021) Facebook's New "Supreme Court" – The Oversight Board and International Human Rights Law. In Custodia Legis Blog, 16 March 2021, https://blogs.loc.gov/law/2021/03/facebooks-new-supreme-court-the-oversight-board-and-international-human-rights-law/
House of the Oireachtas (2008) Joint Committee on the Constitution. First Report. Article 40.6.1.i – Freedom of Expression, July 2008, http://opac.oireachtas.ie/Data/Library3/Library2/DL043973.pdf
Humanist Association of Ireland (2014) Removal of Blasphemy Offence, http://www.constitutionalconvention.ie/AttachmentDownload.ashx?aid=767465d8-802a-e311-96d5-005056a32ee4
IMF (2018) World Economic Outlook, October 2018
Jefferson T (1789) To James Madison from Thomas Jefferson, 6 September 1789. Founders Online, National Archives, https://founders.archives.gov/documents/Madison/01-12-02-0248
Kaminski M, Massaro TM, Norton H (2017) SIRI-OUSLY 2.0: what artificial intelligence reveals about the first amendment. Minn Law Rev 101(6):2481–2525
Kierulf A (2018) Judicial review in Norway: a bicentennial debate. Cambridge University Press, Cambridge
Landemore H (2014) Inclusive constitution-making: the Icelandic experiment. J Polit Philosophy 23(2):166–191
Lansberg-Rodriguez D (2010) Wiki-constitutionalism. The strange phenomenon that's destroying Latin America. The New Republic, 25 May 2010
Lenihan B, Honohan P (2010) Letter of Intent from Brian Lenihan, Ireland's Minister for Finance and Patrick Honohan, Governor of the Central Bank of Ireland, to the International Monetary Fund, 3 Dec. 2010), http://www.imf.org/external/np/loi/2010/irl/120310.pdf [https://perma.cc/E9EQ-Y998]
Lessig L (2016) On Iceland's Crowdsourced Constitution. https://medium.com/equal-citizens/on-icelands-crowdsourced-constitution-ad99aae75fce

Massaro TM, Norton H (2016) Siri-ously? Free speech rights and artificial intelligence. Northwest Univ Law Rev 110(5):1169–1194
Massaro TM, Norton H (2021) Free speech and democracy: a primer for twenty-first century reformers. UC Davis Law Rev 54(3):1631–1685
Menneskerettighetsutvalget [Human Rights Committee] (2011) Rapport fra Menneskerettighetsutvalget om menneskerettigheter i Grunnloven, avgitt 19. desember 2011 https://stortinget.no/globalassets/pdf/dokumentserien/2011-2012/dok16-201112.pdf
Merton RK (1936) The unanticipated consequences of purposive social action. Am Sociol Rev 1(6): 894–904
Meuwese A (2013) Popular constitution-making, the case of Iceland. In: Galligan DJ, Versteeg M (eds) Social and political foundations of constitutions. Cambridge University Press, New York, pp 469–496
Ministry of Culture (2020) Mandate for the Freedom of Expression Commission. https://www.regjeringen.no/en/topics/culture-sports-and-non-profit-work/innsiktsartikler/ytringsfrihetskommisjonen/mandate-for-the-freedom-of-expression-commission/id2695703/
NOU (1999) “Ytringsfrihed bør finde Sted”: forslag til ny grunnlov § 100, NOU 1999:27. Statens Forvaltningstjeneste, Statens Trykning, Oslo
O’Mahony C (2012) This so-called constitutional convention is a charade. Irish Times, 7 June 2012
Oddsson D, Mathiesen ÁM (2008) Letter of intent from Davíd Oddsson, chairman of the central Bank of Iceland, and Árni M. Mathiesen, Iceland’s Minister of Finance, to Dominique Strauss-Kahn, Managing
Persily N, Tucker JA (2020) Social media and democracy. The state of the field, prospects for reform. Cambridge University Press, New York
Public Submissions to the Convention on the Constitution (2014), http://www.constitutionalconvention.ie/Submissions.aspx
Redeker D, Gill L, Gasser U (2018) Towards digital constitutionalism? Mapping attempts to craft an internet bill of rights. Int Commun Gazette 80(4):302–319
Referendum Commission (2019) Report on the referendum on blasphemy, February 2019, https://www.refcom.ie/previous-referendums/referendum-on-blasphemy/Report-on-the-referendum-on-blasphemy.pdf
Sajó A (2005) Constitution without the constitutional moment: a view from the new member states. Int J Const Law 3(2–3):243–261
Schauer F (1983) Free speech and the argument from democracy. Nomos 25:241
Scheppele KL (2008) A constitution between past and future. William & Mary Law Rev 49(4):1377
Sérfræðingahópur (2012) Skilabréf sérfræðingahóps um tillögur stjórnlagaráðs að nýrri stjórnarskrá, 12 November 2012, https://www.althingi.is/pdf/skilabref_fylgiskjol.pdf
Skach C (2005) Borrowing constitutional designs. Harvard University Press, Cambridge
Stjórnlagaráð [Constitutional Council] (2011a) Frumvarp til stjórnarskipunarlaga ásamt skýringum [Constitutional proposal with explanatory notes], http://www.stjornlagarad.is/other_files/stjornlagarad/Frumvarp_med_skyringum.pdf
Stjórnlagaráð [Constitutional Council] (2011b) Stjórnlagaráðstíðindi 2 – Umræður á ráðsfundum, 14.-19. ráðsfundur [Transcripts of discussions at plenary sessions 14–19], http://www.stjornlagarad.is/other_files/stjornlagarad/stjornlagaradstidindi2b.pdf
Suteu S (2015) Constitutional conventions in the digital era: lessons from Iceland and Ireland. Boston College Int Comp Law Rev 38(1):267
Suzor N (2018) Digital constitutionalism: using the rule of law to evaluate the legitimacy of governance by platforms. Soc Media Soc 4:205630511878781. https://doi.org/10.1177/2056305118787812
Suzor N (2020) A constitutional moment: how we might reimagine platform governance. Comput Law Secur Rev 36:105381. https://doi.org/10.1016/j.clsr.2019.105381
The Associated Press (2019) Facebook blocks page of ex-Ecuadorian leader Rafael Correa. ABC News. https://abcnews.go.com/International/wireStory/facebook-blocks-page-ecuadorian-leader-rafael-correa-62369883

The Convention on the Constitution (2014) Sixth Report. The Removal of the offence of blasphemy from the Constitution, January 2014, http://www.constitutionalconvention.ie/AttachmentDownload.ashx?mid=687a658f-b2a2-e311-a7ce-005056a32ee4

The Federalist Papers: No. 49 (1788) Method of Guarding Against the Encroachments of Any One Department of Government by Appealing to the People Through a Convention. https://avalon.law.yale.edu/18th_century/fed49.asp

The Guardian (2015) Ecuador's president wages social media counterattack aimed at 'defamers' https://www.theguardian.com/world/2015/feb/02/ecuador-president-social-media-counterattack

Þórhallsson P (2011a) Minnisblað til stjórnlagaráðs, 20 May 2011, http://www.stjornlagarad.is/servlet/file/Pall_umsogn.pdf?ITEM_ENT_ID=34723&ITEM_VERSION=1&COLLSPEC_ENT_ID=127

Þórhallsson P (2011b) Minnisblað til stjórnlagaráðs, 11 July 2011, http://www.stjornlagarad.is/servlet/file/Pall_umsogn_02.pdf?ITEM_ENT_ID=34775&ITEM_VERSION=1&COLLSPEC_ENT_ID=127

Tooze A (2018) Crashed: how a decade of financial crises changed the world. Penguin Books, London

Tushnet M (1996) Defending the indeterminacy thesis. Quinnipiac Law Rev 16(2):339–356

Tushnet M (2008) Some skepticism about normative constitutional advice. William & Mary Law Rev 49(4):1473–1495

Tushnet M (2016) New institutional mechanisms for making constitutional law. In: Bustamante T, Gonçalves Fernandes B (eds) Democratizing constitutional law. Springer, Cham, pp 167–183

Tushnet M (2021) The Kids are Alright: The Law of Free Expression and New Information Technologies. https://ssrn.com/abstract=3714415

UN Special Rapporteur on the promotion and protection of the right to freedom of opinion and expression (2011) Report of the Special Rapporteur on the promotion and protection of the right to freedom of opinion and expression, Frank La Rue, A/HRC/17/27, 16 May 2011

Venice Commission (2012) Opinion on the Draft New Constitution of Iceland Adopted by the Venice Commission at its 94th Plenary Session (Venice, 8–9 March 2013)

Venice Commission (2017) Georgia - Opinion on the draft revised Constitution as adopted by the Parliament of Georgia at the second reading on 23 June 2017, adopted by the Venice Commission at its 112th Plenary Session (Venice, 6–7 October 2017)

Wikipedia (2021) The 2010–2013 Icelandic constitutional reform, https://en.wikipedia.org/wiki/2010%E2%80%932013_Icelandic_constitutional_reform#The_assembly's_proposals

Wu T (2018) Is the first amendment obsolete? Mich Law Rev 117(3):547–581

Ytringsfrihetskommisjonen (2021). https://www.ykom.no/

**Kári Hólmar Ragnarsson** is an assistant professor of law at the University of Iceland in Reykjavík, Iceland where he teaches international law, human rights and constitutional law. He earned his Mag. Jur. law degree at the University of Iceland and practiced law as partner at Réttur – Aðalsteinsson & Partners in Reykjavík, including in the aftermath of the 2008 financial crisis. Kári then completed his LL.M. and S.J.D. at the Harvard Law School. His dissertation centered on socio-economic rights and neoliberalism. His research interests include law and political economy, socio-economic rights, constitution-making, human rights and climate change.

# Part II
# Regulating Freedom of Speech After the Technology Shift

# *Let the Robot Speak!* AI-Generated Speech and Freedom of Expression

**Katja de Vries**

## Contents



**Abstract** Up until very recently, AI-generated, or more precisely, machine learning (ML)-generated content was still in the realm of sci-fi. A recent series of important inventions gave AI the power of creation: Variational Autoencoders (VAEs) in 2013, Generative Adversarial Networks (GANs) in 2014, and Generative Pre-trained Transformers (GPT) in 2017. Synthetic products based on generative ML are useful in diverse fields of application. For example, generative ML can be used for the synthetic resuscitation of a dead actor, or a deceased loved one. Can ML be a source of speech that is protected by the right to freedom of expression in Article 10 ECHR? In contrast to a tool, such as a pen or a typewriter, ML can be such a decisive element in the generative process, that speech is no longer (indisputably) attributable to a human speaker. Is speech generated by a machine protected by the right to freedom of expression in Article 10 ECHR? I first discuss if ML-generated utterances fall within the protective scope of freedom of expression (Article 10(1) ECHR). After concluding that this is the case, I look at specific complexities raised by ML-generated content in terms of limitations to freedom of expression

K. de Vries (✉)
Uppsala University, Department of Law, Uppsala, Sweden
e-mail: katja.devries@jur.uu.se

 
S. Hindelang, A. Moberg (eds.), *YSEC Yearbook of Socio-Economic Constitutions 2021*, YSEC Yearbook of Socio-Economic Constitutions (2022) 2021: 93–116,
https://doi.org/10.1007/16495_2021_38, Published online: 10 April 2022

(Article 10(2) ECHR). The first set of potential limitations that I explore are those following from copyright, data protection, privacy and confidentiality law. Some types of ML-generated content could potentially circumvent these limitations. Second, I study how new types of content generated by ML can create normative grey areas where the boundaries of constitutionally protected and unprotected speech are not always easy to draw. In this context, I discuss two types of ML-generated content: virtual child pornography and fake news/disinformation. Third, I argue that the nuances of Article 10 ECHR are not easily captured in an automated filter and I discuss the potential implications of the arms race between automated filters and ML-generated content.

## 1 Machines That Create New Utterances

Article 10 of the European Convention on Human Rights (ECHR) safeguards the freedom "to hold opinions and to receive and impart information and ideas without interference by public authority and regardless of frontiers." In this chapter, I explore the question of whether the right to freedom of expression (Article 10 ECHR) protects the content that is generated by a machine with limited or no human guidance. In Sect. 2 of this chapter, I argue that there is no good reason why machine-generated speech, which could equally well contribute to a free exchange of ideas as human-generated speech, should be categorically excluded from the protective scope of freedom of expression (Article 10(1) ECHR). I contrast this to copyright law, where works created by machines without any meaningful human input are unprotected works that fall in the public domain. In Sect. 3, I argue that, in terms of *limitations* to freedom of expression arising from "the rights of others" (Article 10(2) ECHR), machine-generated speech could be in some cases less constrained than human-generated speech. Machine-generated speech often will be an orphaned form of speech that is, for example, not tied to an identifiable person (data protection law) or an author (copyright law) whose rights could limit freedom of expression. In terms of limitations that arise from "the protection of .... morals" (Article 10(2) ECHR), machine-generated speech could turn out to be challenging because of its potential to be tailored to balance exactly on the legal boundary of what is acceptable (for example, with regard to machine-generated imagery bordering on child pornography). Yet, it is also likely that automated filters will be increasingly used to combat undesirable machine-generated speech, such as harmful disinformation or child pornography, and that this will result in over-blocking as well as an arms race between machine-generation and machine-filtering of speech. The legal space granted by Article 10 ECHR for machine-generated speech to be heard may be pre-emptively muffled and stifled by overzealous automated filtering systems.

Before diving into the discussion of Article 10 ECHR in relation to machine-generated speech, I will start out in this section with the very basics: what do I mean with a machine that creates utterances with limited or no human guidance?

Almost all human speech is somehow mediated by tools such as pens, computers, and megaphones. In day-to-day understanding, such tools are considered to be neutral media that merely transmit the ideas of a human enunciator. Only in the hand of a human will a pen, a computer or a megaphone produce something worth protecting. It is this common sense understanding that is also leading within the law. For example, in copyright law, the idea that authorship can be attributed to a communication tool was until recently completely preposterous – and to a large extent, it still is. Obviously, Ernest Hemingway, not the typewriter that he used to write it down, is the author of *A Moveable Feast*. To any copyright lawyer, this goes without question.

However, in philosophy and media theory, this common-sense understanding of communication equipment as neutral media[1] and expression tied to an isolated human individual[2] has been challenged. Expressions emerge within and through material and symbolic surroundings. Communicative tools, which even include language itself,[3] influence the content of what is expressed, as McLuhan famously wrote: *the medium is the message*.[4] The agency distribution between human authors and their communicative tools is not as clear-cut as the common sense understanding would have it. In the movie *Mulholland Drive* (2001) by David Lynch, there is a scene in a theatre where the singer Rebekah Del Rio sings the song *Llorando* a cappella.[5] The scene contains many close-ups and both the face and the voice of the singer express enormous emotional intensity. Then the singer suddenly collapses while the song continues. The scene has been interpreted by the philosopher Zizek[6] as an illustration of the fact that all utterances, even those that seem as pure and unmediated as one's own voice, are to a certain extent external and alien to the individual subject making the utterance.

The philosophical and media theoretic musings on the muddled agency distribution between human enunciators and their communication tools never impacted much on law: in practice, the individual human impact on any utterance worth of protection always used to be decisive in comparison to the impact of communicative tools. However, following recent developments in the field of artificial intelligence (AI) this decisive role of humans is no longer undisputed.

Can machines nowadays, or in the near future, have a decisive, (partly) autonomous role in creating[7] utterances deserving some form of legal protection? Can AI

[1] Kittler (1986), Hayles (1999).

[2] Derrida (1982).

[3] Heidegger (2001), p. 188: "*Language speaks.*"

[4] McLuhan (1994).

[5] https://www.youtube.com/watch?v=uHQnb3HS4hc.

[6] Žižek et al. (2006).

[7] De Vries (2020).

and machine learning (ML) models—currently AI's most prolific branch—generate pictures, texts or other informational patterns that seem to be created by a human? Or depict something that seems to be captured from reality, while in fact merely existing in "machine imagination"?[8]

Until recently AI and ML had a very limited *generative* capacity. ML can be described as an indirect form of programming: instead of instructing machines what to do, ML allows machines to learn rules (or "algorithms" or "models"') from examples. The big breakthroughs in ML in the early 2010s took place in the field of *discriminative* ML, endowing machines with the capacity to create complex, often multi-layered ("deep") rules that allow them to distinguish, classify and recognize. Smart cameras, profiling software, algorithmic decision support software, etc.: it all runs on discriminative ML algorithms that are specialized in discriminative tasks such as differentiating men from women, fraudulent financial transactions from normal ones, terrorists from ordinary travellers, the written letter "A" from the written letter "B," or a brain scan of a healthy brain from one that has a tumour. ML machines are never explicitly instructed about how to distinguish categories, but merely provided with large quantities of labelled examples ("this is an image a woman," "that is an image of is a man," etc.) from which they extract a discriminative rule. Discriminative ML is the variety of ML that is still most widespread in our current world. During most of the 2010s, the dominant mantra was that ML was good at recognizing things but not at creating. Several recent technological breakthroughs in the field of *generative* ML have changed that and given AI the power of creation, including the invention of *Variational Autoencoders* (VAEs) in 2013,[9] of *Generative Adversarial Networks* (GANs) in 2014[10] and a series of highly successful generative text models called *Generative Pre-trained Transformers* (GPT in 2017, GPT-2 in 2019 and GPT-3 in 2020[11]). From 2017 onwards there has been an explosive surge of interest in generative ML. Generative ML also functions through rule extraction from examples—only here the examples are used as input to create a generative rule, that is, an algorithmic recipe for the creation of convincingly realistic new varieties in relation to the training examples. While generative ML could in principle be used for the creation of any informational pattern, such as DNA strings, music or food recipes, most attention currently goes to the creation of images (Fig. 1) and text. The examples of generative ML presented on the website https://thisxdoesnotexist.com/ (last accessed 28 April 2021) belong mostly to these two categories and include links to websites that dream up non-existing cat pictures, food blogs, lyrics, newspaper articles and scenes for *The Office*. In the realm of text generation, it is the aforementioned GPT-3 that is currently the most advanced ML model. GPT-3 can finish a text when prompted with a few opening sentences such as:

---

[8] Giles (2018).

[9] Kingma and Welling (2013).

[10] Goodfellow (2014).

[11] GPT-3 (2020); Heaven (2021).

**Fig. 1** Faces of people that do not exist. Generated on January 30, 2020 at https://www.thispersondoesnotexist.com/. Underlying model: StyleGAN by NVIDIA, public release December 2019. The images are created without human intervention and are, according to the creator of the website, not copyright protected

> In a shocking finding, scientists discovered a herd of unicorns living in a remote, previously unexplored valley in the Andes Mountains. Even more surprising to the researchers was the fact that the unicorns spoke perfect English.

When prompted with these opening lines written by a human, GPT-3 continued the story as follows:

> "They also were found to have perfectly coiffed hair and wore what appeared to be Dior makeup." "We were shocked to discover the unicorns," said anthropologist Daniel St. Maurice. "They were like nothing we had ever seen before. We had heard legends of the unicorns, but never thought they actually existed." When the scientists first arrived in the valley, the unicorns were surprised and startled by the presence of humans, but were also excited. The unicorns welcomed the researchers and explained that they had been waiting for them for a very long time.[12]

Sometimes GPT-3 generates nonsensical gibberish, sometimes it outputs highly coherent texts like in the example. In July 2020 computer science student Liam Porr posted a blog post entitled "*Feeling unproductive? Maybe you should stop overthinking*" on the website *Hacker News* under a fake name.[13] The post, which quickly became the most-read piece on Hacker News and was read by tens of thousands, was mostly generated by GPT-3. Only the title and first paragraph were written by Porr himself. Almost none of the readers suspected that the post was AI-generated. One could of course argue that text-generation in a fluffy domain like self-help is a much easier Turing-test to pass than, for instance, a piece of investigative political journalism. Providing a prompt to GPT-3 that is likely to elicit a good piece of writing might be an art in itself. When *The Guardian* wanted to publish an op-ed written by GPT-3, they asked Porr to create a prompt to start GPT-3's writing process. Porr prompted GPT-3 to expand on why AI will not destroy humans and the output was again impressive. The human editor commented[14]:

> GPT-3 produced eight different outputs, or essays. Each was unique, interesting and advanced a different argument. The Guardian could have just run one of the essays in its

[12] Heaven (2021).

[13] Hao (2019).

[14] GPT-3 (2020).

> entirety. However, we chose instead to pick the best parts of each, in order to capture the different styles and registers of the AI. Editing GPT-3's op-ed was no different to editing a human op-ed. We cut lines and paragraphs and rearranged the order of them in some places. Overall, it took less time to edit than many human op-eds.

The fact that machines have started to output coherent products of "machine imagination" raises many legal questions, particularly in the realm of intellectual property (IP) rights (*Can a generative ML-model be an author? Or an inventor?*) and freedom of speech (*Can ML-generated speech be constitutionally protected?*). Currently, such models often need a significant amount of human curation and editing: during the learning stage (model creation) training examples need to be selected and tweaked until the model is capable of producing successful output, and once the model is ready and in use the produced output will often need some human cherry-picking, editing and brushing-up. Yet, it is no longer always the case that the human input is decisive or more substantial than that of the machine. This makes that the muddling of agency between humans and communication tools, which used to be an issue that only excited some philosophers and media theorists, suddenly becomes relevant in law. Is a voice that *seems* human but actually is machine-generated worthy of legal protection? Currently, in most cases of ML-generated content, the human input is still decisive. Yet, there are instances where this is no longer the case, and their amount is likely to increase in the near future. The question is if this lack of human input is relevant from the perspective of Article 10 ECHR.

## 2 Does ML-Generated Speech Fall Under the Protective Scope of Freedom of Expression (Article 10 ECHR)? A Juxtaposition with the Protective Scope of Copyright Law

Within intellectual property (IP) law there is a rather broad consensus that only a *human* can be an author or inventor[15] and that outputs *solely* generated by ML fall in the public domain. The more interesting IP question is the reverse: if output is *not* solely ML-generated, how much and what kind of input is needed from the human contributor to be named the human author or inventor of a work or invention created predominantly by AI? To put it more concretely: can one claim human authorship based on the human decisions going into the creation of a generative model (for example, the human selection and curation of training examples resulting in *StyleGAN*, Fig. 1, or *GPT-3*), the human prompting of particular output (as Porr did for the *Hacker News* blogpost and *The Guardian* op-ed) or the human edits on ML-generated output (such as my *selection* of 4 images in Fig. 1, or the edits by the human editor of the *GPT-3* piece in *The Guardian*)? Answering these copyright questions goes beyond the scope of this paper focusing on freedom of expression. It

[15] Gervais (2019); European Commission (2020a); Craig and Kerr (2019).

is, however, illuminating to juxtapose the copyright and freedom of expression stance on the role of the human contribution in ML-generated outputs.

Given the broad consensus among legal scholars that copyright protection only can be attributed to a *human* author, it might be seductive to think that the same goes for freedom of expression[16]: that it only protects *human* speakers and their utterances. Article 10 (1) ECHR opens with the word "Everyone...":

> Everyone has the right to freedom of expression. This right shall include freedom to hold opinions and to receive and impart information and ideas without interference by public authority and regardless of frontiers. (...).

The word "everyone" seems to support the assumption that the protective scope of freedom of expression does not include ML-generated utterances. Read against the background that the title of this convention—the European Convention for *Human* Rights—it seems natural to assume that "everyone" should be understood as meaning "every natural person." Case law[17] shows that the word "everyone" also includes, at least to a certain extent, also corporations and enterprises ("corporate persons"). Stretching the word "everyone" to also include the rights of ML systems would, however, be stretching the legal wording too far because companies are hierarchically governed organizations, with the upper echelon made up by single human beings while autonomous ML systems are not steered by humans. Such a stretch would also be incompatible with Article 35 § 3(a) ECHR, which requires that applicants to the European Court of Human Rights are affected victims of an infringement. An applicant could not apply on behalf of an ML system without herself being victimized by the infringement.

Does this mean that ML-generated utterances are excluded from the protective scope of Article 10(1) ECHR? While this question has hardly been dealt with in the context of Article 10 ECHR, a substantial amount of research has been devoted to this question in the context of the constitutional protection of free speech in the US in the First Amendment. Despite the fact that the protection of free speech in the First Amendment and of freedom of expression in Article 10 ECHR is very differently formulated, it has been noted that they have many similarities, especially in terms of outcome: they often will protect the same expressions.[18] Partly these similarities might result from the fact that both rights have been influenced by Article 19 of the International Covenant on Civil and Political Rights (ICCPR) which protects freedom of expression at an international level.[19] This warrants a closer look at the US protection to understand the European one. The First Amendment reads:

---

[16] I will use the notions "freedom of expression" and "free speech" interchangeably, although it should be noted that the former is rooted in Art. 10 the European Convention of Human Rights and the latter in the First Amendment of the US Constitution.

[17] Sunday Times v. the United Kingdom (No. 1), 26.04.1979, no. 6538/74. See also: Wilcox (2016).

[18] Heller and van Hoboken (2019).

[19] Ibid.

> Congress shall make no law respecting an establishment of religion, or prohibiting the free exercise thereof; or abridging the freedom of speech, or of the press; or the right of the people peaceably to assemble, and to petition the Government for a redress of grievances.

While the First Amendment is formulated without reference to an "everyone" who holds a right, US case law and legal scholarly literature suggest that the freedom of speech protection, such as Article 10 ECHR, only applies to natural persons and corporations.[20] In terms of protective scope (also known as "coverage" in the US) the US First Amendment protection of freedom of speech and the ECHR protection of freedom of expression are rather alike. There is a general consensus among US scholars[21] that First Amendment protection also covers ML-generated speech. Due to the similar protective scope of free speech and freedom of expression, many of the arguments raised by US scholars can be transposed into the context of the ECHR.

So why are MR-generated utterances likely to fall inside the scope of Article 10 ECHR, despite the fact that its protection targets natural and corporate persons? First, because the *source* of the *opinions*, *ideas* and *information* named in Article 10 is not further defined. The protection of freedom of expression, unlike copyright protection, is not based on an assessment of the originality of an utterance or the process leading up to its creation. There is no reason why a *human* who holds, shares, or receives *ML-generated* opinions, ideas or information would fall outside the scope of Article 10. A second reason why the protective scope of Article 10 also includes ML-generated utterances is that the protection of Article 10 is, precisely like the constitutionally protected freedom of speech in the US, *multi-lateral*: it equally protects the speaker, the distributor, and the receiver of information. Freedom of expression is, at its very core, defined by its opposite: censorship and other forms of governmental interference in the exercise of this freedom. The impact of "the imposition of prior restraints on publication"[22] does not only affect the one holding opinions, the "speaker"—it equally affects the one "imparting," for example by trying to get something published, or the reader, the one trying to receive information. Freedom of expression thus "constitutes one of the essential foundations of a democratic society and one of the basic conditions for its progress and for each individual's self-fulfilment."[23] Viewed from the angle of censorship, it is clear that an ML-generated opinion can be equally protected by freedom of expression as a human opinion. If a government had tried to prohibit *The Guardian* from publishing GPT-3's op-ed, this would be "as problematic from the perspective of a reader as a government that censors a political novel written by Tolstoy."[24] Article 10, according

[20] Benjamin (2021); Lamo and Calo (2019); Massaro and Norton (2015); Massaro et al. (2016).

[21] Benjamin (2021); Lamo and Calo (2019); Massaro and Norton (2015); Massaro et al. (2016); Norton (2017); Kaminski (2017); Witt (2016); Wu (2012); Benjamin (2012).

[22] European Court of Human Rights, The Observer and Guardian v. United Kingdom (26 November 1991), Application No. 13585/88, para. 60.

[23] European Court of Human Rights, E.S. v. Austria (25 October 2018), Application No. 38450/12, para. 42.2. See also: Handyside v. the United Kingdom (7 December 1976, Series A No. 24), and Fressoz and Roire v. France ([GC], No. 29183/95, §45, ECHR 1999-I).

[24] Kaminski (2017), p. 610.

to the European Court of Human Rights, thus entails that "the public has a right to receive information of general interest."[25] As Lamo and Calo[26] put it, there are "many enjoyable bots that make the internet a brighter, funnier, and more interesting place," which means that "the First Amendment could, for example, protect the rights of internet users who wish to read tweets from their favorite bots."

Given that Article 10 does not pose any requirements on the nature of the protected opinions, ideas or information, and that its protection is multi-lateral, *most* cases of ML-generated speech will fall under its protective scope. Let us imagine, however, a sci-fi scenario where GPT-3s op-ed is published in a newspaper that only has other robots as its readers. It is in this scenario that the question of the human element, which is so central in copyright law, is likely to become relevant. Such a publication would only fall under the protective scope of Article 10 if a natural or corporate person has been sufficiently involved in the writing or publishing of the op-ed. It should be noted that this scenario is in fact less outlandish than it might sound. While *The Guardian for Robots* might seem like a sci-fi element taken from an Asimov novel, it is likely that a substantive amount of the output of generative ML will not be directed at a human audience. Instead, it will serve as input for other AI systems to improve (*ML-generated training data*) or obstruct (*adversarial examples*) its functioning. Why would you want to use ML-generated data, also known as *synthetic* data, to train other AI systems? To make ML systems work they need to be "fed" with abundant amounts of high-quality training data from which they can, bottom-up, build relevant models. Such training data are not always easy to obtain. This is where synthetic training data can be of use. For example, if one wants to train a smart camera to recognize emotions in human faces, one could use non-existing portrait pictures (see Fig. 1) as training examples. Or, if you want to build an ML model that summarizes newspaper articles, it potentially could be trained on newspaper articles and corresponding summaries generated by GPT-3. Synthetic examples could thus significantly boost the learning process of discriminative ML[27] while avoiding some of the potential problems such as bias and the personal nature of data.[28] In contrast, ML-generated data can also be used to obstruct the functioning of other AI systems. Generative ML allows for the creation of "adversarial examples"[29]: data that act as optical illusions for AI. Adversarial examples can be created by using generative ML to alter data in a way that will go undetected by the human eye while fundamentally changing how the data are perceived by a discriminative AI system. For example, by making generative ML altering some pixels in the portrait images in Fig. 1, an AI system might be lured to miscategorize the images as elephants or turtles. Exposing AI systems to such

---

[25] European Court of Human Rights, *Társaság a Szabadságjogokért v Hungary*, App no 37374/05 (ECtHR 14 April 2009), para. 26.

[26] Lamo and Calo (2019).

[27] Ye (2018).

[28] Kaloskampis (2019), Bellovin (2019).

[29] Goodfellow (2018).

adversarial data, during its training process or when it is operational, can pervert and obstruct its functioning. Both in the set-up with synthetic training data and adversarial examples, the intended *receiving* audience is other AI systems. On the *speaker* side of the utterance, however, there is clear human involvement, namely the one *using* generative AI to create utterances that strengthen or break the receiving AI. This means that even in these situations ML-generated utterances could fall under the protective scope of Article 10 ECHR.

## 3 Limitations: Legitimate Interferences in the Freedom to Machine-Generated Expression

In the previous section, I argued that the protective scope of freedom of expression as formulated in Article 10 (1) ECHR will cover most ML-generated utterances. However, that an ML-generated utterance falls inside the scope of Article 10(1) does not mean that it cannot be restricted or that no interference in its exercise is allowed. The real *content* of the right to freedom of expression lies in its *limitations* (Article 10(2) ECHR):

> The exercise of these freedoms, since it carries with it duties and responsibilities, may be subject to such formalities, conditions, restrictions or penalties as are prescribed by law and are necessary in a democratic society, in the interests of national security, territorial integrity or public safety, for the prevention of disorder or crime, for the protection of health or morals, for the protection of the reputation or rights of others, for preventing the disclosure of information received in confidence, or for maintaining the authority and impartiality of the judiciary.

Freedom of expression does not mean that one has the right to spread whatever falls in its protective scope.[30] Falling inside the protective *scope* of freedom of expression does not mean that one also actually is *protected* by Article 10 ECHR. There can be many *legitimate* reasons why an opinion, idea or information should *not* be held, shared, or received. What the right to freedom of expression aims to prohibit is *illegitimate* interference in its exercise. This requires that interference is lawful (based in law), pursues a legitimate purpose, and passes the substantive proportionality test following from the "necessary in a democratic society"--requirement (Is the restriction relevant and sufficient in relation to its legitimate aim? Is it desirable in a democratic society?). If an interference in freedom of expression is legitimate or not, does not depend in *any structural way* on if the expression originates from a human mind or an ML system. For example, let us assume that there is a properly formulated national law prohibiting theft. It follows from Article 10(2) ECHR that the "prevention of crime" is a legitimate purpose, and as long as the interference also passes the "necessary in the democratic society"-test, it will be legitimized to interfere in the exercise of freedom of expression. Bank

[30] Axberger (2019), p. 16.

robbers twisting their voice to sound like the bank director and misleading employees into transferring money to them cannot claim freedom of expression, nor bank robbers using an ML-generated impersonation of a bank director's voice[31]; nor criminals using adversarial examples to undermine the workings of an AI system for the purpose of theft. While there is no *structural* difference in the legitimized interferences with ML-generated and human speech, there are some *aspects* of (certain types of) ML-generated utterances that can impact Article 10(2) and that I will discuss below. The first aspect that I discuss is how ML-generated content can avoid two possible sources of limitations on freedom of expression: limitations following from copyright and privacy rights. A second aspect is that ML-generation can result in new types of content, blurring or challenging the normative grounding for certain limitations. I will illustrate this by exploring, firstly, how ML-generated erotic imagery challenges what should be categorized as child pornography, and second, how ML-generated news ("deepfakes") raises questions about the boundaries between legitimate limitations to the spreading of harmful disinformation and freedom of expression. Such normative grey zones ("greyfakes"[32]), force the legislator to revisit the normative and societal underpinnings of the limits to freedom of expression. A final important aspect of ML-generated content in relation to Article 10(2) ECHR is how the limitations are imposed, and the impact of the arms race that is likely to arise between preventive automated filtering systems and ML-generated content.

## 3.1 *Is ML-Generated Speech Less Limited by the Rights of Others than Human-Generated Speech?*

Two important categories of legitimate aims to limit freedom of expression are for *"the protection of the reputation or rights of others"* and for *"preventing the disclosure of information received in confidence"* (Article 10(2) ECHR). The first category includes limitations following from copyright, data protection and privacy rights. The second one relates to data that were disclosed in a confidential setting, for example to a medical practitioner or a priest.

One important incentive to use ML-generated data is that they can be disseminated in a more unrestrained way because the connection to their origins and originators has been diluted. It is speech that is orphaned, that is, not tied (closely) to a human individual as its origin. For example, if the portrait pictures in Fig. 1 would have been made by a human portrait photographer and depicted real living humans, reproducing them in this chapter would have been more legally complicated. The images would have been protected by the copyright of the photographer, would have qualified as personal data and protected by data-protection law, as well

[31] Stupp (2019).

[32] Ajder (2019).

as portrait rights (Article 8 ECHR). An important allure of ML-generated content is precisely the freedom that follows from its disconnect to reality or original works while preserving the statistical properties of their originals. ML-generated content mimics reality without being directly derived from it. As products of so-called machine imagination, the hope invested in ML-generated synthetic data is that they can no longer be traced back to an individual and qualify as anonymized. Works that are fully ML-generated and sufficiently different from the ones on which the generative model was trained would qualify as novel, independent ones and fall in the public domain (see above, Sect. 2). If the level of disconnect is sufficient to avoid any copyright, data protection, privacy or confidentiality limitations is a factual question that will have to be answered on a case-by-case basis. However, one could imagine that, for example, a psychologist would like to publish a book about therapy sessions with her clients. While she is bound by confidentiality, a model trained on her actual notes might be able to "dream up" non-existing sessions that still convey the vibe and atmosphere of her actual sessions. It is clear that there is a fine line between the imagined sessions being too close to their originals (and thus disclosing confidential information) and being too detached (resulting in nonsensical and uninformative descriptions).

Not all ML-generated content is new content that is detached from its original. Instead ML-generated content often aims to be as closely connected as possible to a real individual, only extending a bit into novel directions. For example, so-called video or voice *deepfakes*[33] aim to resemble a living or deceased person as closely as possible to create realistic alternative realities where a politician says things that she never said (so-called fake news[34]), where the synthetic voice of a deceased person continues to voice new thoughts as if the person never died (as a consolation to mourning family[35]), or where a deceased actor continues acting through a synthetic alternate (additional commercial exploitation[36]). Given the potential high impact and sensitivity, creating and sharing deepfakes of living or deceased individuals, when framed in terms of freedom of expression, can result in hard clashes with data protection and privacy rights (Article 8 ECHR), and call for a reconsideration of those rights in relation to deceased individuals (which currently are often not granted a high level of protection, or even have no protection at all[37]).

While there are many reasons that make it attractive to use ML-generated content, it is likely to be an addition to human speech and not replace it. Overall, it is thus unlikely that classical clashes between freedom of expression and copyright, data protection, privacy or confidentiality will diminish. People will continue to claim their multi-lateral right to freedom of expression when sharing and receiving pirated copies of copyrighted material. People will continue to struggle over the balance

---

33 Ajder (2019).

34 Chesney and Citron (2019); Roth (2021).

35 Mai (2020).

36 Guerrasio (2019).

37 Harbinja (2017); Buitelaar (2017).

between the right to be delisted or "forgotten"[38] and the multi-lateral right of freedom of expression of journalists, publishers, search engines presenting search results and readers and search engine users receiving information.[39] The existing types of conflicts are not likely to diminish. However, when used in particular application niches, ML-generated speech is less likely to be limited by copyright, data protection, privacy and confidentiality laws.

## *3.2 ML-Generated Content: Normative Grey Zones for Freedom of Expression?*

Limitations to freedom of expression imposed by the legislator always have some normative, cultural or societal grounding. When does the negative impact of freedom of expression outweigh its positive impact? What is normatively most valuable? This is a difficult question that cannot be answered in a universal way. When technology allows for the creation of new types of content, new normative grey zones can emerge that challenge existing consensus about the right balance between freedom of expression and other rights and interests. Two such normative grey zones are ML-generated child pornography and ML-generated fake news. Below I will discuss how ML-generation can complicate the boundary between protected and unprotected content, and how this calls for a renewed reflection on the purpose of particular limits to freedom of expression.

### 3.2.1 ML-Generated Child Pornography

In Article 10(2) ECHR one of the legitimate aims to limit freedom of expression is "*for the protection … morals.*" Moral standards change over time and differ across Member States, and using the margin of appreciation doctrine the Court has shown reluctance to interfere with national limitations based on the protection of sexual morality.[40] Child pornography, however, is an area about which there has grown a general consensus that it should not fall under the protection of freedom of expression. In the last decades a growing amount of legislative documents to fight the sexual exploitation of children and child pornography has been adopted, including the Child pornography Directive 2011/92/EU, the Council of Europe's Lanzarote Convention (2007) on the protection of children against sexual exploitation and sexual abuse, and recent Regulation 2021/1232/EU on temporary derogations from ePrivacy Directive 2002/58/EC for combating online child sexual abuse From the perspective of freedom of expression a longstanding discussion is how far-stretching

---

[38] European Court of Justice (ECJ), *Costeja*, Case C-131/12, 13 May 2014.

[39] Kulk and Borgesius (2018).

[40] *Handyside v. the United Kingdom* judgment of 7 December 1976, A 24.

the criminalization of the possession and creation of child pornography should be. Is Nabokov's Lolita child pornography? Artistic images of naked children? Pornography involving individuals that are older than 18 but look as if they are younger? Graphic novels? The discussion around so-called "virtual" child pornography, that is, pornography with simulated depictions of children or adults that look like children, has been ongoing for a long while. Article 20(3) of the Lanzarote convention expresses the controversial status of virtual child pornography by allowing contracting countries to reserve the right to abstain from criminalizing the production and possession of pornographic material of non-existing children and adults that look like children.

- consisting exclusively of simulated representations or realistic images of a non-existent child.
- involving children who have reached the age set in application of Article 18, paragraph 2, where these images are produced and possessed by them with their consent and solely for their own private use.

In contrast Article 2(c) of Child pornography Directive 2011/93/EU is very clear that child pornography also includes simulated variants as well as material made by adults that appear to be children:

> 'child pornography' means: (i) any material that visually depicts a child engaged in real or simulated sexually explicit conduct; (ii) any depiction of the sexual organs of a child for primarily sexual purposes; (iii) any material that visually depicts any person appearing to be a child engaged in real or simulated sexually explicit conduct or any depiction of the sexual organs of any person appearing to be a child, for primarily sexual purposes; or (iv) realistic images of a child engaged in sexually explicit conduct or realistic images of the sexual organs of a child, for primarily sexual purposes.

The moral debate here is if virtual child pornography, where no real children are victimized during the creation, should be criminalized. Reasons for criminalizing virtual child pornography are to prevent the normalization of child pornography, the possibility that such virtual pornography can be used as bait to seduce children into real sexual acts and that real child pornography might falsely claim to be a virtual one. The normative question is if these harms are sufficiently serious to legitimize a restriction on freedom of expression. In 2002 the US Supreme Court[41] struck down two provisions in the Child Pornography Prevention Act of 1996 as being overbroad prohibitions of child pornography that also included sexually explicit images that appeared to depict children but were actually produced without using any real minors. The Court held that "the visual depiction (...) of teenagers engaging in sexual activity (...) is a fact of modern society and has been a theme in art and literature for centuries."[42] The Child Pornography Prevention Act 1996 was thus deemed to be an unconstitutional abridgement of free speech.

> the Court rejected the government's *secondary-effects argument* that such depictions encourage child sexual abuse by whetting the appetites of pedophiles and luring children

---

[41] US Supreme Court, *Ashcroft v Free Speech Coalition* (122S.Ct. 1,389 (2002)).

[42] *Idem*, p. 235.

to participate in sexual acts. Additionally, the Court dismissed the government's claim that juries struggle to distinguish between actual and virtual children and that, because it can be very difficult to distinguish between actual and virtual child pornography, if virtual child pornography is not banned, it might provide a convenient defense for those charged with using actual children in the production of pornography.[43]

The US government reacted to the *Ashcroft* judgment by creating new legislation, the PROTECT Act 2003, that excludes virtual child porn by only criminalizing any digital image "that is, or is indistinguishable from, that of a minor engaging in sexually explicit conduct," while simultaneously placing the burden to prove that the child pornography is virtual on the defendant.

Another interesting case in relation to virtual pornography is the Swedish *Manga-case*.[44] The suspect, in this case, was a translator and expert of *Manga* comics, a Japanese drawing style where the characters have a child-like appearance. During a custody battle with his former wife, the police had searched his computer and, amidst tens of thousands of Manga drawings had found 39 drawings that had a child pornographic character. The Manga expert was found guilty of possessing illegal child pornography by a district court in 2010 and a higher court in 2011. If the drawings could *not* be qualified as child pornography, their possession would be covered by the constitutional protection of freedom of expression as protected in the Swedish *Instrument of Government* (chapter 2, section 1–1) in a way that closely resembles the protection of Article 10 ECHR. Thus, the core question was if these drawings qualified as child pornography and therefore would fall outside the protection of freedom of expression. The operative concept in the *Manga* ruling was if the drawings were *realistic* (*verklighetstrogen*). The Court refers here to Article 2 (c) of the Child pornography Directive 2011/93/EU, which defines child pornography as "realistic images of a child engaged in sexually explicit conduct." Of the 39 images, only 1 drawing was deemed to be sufficiently realistic to qualify as child pornography. However, due to his profession as a Manga expert, the Court considered that the possession of one such picture was defensible and found him not guilty. Meanwhile, speculation about what qualifies as a realistic, child pornographic Manga depiction abounds. The mysterious "drawing 39" is, now that it is qualified as child pornography, kept secret. This creates a curious situation where the boundary between protected speech and illegal child pornography is unclear.[45] Some pointers as to what differentiates "drawing 39" from the other 38 images can be found in section 22 of the judgement (*translation and italics mine*):

Despite the fact that these 38 drawings can be qualified as offensive, *the risk of identification* and thus also the risk of violating children, in general, should be significantly less in the case of such images than in the case of realistic images with sexual content. With regard to the images in question, it seems obvious that they do not represent real abuse. The fact that there are pornographic cartoons with themes that can make one's thoughts wander towards children is hardly such a violation of children in general that it justifies the relatively

[43] Mclean (2017), p. 222.

[44] Supreme Court of Sweden, NJA 2012s. 400 (*Mangamålet*).

[45] Westrin (2013).

> far-reaching restriction on freedom of expression and information that would follow from the criminalization of such unrealistic cartoons without any exception. Nor is such a restriction justified by the reason that one wants to avoid the risk of children being tempted to participate in sexual acts. In addition, manga drawings have a strong foothold in Japanese culture, and against this background, there is reason to consider the importance of the widest possible freedom of expression and information.
>
> The foregoing leads to the conclusion that criminalization of possession of the 38 subscriptions now concerned would go beyond what is necessary in view of the purposes which have given rise to the penal provision.

While the Swedish Court raises many arguments similar to the *Ashcroft* ruling of the US Supreme Court, it is interesting to note that the Swedish Court considers *the risk of identification* as a crucial element in distinguishing between realistic child pornography and unrealistic child pornographic imagery protected by freedom of expression.

One important domain for applications for ML-generated deepfakes is pornography. While services such as *Deepnude*, converting any dressed picture into a nude one,[46] and *Naughty America*, personalizing pornography with generative ML,[47] are in the limelight of public attention, it is highly likely that *deepfake* technology will also be used to create child pornography with non-existing but convincingly realistic children.

To anticipate the questions that might arise from ML-generated child pornography, it is illuminating to look at how such questions have been dealt with in the pre-*deepfake* era and the different perspectives that have been taken on virtual pornography and the degree of realism that virtual pornography needs to have to be criminalized. What makes ML-generated content different from hand-drawn child pornography or pornography that is simulated with more basic computer software, is first, that it allows for very sophisticated manipulation of how realistic and identifiable images are, and second, that it allows for a very easy translation of imagery from one style to another, such as transposing real footage in a manga-styled cartoon, and the other way around. This means that the reasons behind the current boundaries between constitutionally protected speech and illegal child pornography will have to be revisited: what is it that we consider so harmful that it does not deserve constitutional protection from freedom of expression? Based on this normative re-evaluation the current definitions and boundaries will have to be refined to match the fine-grained possibilities of generative ML. The definition of child pornography as defined in Article 2(c) of Child pornography Directive 2011/93/EU is unchallenged within the EU and is, for example, the definition on which Regulation 2021/1232/EU builds, allowing Internet providers to derogate from the surveillance and automated filtering prohibitions of ePrivacy Directive 2002/58/EC for the purpose of combating online child sexual abuse. The question is how the word "realistic" (Article 2(c)-iv, Child pornography Directive 2011/93/EU) in

---

[46] Cole (2019).

[47] Roettgers (2019).

relation to child pornographic images will be defined in case law and which forms of ML-generated content will not be deemed realistic enough to classify as child pornography.

### 3.2.2 ML-Generated Fake News

Generative ML is not only distinguished by its fine-grained possibilities of operating on the thin line between machine fantasy and convincing realism, but also by the possibilities it opens for the massive production of such content. This challenges the classical understanding of freedom of expression as a negative abstention right: that democracy and the open market of ideas work at their best when the State abstains from censorship and other interferences. Faced with an ever- increasing flood of what has been termed disinformation and other harmful content on the Internet, governments are put in a strange double-bind: to preserve a climate where some meaningful exchange of ideas, information and opinions could take place, governments increasingly would need to preventively filter away the avalanche of undesirable content that could transform the Internet in a place overrun with unreliable, unstructured and disgusting content. However, creating such an extensive preventive filtering system would involve extensive normative decision making as well as reliance on unreliable automatic filtering systems (see below, Sect. 3.3). This would *also* destroy the open exchanges of ideas, information, and opinions that freedom of expression aims to preserve.

Within the EU disinformation is defined as "verifiably false or misleading information created, presented and disseminated for economic gain or to intentionally deceive the public."[48] The difficulty here is that this definition will only cover the very extreme cases of misleading information. Much of ML-generated news will fall in a normative grey area. Moreover, the fine-grained possibilities for fine-tuning content that can mislead discriminative ML systems (see above, "adversarial examples") is likely to create increasing challenges for ranking algorithms like Google search results. Keeping the Internet clean and neutral can become more difficult as the amount of ML-generated content grows. In the recent Commission proposal for a Digital Services Act (2020) this struggle between State intervention and abstention is clearly present. The key goals of the Digital Services Act (DSA) include that citizens are less exposed to illegal content and that systemic risks, such as manipulation or disinformation, are mitigated to benefit society at large.[49] In the explanatory memorandum of the DSA proposal it says:

> There is a general agreement among stakeholders that 'harmful' (yet not, or at least not necessarily, illegal) content should not be defined in the Digital Services Act and should not

[48] Communication from the Commission to the European Parliament, the Council, The European Economic and Social Committee of the Regions. Tackling online disinformation: a European Approach. COM (2018) 236 final Brussels, 26/4/2018.

[49] European Commission (2020b).

> be subject to removal obligations, as this is a delicate area with severe implications for the protection of freedom of expression. However, the way algorithmic systems shape information flows online is an area of concern among a wide category of stakeholders.[50]

And

> The new Regulation prohibits general monitoring obligations, as they could disproportionately limit users' freedom of expression and freedom to receive information.[51]

The distinction between illegal and harmful content is, viewed from the perspective of ML-generated content, a crucial one. In practice, it might be a line that is difficult to draw, especially if the identification of these categories of content needs to be operationalized and implemented in automated filters and content flagging systems.

### 3.3 *Catch Me If You Can! The Arms Race Between Automated Filters and ML-Generated Content*

When freedom of expression and AI are mentioned together it is mostly in the context of *AI-fuelled automated content moderation* by means of *ranking*, such as in Google search results, or by *filtering* the content. Automated content filters can be used to censor illegal or harmful content, such as copyright-infringing works or undesirable disinformation ("fake news").[52] Should filters be embraced as the only proper tool to fight illegal, disgusting and politically destabilizing content? Or are filters useless and even dangerous Molochs that will result in over-blocking and censorship?[53] This debate has been fuelled by the introduction of the controversial Article 17 of the Directive on Copyright in the Digital Single Market 2019/790 (DSM Directive), which seems to implicitly mandate that content-sharing service providers such as YouTube, Twitter and Facebook have to use automated filters to prevent the uploading of copyright-infringing content.[54] Recent case law from the CJEU such as the *Eva Glawischnig-Piesczek v Facebook Ireland* ruling (2019), the Opinion of Advocate-General Saugmandsgaar Øe (2021) in the pending CJEU case of *Poland v European Parliament and Council of the European Union* and legislative proposals at the EU level such as the proposed Digital Rights Services Act (2020) raise doubts about the preventive use of upload-filters to prevent defamation and disinformation and prohibit general monitoring obligations to protect their users' fundamental rights. It will be extremely interesting to see what the CJEU decides in

[50] COM(2018) 236 final Brussels, 26/4/2018, p. 9.

[51] COM(2018) 236 final Brussels, 26/4/2018, p. 13.

[52] Helberger et al. (2019); Marsden and Meyer (2019).

[53] CJEU, Case C-401/19, *Republic of Poland v European Parliament and Council of the European Union*, action brought on 24 May 2019.

[54] Spoerri (2019).

the action brought on by Poland asking for the annulment of Article 17 as being incompatible with freedom of expression. In his Opinion regarding this action Advocate-General Saugmandsgaar Øe writes that Poland's action should be dismissed because, in his view, the monitoring and filtering obligations in Article 17 contain enough safeguards with regard to freedom of expression. One of the aspects highlighted by the A-G is that it follows from DSM Directive that providers should only use filtering and monitoring technologies conform to "best industry practices" and the "state of the art" (section 66 of the Opinion) and in compliance with the principle of proportionality (section 67). To avoid the risk of over-blocking and be compliant with the right to freedom of expression there has to be "a 'fair balance' between the effectiveness of filtering and its collateral effect" meaning that copyright holders cannot "require absolute effectiveness – and thus 'zero risk' of copyright infringement – where this would have the effect of blocking a significant amount of lawful content" (section 184). Furthermore, the A-G suggests that a provider may "only be required to filter and block information which has first been established by a court as being illegal or, otherwise, information the unlawfulness of which *is obvious from the outset*, that is to say, it is *manifest*, without, inter alia, the need for contextualisation" (section 198).

The question is if such a balanced and cautious approach will be possible in practice. Providers will have to create filters that meet will a whole range of different legal and commercial demands: filtering out illegal material that is, for example, child pornography or obviously infringing on copyright, as well as material that is unattractive for users. Moreover, providers operating globally will have to juggle enormous amounts of different cultural and political standards. The risk is that filters will become the lowest common denominator. The expected avalanche of ML-generated content on the Internet in the near future adds an extra dimension to the already complex debates with regard to pro-active automated filtering. ML-generated content has the capability for fine-grained adjustments that can manipulate automated content ranking and filtering systems. This could not only lead to an advanced arms race between ML-generated content producers and automated filter creators but also result in a paradoxical situation where filters end up over-blocking content created by humans (missing out on subtle parodies, etc.) and under-blocking ML-generated content.

## 4 Conclusions

In this chapter, I looked at some of the questions raised by generative ML from the perspective of freedom of expression (Article 10 ECHR). I first looked if ML-generated utterances fall within the protective scope of freedom of expression (Article 10(1) ECHR). After concluding that this is the case, I looked at specific complexities raised by ML-generated content in terms of limitations to freedom of expression (Article 10(2) ECHR). First, I explored how ML-generated content can circumvent limitations arising from copyright, data protection, privacy and confidentiality law. Second, I studied how new types of content generated by ML can create normative grey areas where the boundaries between what falls in and outside of constitutionally protected speech are not always easy to draw. In this context, I discussed two types of ML-generated content: virtual child pornography and fake news/disinformation. Third, I looked at the arms race between automated filters and ML-generated content. The conclusions drawn from the analysis in this chapter are that ML-generated content is protected under Article 10 ECHR and that the implications thereof deserve attention. Although there are no categorical differences between the constitutional protection of freedom of expression of human and ML-generated utterances, there are some general tendencies that should be studied, namely the normative grey areas with regard to ML-generated content and the question of how to control it with algorithmic or other forms of regulation – as it has the inherent capacity for fine-tuned metamorphosis and adaptation.

To return to the scene from *Mulholland Drive* mentioned in the first section: when a voice touches us humans profoundly and sounds like a meaningful message coming from a human individual we might be profoundly startled when it turns out that this was not its source. There is, however, no reason to discard voices of ML-origin in a categorical way. In fact, they might sometimes turn out to be pleasantly unconstrained by the rights of others and more prolific than their human counterparts. What makes ML-generated speech stand out in comparison to its human counterpart is not its content. Like human speech, it can be bad or good, disgusting or elevating, profound or prosaic. The difference lies in how easily ML-speech can be generated, tailored and disseminated. To prevent the public exchange of ideas to be flooded with ML-generated speech some kind of automated filtering will be needed – and the big question is if such automated systems ever will be able to encompass the subtleties of law without losing all of their efficacy.

## References


Ajder H (2019) The ethics of deepfakes aren't always black and white. The Next Web. Online available at: https://thenextweb.com/podium/2019/06/16/the-ethics-of-deepfakes-arent-always-black-and-white/

Axberger H-G (2019) Ytttrandefrihetsgrundlagarna. Yttrandefrihetens gränser efter 2019 års grundlagsreform. Nordstedts Juridik, Stockholm

Bellovin SM, Dutta PK, Reitinger N (2019) Privacy and synthetic datasets. Stanford Technol Law Rev 22:1–39

Benjamin SM (2012) Algorithms and speech. Univ Pa Law Rev 161:1445–1494

Benjamin SM (2021) The first amendment and algorithms. In: Barfield W (ed) The Cambridge handbook of the law of algorithms. Cambridge University Press, Cambridge, pp 606–631

Buitelaar J (2017) Post-mortem privacy and informational self-determination. J Ethics Inf Technol 19(2):129–142

Chesney R, Citron DK (2019) Deep fakes: a looming challenge for privacy, democracy, and national security. Calif Law Rev 107:1753–1820

Cole S (2019) This Horrifying App Undresses a Photo of Any Woman With a Single Click. Vice - Motherboard, Online available at: https://www.vice.com/en/article/kzm59x/deepnude-app-creates-fake-nudes-of-any-woman
Craig CJ, Kerr IR (2019) The Death of the AI Author. Available at SSRN 3374951
De Vries K (2020) You never fake alone. Creative AI in action. Inf Commun Soc 23(14):2110–2127
Derrida J (1982) Signature, event, context. In: Margins of philosophy. University of Chicago Press, pp 307–330
European Commission (2020a) Trends and Developments in Artificial Intelligence – Challenges to the Intellectual Property Rights Framework. Luxembourg
European Commission (2020b) The Digital Services Act: ensuring a safe and accountable online environment. Online available at: https://ec.europa.eu/info/strategy/priorities-2019-2024/europe-fit-digital-age/digital-services-act-ensuring-safe-and-accountable-online-environment_en
Gervais D (2019) The machine as author. Iowa Law Rev 105:2053–2106
Giles M (2018, February 21) The GANfather: the man who's given machines the gift of imagination. MIT Technology review. Online available at: https://www.technologyreview.com/s/610253/the-ganfather-the-man-whos-given-machines-the-gift-of-imagination/
Goodfellow I (2018) Defense Against the Dark Arts: An overview of adversarial example security research and future research directions. arXiv preprint arXiv:.04169
Goodfellow I et al (2014) Generative adversarial nets. Adv Neural Inf Proces Syst:2672–2680
GPT-3 (2020) A robot wrote this entire article. Are you scared yet, human? GPT-3, The Guardian. Online available at: https://www.theguardian.com/commentisfree/2020/sep/08/robot-wrote-this-article-gpt-3
Guerrasio J (2019) 64 years after James Dean's death, the actor will star in a new movie. Some in Hollywood are horrified but the advances in visual effects could make it commonplace. Business Insider. Online available at: https://www.businessinsider.com/james-dean-posthumous-casting-in-new-movie-through-visual-effects-2019-11?r=US&IR=T
Hao K (2019) A college kid's fake AI-generated blog fooled tens of thousands. This is how he created it. MIT Technology Review. Online available at: https://www.technologyreview.com/2020/08/14/1006780/ai-gpt-3-fake-blog-reached-top-of-hacker-news/
Harbinja E (2017) Post-mortem privacy 2.0: theory, law, and technology. Int Rev Law Comput Technol 31(1):26–42
Hayles K (1999) How we became posthuman. Virtual bodies in cybernetics, literature, and informatics. University of Chicago Press, Chicago
Heaven WD (2021) Why GPT-3 is the best and worst of AI right now. Open AI's language AI wowed the public with its apparent mastery of English – but is it all an illusion? MIT Technol Rev 124(2):34–35
Heidegger M (2001) Poetry, language, thought. Harper & Row, New York
Helberger N, Eskens S, Drunen M, Bastian M, Möller J (2019) Implications of AI-driven tools in the media for freedom of expression. Council of Europe - Institute for Information Law (IViR, Amsterdam), Strasbourg
Heller B, van Hoboken J (2019) Freedom of Expression: A Comparative Summary of United States and European Law (report). Transatlantic Working Group
Kaloskampis I (2019) Synthetic data for public good. UK's Office for National Statistics
Kaminski ME (2017) Authorship, disrupted: AI authors in copyright and first amendment law. UC Davis Law Rev 51:589–616
Kingma DP, Welling M (2013) Auto-encoding variational bayes. arXiv preprint arXiv:1312.6114
Kittler F (1986) Gramophone, film, typewriter. Stanford University Press, Stanford
Kulk S, Borgesius FZ (2018) Privacy, freedom of expression, and the right to be forgotten in Europe. In: Polonetsky J, Tene O, Selinger E (eds) Cambridge handbook of consumer privacy. Cambridge University Press, Cambridge, pp 301–320
Lamo M, Calo R (2019) Regulating bot speech. UCLA Law Rev 66:988–1028

Mai Q (2020) A mother who lost her only daughter decides to make her into an AI. People, Online available at: https://docs.google.com/document/d/1A4jZI2FjCDNdwfRhjJh68a4QCvfUF-hTWBIHUjEnR9I/mobilebasic?form=MY01SV&OCID=MY01SV and https://mp.weixin.qq.com/s/gY_KetYopg-FZZ8BXaUwvA
Marsden C, Meyer T (2019) Regulating disinformation with artificial intelligence: effects of disinformation initiatives on freedom of expression and media pluralism. European Parliament
Massaro TM, Norton H (2015) Siri-ously? Free speech rights and artificial intelligence. Northwest Univ Law Rev 110:1169–1194
Massaro TM, Norton H, Kaminski ME (2016) Siri-ously 2.0: what artificial intelligence reveals about the first amendment. Minnesota Law Rev 101:2481–2525
Mclean C (2017) The uncertain fate of virtual child pornography legislation. Cornell J Law Public Policy 17:221–246
McLuhan M (1994) Understanding media. The extensions of man. MIT Press
Norton H (2017) Robotic speakers and human listeners. Seattle Univ Law Rev 41:1145–1152
Roettgers J (2019) Naughty America wants to monetize Deepfake porn. Variety. Online available at: https://variety.com/2018/digital/news/deepfake-porn-custom-clips-naughty-america-1202910584/
Roth A (2021) European MPs targeted by deepfake video calls imitating Russian opposition. The Guardian. Online available at: https://www.theguardian.com/world/2021/apr/22/european-mps-targeted-by-deepfake-video-calls-imitating-russian-opposition
Spoerri T (2019) On upload-filters and other competitive advantages for big tech companies under Article 17 of the directive on copyright in the digital single market. J Intell Prop Inf Technol E-Commer Law 10:173–186
Stupp C (2019) Fraudsters used AI to Mimic CEO's voice in unusual cybercrime case. Scams using artificial intelligence are a new challenge for companies. The Wallstreet Journal. Online available at: https://www.wsj.com/articles/fraudsters-use-ai-to-mimic-ceos-voice-in-unusual-cybercrime-case-11567157402
Westrin S (2013) "I skuggan av teckning 39" ("In the shadow of drawing 39"). Svenska Dagbladet
Wilcox V (2016) A Company's right to damages for non-pecuniary loss. Cambridge University Press
Witt L (2016) Preventing the rogue bot journalist: protection from non-human defamation. Colorado Technol Law J 15:517–548
Wu T (2012) Machine speech. Univ Pa Law Rev 161:1495–1533
Ye G et al (2018) Yet another text captcha solver: a generative adversarial network based approach. In: Proceedings of the 2018 ACM SIGSAC Conference on Computer and Communications Security, ACM, pp 332–348
Žižek S, Fiennes S, Rosenbaum M, Misch G, Wieser R, Schnorr R et al (2006) The pervert's guide to cinema

## *Legislation, Regulation, and Policy Documents*

Regulation 2021/1232/EU of the European Parliament and of the Council of 14 July 2021 on a temporary derogation from certain provisions of Directive 2002/58/EC as regards the use of technologies by providers of number-independent interpersonal communications services for the processing of personal and other data for the purpose of combating online child sexual abuse
Proposal for a Regulation of the European Parliament and of the Council on a Single Market For Digital Services (Digital Services Act) and amending Directive 2000/31/EC. COM(2020) 825 final

Directive 2019/790 of the European Parliament and of the Council of 17 April 2019 on copyright and related rights in the Digital Single Market and amending Directives 96/9/EC and 2001/29/EC

Communication from the Commission to the European Parliament, the Council, The European Economic and Social Committee of the Regions. Tackling online disinformation: a European Approach. COM(2018) 236 final Brussels, 26/4/2018

Council of Europe Convention on the Protection of Children against Sexual Exploitation and Sexual Abuse, CETS No.201, Lanzarote, 25/10/2007

Directive 2011/92/EU of the European Parliament and of the Council of 13 December 2011 on combating the sexual abuse and sexual exploitation of children and child pornography, and replacing Council Framework Decision 2004/68/JHA

PROTECT Act (Prosecutorial Remedies and Other Tools to end the Exploitation of Children Today Act), 108-21, 108th Congress session (2003)

Child Pornography Prevention Act, H.R. 4123 (IH), 104th Congress 2d session (1996)

## Case Law

CJEU, Case C-18/18, Eva Glawischnig-Piesczek v Facebook Ireland Limited, ECLI:EU:C:2019:821

CJEU, Case C-401/19, Republic of Poland v European Parliament and Council of the European Union, action brought on 24 May 2019. Opinion by A-G Saugmandsgaar Øe, ECLI:EU:C:2021:613

CJEU, Case C-131/12, Costeja, ECLI:EU:C:2014:317

ECtHR, E.S. v. Austria, 25 October 2018, Application No 38450/12

ECtHR, Fressoz and Roire v. France ([GC], No. 29183/95, 1999-I)

ECtHR, The Observer and Guardian v. United Kingdom, 26 November 1991, Application No. 13585/88

ECtHR, *Sunday Times v. the United Kingdom (No. 1)*, 26 April 1979, no. 6538/74

ECtHR, *Handyside v. the United Kingdom*, 7 December 1976, A 24

US Supreme Court, *Ashcroft v Free Speech Coalition* (122S.Ct. 1389 (2002)

Supreme Court of Sweden, NJA 2012 s. 400 (Mangamålet)

**Katja de Vries** is an assistant professor in public law at Uppsala University specializing in Law and AI. She is also affiliated with the Swedish Law and Informatics Research Institute (Stockholm) and the Center for Law, Science, Technology and Society (Brussels). Her current research focuses on the challenges that AI-generated content ("deepfakes" or "synthetic data") poses to data protection, intellectual property, and other fields of law.

# Private Life, Freedom of Expression and the Role of Transnational Digital Platforms: A European Perspective

**Sten Schaumburg-Müller**

## Contents



**Abstract** Transnational digital platforms have contributed greatly to freedom of expression, not least including easy access to information. However, they have also enhanced private life infringements such as the unconsented distribution of nudity, sexual activities and fake porn.

We may look to the European Court of Human Rights (ECtHR) which has dealt extensively with the balancing of freedom of expression and the protection of private life. The Court has developed a set of criteria to balance the rights; The criteria are not perfect, but they are workable, and they include criteria such as 'contribution to a debate of general interest' and 'the methods involved' when collecting and distributing information, including pictures.

However, companies including transnational digital platforms, are not legally bound by international human rights law, only states are. To address this, the UN has developed United Nations Guiding Principles to Business and Human Rights. These Principles do not create legal obligations, but duties including the duty to address human rights adverse effects of their activities. So far, the transnational digital platforms have done little, if anything at all, to address private life infringements.

S. Schaumburg-Müller (✉)
University of Southern Denmark, Odense, Denmark
e-mail: stsm@sam.sdu.dk

 
S. Hindelang, A. Moberg (eds.), *YSEC Yearbook of Socio-Economic Constitutions 2021,* YSEC Yearbook of Socio-Economic Constitutions (2022) 2021: 117–144,
https://doi.org/10.1007/16495_2022_40, Published online: 8 April 2022

As of late, Facebook has indeed established an Oversight Board and declared its commitments to the UN Guiding Principles. This is a step in the right direction but overtly insufficient, as it solely addresses infringements of freedom of expression, but not any other human rights infringement such as violation of private life.

## 1 Introduction

New technologies bring new opportunities and new challenges. To mention one example, cars have made transport a lot easier and accessible to millions—a great advantage—but they have also carried with them problems of injured and killed people, pollution and climate deterioration. The same goes for the Internet and the ensuing technologies. They have led to tremendous advantages in terms of freedom of expression, also in the broad sense of the term, including, among others, access to information.[1] However, the development is not without problems and challenges. In the present contribution I shall focus on private life problems in terms of private life infringing content uploaded by third parties. The uploading of nudity, sexual activities and fake porn photos and videos is widespread, often without consent, and this poses a challenge for an effective and real protection of private life, especially because the uploaders are often anonymous, and the uploads often appear in semi-closed circles.

The so-called ‘umbrella complex’ from Denmark may serve as an example. Two or three videos, depicting a 15-year-old couple having various forms of sex, were shared more than 1,000 times on Facebook Messenger, and according to the information more than year passed from the moment of Facebook’s receiving a complaint to the reporting of the sharings to the police. Eventually the police took action, and many of the young sharers have been sentenced.[2] However, the reaction was slow, the platform was not involved, and as it appears, the videos are still shared through various online platforms, including Messenger.

Protection of private life (or privacy) and of freedom of speech are universally acknowledged as basic human rights,[3] and in Sect. 2 I shall take a closer look at the relevant case law from the European Court of Human Rights (ECtHR), which has dealt extensively with the balancing of the two specific rights for the past almost 20 years. Thus, the present contribution takes a European perspective, thus leaving

---

[1] I use the term ‘freedom of expression’, indirectly referring to the Covenant on Civil and Political Rights (CCPR), Article 19, and the European Convention on Human Rights (ECHR), Article 10: It covers the right to express opinions *and* the right to seek, receive and pass on information.

[2] The leading case: UfR [the weekly law journal] 2019, p. 132H: The Supreme Court decided for 40 days of suspended imprisonment and DKK 10,000 and 2,000 (apprx. € 1,350 and 270) in tort to the two depicted youngsters.

[3] Universal Declaration of Human Rights Article 12, CCPR Article 17; American Convention on Human Rights Article 11, Arab Charter Article 17(8).

out advantages and challenges in other parts of the world, be it countries with a more authoritarian tradition[4] or countries with a much weaker state structure and with, perhaps, weaker protection of private life.[5] The purpose of the section is, one, to show that it is possible to balance the two sometimes conflicting rights—the balancing is not perfect, but it is a genuine, well thought and well established balance—and two, to establish a base from which the performance of states (and indirectly of digital platforms) can be measured.

The European Convention of Human Rights (ECHR) is a piece of international law, creating direct obligations only for state parties. However, large online media obviously play a highly important part in rendering it possible for millions of people to share information—including the sharing of private life infringing photos and videos. The role of companies in relation to human rights is dealt with by the United Nations Guiding Principles on Business and Human Rights (UNGP), and in Sect. 3 I shall take a closer on the implications of the principles for online media and their role in providing easy access to sharing of all sorts of information, including private life infringing photos and videos. The recent attempt by Facebook to live up to the UNGP duties is dealt with in Sects. 3.2 and 3.3.

In Sect. 4 I shall outline some conclusions as to the duties and obligations for (European) states and digital platforms in relation to the protection of private life and the balancing with freedom of expression.

## 2 Private Life, Freedom of Expression and Possible Collisions

### 2.1 *Private Life*

Article 8 of the ECHR protects private and family life, home and correspondence. When dealing with online activities such as the posting of nudity, sexual activities and fake porn, private life is the important part, whereas family life, home and correspondence may only be relevant in more exceptional cases. According to case law, 'private life' is a broad concept: '(T)he concept of 'private life' is a broad term not susceptible to exhaustive definition. It covers the physical and psychological integrity of a person. It can therefore embrace multiple aspects of the person's physical and social identity. 'It extends in particular to aspects relating to personal identity, such as a person's name or picture', as the Grand Chamber recently stated.[6] The Court moves on to explain that 'private life' is not only the right to be left alone,

[4]See, e.g. Amnesty International (2020).

[5]In the African Charter of Human and Peoples' Rights there is no protection of private life, in contradistinction to the ICCP and the ECHR.

[6]*López Ribaldo and Others v.* Spain, nos. 1874/13 and 8567/13, § 87, 17 October 2019. References to case law excluded in the quote.

but also encompasses aspects of the 'private social life'.[7] This latter aspect is less important when dealing with the posting of sexual activities or fake porn, but ought to be mentioned, as it indicates the broad scope of the protection in Article 8. I therefore use the term 'private life', first, because this is the term used by the ECHR and the Court, and second, and perhaps more importantly, because it indicates a broader conception than merely the right to be left alone.[8]

Included in the protection of private life is also reputation[9] and even group defamation.[10] One may question whether defamatory speech relates to private life—after all, it rather connects to social capital than to private life. At any rate, the Court has decided that defamatory speech also falls under the scope of Article 8, which is line with the broad conception of private life. Besides, in other human rights instruments the protection of honour and reputation is explicitly mentioned in connection with private life protection.[11] Defamation of individuals and of groups[12] appears to be a widespread phenomenon on social media platforms, etc. and is equally important as the posting of nudity, sex and fake porn.

As already indicated in the *López Ribaldo* judgment, pictures fall within the scope of Article 8. In *Von Hannover no. 2*, the Grand Chamber emphasises the importance of a person's right to control the publication of photos: 'Regarding photos, the Court has stated that a person's image constitutes one of the chief attributes of his or her personality, as it reveals the person's unique characteristics and distinguishes the person from his or her peers. The right to the protection of one's image is thus one of the essential components of personal development. It mainly presupposes the individual's right to control the use of that image, including the right to refuse publication thereof'.[13] The photos in question were rather inobtrusive, pictures from a holiday resort in a public street. Photos generally constitutes a more intensive use of personal information: 'The publication of a photograph must, in the Court's view, in general be considered a more substantial interference with the right to respect for

[7] Ibid., § 88.

[8] See an early indication by the former Commission in *X. v. Iceland*, no. 6825/74 (no §), 18 May 1976: 'For numerous Anglo-Saxon and French authors the right to respect for "private life" is the right to privacy, the right to live, as far as one wishes, protected from publicity (. . .) In the opinion of the Commission, however, the right to respect for private life does not end there. It comprises also, to a certain degree, the right to establish and to develop relationships with other human beings, especially in the emotional field for the development and fulfilment of one's own personality'.

[9] E.g. the Grand Chamber judgments *Morice v. France*, no. 29369/10, 23 April 2014, and *Medžlis Islamske Zajednice Brčko and Others v. Bosnia-Herzegovina*, no. 17224/11, 27 June 2017.

[10] As indicated in the Grand Chamber judgment *Aksu v. Turkey*, no. 4149/0441029/04, § 58, 15 March 2012 [GC].

[11] CCPR Article 17; ACHR Article 11, where in fact 'honor and reputation' is mentioned in § 1, prior to private life in § 2.

[12] I prefer to avoid the term 'hate speech', which is too imprecise and ambiguous. Besides, it indicates that hate is a relevant factor, which is not always the case. E.g. according to CERD, Article 4(a) 'racist hatred' is only one element in addition to 'racial superiority', 'incitement to racial discrimination', 'financing of racist activities', etc.

[13] *Von Hannover v. Germany no. 2*, nos. 40660/08 and 60641/08, § 96, 7 February 2012.

private life than the mere communication of the person's name'.[14] Nudity, pornographic pictures and film, and fake porn obviously falls under Article 8, and using pictures aggravates the intrusion, or to put it differently, here the interest in controlling the personal pictures is of a stronger character. Please note that the protection of private life is not an absolute right (see below this section and Sect. 2.3). However, the protection against unauthorised use of nude pictures must be stronger than the protection of photos merely depicting a personal portrait.

Also, fake porn, with or without manipulated pictures, falls within the scope of Article 8. In *K.U. v. Finland* an advertisement on an Internet dating site simulated an invitation from a real life 12-year-old boy for intimate relations. No penal sanction was possible according to the then prevailing Finnish law, and the ECtHR states: 'There is no dispute as to the applicability of Article 8: the facts underlying the application concern a matter of "private life," a concept which covers the physical and moral integrity of the person (see X and Y v. the Netherlands, cited above, § 22). Although this case is seen in domestic law terms as one of malicious misrepresentation, the Court would prefer to highlight these particular aspects of the notion of private life, having regard to the potential threat to the applicant's physical and mental welfare brought about by the impugned situation and to his vulnerability in view of his young age'.[15] Young age is not a *condition* sine qua non for the application of Article 8 in cases of fake porn, but of course tender age renders it so much more important for the Member State to provide protection against private life interferences.

As can be seen from the above-mentioned judgments, *López Ribaldo*, *Von Hannover no. 2* and *K.U. v. Finland*, the state has a positive obligation under Article 8. Not only must the state be sure not to interfere in the private life of its citizens and inhabitants; the state must also be sure to guarantee its protection against third parties' intrusions. In *Söderman v. Sweden* the Grand Chamber states, that 'in addition to this primarily negative undertaking, there are positive obligations inherent in an effective respect for private or family life. These obligations may involve the adoption of measures designed to secure respect for private life even in the sphere of the relations of individuals between themselves'.[16] In *Söderman* a stepfather had filmed the young teenage stepdaughter in the bathroom, and there were neither criminal nor civil remedies available against this kind of behaviour. The Court admits a certain margin of appreciation when it comes to the question of *how* to protect against third parties' private life intrusion.[17] However, it is crucial that there is an effective remedy at hand, and in more gross cases, such as sexual misrepresentation of a minor, engaging criminal law is required: '(E)ffective deterrence against grave acts, where fundamental values and essential aspects of private life are at stake, requires efficient criminal-law provisions', *K.U. v. Finland*, § 43.

---

[14] *Eerikäinen v. Finland*, no. 3514/02, § 70, 10 February 2009.

[15] *K.U. v. Finland*, no. 2872/02, § 41, 2 December 2008.

[16] *Söderman v. Sweden*, no. 5786/08, § 78, 12 November 2013.

[17] *Söderman*, §§ 79–85.

Under § 2 of Article 8, private life protection is not absolute, irrespective of whether the state's obligation is negative or positive. Interferences are acceptable if they (1) are in accordance with the law (no arbitrary interference), (2) they are 'necessary in a democratic society', and (3) pursues a legitimate interest such as 'the protection of the rights and freedoms of others'. It is not necessary in a democratic society to prohibit dissemination of private information of *all* kinds. As an example, if a member of parliament is dating a member of a terrorist group, this is one the one hand private information, as love affairs are private, but on the other such a piece of information is of common interest. Freedom of expression is included in 'the rights and freedoms of others', and this right includes, among others, the right to receive and impart information. Freedom of expression is dealt with below Sect. 2.2, and the possible collision of the two sometimes opposing rights is dealt with in Sect. 2.3.

In conclusion:

- Distribution of nudity, depiction of sexual activities and fake porn falls under the scope of Article 8. (So do expressions which relates to the honour and reputation of others and expressions relating to groups; relevant but not specifically addressed in this contribution).
- The state has a positive obligation to provide effective remedies against third parties' private life intrusions.
- To a certain extent, the choice of remedies lies within the state's margin if appreciation. However, severe private life intrusion requires remedies under criminal law.
- The protection of private life must be balanced with the equally important right of freedom of expression.[18]

## 2.2 Freedom of Expression

The scope of Article 10 is equally broad. It covers 'freedom to hold opinions and to receive and impart information and ideas without interference by public authority and regardless of frontiers', Article 10, § 1. Thus, what is covered is not only the classical right to voice one's opinion, but also the right to receive and disseminate information, including pictures. Article 10 covers as diverse situations as the closure of an art exhibition,[19] the disturbing of fox hunting,[20] journalists buying illegal firework[21] and a man walking around naked.[22] From the outset, the Court has emphasised that protection under Article 10 'is applicable not only to information

[18] The balancing exercise is dealt with below, Sect. 2.3.

[19] *Müller and Others v. Switzerland*, no. 10737/84, 24 May 1988.

[20] *Hashman and Harrup v. The United Kingdom*, no 25594/94, 25 November 1999.

[21] *Mikkelsen and Christensen v. Denmark*, no. 22918/08, 24 May 2011 (admissibility decision).

[22] *Gough v. the United Kingdom*, no. 49327/11, 28 October 2014.

or ideas that are favourably received or regarded as inoffensive or as a matter of indifference, but also to those that offend, shock or disturb. Such are the demands of pluralism, tolerance and broadmindedness without which there is no "democratic society"'.[23] The 'offend, shock and disturb' doctrine was employed for the first time in *Handyside v. the United Kingdom*, no. 5493/72, § 49, 7 December 1976, dealing with 'The Little Red Schoolbook', a rather provocative Danish book, directed at school pupils, including pictures of genitals etc. Thus, pictures, including offending pictures, fall under the scope of Article 10. As for the outcome in *Handyside*, the Plenary Court found no violation of Article 10, which is not of an absolute character. Articles 8 and 10 share the features of being broad in scope with the option of lawful interference under § 2. (See below and Sect. 2.3).

As already indicated, the dissemination of pictures is covered by Article 10. 'The Court notes that it has consistently held that freedom of expression includes the publication of photographs. Similarly, freedom of expression has been considered to include the broadcasting of videos', *Alpha v. Greece* on the publication of videos filmed with hidden camera.[24] Thus, the dissemination of even pictures and videos that may be shocking or offending due to their sexual or pornographic nature falls under the scope of Article 10, and photos and videos are covered even if the shooting has been carried out covertly. The remaining question is the balancing of the competing rights, private life protection and freedom of expression. See below Sect. 2.3.

Similar to Article 8, Article 10 may also bring about positive obligations for the state. However, there are numerous cases dealing with positive obligations under Article 8 (see above Sect. 2.1), but few dealing with positive obligations under Article 10. This probably connects to the fact that third parties regularly infringe on the private life of others, e.g. by dissemination private information, by attacking the honour of others, etc. whereas third parties only more rarely infringe on the freedom of speech of others. In a few cases, the Court has dealt with positive obligations under Article 10, and only in very few cases, the Court has found a violation.[25]

As a point of departure media have no obligation to disseminate everybody's opinions and all sort of information which someone may want to publish. In *Remuszko v. Poland* the Court states the following: '(p)rivately owned newspapers must be free to exercise editorial discretion in deciding whether to publish articles, comments and letters submitted by private individuals or even by their own staff reporters and journalists. The State's obligation to ensure the individual's freedom of expression does not give private citizens or organisations an unfettered right of access to the media in order to put forward opinions'.[26] The same, of course, goes for

[23] *Couderc and Hachette Filipacchi Associés v. France*, no. 40454/07, § 88, 10 November 2010 [GC].

[24] *Alpha Doryforiki Tileorasi Anonymi Etairia v. Greece*, § 38, no. 72562/10, § 38, 22 February 2018.

[25] See below for case law.

[26] *Remuszko v. Poland*, no. 1562/10, § 79, 16 July 2013.

dissemination of pictures and videos. As a point of departure, privately owned media exercises editorial discretion.[27]

There are exceptions. There may for example be a right of reply, which is not necessarily a violation of Article 10 although it is a restriction of the editorial discretion. It is a minor exception, and it 'flows from the need not only to be able to contest untruthful information, but also to ensure a plurality of opinions, especially on matters of general interest such as literary and political debate', as the Court states in *Kaperzynski v. Poland*.[28] Thus, there may be cases in which lack of securing a reply, e.g. by rejecting a request before a court, amount to a violation of the state's positive obligation under Article. 10 This is uncontroversial and undramatic.

In the other end of the scale, the state may violate its positive obligation by not offering protection to media and individual journalist under violent attacks. In *Özgür Gündem v. Turkey*, the Court holds that the Turkish state has violated Article 10 by not offering any protection against several violent attacks on the premises of a newspaper and against its journalists.[29] Similarly, in *Dink v. Turkey* the Court holds the Turkish state responsible for not taking any measure to protect an journalist of Armenian origin, who was assassinated by ultranationalists.[30] The Court also finds a violation of Article 10 in a sentence passed to the journalist for voicing his opinion on the Armenian question. In the present context, the failure to offer protection is relevant, as it implies a positive obligation under Article 10.

Does the state have positive obligations apart from the exceptional and dramatic cases? Yes, to some extent. If a dismissal of an employee is solely founded on her legal expressions, failure to consider freedom of expression by the relevant courts and authorities may amount to a violation of Article 10,[31] Similarly, failure to consider freedom to receive information when dealing with the landlord's noticing a tenant for putting up a satellite disc may amount to a violation of the state's positive obligation under Article 10.[32] In two particular cases, the Court has dealt with the balancing of third parties' discretionary power to reject (or delete) content based on internal policies on the one hand and the states' obligation to guarantee freedom of expression, including the right to receive and impart information, on the other. In *Appleby and Others v. the United Kingdom* most of the city centre was privatised by a shopping mall, including parking lots and walkways, and the company did not allow pamphlet distributions, etc. A local NGO challenged the restrictions, and

[27] The Danish Press Council regularly receives complaint from people whose letter to the editor has not been published and whose interview has not been broadcast etc., and the Press Council regularly dismisses this kind of complaints. Freedom of expression is also freedom of the press, and as a point of departure no one can require specific information to be published.

[28] *Kaperzynski v. Poland*, no. 43206/07, § 66, 3 April 2012.

[29] *Özgür Gündem v. Turkey*, no. 23144/93, 16 March 2000.

[30] *Dink v. Turkey*, nos. 2668/07, 6102/08, 30079/08, 7072/09, 7124/09, § 138, 14 September 2010. The Court also found a violation of Article 2. In the present context, the state's violation of its positive obligations under Article 10 is in focus.

[31] *Fuentes Bobo v. Spain*, no. 39293/98, 29 February 2000.

[32] *Khurshid Mustafa and Others v. Sweden*, 23883/06, 16 December 2008.

eventually the case ended up before the ECtHR. The Courts states that '(w)here, however, the bar on access to property has the effect of preventing any effective exercise of freedom of expression or it can be said that the essence of the right has been destroyed, the Court would not exclude that a positive obligation could arise for the State to protect the enjoyment of the Convention rights by regulating property rights. A corporate town where the entire municipality is controlled by a private body might be an example'.[33] Thus, the privatisation of crucial space may interfere with rights under Article 10. In the present case, however, the Court finds no violation based on the following: '(T)he restriction on the applicants' ability to communicate their views was limited to the entrance areas and passageways of the Galleries. It did not prevent them from obtaining individual permission from businesses within the Galleries (the manager of a hypermarket granted permission for a stand within his store on one occasion, author's note) or from distributing their leaflets on the public access paths into the area. It also remained open to them to campaign in the old town centre and to employ alternative means, such as calling door-to-door or seeking exposure in the local press, radio and television'.[34] The pamphlet distributors were in fact able to express their views and collect support, although it may have been less efficient, compared to a situation where the entire shopping centre, car parks and walkways for free spaces for expressions. In conclusion, the Court does not rule out that a private party's limitation of freedom of expression may amount to a positive obligation for the state to interfere to secure effective freedom of speech (including imparting and receiving information). However, the limitations must be of a comprehensive character before Article 10 comes into play.

In *Remuszko v. Poland* the Court elaborates on the relevant criteria: 'In the determination of the existence and scope of the positive obligations of the State arising under Article 10 of the Convention, the Court has had regard to the subject matter of the case, to its capacity to contribute to the public debate, to the nature and scope of restrictions imposed on the exercise of freedom of expression, and to the availability of alternative means by which that liberty could be exercised, as well as to the weight to be given to the competing rights of other persons or of the general public'.[35]

As for *the subject matter*, the dispute in *Remuszko* was whether a journalist and writer had a right to advertise his recent book, or reversely whether the editors had an obligation to publish the advertisements—and the state an obligation to secure the respective rights and obligation. In commercial cases, there is a wide margin of appreciation, and the Court found no violation of Article 10.

As for the *capacity to contribute to the public debate*, it is clear that matters of genuine public interest enjoy strong protection under Article 10. The dissemination of pictures and videos of private character does not enjoy a strong protection but

[33] *Appleby and Others v. the United Kingdom*, no. 44306/98, § 47, 6 May 2003.

[34] *Appleby and Others*, § 48.

[35] *Remuszko v. Poland*, no. 1562/10, § 65, 16 July 2013.

must be seen in relation to adverse rights under, among others, Article 8. In addition, this criterion is not the only one, as can be deduced from *Appleby and Others* (and the other listed criteria, see below). In *Appleby and Others*, the issue was obviously of public interest—in fact, it was a protest against further privatisation and development of the commons of the city.

*The nature and scope of restrictions imposed on the exercise of freedom of expression* is obviously a relevant criterion. How far reaching are the restrictions? Do they amount to an absolute restriction or do they not? This hinges on the following, *the availability of alternative means by which that liberty could be exercised.* As stated above, the point of departure is third parties' and media's right of deciding their own policies. Even if the alternatives are less effective, the point of departure prevails. Only if the restrictions amount to something close to an absolute restriction, Article 10 comes into play.

Finally, *the weight to be given to the competing rights of other persons or of the general public* is important. It could be property rights as in *Appleby*, and right to private life where the activity consists in distributing nude pictures, sex videos and fake porn. Although these products may be in high demand among a certain audience, the competing rights are strong, and the interests of the general public is weak. The distribution of private pictures does not contribute to a debate of general interest. (See also below Sect. 2.3 on the balancing of private life and freedom of expression).

In conclusion, the state may indeed have a positive obligation under Article 10. However, when it comes to interfering with competing rights, the positive obligation under Article is relatively weak. See also below Sect. 2.3.

Considerations on the states' positive obligations under Article 10 is, of course, relevant in relation to large online platforms which may be criticised for blocking or deleting material uploaded by users of the platform. It is somewhat beyond the scope of the present contribution to go into details of this relevant and interesting discussion. Presently, it suffices to point out the following: *First*, states may have positive obligations under Article 10, which could include securing that online platforms do not arbitrarily delete legal (or perhaps better: human rights abiding) material; and *second*, the states' obligations—and hence indirectly, the platforms' possible obligations not to block or delete uploaded material—must be weighed against other rights, including the right to private life.

- Distribution of nudity, depiction of sexual activities and fake porn falls under the scope of Article 10. (So do expressions which relates to the honour and reputation of others and expressions relating to groups; relevant but not specifically addressed in this contribution).
- Freedom of expression is not absolute and must be balanced, among others, with the equally important right to private life protection.
- The state has positive obligations also in relation to Article 10, although infringements are rare. The state must make sure that persons are not illegitimately precluded from receiving and disseminating information and opinions.

## 2.3 Balancing Private Life and Freedom of Expression

As stated above, freedom of expression includes the publication of photographs.[36] This covers still photographs and videos, also in distorted forms.[37] Thus, as a point of departure the production and dissemination of nudity, porn and fake porn falls under the scope of Article 10. 'However, (t)his [the publication of photos, author's note] is nonetheless an area in which the protection of the rights and reputation of others takes on particular importance, as the photographs may contain very personal or even intimate information about an individual or his or her family'.[38] The rights and reputation of others may legitimise an interference under Article 10, § 2, and the protection of private life under Article 8 is, of course, a relevant right.

Perhaps the possible clash between Article 8 and Article 10 was not fully realised in ECtHR case law until *Von Hannover v. Germany*, no. 59320/00, 24 June 2004. The question was whether the publication of various pictures of the Monegasque princess Caroline von Hannover violated the right to private life. The German courts held that the princess was a public figure '*par excellence*',[39] and that the publication of those photos which portrayed the princess in non-secluded places were acceptable. However, the ECtHR decides that the publication violates Article 8, based on a number of arguments of which two are particularly relevant for the present context: *First*, the pictures did not make any contribution to a debate of general interest.[40] The photos merely depicted the princess in her private capacity, and 'the curiosity of a particular readership regarding the details of the applicant's private life, cannot be deemed to contribute to any debate of general interest to society'.[41] It is important to note that the pictures are, as a point of departure, covered by Article 10. It is not the case that pictures and other information aimed at satisfying the curiosity of a particular readership is not covered by Article 10. But when balancing against the rights under (among others) Article 8, it is paramount whether the information contribute to a debate of general interest. *Second*, the Court emphasises the atmosphere of continual harassment.[42] There is a difference between accidentally appearing on a photo depicting various persons in a public place and the continual harassment by paparazzo photographers hardly leaving any private life protection when persons are privately socialising. For the present purpose, this aspect of continual harassment is important. Persons, mainly adolescent girls and women, who continually appear in nude, sex and fake porn uploads, are continually being harassed by continuing intrusions in their private life.

---

[36] As stated in *Couderc and Hachette Filipacchi Associés v. France*, no. 40454/07, § 89, 10 November 2015 GC.

[37] *Independent Newspapers Limited v. Ireland*, no. 28199/15, 15 June 2017.

[38] *Couderc*, ibid.

[39] '(E)ine "absolute" Person der Zeitgeschichte', *von Hannover*, § 19.

[40] *Von Hannover*, § 60.

[41] § 65.

[42] §§ 59 and 68.

When dealing with cases of possible collisions of Articles 8 and 10, the Court states that '(i)n cases which require the right to respect for private life to be balanced against the right to freedom of expression, the Court considers that the outcome of the application should not, in theory, vary according to whether it has been lodged with the Court under Article 8 of the Convention by the person who was the subject of the news report, or under Article 10 by the publisher. Indeed, as a matter of principle these rights deserve equal respect'.[43] In 2010, the Court was criticised exactly for not doing this, i.e. for addressing the balancing exercise differently, depending on whether the case was brought before the Court as a private life case or a freedom of expression case.[44]

To deal with this problem, the Court developed six criteria when dealing with the balancing exercise. This was done by the Grand Chamber in two cases, *Axel Springer v. Germany*, no. 39954/08, and *Von Hannover v. Germany no. 2, nos.* 40660/08 and 60,641/08, both passed 12 February 2012. The criteria may not be extraordinarily brilliant.[45] However, they are systematically employed by the Court ever since the 2012 judgments, and they work, especially in relation to the publication of photos and other private life information.[46]

The criteria are as follows:

a. Contribution to a debate of public interest.[47]

It is obvious that nudity, sex and fake porn does not normally contribute to a debate of public interest. Rather, it serves the curiosity of a particular audience. As noted, such elements will normally fall under the scope of Article 10, but when balancing the involved rights Article 8 prevails. In general, nudity and sex may be subjects of public debates. After all, sex is an important part of human life, and all sorts of aspects may be up for discussion. The balancing requirement appears when persons are depicted without their consent, which is often the case with nudity, depiction of sexual activities and fake porn.

b. How well known is the person concerned and what is the subject of the news report?[48]

This is actually two criteria. The first, how well known is the person concerned, is irrelevant when dealing with the publication of nude pictures, etc. Obliviously, in many situations it is relevant whether person concerned is prime minister or totally

---

43 *Couderc*, § 91.

44 Smet (2010), pp. 185, 197 and 235 with further references.

45 Schaumburg-Müller (2013).

46 They may work less well in cases of clashes between private life protection against insults and freedom of speech, see *Morice v. France*, no. 29369/10, 23 April 2014 [GC] and *Medžlis Islamske Zajednice Brčko and Others v. Bosnia-Herzegovina*, § 88, no. 17224/11, 27 June 2017 [GC].

47 See, e.g. *Couderc*, §§ 96–116.

48 *Couderc*, §§ 117–129.

unknown. But even prime ministers' sex life is private,[49] and depictions are protected by Article 8, outweighing Article 10.

In contradistinction, the subject of the report is highly relevant. Even pictures that would normally fall under the protection of Article 8 such as one person have an intimate relationship with another, may be protected by Article 10, e.g. when the prime minister is dating a member of a terrorist group. Still, as regards pictures of the relationship in sexual action, Article 8 will outbalance freedom of expression.

c. Prior conduct of the person concerned[50]

This criterion is somewhat tricky. *First*, if a person has voluntarily served as a nude model for publication, Article 8 weighs much less. Still, Article 8 is relevant, and in the case of the use of a non-pornographic nude picture in a fake porn context is, private life protection is likely to prevail. In addition. There are copyright and contractual issues to be considered. *Second*, if a person previously has served as voluntary nude model or the like, this is not a free pass to infringe on that person's private life in other situations. In relation to this criterion, the Court is not always clear as to what exactly the prior conduct, e.g. of exposing private information through the media, implies for future media intrusion. At any rate, since nudity, sex and fake porn are heavy private life intrusions, prior conduct cannot be of any particular importance—apart from prior consent, of course.

d. Method of obtaining the information and its veracity[51]

Like point b. above, this point consists of two criteria. Method of obtaining the information relates to paparazzo photographers and other clandestinely shooting of photos and films. Given the present-day circumstances where almost everybody has a smartphone enabling them to always shoot photos and videos, this is a highly relevant criterion. In the case of dissemination of nude and sex photos and videos when recorded unknown to the persons appearing, private life protection is likely to prevail over freedom of expression.

As for veracity, this criterion is relevant in fake porn situations. An unproblematic head shot, e.g. from a personal website may be photo shopped into a pornographic context, making it look like the person is engaged in pornographic activities.[52] Pictures does not have to be involved, see *K.U. v. Finland*, in which a sexual interests was feigned. This, of course, falls under the scope of Article 8, and private life considerations outbalance freedom of expression. The veracity criterion does not imply that if true, freedom of expression prevails. It merely points out that the manipulation of pictures, etc. may in itself tip the balance in favour of private life protection. In the case of a published head shot, the picture will as a point of

[49] *Ojala & Etukeno Oy* v. Finland, no. 69939/10, 14 January 2014.

[50] *Couderc*, § 130.

[51] *Couderc*, §§ 131–136.

[52] An example from Danish case law: six-month imprisonment for, among others, photo shopping a portrait of a young girls on to a masturbation site, UfR (Weekly Law Reports] 2015, p. 2561.

departure be open for media use[53]—with due respect to copyright—but not for postings in fake porn, no matter how pretty the face.

e. Content, form and consequences of the impugned article[54]

This is a rather loose compilation of criteria, perhaps serving as serving as a kind of safe, if all relevant criteria were not caught by the previous categories.

As regards *content*, it is difficult to identify anything in addition to point b. 'what is the subject of the report?'. As regards *form*, this seems mainly to be relevant when dealing with traditional, professional media which decides their form of reporting—with due regard to ethics of journalism and professional standards. Since *Jersild v. Denmark,* no. 15890/89, 23 September 1994, the Court has consistently held that not for the courts, neither national courts nor the ECtHR, to make a decision as to the format of the reporting. This position is reiterated in *Couderc*, § 131. In relation to the posting of nudity, pictures and videos with sexual content and fake porn, the content is in itself private and very unlikely to be outweighed by freedom of expression. Still, the format may be aggravating if the pictures or videos are accompanied with derogatory remarks, enticement to further postings, etc.

As for the *consequences*, unconsented dissemination of nudity, depiction of sexual activities and fake porn may have severe implications.[55] In a set of more than thousand criminal cases dealing with the dissemination of one or a few videos of a minor couple having sex—the so-called umbrella complex—the Danish Supreme Court notes that the participating girl suffers from posttraumatic reactions including anxiety and panic reactions, medium to severe depression and a reduction of her cognitive functions. The impact on the participating boy is less severe; still, he has huge social problems, problems of finding jobs and continuously in need of psychological assistance.[56]

The sixth criterion is the severity of the sanction imposed. For the present purpose, this is not relevant. The Court will, of course, take proportionality into consideration, but this is of no importance to the balancing of the involved rights.

To conclude:

- The dissemination of nude pictures, depictions of sexual activities and fake porn fall under the scope of Article 8 protecting private life *and* freedom of expression as it entails receiving and imparting information.
- When balancing the two rights there is little, if anything, in favour of freedom of expression. It does not contribute to a debate of general interest, it is often obtained clandestinely, and the consequences of the dissemination potentially has severe consequences for the involved—whereas, conversely, the prohibition of the dissemination has no impact on the functioning of a democratic society.

[53] E.g. *Schüssel v. Austria* (dec.), no. 42409/98, 21 February 2002.

[54] *Couderc*, §§ 137–150.

[55] For more elaborate research on the consequence, see, e.g. Bates (2017) and Ruvalcaba and Eaton (2020).

[56] UfR [Weekly Law Review] 2019, p. 1232.

Consented nude pictures, and depictions of sexual activities are widely accessible, and there is no need for access to unconsented material.
- There is an abundance of case law dealing with the balancing exercise. The collision is illuminated, illustrated and clarified as regards many aspects. It is not pristine land for newcomers.

## 3 Internet Platforms and Private Life Infringing Content

Companies are not bound by international human rights law, states are. Yet companies play an important part in relation to human rights, be it positively by, e.g. creating jobs, economy and welfare, or negatively by, e.g. supporting human rights oppressive regimes or directly participating in human rights adverse activities. For large Internet platforms, this is not different. The platforms provide unprecedented access 'to seek, receive and impart information and ideas of all kinds, regardless of frontiers', a basic human right, here quoted from CCPR Article 19. On the other hand, there may be negative human rights impact, e.g. by providing easy access to the sharing of unconsented content such as nudity, sexual activities and fake porn.

This situation—i.e. great impact, but no corresponding human rights liability—has been addressed by the United Nations Guiding Principles to Business and Human Rights[57] (UNGP or Guiding Principles). The Guiding Principles reiterate that business companies do not have legal obligations under international human rights law, and they emphasise that the principles do not create new obligations under international law. What they do is sketching out some rules and principles which, first, are relevant and operational for companies. After all, since human rights obligations are formulated as state obligations, they do not automatically translate into instructions for business companies. Second, the Guiding Principles are apt for assessment. It is not so difficult to assess whether, in fact, a particular company is living up to the recommended standards. Failure to do so does not prima facie bring about legal sanctions, but assessments are interesting for companies, stakeholders and states. Companies which do want to respect human rights now have guidelines assisting them in fulfilling their aspirations, stakeholders may use the guidelines as a platform for praise or critique, and states may use them for turning them or some of them into hard sanctionable law and due diligence legal requirements.

In the following I shall take a closer look at the relevant parts of the Guiding Principles, Sect. 3.1, and in Sect. 3.2 I shall analyse Facebook's recent commitment to UNGP and the decisions by the recently established Oversight Board. In Sect. 3.3 I assess whether Facebook does live up to its newly declared commitment to the UNGP.

[57] United Nations, 2011. https://www.ohchr.org/documents/publications/guidingprinciplesbusinesshr_en.pdf.

## 3.1 UNGP

The Guiding Principles are divided into three sections: I. The state duty to protect human rights, II. The corporate duty to respect human rights, and III. Access to remedies. Each section is divided into Foundational principles (A) and Operational principles (B), and each paragraph is followed by a commentary going more into details. Thus, the UNGP is a useful tool for the various stakeholders, states, companies, and others.

It could be considered superfluous for the Guiding Principles to deal with state duties, as state obligations are already dealt with by international human rights instruments. However, the UNGP sets out the state duties[58] in more details and related to business enterprises. Thus, states 'must protect against human rights abuse within their territory. . . . This requires taking appropriate steps to prevent, investigate, punish and redress such abuse through effective policies, legislation, regulations and adjudication'.[59] This duty may reach further than the state obligation under the present international human rights law regime. As an example, a state should consider its duty to legislate Internet platform liability and to create ways of forcing or nudging the platforms to, among others, protect private life. Obviously, this duty could be fulfilled through effective EU law.[60] The states also have a duty to 'set out clearly the expectation that all business enterprises . . . respect human rights throughout their operations'.[61] As examples this could be done through a 'welcome communication' once an international digital platform has established itself within the jurisdiction of the states, and it could be done through contracts and permissions, including human rights performance as a part of the contracts or the permission.[62] Besides, the states have a duty to assess the adequacy of the relevant law, e.g. the adequacy of the laws pertaining to digital violations of private life.[63] The states also have a duty to provide 'guidance to business enterprises on how to respect human rights throughout their operations'.[64] As for digital violations of private life, states

[58]The UNGP uses the term 'duty'. A UNGP duty is not a legal obligation under international law, but a duty nevertheless, and many UNGP duties may be more closely regulated in domestic law and eventually turned into legal obligations.

[59]UNGP I.A.1.

[60]As for copyright infringements, the EU has required Member States to provide liability for 'online content-sharing service providers', Directive (EU) 2019/790 of 17 April 2019 on copyright and related rights in the Digital Single Market, Article 17. The EU could direct the Member States to provide liability for online media also for (gross) private life infringements. Here, the EU seems to take a softer approach, cf. the Proposal for a Regulation on a Single Market for Digital Services (Digital Services Act) 15 December 2020.

[61]UNGP I.A.2.

[62]The commentary to I.A.2 relates to the performance abroad of home business enterprises, but the opposite is also relevant. States want to attract foreign investment, and this should be done in a human rights respecting way.

[63]UNGP I.B.3.a.

[64]UNGP I.B.3.c.

should provide guidance for the digital platforms as to how to avoid violations and at the same time respect freedom of expression. The idea is that states have experience with this balancing exercise, and states ought to be pro-active in informing companies operating in and out of the country as how to best handle the situation. To my knowledge, states have done little if anything in this respect.[65]

As for business enterprises, they 'should respect human rights'.[66] This indicates, one, that there is a part to play for corporate enterprises, and two, that the duty is not a binding obligation, but a recommendation for relevant action. Still, the recommendations may have a spillover effect into national law and international human rights law. Companies carrying out their duties under the UNGP will more easily be left off the legal complicity hook.[67] Respecting human right entails that business enterprises 'should avoid infringing on the human rights of others *and* should address adverse human rights impacts with which they are involved'.[68] The Guiding Principles acknowledges that there is a distinction between directly infringing human rights, including the right to private life, and indirectly impacting human rights in an adverse way.[69] This distinction may be highly relevant to legal liability and complicity, but as for duties under the UNGP both situations are covered. One may discuss whether providing easy access for upload of private life infringing material is direct or indirect,[70] but in relation to the UNGP this is not important. The business enterprise has duties in either case.

'The responsibility of business enterprises to respect human rights refers to internationally recognized human rights – understood, at a minimum, as those expressed in the International Bill of Human Rights ...'.[71] Above in Sect. 2 I have

---

[65] According to Danish penal law, anyone who is inciting, advising or somehow participating in the act may be sentenced. It is clear that digital platforms are involved, i.e. participating in the act by providing a platform and by not taking action against illegal content. So far, no digital platforms have been prosecuted. It does not seem as if this is due to thorough considerations, but rather a result of the police and the prosecutor being slow and somewhat reluctant to prosecute digital crimes. Initially, it appeared that the police and the prosecution brushed aside digital crimes as if they were not real crimes. This has changed, and now the police investigate, and the prosecution prosecutes digital violations of the various private life provisions. Still, there is no prosecution of online media, although the penal provisions are there, and the prosecutor has an obligation to prosecute criminal acts. (There is a certain element of passive complicity, which is relatively complicated, see Holst (2015) and Schaumburg-Müller (2018)).

[66] UNGP II.A, § 11.

[67] UNGP II.A, Commentary re § 17.

[68] UNGP II.A, § 11 (my italics).

[69] UNGP II.A, § 13.

[70] See Buhmann and Olivera (2020), p. 129.

[71] UNGP II.A, § 12 which also mentions 'the principles concerning fundamental rights set out in the International Labour Organization's Declaration on Fundamental Principles and Rights at Work' which for the present purpose is of little relevance. 'International Bill of Rights' refer to the 1948 Universal Declaration of Human Rights and the two 1996 covenants, both in force from 1976, the one on civil and political rights, CCPR, and the one on social, economic and cultural rights, CSECR.

analysed the relevant case law of the ECtHR, although the European Convention is not mentioned in the UNGP. As a point of departure, it will suffice to include the International Covenant on Civil and Political Rights (CCPR) when business enterprises seek to carry out their duties under the UNGP. Still, the European Convention may be relevant, cf. the wording 'as a minimum', the ECtHR has the most elaborated case law on the balancing of the right to private life and freedom of expression, and when operating in Europe, the ECHR is of course relevant, since the European states are obliged to protect the rights as indicated in the Convention.

The UNGP are for all business enterprise, large and small, national and international. Still, the duties vary according to scale and adverse human rights impact.[72] Even a smaller locally operating company has duties under the UNGP, but large multinational enterprises have stronger duties, their impact being larger—and hence, the possible adverse impact. They have the resources for carrying out in depth due diligence activities, which includes processes 'to identify, prevent, mitigate and account for how they address their impacts on human rights'.[73]

The UNGP are made generally for all business enterprises, perhaps with the mining industry in mind. There is no special regard for digital platforms which provides virtual space for third party uploading. However, the same duties apply. The large digital platform companies have a duty to address the possible adverse effects of their activities, including the possibility of private life infringement on a much larger scale than what was possible in the good old analogue world. This implies that large companies such as Google and Facebook should have processes and activities in place. First, they should identify adverse human rights impacts. This may be a large undertaking, given the prevalence of the company activities and the diversity of uploads—not to mention the companies' own activities such as gathering personal data, which is not the focus of the present contribution. Second, the companies should work to prevent human rights infringements, including using their leverage to influence relevant actors.[74] This is no easy task, either; still, large companies have the capacity to include internal and external expertise[75] to come up with human rights abiding solutions to, e.g. infringements of private life. It is immaterial as to whether the adverse human rights effects were intended or foreseen, which they most often are not. The problem is that large enterprises have all sorts of effects throughout the societies in which they operate. Adverse effects are not easily anticipated, and it is probably even more difficult to deal with them. But exactly doing that is a duty under the UNGP. The business enterprises should also mitigate adverse effects and account publicly for their efforts.

Lastly, business enterprises should have in place '(p)rocesses to enable the remediation of any adverse human rights impacts they cause or to which they

[72] UNGP, II.A, § 14.

[73] UNGP, II.A, § 15(b).

[74] UNGP, II.B, § 19(b)(ii) including the Commentary.

[75] As recommended in § 18(a).

contribute'.[76] This duty is elaborated in the Remedy section, which mainly deals with state duties to provide effective remedies. However, there are also duties for business enterprises which 'should establish or participate in effective operational-level grievance mechanisms for individuals and communities who may be adversely impacted',[77] and these mechanisms should be effective.[78] The idea is, of course, that individuals and communities should have access to a complaints procedure. Seen from the company perspective it is a way of accessing information on (unintended) adverse human rights effects, and to be able to prevent escalating harms.[79] Engaging in remedy procedures is not an alternative to state run judicial mechanisms; the overall idea of the UNGP is exactly that states have the primary duty to protect human rights, which includes, among others, proper procedures in cases of (alleged) human rights violations. Still, the business enterprises have a (non-legal) duty to respect human rights, which, among others, includes having relevant complaint procedures.

It is beyond the scope of this contribution to go into details of the question whether the various digital platforms live up to the UNGP recommendations. On the other hand, it is not difficult to gather that, largely, they do not.[80] Suffice it to mention two cases, involving unconsented dissemination of nudity and sexual activities. In the so-called umbrella-complex, briefly mentioned in the Introduction, the videos disclosing explicit sex scenes with a 15-year-old couple were shared more than 1,000 times on Facebook Messenger, and more than a year passed from the moment of Facebook receiving a complaint until informing the police. Whether Facebook did anything to prevent the illegal sharing, is not publicly known, and besides the videos are still shared on Messenger. In another case, Danish nude models were used as thumbnails and popped out in the feed of users of Reddit. Eventually, the media agreed to stop the dissemination, but it seems that there was no consideration whatsoever as to the lawfulness of the pictures in the first place. As John Ruggie—who was UN Special Rapporteur on the UNGP—cites in relation to Facebook's hesitant stance towards human rights abiding performance: 'It is difficult to get a man to understand something when his salary depends upon his not understanding it'.[81] In other words, human rights considerations may not count much when weighed on an economic scale.

[76] UNGP, II.A, § 15(c).

[77] UNGP, III.B, § 29.

[78] UNGP, III.B, § 30.

[79] UNGP, III.B, § 29, Commentary. From my own experience, working as a legal advisor for YWCA, Lusaka, Zambia 1997–2000, complaints procedures provide valuable information from real life experience.

[80] See also Buhmann and Olivera (2020), p. 133: 'To honour their corporate responsibility to respect human rights, companies in the ICT sector need to much more seriously consider their own human rights impacts and their role in facilitating such impacts'.

[81] Ruggie is quoting Upton Sinclair in a post on 15 November 2018, 'Facebook in the Rest of the World'. https://media.business-humanrights.org/media/documents/files/documents/John_Ruggie_Facebook_15_Nov_2018.pdf.

Interestingly, by March 2021 Facebook has declared its commitment to the Guiding Principles, and Facebook has set up an Oversight Board which can receive complaints and deliver decisions that Facebook must follow. The section below provides a closer look.

## *3.2 Facebook's Commitment to the UNGP and the Oversight Board*

On 18 March 2021, Facebook announced its commitment to human rights and the duties outlined in the UNGP[82]—alongside with other commitments to, e.g. Global Network Initiative and OECD Principles on Artificial Intelligence, which will not be commented here. Critically, one may note that it took long. The UNGP was endorsed by the UN Human Rights Council in 2011, and already in 2008, the ideas were developed,[83] and one of the ideas is exactly to carry out human rights diligence from the outset, as it is not easy, or perhaps impossible, to foresee all human rights implications. However, previously, Facebook was not committed to anything of the sort. As Mark Zuckerberg stated earlier on: 'Governments sometimes order us to remove content they believe is illegal but doesn't violate our Community Standards. [. . .] We fight to protect our community from unnecessary or overreaching government intervention'.[84] This is a craving for corporate self-determination rather than respect for democratically elected governments and internationally agreed human rights. Another Zuckerberg quote shows a similar thrust: '(A) lot of times people are just . . . too careful. I think it's more useful to . . .make things happen and then . . . apologize later than it is to make sure that you dot all your i's now and then . . . just not get stuff done'.[85] This is far from human rights due diligence, and one may question the sincerity of the commitment. However, it is for the future to show how it will be carried out, and the present commitment is commendable and praiseworthy.

By 2021 Facebook has established an Oversight Board. It operates within the Facebook enterprise, independent in the limited sense that it is not bound by decisions by Facebook board of directors apart, of course, from the decision to establish the board and setting out its bylaws. Presently, the Board has six so-called trustees, responsible for the running of the Board, including finance and the appointing of members. Presently, the Board has 20 members from around the world, it runs under a Charter, and its stated purpose is to 'protect free expression

---

[82] https://about.fb.com/wp-content/uploads/2021/03/Facebooks-Corporate-Human-Rights-Policy.pdf.

[83] A/HRC/8/5, 'Respect and Remedy: A Framework for Business and Human Rights. Report of the Special Representative of the Secretary-General on the issue of human rights and transnational corporations and other business enterprises, John Ruggie' 7 April 2008.

[84] Quote 15 March 2015 from the official Facebook homepage. The quote is no longer accessible.

[85] Quote from Ruggie, 'Facebook in the Rest of the World', 15 November 2018.

by making principled, independent decisions about important pieces of content and by issuing policy advisory opinions on Facebook's content policies'.[86]

From January 2021, the Oversight Board has been functioning with ten decisions in total per 5 May. The original idea was that the Oversight Board was to make decisions as to whether Facebook's actual decisions, e.g. in relation to the deletion of uploads, are in line with Facebook rules.[87] This is a purely internal exercise. However, the Board has also engaged international human rights as the basis of its decision making, which makes sense in relation to Facebook's official commitment to the UNGP, etc. So far, most of the decisions relate to hate speech in the broad sense of term, including what falls under Facebook's community standards 'Dangerous individuals and organizations'.[88] One is on nudity, one on misinformation and one on incitement to violence.[89] In relation to human rights standards, in each case the Board indicates the relevant human rights law and CCPR Article 19 is cited in all cases. Article 19 is *the* international freedom of expression clause, using the same format as the corresponding Article 10 of the European convention, Article 19 being somewhat shorter: Freedom of expression constitutes the point of departure, it includes the right to seek,[90] receive and impart ideas and information, and the right may be limited if (1) it is provided by law, (2) pursues a legitimate aim such as the 'respect of the rights or reputations of others'[91] and is necessary to achieve the aim. The three-step test is similar to the one in ECHR Article 10, except that the European version requires necessity 'in a democratic society', which does not pertain to the global convention, since many countries are not democratic. Neither are companies, for that matter. In addition, CCPR Article 20 prohibits propaganda for war and '(a)ny advocacy of national, racial or religious hatred that constitutes incitement to discrimination, hostility or violence'. As for the latter, this in line with the ECtHR's interpretation of Articles 10 and 17 (the misuse clause).

The Board applies the three-step test in each case.

As for *legality*, in several cases the Board criticises Facebook's rules for being too broad and vague.[92] This pertains especially to the 'Community Standards on Dangerous Individuals and Organizations', and generally, the Board criticises the rather messy communication with various standards in various places, internal standards not communicated to the public, continuous alterations of the standards and in one

[86] Info and quote from https://oversightboard.com/governance/.

[87] Oversight Board Charter, Section 2. Basis of Decision Making.

[88] Case Report 2020-001-FB-UA 28 January 2021 (hereafter 2020-1 plus date), 2020-02, 2020-03, 2020-05 (all 28 January), 2020-07 12 February 2021-02 13 April, 2021-03 29 April.

[89] 2020-04 28 January (*Nudity and breast cancer*), 2020-6 28 January (*'Harmless drug'*) and 2021-01 5 May (*Trump*).

[90] To seek is not included in the European version, see, e.g. *Magyar Helsinki Bizottság v. Hungary*, no. 18030/11, 8 November 2016 [GC] interpretation hardships.

[91] CCPR, Article 19(3)(a).

[92] 2021-1, 2021-3, 2020-6, 2020-5, 2020-4.

case, lack of translation into the relevant language.[93] In six cases out of ten the legality requirement is not fulfilled. Compared to the ECtHR judgments, this is a large percentage. By far, most Article 10 cases hinges at the necessity requirement, with a smaller part related to the legality requirement. This indicates, perhaps not surprisingly, that Facebook has a legislation problem.[94] After all, Facebook is a commercial company, not a state with historical experience in legislation. Interestingly, the legality requirement does not only pertain to the standards, but also to the sanctions. In 2021-1 (*Trump*) the Board criticises the eternal ban for not having any backing in Facebook's standards.[95]

As for a *legitimate aim*, this requirement is fulfilled in most cases. In European case law Article 10 has never been violated solely because the aim of the sanction was not legitimate. In 2021-2 (*Zwarte Piet*) the Board states that 'it is not a legitimate aim to restrict expression for the sole purpose of protecting individuals from offense' (with a reference to UN Special Rapporteur on freedom of expression, report A/74/486, § 24). This makes sense: Rights and reputation of others are the pertinent requirements, cf. CCPR Article 19(3)(a), but there is no right not to be offended. Critically, it can be noted that Facebook's community standards on nudity does not live up to this requirement: 'We restrict the display of nudity or sexual activity because some people in our community may be sensitive to this type of content'. This is exactly to protect someone from being offended, which according to the Board's remark is *not* a legitimate aim. The standards continue: '*Additionally*, we default to removing sexual imagery to prevent the sharing of non-consensual or underage content' (my italics). There is something with the priority here:[96] According to Facebook, gross private life infringements such as the unconsented dissemination of nudity, sexual activities and fake porn are only additional to offending some people in seeing, e.g. female nipples.

One may argue that Facebook has a right to decide on its policies, including banning of nudity, a right which would be similar to the traditional media's right of editorial discretion.[97] However, Facebook is a social media providing space for uploaders, not a traditional edited media with strong editorial rule (and corresponding strong editorial liability). Besides, Facebook has now decided that their policies and decisions should be coherent and in line with the UN Guiding Principles.

As for the *necessity* test, the Board states that although 'companies do not have the obligations of Governments, their impact is of a sort that requires them to assess

---

[93] 2021-3 (*'RSS is the new threat'*).

[94] Obviously, it is not legislation in the strict sense. However, it resembles; Facebook and other digital platforms offer a public space, and therefore their terms of use are not merely contract conditions, but also a relevant regulation of public affairs.

[95] This in line with the ECtHR, e.g. in *Hashman & Harrup v UK*, no. 25594/94, 25 November 1999 [GC].

[96] Note that according to the UNGP, II.B, § 24.

[97] See *Remuszko v Poland*, above Sect. 2.2.

the same kind of questions about protecting their users' right to freedom of expression'.[98] This implies, one, that companies do not have to live up to the rather strict necessity requirements pertaining to state sanctions, and two, that companies nevertheless must engage in some kind of necessity consideration. Not any policy will do. This leaves the Board with the difficult task of establishing the particular necessity threshold for Facebook.[99]

### 3.3 *Assessment – Facebook, the Oversight Board and the UNGP*

No doubt, the Oversight Board and its decisions bring Facebook in better line with the UN Guiding Principles. The Board engages relevant human rights law and has embarked on the necessary but difficult task to establish the company's duties under the UNGP in more details. It is a basic idea of the UNGP that states have a duty to protect, in some details spelled out under international law, and that companies have a duty to respect. Those duties are only somewhat similar to state duties. They are similar in the sense that they share a common normative background in, among others, the Universal Declaration of Human Rights and the two 1966 human rights covenants. However, companies are not states, they are not full subjects of international law, and they have other functions. Still, and this is crucial according to the UNGP, companies do have duties in relation to human rights. The UNGP including the preparatory work and the commentaries have laid the general foundation, but it is up to future organisations such as the Oversight Board, to translate the duties into more detailed operational requirements. One may compare this situation to the one when states had agreed on generally formulated human rights, leaving it for future decisions by courts and other institutions to fill in the details.[100]

However, the set-up has some serious shortcomings:

*First*, only users of Facebook—and Facebook itself—can submit a complaint to the Board.[101] This is not in line with the UNGP that emphasises the importance of including stakeholders in the whole human rights' due diligence process, and it leaves out persons who may be adversely affected by the company's activities from having access to complaints procedures. As noted above, complaint and remedy procedures are not only for the sake of each complainant, but also for the gathering of information in relation to the company's human rights impact. By not allowing for

[98] 2020-3. The Board refers to the UN Special Rapporteur on Hate Speech, A/74/486, § 41.

[99] Similar to the case law of the ECtHR which has continuously elaborated on the 'necessary in a democratic society' test in relation to state sanctions from European countries.

[100] As an example, the ECHR was agreed upon in 1950 with a commission to receive complaints, but no court. Now the Court has passed approx. 20,000 judgments, which gives a much more precise picture of state obligations under the Convention.

[101] Charter of the Oversight Board, Article 2.

all affected to make a complaint, Facebook will not get sufficient knowledge in relation to adverse human rights effects.

This connects to the *second* shortcoming: There is an unbalanced approach to human rights issues that involve private life protection as well as freedom of expression. Private life protection is, of course, not the only consideration, but it is the focus of the present contribution. Alas, it not the focus of neither Facebook, nor the Oversight Board. According to Facebook, the role of the Board is to 'ensur (e) respect for free expression, through independent judgment',[102] further elaborated: 'The Oversight Board was created to help Facebook answer some of the most difficult questions around freedom of expression online: what to take down, what to leave up, and why. The board uses its independent judgment to support people's right to free expression and ensure those rights are being adequately respected'.[103] As indicated above Sect. 2, the ECtHR has for the past almost 20 years grappled with the difficult balancing of private life protection and freedom of expression. Facebook has not even started, and it is unlikely that the Oversight Board will receive cases involving (alleged) private life infringements, and therefore unlikely that the Board will engage in serious balancing of the two equally important rights.

It appears that preferential approach to the private life vs. freedom expression complex is not limited to Facebook. The UN Human Rights Committee General Comment on freedom of expression[104] does not mention the right to the private life, and it emphasises that restrictions must not be overbroad.[105] It is, of course, highly relevant to state that freedom of speech must not be overly restricted. However, it is not only a question of limiting freedom of speech, but also of securing the right to private life. The same critique could be directed at the recent EU proposal for a regulation on digital service.[106] It replicates the imbalance by taking freedom of expression as the important point of departure—and, of course it is important—but without seriously considering private life.

*Third*, one may question whether the Oversight Board is truly an independent body. Without going into details, suffice it to state the UNGP calls for companies to establish 'effective operational-level grievance mechanisms for individuals and communities who may be adversely impacted'.[107] The complaints procedure does not have to be totally disconnected from the company; in fact, the UNGP recommends non state grievance mechanisms with company involvement. Importantly,

---

[102] Headline, https://oversightboard.com.

[103] Quoted from https://oversightboard.com/ accessed 12 May 2021.

[104] GC no. 34 of 29 July 2011.

[105] Ibid., § 34.

[106] Proposal for a Regulation of the European Parliament and of the Council of a Single Market for Digital Services (Digital Services Act) and amending Directive 2000/31/EC, 15 December 2020, COM (2020) 825 final.

[107] UNGP, III.§ 29.

company run grievance mechanisms are not meant to be the only procedures.[108] Therefore, although the independence of the Board may be questioned, this is not of paramount importance.

As indicated above, Facebook does have rules regarding the display of nudity and sexual activities, which as a point of departure are prohibited. One may therefore ask whether this is not sufficient for the protection of private life. Why go into details with the balancing problems, if this is dealt with, clear cut and no shaking hand?

The answer is that rules are exactly rules. Sometimes they are followed, sometimes they are not, and sometimes they are implemented, sometimes they are not. It is obvious that rules are normally not followed 100%, in which case the rules would be redundant. In the case of Facebook, it is obvious that users do not always abide by the rules.[109] In addition, and importantly, rules may not be implemented. In some cases, rules are mere window dressing only meant to show off; in other cases, implementation is well intended. Still, it is very unlike that implementation is perfect. This may be due to rule inconsistency, lack of resources, lack of willingness to allocate sufficient resources, etc. These phenomena are well known from state rules, and the situation is not altogether different from that of a company. Facebook's rules are not always consistent, there is obviously technical challenges in managing the number of postings, and Facebook may not have given high priority to rule managing compared to, say, profit making. In two of the Oversight Board cases, Facebook readily admits that the postings were removed by mistake,[110] and in in some cases, the Board points out that the internal guidelines differ from the overall general rules, available to the public.

Hence, adjudication is important. It serves in establishing a legal regime,[111] it serves to solve unavoidable interpretative problem, it may serve to point out more systematic inconsistency, and it serves to sanction rule deviation. In this light, the Oversight Board is a step in the right direction, bringing an independent adjudicative body into the loop. However, as stated above, the Board is not provided with across-the-board adjudicative power, as it can only receive complaints from Facebook and Facebook customers, leaving out other stakeholders who may be adversely affected by Facebook's activities. In conclusion, Facebook does not live up to the duties under the UNGP, which requires, among others, concern for *all* human rights, not only freedom of expression, human rights due diligence procedures from the outset and pertaining to all operations, and remedies for all adversely affected, not only for some.

---

[108] See also a hesitant backing, Douek (2019), who points out that the Oversight Board may succeed in improving the legislative process and contributing to a public debate on the prevailing rules.

[109] In the third quarter of 2020, 12.4 million pictures (allegedly) violating Facebook standards were removed.

[110] 2020-4 (*Breast cancer*) and 2021-3 (*RSS*).

[111] Hart (1961), p. 94.

## 4 Conclusions

European states have positive obligations under ECHR Article 8 (and CCPR Article 17) to effectively protect private life. This requires having legal provisions in place, in gross cases criminal provisions, and efficient procedures. However, the legal framework is prerequisite, but is not in itself sufficient. If the enacted laws are not properly implemented, private life is not properly protected. It beyond the scope of the present contribution to state whether all European states live up to their obligations. As an indication of the score, Denmark may be an illustrative example. Denmark is a human rights abiding country (perhaps with a less convincing record when it comes to immigrants), the ECHR was incorporated into Danish legislation in 1992, and Danish courts take the ECtHR case law seriously.[112] Still, not until the so-called umbrella complex, starting off around 2016, section 264d of the Penal Code was engaged in cases of digital sex offenses. Section 264d is the private life provision, criminalising the unwarranted dissemination of private information, including pictures. The police seemed hesitant, the prosecution seemed hesitant, perhaps because it was a new area, perhaps because digital offenses were seen as only virtual and not real compared to, e.g. physical sexual assaults. This situation has improved considerably, but one may still question whether the prosecution always live up the requirements under Article 8. In addition, so far there has been no prosecution of platform companies, which according to Danish penal law may be complicit in the vast amount of private life infringements via their respective services. So far, no digital platform has been prosecuted even in cases when the company obviously was aware of the illegal content.[113]

States have positive obligations also under Article 10. When companies such as Facebook provide a highly important part of the communication infrastructure, and the company bans the users from access, does this involve any Article 10 considerations? On the one hand, to bring about a positive obligation under Article, the situation must be quite serious. As a point of departure, Facebook users have other means to communicate, although they may not be as efficient, cf. *Appleby and Others v. the UK*. On the other hand, it would certainly be in line with Article 10 if states took the quasi-monopoly situation into consideration and, at least, made some considerations as to possible legal regulations as regards the question whether the companies ought to have any obligations to accept entirely legal uploads. It is not an easy question, but is it not made easier, let alone solved, by not giving it any political and expertise considerations.

As for the UNGP, states have duties, among others, to provide state and non-state grievance mechanisms. My immediate impression is that states are far from fulfilling

[112] There is an abundance of published case law relating to freedom of speech. All courts painstakingly take the relevant ECHR Article 10 criteria into consideration, and Denmark has not lost a freedom of speech case since *Jersild*, no. 15890/89, 24 Sep 1994, dealing with the media's right to disseminate publicly relevant information.

[113] Which may be a requirement under the E-Commerce Directive, 2000/31/EC, Article 14.

their UNGP duties. State grievance procedures may be slow, reluctant and in some countries perhaps hardly existing, but even with criminal procedures right in place, this may not be the best way of dealing with private life infringements. Faster procedures, less formal, and procedures which include stakeholders may in some cases be preferable; and they are part of the UNGP state duties. In addition, states could consider making the human due diligence process a mandatory requirement. According to the UNGP, states have also a duty to provide guidance to companies, as to how companies can live up to their human rights duties. To my perception, states do no nothing of the sort in relation to digital platforms' duties in relation to adverse human rights impact.

Companies have a range of duties under the UNGP, one being to establish or to assist in establishing grievance mechanism. Facebook has recently embarked on this route, but as mentioned, the limited access and the freedom of expression favouring approach renders it insufficient. Besides, there are other duties: Bringing in human rights considerations in the first place, and not only some, but all relevant human rights, including the right to private life. It seems as if only very few online platforms have even started. The companies also have a duty to engage in human rights due diligence processes. Facebook has declared its commitment, which is a good start, but only a start. Many other platforms have, to my knowledge, not even realised that there is more to the business than freedom of expression and profit (and side bonusses such as exciting nude pictures, etc.).

There is still a long way go. But securing potentially conflicting rights is not impossible, as the case law of the ECtHR has shown.

## References

Amnesty International (2020) Let Us Breathe. Censorship and Criminalization of Online Expression in Viet Nam. Amnesty International

Bates S (2017) Revenge porn and mental health: a qualitative analysis of the mental health effects of revenge porn on female survivors. Fem Criminol 12(1):22–42

Buhmann K, Olivera R (2020) Human rights and social media platforms: the corporate responsibility to respect human rights in regard to privacy infringements involving photo posting. Aust J Human Rights 26(1):124–141

Douek E (2019) Facebook's "oversight board": move fast with stable infrastructure and humility. North Carolina J Law Technol 21(1):1–77

Hart HLA (1961) The concept of law. Oxford University Press

Holst NS (2015) *Strafbar passivitet* [Criminal complicity]. DJØF Publishing

Ruvalcaba Y, Eaton AA (2020) Nonconsensual pornography among U.S. adults: a sexual scripts framework on victimization, perpetration, and health correlates for women and men. Psychol Violence 10(1):68–78

Schaumburg-Müller S (2018) "Strafansvar for indholdet af onlinemedier - Om formidleransvar for medier, der ikke er omfattet af medieansvarsloven" [Criminal liability for online media content. Provider liability for media not covered by the media liability act]. UfR [Week Law Rev] 2018: 113–123

Schaumburg-Müller S (2013) Privacy and publicity. In: Gammeltoft-Hansen T et al (eds) Protecting the rights of others. Festschrift to Jens Vedsted-Hansen. DJØF Publishing, pp 389–406

Smet S (2010) Freedom of expression and the right to reputation: human rights in conflict. Am Univ Int Law Rev 26(1):184–236

**Sten Schaumburg-Müller** is a law professor at the University of Southern Denmark. He holds a PhD and a Dr. jur. (habilitation), and his main areas of interest are media law, human rights law and legal philosophy.

# The Freedom of speech in the Digital Era: Leveraging Its Constitutional and Social Ramifications

**Anna Aurora Wennäkoski**

**Contents**



**Abstract** Freedom of speech in the digital era comes with a number of open issues, including the role of regulation, of the markets as well as that of the public sphere. In many of the related issues, tensions of constitutional and social nature resurface. This is also the case with some of the recently introduced EU policy initiatives and legal rules to digital speech. While they seem to give ground to EU wide rules on some important issues, their reach can remain limited without a constitutional and social understanding of the matters at hand. Thus, it appears in many ways beneficial to have a wider outlook and analysis of these topics, including the constitutional and social ramifications of regulating freedom of expression today. This article sets an example to that and joins these threads together in its analysis. By doing so, the work aims to contribute towards obtaining a wider outlook into an evolving domain which has global implications.

---

The opinions expressed are those of the writer.

---

A. A. Wennäkoski (✉)
University of Helsinki, Helsinki, Finland
e-mail: anna.wennakoski@helsinki.fi



S. Hindelang, A. Moberg (eds.), *YSEC Yearbook of Socio-Economic Constitutions 2021*, YSEC Yearbook of Socio-Economic Constitutions (2022) 2021: 145–174,
https://doi.org/10.1007/16495_2021_36, Published online: 10 April 2022

## 1 Introduction

Digitalization comes with a set of challenges to freedom of speech. Surely, not *all* (speech) issues are related to digitalization; nor do they all reach a constitutional level, but new contexts have continued to rise new confrontations. Alongside traditional means of mass communication, there has, by today emerged a panoply of different new means of electronic communications.[1] Technology has, in various manners, become a vital part in news production,[2] and different technologies have already transformed the ways in which news are produced. This has also been predicted to continue.[3] New convergence has also meant changes in both the production and the consumption of media.[4] There are also multimedia markets involving different sensory elements.[5] Already for a while, not only technology, but also the audience itself, has permeated from offline contexts to online.[6] Hence, the novel technologies alter both the notion of freedom of speech as well as social conditions of speech.[7] Thus, arguably, how technological and social advances interconnect, is compounded.[8]

While the policy and regulatory demands have been mounting, so far, the (regulatory) solutions have been mostly national or companies have had their own policies based on which they operate and guide users. Moreover, considerable power has concentrated to certain platforms and private entities. Yet, at the same time, the media landscape has already changed from national to global. This includes on the one hand the ways in which citizens can participate in public debates, increasingly also as producers of information, and on the other hand, the ways in which power in the industry concentrates to a limited number of actors, affecting media pluralism and citizens' possibilities to retrieve information.[9] These also bring forth the interesting questions on the nature of the medias. Importantly, one can ask whether the media itself has a freedom of speech or whether it is (merely) a vehicle to advance that.[10]

The regulatory and policy work in this space remains unfinished. Simultaneously, the (global) social problems have not vanished. Moreover, often we also come across

---

[1] Rosendahl (2007), p. 5.

[2] Hutchison (1999), p. 63.

[3] Bell (2016).

[4] Jenkins (1992), and Jenkins (2008), p. 16.

[5] Suthersanen (2001), p. 92.

[6] Livingstone (2003). pp. 4–7.

[7] Balkin (2004). p. 2.

[8] Hutchison (1999), p. 50.

[9] Draft Report on media pluralism and media freedom in the European Union (2017/2209(INI)) Committee on Civil Liberties, Justice and Home Affairs Rapporteur: Barbara Spinelli, 2017/2209, at E.

[10] Paukku (2006a), p. 48.

with several constitutional questions. These are also issues which decision makers certainly need to face.[11]

## 2 New Medias and Markets

### 2.1 *Role of the (New) Medias*

The media industry has indeed changed. Often today, even the publishing of news can have a "hybrid character"[12] that typically deploys a profit generation formula that is author-subsidized.[13] Along with that, there is also an issue on the nature of social media. That is, whether social media is a "media" and if so, what kind. In Germany, the Network Enforcement Act draws a distinction between "social networks"[14] and more traditional media, a social media platform being "for profit" and "where users can share content," but even with these, the distinction is difficult to make, since what does "for profit" today mean? From a wider perspective, the issue is the changed value of information within our society.[15] And yet, viewpoints might diverge.[16] Thus, perhaps no easy unanimity at sight. This appears pertinent particularly in terms of how to monitor the new commercial platforms.

Also, liability issues in these new media spaces remain complex. After declaring that the issue of liability over third-party content in law is still one of the most difficult unresolved issue,[17] the Council of Europe (CoE) prompted to adapt a recommendation on the topic.[18] Further, the CoE draft modernized Convention 108[19] puts significant role in the protective role of the state in the execution, i.e., providing protection to its citizens, which can be seen as a classical approach (akin to the responsibility to protect under public international law).[20] This comes then back to issue of the role of state.

---

[11] Hutchison (1999), p. 62.

[12] See also Pihlajarinne (2012), p. 12 referring to C 324/09 Loreal SA etc. v. Ebay.

[13] At https://www.ibpa-online.org/page/hybridpublisher.

[14] See Council of Europe, European Court of Human Rights, European Data Protection Supervisor, and European Union Agency for Fundamental Rights (2018) Handbook of European Data Protection Law, p. 361, referring to WP29 opinion 5/2009 on online social networking WP163, 12 June 2009, p. 4.

[15] Saarenpää (1995), p. 588.

[16] Hirshman and Holbrook (1992), p. 25.

[17] CoE (2018), p. 43.

[18] Council of Europe Recommendation CM/Rec(2018)2 on the roles and responsibilities of internet intermediaries.

[19] Draft Recommendation of the Committee of Ministers to Member States on the Roles and Responsibilities of Internet Intermediaries, finalized by the MSI-NET on 19 September 2017.

[20] See Shaw (2003), pp. 694 and 704.

According to a study by the European Commission, nationally the solutions by the broadcasters vary because of different normative and business structures. While in the majority, there are codes of conduct in place and a duty to allow third parties to respond. Also impartiality and transparency in terms of ownership and the protection of children as well as limits to commercial features are common.[21] Often, platforms and sites moderate content themselves, either *ex ante* or *ex post* (that is prior or post publication). Moreover, many companies have drafted social media policies.

In literature, *Ananny* has argued that there is a duty based on ethics to also provide updates and corrections, albeit the (technical) execution of such a duty would come down to algorithms.[22] Yet, there have also been expressions that the rules on content which were crafted for traditional media would not be applicable online.[23] Also, besides censorship concerns, limiting access to content can also cause intellectual property and human rights concerns.[24]

To that, *Hardt* argues that newspapers should not be the ones to remain responsible for overall societal issues.[25] But platforms are not newspapers. Nonetheless, there are several challenges involved, including finding the original poster. Blocking content might also be problematic from a due process perspective.[26] Additionally, too tight timeframes within which harmful content should be removed can pose a practical challenge.[27] This way too, constitutional issues might arise, as due process is inscribed in several national constitutions. But this too, can be based on supranational rules, as in the European Convention on Human Rights (ECHR).[28]

Surely, as we saw above, there appears to be some salience for states to take action, as freedom of speech is a matter of constitution. But what about the company-level acts? Are they to be comprehended as acts of common good, or as a matter of public policy taken into the private entities? To that, one element is also media ownership. On the other hand, there is concentration, which has provided ground for worry over the independence of medias.[29] Politically, this can also be linked to the rise of different movements (such as populism or authoritarianism). However, it should not be deduced that state-owned medias would be automatically "superior" as such. Rather, as the EU Commission has noted, concentration of any kind can be problematic. Hence, Member States must ensure that medias "are independent,

[21] European Commission (2018) A multi-dimensional approach to disinformation. Report of the independent High-level Group on fake news and online disinformation; March, p. 16.

[22] Ananny (2015), pp. 13–14.

[23] OSCE 2012, p. 199.

[24] At http://www.circleid.com/posts/20171016_civil_society_call_for_deletion_of_eu_internet_filtering_provision/.

[25] Hardt (2001), p. 155.

[26] Mujić et al. (2012), p. 38.

[27] Pallero and Pirkova (2020), p. 30.

[28] European Convention on Human Rights, Article 6.

[29] See: OSCE Report 2012 "Freedom of Expression on the Internet."

transparent and well-funded."[30] Audio-visual services and media pluralism have also been subject to public consultations in the EU and the results seem similar to the above.[31]

Within its case law, the CJEU has also emphasized media pluralism.[32] While underscoring the need to maintain media pluralism, the EU Parliament has also voiced that in itself that would not suffice to ensure as such that content is diverse, wherefore there is a need for novel measures that guarantee pluralism, diversity as well as objective and timely information transmission.[33] Also the idea of establishing independent media councils has been put forth.[34] While simultaneously, these discussions are about fundamental debates on the rule of law and democracy in contemporary societies.[35] Thus, also broader themes of public policy that would need to be addressed. We will revert to these.

## 2.2 *Role of the Markets*

Along the years, audiovisual policies tendencies (dirigist vs. liberal) have been pulling into different directions. This has affected the opening of the markets, the free flow of information and of services, and the commercialization of the offering; the latter which has also been seen as a threat to cultural pluralism (especially in smaller Member States).[36] More recently, media politics have increasingly become legally and market oriented.[37] To that, *Curran* has argued that it is the free market that has led to a high concentration in media ownership. Curran has presented as alternatives (a) "a centrally controlled market economy," (b) "a mandated market economy," (c) "a regulated market economy," and (d) "a regulated mixed economy, composed of public, civic and market sectors," without, however, seemingly purporting anyone of them above the others.[38]

---

[30] Media pluralism and democracy: Outcomes of the 2016 Annual Colloquium on Fundamental Rights, pp. 3–7.

[31] At https://ec.europa.eu/digital-single-market/en/public-consultations-media-issues Last accessed on January 10, 2021.

[32] Case C-288/89 Stichting Collectieve Antennevoorziening Gouda and others v Commissariaat voor de Media. ECR 1991 Page I-04007, para. 23–25.

[33] Report on concentration and pluralism in the media in the European Union (2007/2253(INI)), at Q.

[34] Vīķe-Freiberga et al. (2013), p. 7.

[35] See rather similarly Hyttinen and Tapani (2018), p. 61.

[36] See Case C-288/89 Stichting Collectieve Antennevoorziening Gouda and others v Commissariaat voor de Media. ECR 1991 I-04007, para. 23. and case C-23/93 TV10 SA v Commissariaat voor de Media. ECR 1994 I-04795, para. 23 and 25. See also Paukku (2006a), p. 59.

[37] Paukku (2006b), p. 118.

[38] Curran (1991), pp. 47–52.

However, looking at this from a purely market point of view would be blindsided. For example, *Pickard* has importantly noted that there are demands regarding information which cannot emanate from the market. To that, Pickard's cure seems to point to a model where commercial concentration is curtailed and where there would be protection of the public interest instead.[39] However, it is important to keep in mind that there are typically a number of issues involved.

One problem is the privatization of computational power, or as *Anderson* puts it "the legitimacy of private power," when he writes about new constitutionalism in which a political onus would be put on the constitution, as opposed to a more typical liberal approach of the constitution.[40] Yet, politicizing a constitution might seem just as—if not even more—dangerous a tool.

Furthermore, often many of the most powerful platforms and sites are non-Europeans, which has resulted in issues on the extraterritorial reach of EU rules. Another issue is whether global agile business models are bluntly "killing" local journalism. This brings us back to the issue of media pluralism. Hence, there are also ownership issues that link to the market and its pluralism. *Mylly* has argued for a case law which would focus on the role of private power in information resources, including communications infrastructures.[41] Mylly puts the onus of advancing the media pluralism on governments along with the judiciary.[42] Along those lines, *Belshaw* has posited it is for the government to set the example on to what extent society embraces information and its values.[43] These postures would thus seem to give leeway to supranational actions. Yet, on a European scale, they are also linked to the rule of law.

Thus, this discussion is, however, by no means limited to Europe. But the sub-questions can be slightly different. For instance, in Africa, the right to receive communication without interference has been sometimes through long battles at (constitutional) court.[44] This also demonstrates the global (human rights) implications of the matter. In addition, copyright issue can arise, such as what the recent law in Australia shows.[45] Also, (other) property rights might be involved.[46] Sometimes, they can obstruct expressions by others. One example from Europe is the Familiapress case, which according to *Mylly* demonstrated that the freedom of expression of a corporation may thereby be in discrepancy with mass communications and the shared value therein. Mylly links this to workable markets, in which

[39] Pickard (2017) The Big Picture: Misinformation Society 11.28.2017 at http://www.publicbooks.org/the-big-picture-misinformation-society/.

[40] Anderson (2005), in particular pp. 113–115.

[41] Mylly (2009), p. 192.

[42] Mylly (2009), p. 170.

[43] Belshaw (1976), p. 321.

[44] See the Zimbabwe Supreme Court in re: Munhumeso 1995 (2) BCLR 125 (ZS) 130.

[45] Treasury Laws Amendment (News Media and Digital Platforms Mandatory Bargaining Code) Bill 2021.

[46] Mylly (2009), p. 154.

panoply of operators necessitates constitutional protection. He views that in the end, there must be a validation of fundamental rights. Mylly seems clear that the media contexts (whether corporate or other) make no exception in this regard.[47] Moreover, we can also read Mylly to be in favor of widening the analysis of public spheres and democracy because it would also enable to scrutinize more critically the "different facets" in the EU's policy areas.[48] This gives salience to this present article too. We will revert to the public sphere.

## 3 The Nature of Freedom of Expression

The rise of the freedom of expression can be associated with several fundamental movements towards a modern society.[49] Doctrinally, a modern view to free speech has argued to have emerged post Second World War, when a fundamental rights-oriented view to the topic rose, including the more precise limitations to this important freedom. Many national constitutions were amended to reflect these changes.[50] Gradually, the protection of freedom of speech rose prominently into several international declarations.[51] Also in case law clear pro-freedom of speech stances proclaimed it essential for both the society and individuals.[52] We will revert to this below. Yet, while *freedom of the press* has featured in the constitutions of several countries since the mid-19th century,[53] compressing it to an international convention under the auspices of the UN failed already decades ago.[54]

> The notion of freedom of press is not identical to freedom of expression. The former can be seen to be composed of "the proprietor's right to print news and comment freely and critically and the right of the public to receive a steady and honest supply of information, but also the right of the individual journalist to tell the public what he knows." Yet, the

[47] Mylly (2009), pp. 168–169, referring to case C-368/95 Vereinigte Familiapress Zeitungsverlags- und vertriebs GmbH v Heinrich Bauer Verlag [1997] ECR I-3689.

[48] Mylly (2009), p. 52.

[49] Siebert et al. (1956).

[50] Neuvonen (2014), pp. 20–21.

[51] Universal Declaration of Human Rights (UDHR) proclaimed by the United Nations General Assembly in Paris on 10 December 1948; the International Covenant on Civil and Political Rights (ICCPR) adopted by UN GA Resolution 2200A (XXI) on 16 December 1966, and in force from 23 March 1976 in accordance with Article 49 of the covenant, The European Convention of Human Rights (ECHR), the Declaration on Fundamental Principles concerning the Contribution of the Mass Media to Strengthening Peace and International Understanding, to the Promotion of Human Rights and to Countering Racialism, apartheid and incitement to war 28 November 1978, the Charter of Fundamental Rights, and the Charter for European Security.

[52] Case of Handyside v. the United Kingdom (7 December 1976), para. 49, case of Zana v. Turkey (25 November 1997), para. 32 and case of Axel Springer v. Germany (7 February 2012), para. 78, and Mylly (2009), p. 185.

[53] Eek (1953), p. 12.

[54] Eek, p. 77.

problem on the nature of the right and its content was pondered upon in connection with the UN planned convention on freedom of information. There too, one of the issues was where to draw the line without clashing with national constitutions. In any event, some amount of governmental support is needed for the freedom of information.[55] As common features of the freedom of information at constitutional level, have been seen the role of courts, the element of rule of law and particular laws on the press.[56] Yet, also already at the time, the cross-border data flows were seen problematic (when hindered).[57] We can note that most of these issues are still present.

While supranational solutions have been more or less declaratory in nature, states have addressed speech issues nationally. We cannot examine them in this article at length, but a few brief examples are given.

For instance, in Germany, restrictions on hate speech are today not only found in the criminal law[58] but also in special acts, such as the more recent law on hate speech, namely, the Network Enforcement Act (*Netzwerkdurchsetzungsgesetz*) which obliges companies to a half-yearly reporting (2 §) and in maintaining “an effective and transparent procedure for handling complaints about unlawful content” (3 §). In case unlawful content is found, it is to be removed within 7 days (3.3 §), subject to a fine of EUR 50,000 (4 §).[59] Some authors claim that this law is putting the onus from public into the private hands.[60] Moreover, the duty to set legal rules to intermediaries in the media sector, which has been seen both ethically and constitutionally mandated in Germany, can also lead to a remodeling of the entire legislative structure on this area.[61] Hence, we find a very delicate issue on the role of the state. While a state might be an appropriate level to tackle issues of regulation, a national act, however, typically lacks international enforcement.

In France, when a new law on fake news was voted,[62] also co-operation mechanisms to remove content, as an obligation to platform hosting providers, were also pondered upon. Some experts saw that such a provision was already in French law—hence the issue whether there is a need to enact a new provision to begin with. The focus in the eventual rule being the possibility to remove content immediately or as expeditiously as possible. Removal of hostile content—including (electoral) funding

---

[55] Eek, pp. 41, 57 and 133.

[56] Eek, pp. 28–29.

[57] Eek, p. 51.

[58] German Federal Criminal Code, § 185. and § 130(1).

[59] At https://www.bmjv.de/SharedDocs/Gesetzgebungsverfahren/Dokumente/NetzDG_engl.pdf?__blob=publicationFile&v=2.

[60] Guggenberg N (2018) How not to regulate social networks WWU Münster Newsportal March 14, 2018 at https://www.uni-muenster.de/news/view.php?cmdid=9436.

[61] Daten Ethik Kommission (2019), p. 208.

[62] Loi organique et loi ordinaire du 22 décembre 2018 relatives à la manipulation de l'information.

to be disclosed on websites more openly—was seen pertinent especially during election period.[63]

> It appears interesting to note that already during the French Restauration era (i.e., between 1814 and 1830), the problem (of a violation) was not so much the thought expressed, but rather, the way in which the expression was made.[64] Does it sound not that far off from what is being tackled today still, given the pre-eminence of various egregious forms of speech today?

In many Member States, media pluralism is seen an important goal. One can distinguish between internal pluralism (each media (channel) offers a plurality of content) and external pluralism (the medias (channels) together do the same).[65] Yet, it also remains contested whether there is any duty of the state to secure media pluralism or (a duty) to honor that. Traditionally, freedom of speech is seen to entail both a negative (duty to respect the right of others) and a positive dimension to fulfill, the latter which is seen particularly (a duty) for the state to fulfill.[66] There is also the complex question of *Drittwirkung*, that is, the third-party effect of fundamental rights[67] which can be direct or indirect as in Lüth.[68]

Yet, to honor that comes with a dilemma of securing sufficient audiences while securing fundamental rights.[69] This in turn also requires a certain vigilance to anticipate forthcoming trajectories of constitutionalism.[70] Hence, we cannot ignore constitutional parameters.

# 4 Balancing Case Law

In the EU media policy, a central trait has been the aim of guaranteeing the free movement of audiovisual services[71] and *mutatis mutandis*, when setting limits to that freedom, the limitation would also need to fulfill the criteria of limiting freedom of speech.[72] Arguably, some case law seem to have shifted from institutional to more

---

[63]Neuman S (2018) France's Macron Says He Wants Law To Combat Fake News. January 4, 2018 at https://www.npr.org/sections/thetwo-way/2018/01/04/575580790/frances-macron-says-he-wants-law-to-combat-fake-news?t=1611048976370.

[64]Garcon (1963), p. 111.

[65]Paukku (2006b), p. 116.

[66]Case of Heinisch v. Germany (21 July 2011), para. 44. See also case of K.U. v. Finland (12 December 2008).

[67]See e.g. Ipsen (1954), pp. 111-198, at 143 and van Dijk and van Hoof (1990), p. 413 and pp. 15–20.

[68]Lüth, BVerfGE 7, 198 (15 January 1958).

[69]Hoikka (2006), pp. 146–149.

[70]Hoikka (2006), p. 153.

[71]Paukku (2006a), p. 59.

[72]Paukku (2006a), p. 66.

functional evaluation (of national media operations).[73] But these are merely some dimensions from the vast case law on the freedom of expression, found both by the CJEU and the ECtHR; the former covering some 350 cases, and the latter about 4,200 cases.[74]

From this body of cases, we can make a few other observations here. First, the protection of expression and free speech is rarely, if ever, absolute, but rather, relative and limited by other rights and freedoms. In essence, it must also co-exist with other fundamental rights. For instance, under Article 10 of the European Convention of Human Rights (ECHR), restrictions (derogations) to it are possible when necessary and prescribed by law.[75] Yet, the exceptions are to be narrowly interpreted.[76] Moreover, the social purpose and its "objectives of general interest" must also be considered when restricting the freedom of expression.[77] It can be noted that shocking and disturbing expressions can also be protected under free speech. This has been justified under the name of tolerance and plurality of views.[78] Finally, there must also be an overall balancing of all interests and circumstances involved.[79] Also in the ECtHR case law, the quest for balance between various human rights is strong.[80] These requirements are also needed to be considered in Member States' praxis.[81] Thus, the balancing of these elements occupies a central place when courts weigh the result in a particular case.

Second, different fundamental rights can pull into opposite directions[82] and the dynamics of limitations work both ways. To illustrate, there are public policy-related limitations which must be considered when weighing in freedom of expression, and vice-versa; EU Member States must consider freedom of expression when limiting free movement of goods and services.[83] Yet, at least for the European Court of Justice (CJEU), in such cases both material and symbolic effects to constitutional

[73] Paukku (2006b), p. 130, referring to case Informationsverein Lentia and Others v. Austria 24.11.1993 A276.

[74] As of January 2021.

[75] C 368/95 Vereinigte Familiapress Zeitungsverlags- und vertriebs GmbH v Heinrich Bauer Verlag, para. 26. Cf. Raitio (2009), p. 314.

[76] Case of the Sunday Times v. The United Kingdom (26 April 1979), para. 65, case of Müller v. Switzerland (24 May 1988), and case of Sokolowski v. Poland (17 December 2004).

[77] Case C-112/00 Schmidberger, para. 80.

[78] Case of Handyside v. UK (7 December 1976), para. 49, and case of Castells v. Spain (23 April 1992), para 42. Note also case of Lingens v. Austria (8 July 1986), para. 41, and case of Vogt v. Germany (26 September 1995), para 52.

[79] Case C-112/00 Schmidberger, para. 81.

[80] See, e.g., case of Groppera Radio AG and others v Switzerland (28 March 1990) and case of Lentia Tele 1 Privatfernsehengesellschaft v. Austria (24 November 1993).

[81] Tiilikka (2012), p. 59.

[82] Hyttinen and Tapani (2018), p. 48.

[83] Case C-260/89 Elliniki Radiophonia Tiléorassi AE and Panellinia Omospondia Syllogon Prossopikou v Dimotiki Etairia Pliroforissis and Sotirios Kouvelas and Nicolaos Avdellas and others. ECR 1991 I-02925, para. 45.

values must not be compromised. This can be useful in terms of allowing constitutional matters to be considered, but can also leave room for too much case-by-case reasoning, and thus legal uncertainty. Furthermore, there are allowed derogations due to freedom of expression and other fundamental values.[84] Some of the same values, such as the requirement of pluralism, can also be found in the case law of the ECtHR.[85]

Third, there are also several national dimensions in the interpretation of freedom of speech. Importantly, behind the notion of freedom of speech as a fundamental right in the EU, one can find several values such as tolerance and the prohibition of censure; with some national nuances.[86] Yet, while a margin of appreciation and a doctrine of consensus could paint a uniformist picture, literature has sought to also remind that plurality readings and end-results are possible—if not more plausible—in system based also largely on a case-by-case reasoning.[87] Moreover, the interpretation of the ECHR by the ECtHR draws its foundation from the constitutional traditions of its Member States.[88] Again, we see constitutional issues rise in importance.

Also, it needs to be noted that the constitutional appeal system under the ECHR with its national variants can be considered rather remarkable.[89] *Schmauch* has remarked from a procedural law standpoint that national constitutional predicaments can be incused from the CJEU's case law in this area.[90] The issue of supremacy of norm broiling down to, according to Schmauch, as to from where the rule(s) in question emanate from (Charter, constitution, committee, etc.).[91] This can also be understood as stances on the hierarchy of sources.

Importantly also, the ECHR has different hierarchical status nationally; while, for instance, relatively high ("equal to or even above national constitutions") in Austria or in the Netherlands, but ordinary law in, for instance, France and Spain.[92] Moreover, in France, the ECHR has been seen as principles that have constitutional

---

[84] Chalmers et al. (2006), pp. 833–834.

[85] See case of Radio ABC v. Austria (20 October 1997) and Demuth v. Switzerland (5 November 2008).

[86] Pere (2015), p. 63.

[87] Neuvonen (2014), p. 25.

[88] See case 29/69 Erich Stauder v City of Ulm - Sozialamt, case 11/70 Internationale Handelsgesellschaft mbH v Einfuhr- und Vorratsstelle für Getreide und Futtermittel. ECR 1970 Page 01125, para. 2. and from literature, e.g., Neuvonen (2014), p. 23.

[89] See van Dijk and van Hoof (1990), p. 90.

[90] Schmauch (2014) at https://svjt.se/svjt/2014/520 at p. 523.

[91] Schmauch, p. 528.

[92] Brückmann (2008), p. 165.

value.[93] While in Germany, the constitutional protection of speech has been voiced[94] but the status there has been more complex.[95]

Also, competences pertaining to freedom of speech (supranational v. national) can vary.[96] Granting competences to supranational level has not been straightforward and lengthy discussions have prevailed, also regarding subsidiarity. In case law, a cautious, narrow approach has been visible even at advocate general level, which according to *Weatherill,* speaks volumes about the constitutional rivalries underpinning the surface.[97] Yet, this has not been limited to freedom of speech. One culmination point being the *Solange* case,[98] in which the German court was reluctant to give up its power to adjudicate.[99] The issue goes back to that of competences and the "Kompetenz-kompetenz quandary."[100] Yet, the scuffle appears to pursue, as the recent *Weiss case* showed.[101]

> Although at first glance the Weiss litigation was about the Public Sector Purchase Programme (PSPP) and the EU's monetary policy; beyond that, it brings forth questions of primacy and sovereignty, that is, the fundamental principles of the EU legal order. From that perspective, the case is by no means alone.[102]

Thus, when looking at freedom of speech, we also need to keep in mind both supranational and national jurisprudence. Yet, again, several constitutional issues emerge.

## 5 EU's Normative Responses

Many of the recent speech related problems are often not limited to national borders. This has not been left unnoticed. For instance, the rise of hate speech has been noted high on the EU agenda.[103] The EU Commission has admitted that we currently live

[93] See Stirn (2008), p. 18.

[94] See case Lüth BVerfGE 7, 198, 15 January 1958.

[95] Brückmann, pp. 182 and 185.

[96] Neuvonen (2014), p. 26. See, e.g., Joined cases 60 and 61/84 Cinéthèque SA and others v Fédération nationale des cinémas français. ECR 1985 -02605.

[97] Weatherill (2006), p. 41, looking also at Opinion of Advocate General in Case C-376/98, para. 4, 89 and 133.

[98] BVerfGE 37, 271 2 BvL 52/71 Solange I-Beschluß.

[99] Ojanen (1998), p. 104.

[100] Besson (2008), p. 63.

[101] Case C-493/17 Proceedings brought by Heinrich Weiss and Others. Published in the electronic Reports of Cases (Court Reports—general).

[102] See also case C-399/09 Marie Landtová v Česká správa socialního zabezpečení. Reports of Cases 2011 I-05573 and Case C-441/14 Dansk Industri (DI). Reports of Cases (Court Reports - general).

[103] General Secretariat of the Council (2017) Taking forward the Strategic Agenda 18-month Programme of the Council (1 July 2017–31 December 2018), p. 8.

in an era where the amount of information is unprecedented and the speed in which news and tweets are produced has become most difficult to keep up with. The Commission associated these difficulties to regaining trust, as it too sees these themes connected to the ways in which democracy operates.[104] Also affirming the need to tackle disinformation, Commissioner Jourová has spoken on securing European values, including media freedom and freedom of expression. On content regulation, Jourová has stressed that similar content prohibitions must apply both online and offline. In tackling disinformation, Jourová stressed digital literacy. Underscoring a comprehensive approach, she also mentioned the European code of practice for social media.[105] Hence, at least policy arguments have not been lacking.

In 2015, the European Commission against Racism and Intolerance (ECRI) adopted a general policy recommendation on hate speech, calling respect for fundamental rights, including tolerance and using "appropriate measures to remove" such content, while also pleading a role of self-regulation.[106] Also the possibility of co-regulation has been alluded to; for example, if they are transparent and allow for authentic participation and have suitable redress tools, co-regulation can offer useful way for governance, while deploring that this is not always the case, as evidenced by the EU code of conduct on hate speech.[107] While co-regulation can be a vehicle to provide more flexibility, it is also a sensitive topic to the industries.[108]

In terms of hardcore regulation, however, on the EU's legislative front, the solutions have been erring more on the side of secondary law. More recently, proposals of the EU Commission, i.e., Digital Markets Act[109] and Digital Services Act[110] were given. These will touch upon the issue of platforms as gatekeepers. Noting the necessity to harmonize the matter,[111] the first proposal would provide "harmonised rules ensuring contestable and fair markets in the digital sector across the Union where gatekeepers are present."[112] The latter proposal aspires to "mitigate risks of erroneous or unjustified blocking speech, address the chilling effects on

---

[104] European Commission (2017b) White Paper on the Future of Europe: Reflections and Scenarios for the EU27 by 2025, p. 13.

[105] Hearing of Commissioner-designate Věra Jourová at the European Parliament 7 October 2019 (AFCO- and LIBE- committees).

[106] ECRI General Policy Recommendation N°15 on Combating Hate Speech - adopted on 8 December 2015.

[107] Pallero and Pirkova (2020), p. 18.

[108] Neuvonen (2012), p. 188.

[109] Proposal for a Regulation of the European Parliament and of the Council on contestable and fair markets in the digital sector (Digital Markets Act) Brussels, 15.12.2020 COM(2020) 842 final 2020/0374 (COD). See Article 2 for a definition of "Core platform service."

[110] Proposal for a Regulation of the European Parliament and of the Council on a Single Market For Digital Services (Digital Services Act) and amending Directive 2000/31/EC Brussels, 15.12.2020 COM(2020) 825 final 2020/0361 (COD).

[111] Proposal COM(2020) 842 final, p. 4 and recital 8.

[112] Proposal COM(2020) 842 final, Article 1.

speech, stimulate the freedom to receive information and hold opinions, as well as reinforce users' redress possibilities."[113] That proposal seeks to focus in-depth on "[t]hree categories of systemic risks," namely, (1) illegal content, (2) "the impact of the service on the exercise of fundamental rights including the freedom of expression and information" which could involve "the design of the algorithmic systems used by the very large online platform or the misuse of their service through the submission of abusive notices or other methods for silencing speech or hampering competition," and (3) "the intentional and, oftentimes, coordinated manipulation of the platform's service" which might involve "bots, and other automated or partially automated behaviours."[114] Already these brief quotations demonstrates not only a panoply of technological ramifications—including competition law—in today's digital speech issues, but also the out-of-datedness of the current directive on electronic commerce[115] to respond to the novel challenges. It is possible to comprehend the proposed Digital Services Act also as a combination of the German view and of the Digital Markets Act. From that perspective, some support to the enforcement and interpretation of the Digital Services Act might come from the German *Netzwerkdurchsetzungsgesetz* (as we saw above). Also, the nomenclature of the two proposals is interesting, namely, the use of "acts." Acts have been classically used by nation states, but not by the EU. One might ask, is the EU stepping here on the footsteps of national regulator? In any event, while some companies might test the waters regarding the application of the above rules (once in force), given the dynamic nature of today's competitive environment, the lines risk remaining blurry at least for a while still.

Yet, in literature, it has already been asked how platform operators are able to recognize content which needs to be removed. This certainly is not an easy task. [116] This can also be seen in case law where it has been inter alia posited that this might lead to lawful communications being blocked, thus compromising free speech.[117] Further, in the ubiquitous online environments, the traditional approach to crimes relating to freedom of speech[118] might need re-evaluation. Yet, there is the entire issue of whether and when to deploy civil or criminal law measures to begin with. Writers have argued that the primary sources (criminal law) should be exhausted first and only after those should there be a pro and contra style balancing, as avenues to maximizing legal certainty.[119]

---

[113] Proposal COM(2020) 825 final, p. 12.

[114] Proposal COM(2020) 825 final, para. 57.

[115] Directive 2000/31/EC of the European Parliament and of the Council of 8 June 2000 on certain legal aspects of information society services, in particular electronic commerce, in the Internal Market ("Directive on electronic commerce") OJ L 178, 17.7.2000, pp. 1–16.

[116] Pihlajarinne (2012), p. 20.

[117] Case C 70/10 Scarlet Extended SA v Société belge des auteurs, compositeurs et éditeurs SCRL (SABAM), 2011 I-11959, para 52.

[118] See Cornils (1999), p. 713.

[119] Hyttinen and Tapani (2018), p. 57.

Yet, in the EU's media policy, the aim of securing freedom of speech must also confront the different aims of the internal market, including those of competition norms, many of which have a relatively heterogonic playing field.[120] To tackle these, it has been articulated that there might be a need for more extensive competences for the EU in this domain.[121] In the new proposed EU rules for digital content, users could seek empowerment to their judicial redress from other countries.[122] This can help to tackle the cross-border element, but remains unsure. Moreover, the Digital Services Act also calls Member States to designate "a Digital Services Coordinator in each Member State" for enforcement.[123] Yet, the complaint mechanism there can appear complex and challenging, as removing content is also context dependent.

Furthermore, arguably, the ways in which speech can be restricted has remained unclearly articulated. This includes nouns such as "extremism," "terrorist propaganda," "harmful" or "racist content," and "hate speech."[124] The recent proposals of the EU do not respond to these. This can be problematic; for instance, in connection with European security in which it has been argued that there is a need to consider the challenges of deliberative democracies.[125]

Thus, so far, the EU legal initiatives in this area have been emerging only relatively recently. In the meantime, this has enabled states to continue addressing speech issues at national level. This has salience, but might remain insufficient, especially given the cross-border nature of new medias, as we saw above. There are also the company level actions which might demand different responses. How the media market will develop remains to be seen. To that, constitution might also provide stability.

## 6 The Role of Constitution and the Contested Constitutionalism

While constitutional elements can be found since the EU's foundation,[126] constitutionalism has also been later developed and observed both on the EU and national level[127]—be it a "waning constitutionalism"[128] or an aspiration to a new constitution, as in the beginning of the millennium (along with the erasure of the pillar

[120] Paukku (2007), p. 130.
[121] Vīķe-Freiberga et al. (2013), p. 4.
[122] COM(2020) 825 final, para. 44 and Article 18.
[123] COM(2020) 825 final, recitals 73–74, and chapter IV of the act.
[124] Mujić et al. (2012), p. 30 and p. 199.
[125] Nuotio (2010), p. 15.
[126] Mutanen (2015), p. 95.
[127] Mäenpää (1996), p. 62 and the references therein.
[128] Rasmussen (2007), pp. 149–156.

structure).[129] Yet, some constitutional elements have remained contested in the EU. Perhaps no wonder, considering the primacy of the EU law vis-à-vis national rules.[130] This is seen in case law too.[131]

In literature, the views diverge. For instance, while some writers have purported that the role of the (planned) EU constitution is a response to the legitimacy[132] or democracy deficit[133] in the EU, others have seen that the EU Charter contributes to the EU's constitutionalism as a process.[134] Further, there are writers who have seen the Charter, the EU's general legal principles, and the ECHR as forming something "equivalent to a constitutional preamble."[135] Some writers even argue that some federalist tendencies have emerged in the EU.[136] One classic counter-argument to such aspirations is that it threatens national sovereignty.[137] No wonder the reluctance to relinquish powers to the EU has been voiced.[138] However, one can also find views that the European constitutionalism is relative and the European model should be distinguished into multiple parts,[139] which, as a view point, reminds *Tebner's* "societal constitution."[140] However, social dimensions in the EU are also still under debate.

The issue of legitimacy remains too.[141] Officially, one can find democratic legitimacy proclaimed in the EU primary law.[142] Despite further proclamations towards enhancing it, such as in the Lisbon treaty (preamble), in literature, some expressed that this did not change much in terms of sovereignty.[143] Certainly, in several instances, the sensitive nature of the issue has been de facto palpable, as illustrated by the right to veto (later abolished) in the Treaty of Amsterdam,[144] or in connection with the Lisbon Treaty where the characteristics of a supranational

---

[129] Salminen (2010), p. 157.

[130] Case 106/77 Amministrazione delle Finanze dello Stato v Simmenthal SpA. ECR 1978 -00629, see in particular para. 21 and 22.

[131] Case 11/70 Internationale Handelsgesellschaft mbH v Einfuhr- und Vorratsstelle für Getreide und Futtermittel.

[132] Tiilikainen et al. (2005), p. 81.

[133] See, e.g., Eurobarometers 64/2005 and 251/2006. And Nieminen (2008), p. 17.

[134] Bischof et al. (2002), p. 19.

[135] Stirn (2008), p. 41.

[136] Mäenpää (1996), p. 62.

[137] Postigo (2013), p. 45.

[138] See, e.g., Salminen, p. 161, referring to matters of criminal justice.

[139] Tuori (2013), pp. 24–26.

[140] Tuori (2013), p. 29, referring to Teubner (2004a), pp. 71–87, and Teubner (2004b), pp. 3–28.

[141] Engström (2011), p. 21.

[142] Vīķe-Freiberga et al. (2013), p. 20, referring to TEU Article 10.

[143] Mutanen (2015), p. 64 referring to Weatherill (2011), pp. 850–851.

[144] See Enhanced cooperation - Summaries of EU legislation at http://eur-lex.europa.eu/legal-content/EN/TXT/?uri=LEGISSUM%3Axy0015.

constitution were ripped off and references were made to national constitutions.[145] Thus, again, we circle back to constitutional issues and national level.

Constructively, constitutionalism can be seen as a continuous task.[146] Yet, that has not taken away the criticism. For the EU, in the beginning, there was no contract of social or political nature, and this deficiency later became subject to criticism. Yet, according to *Engström,* the EU continues to set an example in terms of formal supranational constitutionalization. Nonetheless, it has also made legitimacy experiments of a democratic nature.[147] Moreover, the CJEU has been blamed for exceeding its role in social issues, thus going beyond its limits. Engström further claims that going forward, the EU's constitutionalism would evolve more on its political, rather than on its more mature formal constitutionalism today.[148] Yet, if constitutionalism is truly (all) about reform as Engström claims,[149] then what a better chance to realize that than with digitalization which also reaches speech regulation?

## 7 Deliberative Democracy and Public Sphere: Towards Peaceful Co-Existence?

At the origin, public sphere, as for example as *Habermas* viewed it, was more of an analytic category[150] in which the communicative freedom is institutionalized by a state constitution and regulated to become an administrative power.[151] To Habermas, ideally, a society is able to provide a model legal regime where the constitutional rights and principles accomplish the tasks that the law has provided to them.[152] Thus, there is both normative (political) society and citizen (social) element present.[153] Arguably, there must be a certain socializing for a democratic citizenship, hence a conflation between the political and the social.[154] Yet, while sociologically, the public sphere assumes a role in providing integration in society,[155] at the same time, however, the entire culture being democratic can only be a normative ideal.[156]

145 See Mutanen (2015), pp. 65–66.

146 Engström (2011), p. 25.

147 Engström (2011), pp. 13–14, referring to, inter alia, Walker (2009), p. 162, and Weiler (1999), pp. 226–234.

148 Engström (2011), pp. 21–22.

149 Engström 2011, p. 32.

150 Dahlgren (1991), p. 2.

151 Habermas (1997), p. 176.

152 Habermas (1997), p. 194.

153 Habermas J (1962) Strukturwandel der Öffentlichkeit.

154 Eriksen och Molander (red./eds.) (1997), pp. 133–134.

155 Susen (2011), p. 44, referring to Calhoun (1992), pp 1–48.

156 Balkin (2004), p. 46. See also Dahlgren (1991), p. 3.

From that perspective, the lack of real, authentic, public sphere, at least in its fullest extent, which Habermas[157] aspires, remains undone.[158]

While certainly the EU has had communications projects, from physical infrastructure, such as physical transports, like the TGV trains,[159] to telemarkets,[160] yet, indeed, from a policy standpoint, one can still ask whether there is still a lack of common public space. At least *Lepsius* has strongly voiced of a real lack in this regard.[161] Yet, not all writers share this view, and purport rather that the "common" discussions are taking place but at national level.[162] Then there can be some middle ground in that what exists is a "quasi-public."[163] Or one could also ask, do we have public spheres in plural? Are platforms the new townhalls?

To this, *Dahlgren* does not give answers but identifies four explanatory factors as to how we got where we currently stand, namely: (1) "crisis of the state," (2) "audience segmentation," (3) "new movements," and (4) "available communication technologies."[164] Dahlgren argues that not only is there the discrepancy between how the rulers and the ruled view the public sphere, but this has also taken place simultaneously when mass media gained their dominance in the public sphere.[165] Hence, one way to view this would be more as a shared process, rather than as institutions, but which all the same enables engagement with political life.[166]

To respond to some of these outcries, some EU Member States have introduced digital tools via which citizens can participate in the public debate.[167] This too is mostly at national level, albeit the EU has also introduced some new online tools.[168] However, it has been argued that no silver bullet to truth can be found from private or public actors, and that instead, only a diversified access and public debate will lead to transparency and ultimately, to the truth.[169]

*Voltmer* has argued that public spheres (in plural, as he writes) are today more intertwined with the civil society, which is global, rather than national. This has given salience into a separation of "polis" and "demos," he writes. Therefore, it has also been suggested that "publicness" as a notion would need to be looked at from

[157] Habermas (2011), pp. 59–61.

[158] Schwartz and Peifer (2017), p. 146.

[159] Svallhammar (1995), p. 9.

[160] Svallhammar (1995), p. 146.

[161] Eriksen och Molander (red.) (1997) Jürgen Habermas Diskurs, rätt och demokrati. Daidalos, p. 136.

[162] Mörä (2008), p. 97.

[163] Mylly (2009), p. 186.

[164] Dahlgren (1991), p. 14.

[165] Dahlgren (1991), p. 1.

[166] Crigler and Jensen (1991), p. 191.

[167] Lironi (2018), p. 3.

[168] See, e.g., https://ec.europa.eu/info/law/better-regulation/have-your-say.

[169] de Zayas (2018), p. 46.

the perspective of the new communication environments.[170] One point is that there is no common language or common tv across the entire Europe. Hence, there is also the issue of addressing multiple audiences. Yet, while that was the status quo perhaps a decade ago,[171] today discussions are also taking place in private platforms where the power concentrates. One positive aspect is the ability to engage in conversation with people around the world. Yet, on the flip side, there are different phenomena such as hate speech and even cyber bullying which have emerged.[172] This can also include identity issues, and for example new ways in which identification or relation building in groups can also take place.[173] The effects of which can be positive (as for instance a sense of belonging) but also negative (for example, spurring into incivilities).[174] There could, speculatively, even be a connection between collective identity and the legitimacy of power.[175]

Surely, technological properties can support participatory democracy, or "collaborative democracy," and thus foster economic growth, such as sharing economy in social networks. But also, paradoxically, there can be many ways in which there can be restrictions—from a social standpoint—to individuals.[176] From this angle, the protection of speech turns into protection of participation and inclusiveness, along with human dignity. Indeed, Habermas also wrote about (legal) structures of social life, which can also restrain some spontaneous form(s) of life too.[177] Economic rights can also be implicated, as we saw above.

Further, information technologies have social dimensions. This is something that sociology has looked at more in-depth, focusing for instance on the (psycho)social aspects of information technology.[178] Studies have been conducted on for instance the impact of social media on relationships in general,[179] on teens,[180] and on tweets.[181] Surely, social policy and mass communication interact in a variety of ways. This can include for instance the message flows convening patterns, consensus or giving meaning to opinions and beliefs, and their formation in different ways.[182]

[170] Volkmer (2015)

[171] Mörä (2008), p. 93.

[172] Foxman and Wolf (2013).

[173] Kaakinen (2018), p. 28.

[174] Kaakinen, p. 30 and Rains et al. (2017), pp. 163–178.

[175] Jyränki (2003), p. 73.

[176] Belshaw (1976), p. 163.

[177] Habermas (1986).

[178] Sundeep (1997), pp. 229–260.

[179] Baym (2010).

[180] Boyd (2014).

[181] Marwick and Boyd (2010), pp. 114–33.

[182] Gerbner (1967), p. 50.

Yet, with these (as many other open question), there can be differences between gender, age, and social groups.[183]

Thus, the role of media (vis-à-vis citizens) appears crucial. Yet, freedom of expression is bound to change with cultural changes too.[184] Traditionally, matters of public concern have been afforded a heightened protection. At the background, we can find the idea(l) of the media as "public watchdogs."[185] While today, medias are, arguably, one of the most important sources of *distrust* or *mistrust* for citizens. To illustrate, in a European wide survey, some two-thirds of the respondents indicated that they do not trust medias.[186] Nationally, for instance, two-thirds of French people consider social media sources "unreliable."[187] For example, finding reliable information online can appear tricky.[188] Yet, one must be cautious in generalizing, as this can also be generational. Also, many regional and local variants could be distilled, including between age groups.[189] Further, in a Eurobarometer study, one of the top three most agreed topics amongst the young was combating fake news.[190] To that, some like *Berset* has recommended direct democracy, education, individual critical thinking, and independent media. Yet, this is aggravated by phenomena such as amplification and echo-chambers.[191] *Shotter* has claimed that communications are shaped by social practices. Hence, his views can be associated with social constructivism, as speech being developed by social practices.[192]

At least sociological[193] issues (or legal sociology) in particular appear important not only to the extent that they can elucidate questions underpinning legal system but also because of its ability to provide a deeper and richer image of the human mind and subjective experiences, or act as a "cognitive background."[194] And surely, social media offer multitude ways of communicating and interacting with one another,

---

[183] See, e.g., Carlsson and Weibull (2018), p. 22 And Matikainen and Villi (2013), see, e.g., pp. 32 and 40.

[184] Nyyssönen (2006), p. 107.

[185] Case Lingens v. Austria, (8 July 1986), para 41, case Oberschlick v Austria (23 May 1991) para 58, case of Observer and Guardian v. the UK (26 November 1991) at 59b and case of Magyar Helsinki Bizottság v. Hungary (8 November 2016), para. 168. See also Thorgeirsdottir (2003).

[186] European Commission (2017a) Special Europbarometer 461: Designing Europe's future: Trust in institutions. Globalisation. Support for the euro, opinions about free trade and solidarity Report, p. 14.

[187] Présidentielles 2017: des élections sous influence? At http://www.informatiquenews.fr/presidentielles-2017-elections-influence-51385.

[188] Koskimaa (2001), p. 93.

[189] See, e.g., Nordicom (2012) Medietrender i Norden 2012. Nordicom.

[190] At http://ec.europa.eu/commfrontoffice/publicopinion/index.cfm/Survey/getSurveyDetail/instruments/FLASH/surveyKy/2163 , p. 5.

[191] Vos et Monnet (2018), pp. 20–22.

[192] Bayer and Shotter (1998). Also Shotter (1993).

[193] Cf. Paasilehto (1999), p. 103.

[194] Cotterrell (1998), especially p. 188, fn. 58, citing Professor Hubert Rottleuhner.

either as consumers or as content producers.[195] As problems have been raised a lack of knowledge and comprehension from the part of the technology field,[196] which leaves open whether everyone should know more about technology too.

## 8 Connecting the Dots

If speech is so much a social issue, where does the law fit in then? Some authors have argued that a good constitution can be "enough" to install stable social conditions.[197] However, some writers see that instead of a constitution, the multitude (plurality) of constitutions need to be acknowledged.[198] Alas, at constitutional level, amending the EU Treaties would essentially require unanimity[199] but that does not seem likely to interest all Member States. Although the result of the constitutional treaty would have allowed for more multispeed Europe, the way to get there does not necessarily seem that tempting.[200] But by adopting geometry variable, do we risk losing unity? There is a risk of political instability, vs. to weight in doing nothing. Of course, one could also think of stability as having (carrying) social value. Simultaneously, there is great potential for the EU to purport its values (via for instance uprooting hate speech), although this would mean limitations to the freedom of speech.[201]

Internationally, UNESCO has aimed to promote a view in which freedom of expression is one of the four pillars that knowledge societies should build upon.[202] In the EU too, perhaps with a slightly different angle, as we saw above with, for instance, Commissioner Jourová articulating on the need to promote digital literacy as part of the comprehensive approach. Hence, it does not seem a surprise that at national level, some writings have advocated for more closer ties between or towards the social realm; for instance, in supporting novel takes or hidden scientific needs, or increasing contacts and cooperation, as per a French perspective.[203]

Yet, from a more historical angle, the Roman law already contributed into the preservation of "the idea that law should play a role in the ordering of political and social relationships."[204] In 2001, the EU defined as good governance the principles

[195] Säntti and Säntti (2008), p. 14.

[196] Säntti and Säntti (2008), p. 19.

[197] Riker (1976), pp. 13–15.

[198] See Poiares Maduro (2003), pp. 74–102. And Tuori and Sankari (2010).

[199] Treaty establishing a Constitution for Europe, Article IV-443.

[200] Tiilikainen et al. (2005), pp. 16–17.

[201] Nuotio (2010), p. 19.

[202] UNESCO Building Knowledge Societies At https://en.unesco.org/themes/building-knowledge-societies.

[203] Mattelart et Stourdze (1985), p. 23.

[204] Berman (1983), p. 53.

of openness, participation, accountability, effectiveness, and coherence.[205] Yet, arguably, there needs to be democratic participation, not governance, to enable culture to be democratic as participation allows for both the self and the common to develop.[206] Some writers have proposed as solution to the constitutionalism crisis a "social dialogue" in Europe.[207] *Schulz* has brought about that it has been suggested that there could be a social right to communication.[208] *Neuvonen* has written about communicational fundamental right[209] which points very strongly to law (only). Also procedurally, one typically cannot proceed based on an aktio popularis, that is the personal rights of the person concerned need to be affected. Hence, e.g., in Germany the "eternity clause."[210] Hence, again, there is an (in-)direct connection to constitution. Moreover, these postures also seem to associate the discussion into the constitution and legitimacy too.

Hence, while information technologies enable new ways of news production, on the flip side, this hinges upon matters which are outside of its own field; that is, more of social and/or technological in nature.[211] *Franck* associated this to legitimacy or "democratic entitlement," as he calls it, in democracies, built upon constitutional parameters, a Lockean bargain of a social contract in terms of those representing the people and judges and an "inquisitive press."[212] From a sociological point view *Kessler,* who has looked at Luhmann, writes about the "emergence of territorial differentiations," taking the discussion (back) to the era without clear boundaries or borders[213] and where polycontextuality emerges from "functional differentiation."[214] This could be interesting from a social media standpoint. Another take would be to view the new online communities of speech as an "imagined international community."[215] This seems to fit into the narrative that some authors purport, arguing that a new global community is based not on nation states (*communitas communitatum*) but on individuals (*communitas hominum*).[216] However, before even going as far as conceiving social media (or an online platform) as a state on its own right, and to consider the elements of statehood,[217] any such entity would also need to exercise functions which are normally attributed to a state, such as

[205] European Commission (2001) White Paper: A European Governance. Brussels, 25.7.2001 COM (2001) 428 final.

[206] Balkin (2004), pp. 33–38.

[207] Christodoulidis (2008), p. 78.

[208] Schulz (2011), p. 247.

[209] Neuvonen (2014), p. 30.

[210] See also the German Constitution, Article 38.

[211] Anderson (2012), p. 1009.

[212] Franck (1992), p. 50.

[213] Kessler (2012), p. 83, referring to Luhmann (1997), p. 670.

[214] Kessler (2012), p. 85.

[215] Buchanan and Pahuja (2008), pp. 261, 271.

[216] Domingo (2012), p. 567.

[217] From public international law, see, e.g., case Clerget Cour d'appel de Paris, 5 novembre 1969.

setting up a legal framework, governing the administration, and exercising "all of the public" in that territory and under supervision[218] which seems relatively far from reality.

Yet, although one would not agree to see social media as forming new statehood, one can ask whether new social practices in social media will lead to an entirely novel (social) morality.[219] *Brown* and *Duguid* have noted that along with the rise of information age, there have been predictions on certain "endisms" for instance in terms of different medias, including politics or some traditional state-based authorities.[220] There is a need for (more) understanding of "the contribution of the social fabric" underscoring that the interaction is dynamic.[221] This seems very pertinent indeed. Yet, According to *Norros,* the effect(s) of technology can be seen twofold: as social mediation occurs towards technology (but) which users also impact with their choices.[222] There is also a particular task for each member to comprehend their role as part of a bigger community.[223] Further, along these lines, one could note what *Habermas* wrote about discourse and rules of discourse.[224] Yet, what are those online and how to ensure that those are respected? In some instances, they can be context dependent, which can render them tricky for national legislator to regulate. Partly, it is explained by the fact that some of these practices are relatively new and possibly transitory[225] in nature. Partly, not all citizens might view this similarly. One way to approach this is through a citizen-focused approach, that is, how do citizens view "publicness" or "public" in Europe[226] or, how journalists view it.[227] For citizens, participation can be important in addressing the democracy deficit in the EU.[228] For journalists, it can question not only about securing one's job (vs. automated news production) but also the quality of work. Arguably, no matter how democratized information (and its usages) may be online, quality in journalism is not something it can replace.[229] We can even note research results that indicate a decrease of published journals in its study on the state of democracy.[230] Yet, overall, although this is not simply a legislative or constitutional matter but a social one, legislative moratoriums must be avoided.

---

[218] Stahn (2001), p. 549.

[219] Eriksson (1992), p. 188.

[220] Brown and Duguid (2000), p. 16.

[221] Brown and Duguid (2000), pp. 49–52.

[222] Norros (1996), p. 159.

[223] Berman (2005), p. 485, 516.

[224] Kapulainen and Rudanko (2012), p. 180.

[225] See, e.g., Banakar and Travers (2013), p. 313.

[226] See Sassi (2008), pp. 71–90.

[227] Mörä (2008), pp. 91–114.

[228] Kumpula (2006), p. 105.

[229] Council of Europe (2018) State of democracy human rights and the rule of law role of institutions threats to institutions 2018 Annual report from the Secretary General p. 29.

[230] See Berggruen Institute (2020), p. 18.

# 9 Conclusions

We can argue that certain developments, notably related to digitalization, continue to have such sweeping impact that new measures are needed in protecting speech in the digital era. In that, several constitutional and social dimensions emerge. As we noted above, the regulatory and policy standpoints are complex. Given the cross-border nature of the new media environments, but also the considerable weight of the issues at stake, common policy discussions should not be avoided. In that, the reach of the recently introduced EU measures can remain limited without a constitutional and social understanding of the matters at hand. Thus, a wider outlook and analysis of these topics, including on the notions of constitutional law, democracy, territoriality, and unity is needed to complement the law and the viewpoints. Ultimately in these matters, there are also social causes and consequences, in terms of how speech and the law craft and (de-)construct social order. The law cannot replace these, but it can protect the interests at stake.

# References


Ananny M (2015) Toward an ethics of algorithms: convening, observation, probability, and timeliness. Sci Technol Human Values:1–25

Anderson CW (2012) Towards a sociology of computational and algorithmic journalism. New Media Soc 15(7):1005–1021. https://doi.org/10.1177/1461444812465137

Anderson G (2005) Constitutional rights after globalisation. Hart Publishing, Great Britain

Balkin JM (2004) Digital Speech and Democratic Culture: A Theory of Freedom of Expression for the Information Society. Faculty Scholarship Series. Paper 240

Banakar R, Travers M (2013) Law and social theory, 2nd edn. Hart Publishing

Bayer BM, Shotter J (eds) (1998) Inquiries in social construction: reconstructing the psychological subject: bodies, practices and technologies. SAGE Publications Ltd, London. https://doi.org/10.4135/9780857026019

Baym NK (2010) Personal connections in the digital age. Polity, Cambridge

Bell E (2016) Facebook is eating the world. Columbia Journalism Review. March 7, 2016

Belshaw CS (1976) The Sorcerer's apprentice an anthropology of public policy. Pergamon Press Inc, New York

Berman HJ (1983) Law and revolution: the formation of the western legal tradition. Harvard University Press

Berman PS (2005) From international law to law and globalization. Colum J Transnatl Law 43:485

Besson S (2008) How International is the European Legal Order? Retracing Tuori's Steps in the Exploration of European Legal Pluralism. No Foundations 5 for Kaarlo Tuori

Bischof G, Pelinka A, Gehler M (2002) Austria in the European Union. Contemporary Austrian Studies Volume 10. Transaction Publishers

Boyd D (2014) It's complicated: the social lives of networked teens. Yale University Press, New Haven. http://dl.acm.org/citation.cfm?id=2584525

Brown JS, Duguid P (2000) The social life of information. Harvard Business School Press

Brückmann R (2008) Kindergarten? The Interaction between the German Constitutional Court and the European Court of Human Rights. Finnish yearbook of international law, vol XVII 2006. Martinus Nijhoff Publishers, Leiden/Boston

Buchanan R, Pahuja S (2008) Law, nation and (imagined) international communities. In: Krisnaswamy R, Hawley JC (eds) The Postcolonial and the Global Minnesota 2008
Carlsson U, Weibull L (eds) (2018) Freedom of expression in the digital media culture a study of public opinion in Sweden. Nordicom
Chalmers D, Hadjiemmanuil C, Monti C, Tomkins A (2006) European Union law. Cambridge University Press
Christodoulidis E (2008) European constitutionalism: The improbability of self-determination. No Foundations 5 for Kaarlo Tuori
Cornils K (1999) Internetissä tehtyjen rikosten paikallistaminen. Lakimies 5/1999
Cotterrell R (1998) Why must legal ideas be interpreted sociologically? J Law Soc 25(2) June
Crigler AN, Jensen KB (1991) Discourses on politics: talking about public issues in the United States and Denmark. In: Dahlgren P, Sparks C (eds) Communication and citizenship – journalism and the public sphere. Routledge, reprint 1997
Curran J (1991) Rethinking the media as a public sphere. In: Dahlgren P, Sparks C (eds) Communication and citizenship – Journalism and the public sphere. Routledge, reprint 1997
Dahlgren P (1991) Introduction. In: Dahlgren P, Sparks C (eds) Communication and citizenship – journalism and the public sphere. Routledge, reprint 1997
de Zayas A (2018) Fake News, Fake history, Fake law. UN Special Magazine. Juin
Domingo R (2012) The new global human community. Chicago J Int Law 12(2):567
Eek H (1953) Freedom of Information as a project of international legislation A-B Lundequistska Bokhandeln, Uppsala
Engström V (2011) International organizations, constitutionalism, and reform. In: Klabbers J (ed) Finnish yearbook of international law. Hart, Oxford
Eriksen EO och Molander A (red.) (1997) Jürgen Habermas Diskurs, rätt och demokrati. Daidalos
Eriksson LE (1992) Kritik, Moral och Rätt, Offentligrättsliga institutionen. Helsingfors universitet
Franck TM (1992) The emerging right to democratic governance. Am J Int Law 86(1):50
Garcon M (1963) L'avocat et la Morale. Buchet/Chastel
Gerbner G (1967) Mass media and human communication theory. In: Dance FEX (ed) Human communication theory Holt. Rinehart & Winston
Guggenberg N (2018) How not to regulate social networks WWU Münster Newsportal March 14, 2018 at https://www.uni-muenster.de/news/view.php?cmdid=9436. Last accessed on November 19, 2020
Habermas J (1986) Legitimation crisis (trans: McCarthy T). Heinemann, London
Habermas J (1997) Facts and norms contributions to a discourse theory of law and democracy. Polity Press
Habermas J (2011) Zur Verfassung Europas 66 (2011)
Hardt H (2001) Social theories of the Press: constituents of Communication Research, 1840s to 1920s, 2nd edn. Rowman & Littlefield Publishers, Inc. (Critical Media Studies: Institutions, Politics, and Culture)
Hirshman EC, Holbrook MB (1992) Postmodern consumer research the study of consumption as text. Sage Publications
Hoikka M (2006) Viestinnän moniarvoisuus eurooppalaisena oikeusperiaatteena. In Viestintäoikeuden vuosikirja 2005 Kuka valvoo vapautta Helsingin yliopiston oikeustieteellisen tiedekunnan julkaisuja. Helsinki
Hutchison D (1999) Media policy an introduction. Blackwell Publishers
Hyttinen T, Tapani J (2018) Rikoksen ja rangaistuksen äärellä. Helsingin yliopiston oikeustieteellisen tiedekunnan julkaisuja, Helsinki
Ipsen HP (1954) Gleichheit. In: Neumann FL, Nipperdey HC, Scheuner U (eds) Die Grundrechte: Handbuch der Theorie und Praxis der Grundrechte. Band 2: Die Freiheitsrechte in Deutschland. Berlin, pp 111–198
Jenkins H (1992) Textual poachers: television fans & participatory culture. Routledge
Jenkins H (2008) Convergence culture: where old and new media collide. Revised edn. New York University Press, New York

Jyränki A (2003) Valta ja Vapaus valtiosääntöoikeuden yleisiä kysymyksiä. Kolmas laajennettu laitos. Helsinki

Kaakinen M (2018) Disconnected online: a social psychological examination of online hate. Dissertation, University of Tampere, Tampere

Kapulainen P, Rudanko M (2012) Kriittinen diskurssianalyysi lainsäädännön tutkimuksessa. Business Law Forum, Lakimiesliiton kustannus

Kessler O (2012) World society, social differentiation and time. Int Stud Q 6(1)

Koskimaa R (2001) Kotikirjastojen uudet vaatteet. In: Jussila R, Kalalahti A, Rautoja S (toim./eds) Tieto ja kirja. Suomen tietokirjailijat ry 2001

Kumpula A (2006) Kun oikeustiede ei riitä: Ympäristötiedon rakentuminen ja ympäristöoikeus. In Niemi-Kiesiläinen J et al (eds) Oikeuden tekstit diskursseina. Suomalaisen lakimiesyhdistyksen julkaisuja E-sarja no 13

Lironi E (2018): Harnessing digital tools to revitalize European democracy Carnegie Europe, November 2018 at https://carnegieeurope.eu/2018/11/28/harnessing-digital-tools-to-revitalize-european-democracy-pub-77806

Livingstone S (2003) The changing nature of audiences: from the mass audience to the interactive media user. In: Valdivia A (ed) Companion to media studies. Blackwell Publishing, Oxford. http://eprints.lse.ac.uk/417/

Mäenpää O (1996) Eurooppalainen hallinto-oikeus – Lähtökohtia ja perusteita. Lakimiesliiton kustannus, KATTI 26, Helsinki

Marwick AE, Boyd D (2010) I Tweet Honestly, I Tweet passionately: Twitter users, context Collapse, and the imagined audience. New Media Soc 13(1):114–133. https://doi.org/10.1177/1461444810365313

Matikainen J, Villi M (2013) Mobiilit mediasisällöt Sisältöjen tuottaminen, jakelu ja kulutus sosiaalisessa mediassa. Viestinnän tutkimuskeskus CRC, Sosiaalitieteiden laitos, Helsingin yliopisto

Mörä T (2008) Julkisuuden ihanteet ja journalismin arki: Brysselin -kirjeenvaihtajat EU-koneiston ja kansalaisten välissä. In: Karppinen K, Nieminen H, Mörä T (toim./eds.) (2008) Onko Eurooppa olemassa? Näkökulmia Eurooppalaiseen julkisuuteen ja demokratiaan. Gaudeamus, Helsinki University Press

Mujić Z, Yazici D, Stone M (eds) (2012) Freedom of Expression on the Internet A study of legal provisions and practices related to freedom of expression, the free flow of information and media pluralism on the Internet in OSCE participating States. OSCE

Mutanen A (2015) Towards a Pluralistic Constitutional Understanding of State Sovereignty in the European union? The Concept, Regulation and Constitutional Practice of Sovereignty in Finland and Certain Other EU Member States. Dissertation. University of Helsinki, Faculty of Law

Mylly T (2009) Intellectual Property and European Economic Constitutional Law – The Trouble with Private Informational Power. Publications of IPR University Center. Gummerus Kirjapaino Oy. Vaajakoski

Neuman S (2018) France's Macron says he wants law to combat fake news. January 4, 2018 at https://www.npr.org/sections/thetwo-way/2018/01/04/575580790/frances-macron-says-he-wants-law-to-combat-fake-news?t=1611048976370

Neuvonen R (2012) Sananvapauden sääntely Suomessa. Lakimiesliiton kustannus. Hansaprint. Vantaa

Neuvonen R (2014) Eurooppalaisen sananvapauden ideaali ja todellisuus. In: Tiilikka P (toim./ed) Sananvapaus puntarissa. Viestintäoikeuden vuosikirja 2013. Helsingin yliopiston oikeustieteellisen tiedekunnan julkaisuja

Nieminen H (2008) Eurooppalainen julkisuus tutkimuksen kohteena. In: Karppinen K, Nieminen H, Mörä T (toim./eds) Onko Eurooppa olemassa? Näkökulmia Eurooppalaiseen julkisuuteen ja demokratiaan. Gaudeamus, Helsinki University Press

Norros L (1996) System disturbances as springboard for development of operators' expertise. In: Engström Y, Middleton D (eds) Cognition and communication at work. Cambridge University Press

Nuotio K (2010) Eurooppalaisen integraation uusi painopiste: Vapauden, turvallisuuden ja oikeuden Eurooppa. In: Nuotio K, Malkki L (toim./eds) Vapauden, turvallisuuden ja oikeuden Eurooppa, Helsingin yliopiston oikeustieteellisen tiedekunnan julkaisuja, Forum Iuris

Nyyssönen T (2006) Visuaalinen viestintä sananvapauskäsitysten haasteena. In Viestintäoikeuden vuosikirja 2005 Kuka valvoo vapautta Helsingin yliopiston oikeustieteellisen tiedekunnan julkaisuja. Helsinki 2006

Ojanen T (1998) The European way the structure of national court obligation under EC law. Gummerus. Saarijärvi

Paasilehto S (1999) Legal cultural obstacles to the harmonisation of European law. In: Heiskanen V, Kulovesi K (eds) Function and future of European law. Publications of the faculty of law. University of Helsinki, Helsinki

Pallero J, Pirkova E (2020) 26 recommendations on content governance - a guide for lawmakers, regulators, and company policy makers. Access Now

Paukku E (2006a) Sananvapaus ja joukkoviestinnän sääntely EU:n oikeudessa. In: Viestintäoikeuden vuosikirja 2005 Kuka valvoo vapautta Helsingin yliopiston oikeustieteellisen tiedekunnan julkaisuja. Helsinki (Paukku 2006a)

Paukku E (2006b) Eurooppalaisen mediapolitiikan ja -sääntelyn lähtökohtia. In: Viestintäoikeuden vuosikirja 2005 Kuka valvoo vapautta Helsingin yliopiston oikeustieteellisen tiedekunnan julkaisuja. Helsinki (Paukku 2006b)

Paukku E (2007) Eurooppalaisen mediapolitiikan ja -sääntelyn lähtökohtia. In: Miten vapaa sana. Viestintäoikeuden vuosikirja 2006. Helsingin yliopiston oikeustieteellisen tiedekunnan julkaisuja

Pere T (2015) Suojattu, suvaittu vai sanktioitu Sananvapaus. Dissertation, Helsinki

Pickard V (2017) The Big Picture: Misinformation Society 11.28.2017 at http://www.publicbooks.org/the-big-picture-misinformation-society/

Pihlajarinne T (2012) Nykyaikainen internetviestintä ja tallennuspalvelut – kuka saa vastuuvapauden. In: Vastaako joku viestistä. Viestintäoikeuden vuosikirja 2011, Helsingin yliopiston oikeustieteellisen tiedekunnan julkaisuja

Poiares Maduro M (2003) Europe and the constitution: what if this is as good as it gets? In: Weiler JHH, Wind M (eds) European constitution beyond the state. Cambridge University Press

Postigo M (2013) A political-philosophical analysis of the EU legal order and European integration: federal and cosmopolitan perspectives. In: Neergaard UB, Nielsen R (eds) European legal method – towards a new legal realism. DJØF

Rains SA, Kenski KM, Coe K, Harwood JT (2017) Incivility and political identity on the internet: intergroup factors as predictors of incivility in discussions of news online. J Comput-Mediated Commun 22(4):163–178. https://doi.org/10.1111/jcc4.12191

Raitio J (2009) Tavarakaupan rajoitusperusteet, yleinen, etu ja tilanneherkkyys - mitä uutta. Defensor Legis, 2/2009

Rasmussen H (2007) Denmark's waning constitutionalism. In: Albi A, Ziller J (eds) The European constitution and national constitutions - ratification and beyond. Kluwer Law International, The Netherlands

Riker WH (1976) Comments on Vincent Ostrom's Paper. Public Choice 27:13–15

Rosendahl R (2007) Joukkoviestin oikeudellisena käsitteenä. In: Miten vapaa sana. Viestintäoikeuden vuosikirja 2006. Helsingin yliopiston oikeustieteellisen tiedekunnan julkaisuja. Helsinki

Saarenpää A (1995) Tieto, suoja ja byrokratia – näkökohtia suomalaisen tietosuojan kehityksestä ja tulkinnoista. In: Oikeuskirja. Lapin Yliopiston Oikeustieteiden tiedekunta

Salminen J (2010) Yksityisten oikeudellisen suojelun mahdollisuuden rajat. In: Nuotio K, Malkki L (eds) Vapauden, turvallisuuden ja oikeuden Eurooppa. Helsingin yliopiston oikeustieteellisen tiedekunnan julkaisuja, Forum Iuris

Säntti R, Säntti P (2008) Tiedosta, määrittele ja hyödynnä. In: Aaltonen-Ogbeide T, Saastamoinen P, Rainio H, Vartiainen T (toim. / eds) Silmät auki sosiaaliseen mediaan. Eduskunnan tulevaisuusvaliokunta 2008
Sassi S (2008) Julkisuus kansalaisten silmin. In: Karppinen K, Nieminen H, Mörä T (toim/eds) julkisuuteen ja demokratiaan. Gaudeamus, Helsinki University Press
Schmauch M (2014) Tryck- och yttrandefrihetsgrundlagarna och EU-rätten —en kommentar till en kommentar. Svensk Juristtidning (SvJT) at https://svjt.se/svjt/2014/520
Schulz MS (2011) Values and the conditions of global communication. Curr Sociol 59(2):Monograph 1, March 2011
Schwartz PM, Peifer K-N (2017) Transatlantic data privacy law. Georgetown Law J 106:115
Shaw MN (2003) International Law. Cambridge University Press
Siebert F, Siebert FT, Peterson T, Peterson TB, Schramm W (1956) Four theories of the press: the authoritarian, libertarian, social responsibility, and soviet communist concepts of what the press should be and do. University of Illinois Press
Stahn C (2001) Constitution without a state? Kosovo under the United Nations constitutional framework for self-government. Leiden J Int Law 14(3)
Stirn B (2008) Les sources constitutionnelles du droit administrative. 6ème edition, L.G.D.J
Sundeep S (1997) Implementation of information technology: a time-space perspective. Org Stud 18(2):229–260. https://doi.org/10.1177/017084069701800203
Susen S (2011) Critical notes on Habermas's theory of the public sphere. Sociol Anal 5(1)
Suthersanen U (2001) A comparative review of database protection in the European Union and United States. In: Dessemontet F, Gani R (eds) Creative ideas for intellectual property, CEDIDAC, Fondation pour le Centre du droit de l'entreprise de l'Université de Lausanne
Svallhammar S (ed) (1995) Kommunikationernas Europa. YMER. Svenska Sällskapet för Antropologi and Geographi
Tiilikainen T, Helander P, Heliskoski J (2005) Perustuslaki Edita Helsinki
Tiilikka P (2012) Päätoimittajan vastuu yleisön tuottamasta verkkosisällöstä. Lakimies 1/2012
Tuori K (2013) The relationality of European constitution(s). In: Neergaard UB, Nielsen R (eds) European legal method – towards a new legal realism. DJØF
van Dijk P, van Hoof GJH (1990) Theory and practice on the European convention on human rights, 2nd edn. Kluwer
Vīķe-Freiberga V, Däubler-Gmelin H, Hammersley B, Poiares Pessoa Maduro LM (2013) Report of the High Level Group on Media Freedom and Pluralism, A free and pluralistic media to sustain European democracy
Volkmer I (2015) Rethinking 'public service' in a globalized digital ecology opendemocracy. https://www.opendemocracy.net/ourbeeb/ingrid-volkmer/rethinking-'public-service'-in-globalized-digital-ecology/
Vos A et Monnet V (2018) La Mécanique du Mensonge. Campus News. Magazine Scientifique de l'Université de Genève n 133 Juin 2018
Weatherill S (2006) Cases and materials on EU law, 8th edn. Oxford University Press

## *Reports, Studies*

Berggruen Institute (2020) Renewing democracy in the digital age
Calhoun C (1992) Introduction: Habermas and the public sphere. In: Calhoun C (ed) Habermas and the public sphere. MIT Press, Cambridge, pp 1–48
CoE (2018) State of democracy human rights and the rule of law role of institutions threats to institutions 2018 Annual report from the Secretary General
Council of Europe (2018) Annual report from the Secretary General

Council of Europe, European Court of Human Rights, European Data Protection Supervisor, and European Union Agency for Fundamental Rights (2018) Handbook of European Data Protection Law

Council of Europe Recommendation CM/Rec(2018)2 on the roles and responsibilities of internet intermediaries

Daten Ethik Kommission (2019) Opinion of the Data Ethics Commission. Data Ethics Commission of the Federal Government Federal Ministry of the Interior, Building and Community Berlin, 2019

Draft Recommendation of the Committee of Ministers to Member States on the Roles and Responsibilities of Internet Intermediaries, finalized by the MSI-NET on 19 September 2017

Draft Report on media pluralism and media freedom in the European Union (2017/2209(INI)) Committee on Civil Liberties, Justice and Home Affairs Rapporteur: Barbara Spinelli, 2017/2209

ECRI General Policy Recommendation N°15 on Combating Hate Speech - adopted on 8 December 2015

Eurobarometers 64/2005 and 251/2006

European Commission (2001) White Paper: A European Governance. Brussels, 25.7.2001 COM (2001) 428 final

European Commission (2017a) Special Europbarometer 461: Designing Europe's future: Trust in institutions. Globalisation. Support for the euro, opinions about free trade and solidarity Report

European Commission (2017b) White Paper on the Future of Europe: Reflections and Scenarios for the EU27 by 2025

European Commission (2018) A multi-dimensional approach to disinformation. Report of the independent High Level Group on fake news and online disinformation March

Foxman AH, Wolf C (2013) Viral hate: containing its spread on the internet. St. Martin's Press

General Secretariat of the Council (2017) Taking forward the Strategic Agenda 18-month Programme of the Council (1 July 2017 - 31 December 2018)

Hearing of Commissioner-designate Věra Jourová at the European Parliament 7 October 2019 (AFCO- and LIBE- committees)

Luhmann N (1997) Die Gesellschaft die Gesellschaft. Frankfurt am Main, p 670

Mattelart A, Stourdze Y (1985) Technology, culture and communication a report to the French minister of research and industry. Elsevier Science Publishers B.V, Holland

Media pluralism and democracy: Outcomes of the 2016 Annual Colloquium on Fundamental Rights

Nordicom (2012) Medietrender i Norden 2012. Nordicom

OSCE Report 2012 'Freedom of Expression on the Internet'

Report on concentration and pluralism in the media in the European Union (2007/2253(INI))

Shotter J (1993) Conversational realities. Sage Publications

Teubner G (2004a) Global private regimes: neo-spontaneous law and dual constitution of autonomous sectors? In: Ladeur K-H (ed) Public Governance in the age of globalisation. Ashgate, Aldershot, pp 71–87

Teubner G (2004b) Societal constitutionalism: alternatives to state-centred constitutional theory? In: Joerges C, Sand IJ, Teubner G (eds) Constitutional and transnational governance. Hart, Oxford, pp 3–28

Thorgeirsdottir H (2003) Journalism worthy of the name: a human rights perspective on freedom within the press. Lund

Tuori K, Sankari S (2010) The many constitutions of Europe. Ashgate, Oxford

UNESCO Building Knowledge Societies At https://en.unesco.org/themes/building-knowledge-societies Last accessed on January 16, 2021

Walker N (2009) Reframing EU constitutionalism. In: Dunoff J, Trachtman J (eds) Ruling the world?: Constitutionalism, international law, and global governance. Cambridge University Press, pp 149–177

Weatherill S (2011) The limits of legislative harmonisation - ten years after Tobacco advertising. German Law J 12(3–4):850–851

Weiler J (1999) The constitution of Europe: "Do the new clothes have an emperor?" and other essays on European integration. Cambridge University Press, pp 226–234

**Anna Aurora Wennäkoski** (L.L.M., M.Sc.) is a Senior Specialist at the Ministry of Transports and Communication in Finland. She has over 10 years of professional experience from various legal positions in Finland, France, and the United States. Her research interests include European law, legal theory, freedom of expression, First Amendment, data protection privacy law, and data law.

# Who Watches the Watchmen? Social Media and Election Securitisation

**Dmitry Kurnosov**

## Contents



**Abstract** In the wake of the 2020 presidential election, incumbent Donald Trump voiced dubious allegations of vote fraud. In response to that, social media giants Twitter and Facebook made a dramatic step of attaching corrective statements to the U.S. president's posts. By doing so, they highlighted their power over core political speech. In his 2014 article 'Old-School/New-School Speech Regulation', influential American legal scholar Jack Balkin argued that today speech is often suppressed by private actors, controlling the digital infrastructure, rather than directly by governments.

In a follow-up article 'Free Speech in Algorithmic Society', Balkin suggests that there is a triangular relationship between governments, corporations and end-users. My contribution will discuss this triangulation in the context of electoral speech. In recent years, the threat of foreign interference in elections became a widely discussed issue in established democracies. These discussions specifically highlighted the role of social media. They have also led to an increasingly aggressive policing of election-related content on major platforms such as Facebook and Twitter.

This chapter suggests that securitisation of elections in established democracies occurs primarily as cooperation between private actors and governments. The apparent exclusion of end-users is a worrying tendency. It obscures the distinction between established democracies and competitive authoritarian regimes, ultimately

D. Kurnosov (✉)
University of Helsinki, Helsinki, Finland
e-mail: dmitry.kurnosov@helsinki.fi



S. Hindelang, A. Moberg (eds.), *YSEC Yearbook of Socio-Economic Constitutions 2021*, YSEC Yearbook of Socio-Economic Constitutions (2022) 2021: 175–196,
https://doi.org/10.1007/16495_2022_39, Published online: 8 April 2022

undermining the very democratic legitimacy that needs to be secured. I argue that, given the role of social media companies in the current environment, their obligations go beyond the traditional notions of corporate social responsibility. These companies have de facto assumed the role of a regulator effecting election securitisation in online speech. I suggest that such (self-) regulation could only be proportionate, if internationally recognised standards of free elections are considered.

## 1 Introduction

'Who watches the Watchmen?'—goes the question first asked in Ancient Rome[1] and repeated in contemporary culture to the point of ubiquity. Yet, I believe that it is still worth asking, given the changing constellations of power. Social media companies went from humble beginnings to becoming a key communication space for billions of people. With this power comes the responsibility to police that space from the various harmful content that some of those billions inevitably produce or share.

It has been claimed that the development of the Internet as a communication space has been helped by the immunity from responsibility for the content distributed by users, provided there was an opportunity to take published content down. Examples of such immunity include Section 230 introduced by the Communication Decency Act in the United States, and Article 12 of the Directive 2000/31/EC in the European Union.

However, this approach is increasingly challenged by how social media companies operate, and by how they are regulated. Starting from the 2016 United States presidential election, Internet giants such as Facebook, Twitter and Google take an increasingly aggressive approach towards policing political speech, particularly during electoral campaigns. This tendency culminated in the wake of the subsequent quadrennial American election. First, Twitter and Facebook made a dramatic step of attaching corrective statements to the posts by then-President Donald Trump on respective platforms. Then, following 6 January 2021 in Washington D.C., the President's accounts were blocked. These steps have highlighted the dramatic power that Internet giants hold over core political speech in a contemporary political arena. The power is enabled by a high degree of concentration of market power in the hands of the few companies. Thus, should one of the giants exercise the power to banish a speaker, he or she will be denied access to a large share of their audience. The constellation of these factors has prompted U.S. Supreme Court justice Clarence Thomas to note that '(w)e will soon have no choice but to address how our legal

[1] 'Quis custodiet ipsos custodes?', Satire VI, lines 347–348.

doctrines apply to highly concentrated, privately owned information infrastructure such as digital platforms'.[2]

Back in 2014, influential U.S. legal scholar Jack Balkin questioned[3] if that situation meant that the previous focus on direct government action was no longer relevant. In his opinion, the extent of control by private actors over online speech has made them the principal gatekeepers. Governments, on their part, rely on private controls to indirectly suppress problematic speech.[4] Balkin's argument is further strengthened by the tendency known as 'data extractivism'.[5] Not only social media companies occupy a dominant market position, but they were able to do so through a concerted effort to ensure a continuous data flow from end-users.[6] This effort can have social and political impacts. A recent study has demonstrated that social media algorithms affects the behaviour of politically active end-users.[7] Specifically the algorithms encourage expressions of outrage by providing immediate positive feedback and enabling end-users to cocoon themselves in ideologically homogeneous groups.[8] The online outrage may have negative real-world consequences, deepening political polarisation and even leading to violence.[9] Thus, the 'who watches the watchmen' paradox becomes even more profound. Those entrusted with preventing online harms may be at the same time (at least inadvertently) encouraging those harms.

In his follow-up 2018 article,[10] Balkin contoured a triangular relationship between governments, corporations, and end-users. My contribution will discuss this triangulation in the context of political speech during electoral periods. While there is ample discussion[11] of the general nature of the triangular relation, so far legal literature has rarely touched upon its impact on elections. However, freedom of speech is one of the cornerstones of free and fair elections as defined in global[12] and

[2] Biden v. Knight First Amendment Institute, Thomas J., concurring.

[3] Balkin (2014), p. 2304.

[4] Balkin's approach here aligns with authors noting the tendency of governments to outsource certain functions to private actors. See, for example, Verkuil (2007).

[5] 'Data centered economies foster extractive models of resource exploitation, the violation of human rights, cultural exclusion, and ecocide. Data extractivism assumes that everything is a data source'. Ricaurte (2019).

[6] Morozov et al. (2016).

[7] Brady et al. (2021).

[8] Ibid.

[9] Finkel et al. (2020).

[10] Balkin (2018), p. 1175.

[11] See, for instance, Klonick (2018), Mulligan (2016), Richards (2015), Kreimer (2006).

[12] 'Freedom of expression, assembly and association are essential conditions for the effective exercise of the right to vote and must be fully protected', Human Rights Committee, General Comment 25 (57).

regional[13] human rights law. While some social media companies do acknowledge the importance of human rights instruments in certain contexts (such as the mandate of their oversight institutions), they do not apply them consistently. Therefore, I believe that my contribution will address an important gap in the literature.

The goal of the chapter is to develop theory proposed by Balkin in relation to operation of social media companies as gatekeepers and to apply it to political speech during election periods. To do so, it will address the issue of election securitisation that affects attitudes towards elections in different types of political regimes. In the decades following the Second World War, it was commonplace to divide countries into democracies and non-democracies. Yet, the dividing line has become increasingly vague during the 1990s and 2000s.[14] Although few governments were now ready to portray themselves as undemocratic, there were many more whose commitment to the democratic principle left much to be desired. Their leaders relied on elections to claim legitimacy but were not ready to give up power because of losing at polls. This tendency has prompted theoretical discussions in the political science scholarship. Following these discussions, scholars now distinguish competitive authoritarianism as a type of political regime.[15] Compared to 'conventional' authoritarians, their competitive colleagues do hold elections, but deny opposition a practical chance of winning by denying it a level playing field.

Given that this structural unfairness is a key feature of such regimes, it comes as no surprise that competitive authoritarians pioneered the idea of treating elections as a part of national security. However, recently the threat of foreign interference in elections became a widely discussed issue in established democracies too. These discussions specifically highlighted the role of social media. The high-profile Special Counsel investigation in the United States has led to an inditement of a Russian-based 'Internet Research Agency' for 'interfering with the U.S. political and electoral processes'. In the wake of the investigation, social media companies have taken an increasingly aggressive approach to policing election-related content in established democracies. This approach appears to culminate in long-term[16] removal of Donald Trump from various social media platforms.

Without questioning the rationale for election securitisation, my chapter argues that it should be more nuanced in the context of social media platforms. The oversight bodies of the social media companies have already noticed the tension between human rights instruments. This tension can affect the ability of voters to make an informed opinion about elections, undermining democratic processes. I

---

[13] 'Democratic elections are not possible without respect for human rights, in particular freedom of expression and of the press', Code of Good Practice in Electoral Matters, Organization for Security and Cooperation in Europe and the Venice Commission (2002).

[14] Møller and Skaaning (2010).

[15] Levitsky and Way (2010).

[16] Facebook Oversight Board has questioned the indefinite character of Mr. Trump's suspension from the platform, prompting the social media company to subject it to regular reviews. See Case decision 2021-001-FB-FBR of 5 May 2021.

suggest that election securitisation on social media could be made more proportionate by integrating internationally recognised electoral standards.

The chapter will proceed in three parts. Section 2 will discuss the two works of Balkin and their implications for the regulation of political speech on social media during election periods. Section 3 charts the history of election securitisation and its implications for different types of political regimes. It will also tackle the effects of election securitisation on social media in electoral contexts. Section 4 is going to analyse to what extent the election-related policies of major social media platforms currently align with the internationally recognised electoral standards. It will also suggest how the two can be brought closer.

## 2 The State of Social Media Triangulation

We used to take for granted that censorship was something emanating from the authorities. The figure of censor in the popular imagination meant a government agent exercising 'prior restraint', that is preventing a particular publication. Alternatively, government censorship can suppress a publication already in circulation. Throughout twentieth century government authorities in most countries generally held sway over the media landscape. Thus, the big legal stories of the era involved media outlets battling the governments that sought to prevent the publication of particular documents (the Pentagon papers case) or punish a particular outlet for a publication (New York Times v. Sullivan case). The audio-visual media was often subject of tighter controls, given both the scarcity of broadcasting frequencies and its perceived larger effect on the audience. In some cases, states maintained monopoly on television broadcasting while in others access to broadcasting was regulated to ensure the diversity of media outlets. The rapid development of Internet in 1990s and 2000s coupled with a trend towards deregulation of radio and television markets has changed this equilibrium. Consistent with Marshall McLuhan's maxim that 'the medium is the message', the early Internet seemed to revolutionise access to information and its dissemination. Now, instead of media outlets and professional journalists, ordinary end-users seemed to be empowered. The World Wide Web has brought their costs of access and dissemination to practically zero.[17] Faced with the radical democratisation of media landscape, authorities sought tools to bring it back under control. An early example of such efforts was the Section 230 of the Communication Decency Act in the United States, which absolved network infrastructure companies from responsibility for user-generated content, clarifying that they were not to be treated as publishers of the 'traditional' media. At the same time, this

[17] The justices of the U.S. Supreme Court were quick to note this, opining that '. . .(t)hrough the use of chat rooms, any person with a phone line can become a town crier with a voice that resonates farther than it could from any soapbox. Through the use of Web pages, mail exploders, and newsgroups, the same individual can become a pamphleteer'. Reno v. American Civil Liberties Union (1997).

provision shielded web hosts from responsibility for the act of removing user-generated content. The norm proved remarkably resilient. The only significant changes occurred in 2018, requiring infrastructure owners to remove particular types of objectionable content. The norm has also proved an example for regulators in other jurisdictions. For instance, an analogous provision was introduced in the European Union as part of the Directive 2000/31/EC.

This 'Good Samaritan' clause was intended to incentivise self-regulation in a new seemingly chaotic environment. However, the environment itself would soon change dramatically. With the advent of social media in the late 2000s, the role of intermediaries became ever more prominent. Billions of users became dependent on them both for accessing and distributing information. In his 2014 article 'Old School/New School Speech Regulation' Harvard Law School Professor Jack Balkin has argued that this situation has engendered a new reality when it comes to speech regulation. 'In the second decade of the twenty-first century, the most powerful media companies are platforms like Google and Facebook. These platforms are not primarily designed to publish what the platform owner creates. Instead they create opportunities for end users to publish (Blogger, Tumblr, Twitter), send email and private messages (Gmail, Yahoo! Mail), upload content (YouTube, Pinterest), and share content (Facebook); and they make it easy for end users to find content created by others (Google, Bing)'.[18] Therefore, from the standpoint of a government it made sense to target this infrastructure to suppress undesirable speech in a form of 'collateral censorship'.[19] Balkin argued that governments were precisely doing that by nudging Internet companies to do their bidding in a form of 'digital prior restraint' through filtering, domain seizures and content-blocking.[20] The nudging relied on legal incentives. 'If an intermediary searches for and blocks offending content, or refuses to do business with the relevant speaker, it is held legally harmless. But if it fails to search, block, or stop doing business, it may be held contributorily or vicariously liable for the offending content'.[21]

In his follow-up article, 'Free Speech in the Algorithmic Society' Professor Balkin has additionally highlighted the fact that 'the large private enterprises that constitute the digital infrastructure have the technical and bureaucratic capacity to regulate and govern speech, through blocking, filtering, and removing content, through otherwise controlling access to their facilities, and through digital surveillance'.[22] The ever-growing bureaucracy of the social media companies is response to the demand for governance from both governments and end-users.[23] This demand is natural, however it is overshadowed by the fact that end-users themselves are the central element of the business model of the social media companies. As Balkin

[18] Balkin (2014), p. 2304.

[19] Ibid, pp. 2308–2314.

[20] Ibid, pp. 2318–2324.

[21] Ibid, p. 2325.

[22] Balkin (2018), p. 1175.

[23] Ibid, pp. 1182–1184.

notes, 'monetizing personal data ... is central to many online service companies, which allows them to subsidize the services they perform for end-users'.[24] Based on this phenomenon, he proposes the concept of 'algorithmic nuisance' that 'tries to capture the idea of companies externalizing the socially unjustified costs of algorithmic decision-making onto the populations whose lives are shaped – and opportunities constricted - by algorithmic judgments'.[25] Some scholars move even further by proposing the concept of digital (or social media) extractivism, 'a direct parallel to the natural-resource extractivism that has driven the activities of energy firms and commodity producers across the globe'.[26] 'Traditional' extractivism is associated with environmental ruin and exploitation of indigenous populations. Likewise, digital extractivism claims that insatiable appetite for end-user data results in harm to user experience and ultimately socially problematic outcomes.[27]

These approaches undermine the legitimacy of leaving the social media governance to social media companies. Yet, despite this, judges and regulators continue to empower companies policing of speech. Back in 2014, the Court of Justice of the European Union effectively handed search engines a responsibility to determine if an individual has the right to remove particular items from the search.[28] In 2015, the European Court of Human Rights in *Delfi AS* recognised the responsibility of media companies for policing speech at their forums.[29] The judgment produced this outcome in spite of the dissenting judges referring to the 2014 article of Professor Balkin.[30] These developments resulted in some social media companies expanding their speech-governing bureaucracy by quasi-judicial bodies that according to some scholars already the hallmarks of a human rights review body.[31] Such bodies rely on, inter alia, human rights instruments when interpreting the platforms' terms of use.[32]

[24] Ibid, p. 1162.

[25] Ibid, p. 1165 (internal quotations omitted).

[26] Morozov (2017).

[27] Ibid.

[28] Case C-131/12, Google Spain.

[29] Delfi AS v. Estonia.

[30] 'We regret that the Court did not rely on the prophetic warnings of Professor Jack Balkin', Ibid, Joint Dissenting Opinion of Judges Sajó and Tsotsoria, Para. 2.

[31] Helfer and Land (2021).

[32] The Charter of the Facebook Oversight Board states that 'When reviewing decisions, the board will pay particular attention to the impact of removing content in light of human rights norms protecting free expression'. In its decision on Trump's suspension from the platform, the Board explicitly referred to the International Covenant on Civil and Political Rights and the International Convention on the Elimination of All Forms of Racial Discrimination. In its subsequent decision, the Board ruled that a decision to remove content was both unnecessary and disproportionate in terms of human rights obligations. See Case decision 2021-004-FB-UA of 26 May 2021, https://oversightboard.com/decision/FB-6YHRXHZR/.

Social media have become one of the principal arenas for electoral campaigning.[33] Therefore, the way they self-regulate themselves affects the ability of candidates and parties to communicate with prospective voters. The extent to which voters can inform themselves is also affected. The shifting approaches to the freedom of speech noted by Professor Balkin thus have political repercussions. To assess them I will use the notion of election securitisation to contextualise the (self-) regulation of the social media companies. I am going to discuss external and internal challenges to the election security to set the stage for the proportionality assessment of the election-related provisions of social media policies.

## 3 Election Securitisation: The History and the Present

Election securitisation is understood in this chapter as the process whereby political actors frame elections as a part of national security discourse. Security here can be both internal—guarding from threats within the political community, and external—focusing on outside threats to the aforesaid community. Both concepts are nothing new. Back in 1930s, German American political scientist Karl Loewenstein developed the idea of a 'militant democracy', that is a liberal democratic regime capable of protecting itself. The threats of the day were totalitarian groups eager to exploit freedoms offered by liberal democratic regimes to destroy them. These groups often relied on support of foreign governments, eager to spread their ideology. Examples of the early reliance on militant democracy include Public Order Act of 1936 in the United Kingdom, Foreign Agents Registration Act (FARA) of 1939 and Smith Act of 1940 in the United States. While the other two acts focused on internal threats from totalitarian groups, FARA sought to disclose persons who acted in the interest of foreign governments while engaging in political activities. Therefore, it focused on external threats.

In the wake of the Second World War, militant democracy became constitutionalised in several countries with prior experience of totalitarian government. Perhaps the most vivid examples of such practices can be found in the Federal Republic of Germany. The country's Basic Law gives the authorities an ability to prohibit extremist organisations, including political parties. The latter power has only been exercised twice—in 1950s when the Federal Constitutional Court banned the neo-Nazi Socialist Reich Party and the German Communist Party.[34] Yet, despite the relative caution in applying the measures of militant democracy, Germany highlights the inherent tension between the principle of militant democracy and

[33] For instance, according to the data compiled by the scholars of the Wesleyan University, in the 2020 electoral cycle in the United States, presidential candidates Donald Trump and Joe Biden spend over $360 million of their combined $1.5 billion advertising budget on ads placed on platforms owned by Google and Facebook. See Baum (2020).

[34] Kommers (2006).

electoral procedures. On the one hand, it would be excessive to exclude from the democratic process parties that routinely fail at polls. Doing this would arguably upend the very rationale of elections.[35] On the other hand, it is tricky to establish the precise moment, where an extremist party would present a 'clear and present danger', that would justify the intervention into electoral process. The European Court of Human Rights has faced this question on several occasions. Such cases have primarily originated from post-Communist states and Turkey. The Court has underscored that a mere affiliation with a particular ideology would be insufficient to justify a ban.[36] Instead, it required states to produce evidence of actual conduct in the past or clear danger in the future. It is here, where the relation between militant democracy and electoral politics becomes particularly strained. Arguably, the most consequential case here is *Refah Partisi*. Here the European Court of Human Rights has dealt with the decision of the Turkish judiciary to ban the major Islamist Welfare Party (Refah), which led the country's government in 1996–1997 and at the material time was leading in opinion polls. It was precisely this fact that made arguments in favour of the ban particularly convincing for the European Court.[37] It considered that 'at the time of its dissolution Refah had the real potential to seize political power without being restricted by the compromises inherent in a coalition'.[38] Thus, the Court emphatically relied on relative electoral strength as a benchmark for risk calculation in a militant democracy. This meant elections being not an instrument for allocating political power, but also a barometer of the social health in a political community. If problematic actors begin amassing popular support, then authorities have ground to intervene to stop them. Therefore, election securitisation can affect even those actors that have real prospects of attaining political power.

In practice of the European Court of Human Rights, the reliance on militant democracy is rooted in the acceptance of pluralist democracy as a principle.[39] However, such acceptance can hardly be taken for granted. It is especially so in a situation when multiple countries fail to become consolidated democracies or experience democratic backsliding. Indeed, influential political scientists Stephen Levitsky and Lucan Way argue that a permanent grey area has established itself between democracy and authoritarianism. 'Competitive authoritarian regimes are

---

[35] This logic seems to have underpinned the judgements of the Federal Constitutional Court, which on several occasions has refused to place the ban on the far-right National Democratic Party. Although the party has achieved representation in legislatures of several federal states, it has never been able to breach the electoral threshold for the federal Bundestag.

[36] 'From that point of view, there can be no justification for hindering a political group solely because it seeks to debate in public the situation of part of the State's population and to take part in the nation's political life in order to find, according to democratic rules, solutions capable of satisfying everyone concerned'. United Communist Party of Turkey v. Turkey, Para. 57.

[37] Refah Partisi (Welfare Party) v. Turkey, Para. 107.

[38] Ibid., Paras. 108, 110.

[39] 'Democracy thus appears to be the only political model contemplated by the Convention and, accordingly, the only one compatible with it'. The United Communist Party of Turkey v. Turkey, Para. 45. See also Vidmar (2010), p. 209.

civilian regimes in which formal democratic institutions exist and are widely viewed as the primary means of gaining power, but in which incumbents' abuse of the state places them at a significant advantage vis-à-vis their opponents. Such regimes are competitive in that opposition parties use democratic institutions to contest seriously for power, but they are not democratic because the playing field is heavily skewed in favour of incumbents. Competition is thus real but unfair'.[40] If given instruments of militant democracy or generally of election securitisation, competitive authoritarian regimes are likely to use them in a way that will suit their agenda. For instance, they can use legal tools against political extremists to target political opposition and to prevent it from running in elections. Likewise, competitive authoritarians can use external security considerations to portray their opponents as pawns of foreign adversaries, to limit international election observation and NGO activity. These scenarios are not far-fetched. Indeed, the case-law of the European Court of Human Rights on party dissolution is largely a consequence of Turkey's long-standing practice of dissolving parties of leftist and pro-Kurdish orientation.[41] In some cases, the concerns of competitive authoritarian regimes have been on display in binding international documents on election securitisation. For example, the binding Convention on the standards of democratic elections adopted by a group of Post-Soviet states in 2002 had explicitly stated that '(a)ny direct or indirect participation of foreign citizens, persons without citizenship, foreign legal entities, international public movements, international organizations in activities facilitating or hindering preparation and conduct of elections to the bodies of state power and local self-governments, to other bodies of peoples' (national) representation, elective officials is not allowed'.[42] Notably this norm targets even those foreign entities that facilitated elections. Thus, here election securitisation was not about shielding polls from external threats, but rather aimed at shielding those in power from capacity-building NGOs that were seen as helping the opposition. Therefore, the goal was to ensure that playing field would remain uneven. This means that in absence of commitment to pluralistic democracy, election securitisation can become a tool for undermining international cooperation in democratic development.

Summing up the history of election securitisation, it seems to reflect the relevant political agenda of those in power. While there is an objective need to protect democratic procedures from nefarious actors inside and outside of the political community, securitisation can serve to undermine the pluralistic character of elections. It can occur when it limits the participation of a broad spectrum of political groups in elections or hinders democracy promotion efforts. Therefore, the expansion of election securitisation into new domains such as social media should be taken

[40] Levitsky and Way (2010), p. 5.

[41] See, for instance, The United Communist Party of Turkey v. Turkey, Paras. 9–10, Socialist Party and Others v. Turkey, Paras. 9–15, Dicle for the Democratic Society Party v. Turkey, Paras. 7–24, Democracy and Change Party v. Turkey, Paras. 7–16.

[42] Convention on Standards of Democratic Election, Voting Rights and Freedoms in the Member States of the Commonwealth of Independent States, Article 1.

with a grain of salt. The systemic challenges to social media regulation highlighted in Part I such as market domination and extractivism can further augment the difficulties associated with election securitisation. Jack Balkin noted the tendency of governments to rely on cooperation with Internet companies to achieve the aim of indirectly censoring certain kinds of speech. This tendency can be problematic in the context of election securitisation. If a governing party would rely on social media companies to suppress a particular speaker or a form of political speech it could raise questions of political bias. In some cases, such intervention could be warranted. As noted above, there are situations when extremist groups need to be excluded from the political process. In a similar vein, extreme forms electoral speech may need to be suppressed. However, the determination of what speech is unacceptable during an electoral campaign is a complicated. The European Court of Human Rights[43] has in its case-law determined that media freedom is crucial to electoral campaigning,[44] but also underscored the need to balance between freedom of speech and election regulation.[45]

The issue of social media became a prominent part of election securitisation discussions following the 2016 presidential campaign in the United States. The 2017–2019 Special Counsel investigation led by Robert Mueller has concluded that Russian-based Internet Research Agency 'conducted social media operations targeted at large U.S. audiences with the goal of sowing discord in the U.S. political system'.[46] In particular, on Facebook the agency has purchased 'over 3,500 advertisements, and the expenditures totalled approximately $100,000'.[47] The social media company claimed that accounts controlled by the agency may have reached an estimated audience of between 29 and 126 million Americans.[48] On Twitter the activities of Russian structure have impacted up to 1.4 million users.[49] Internet Research Agency had an explicit political agenda, promoting the candidacies of Donald Trump and Bernie Sanders while opposing the candidacy of Hillary

[43] References to the case-law of the European Court of Human Rights (ECtHR) are given here primarily for illustrative purposes. The Court relies upon same international electoral standards (such as the Code of Good Practices in Electoral Matters) as I suggest for the social media companies. However, I do not claim that the ECtHR judgments are necessarily decisive in the interpretation of these standards.

[44] Freedom of expression is one of the 'conditions' necessary to 'ensure the free expression of the opinion of the people in the choice of the legislature', Orlovskaya Iskra v. Russia, Para. 110.

[45] Nonetheless, in certain circumstances the two rights may come into conflict, and it may be considered necessary, in the period preceding or during an election, to place certain restrictions, of a type which would not usually be acceptable, on freedom of expression, to secure the 'free expression of the opinion of the people in the choice of the legislature', Bowman v. the United Kingdom, Para. 43.

[46] Report On The Investigation Into Russian Interference In The 2016 Presidential Election, Vol. 1, p. 14.

[47] Ibid, p. 25.

[48] Ibid, p. 26.

[49] Ibid, p. 29.

Clinton.[50] The activities of the organisation uncovered by the investigation have led to a criminal indictment by the U.S. federal authorities. The prosecutors allege that the Agency and several related persons have conspired 'to defraud the United States by impairing, obstructing, and defeating the lawful functions of the government through fraud and deceit for the purpose of interfering with the U.S. political and electoral processes, including the presidential election of 2016'.[51]

The outcomes of the Special Counsel Investigation and related criminal charges raise several issues pertinent to election-related speech on social media. It is notable that although influenced by foreign actors, people on social media exercised their right to political speech. Thus, the content itself was not problematic. Rather, the effects of social media extractivism amplified the scope of the election interference by the Internet Research Agency. It could expect to produce an 'echo chamber' effect[52] by ramping up highly partisan content. Doing so aligned with other alleged facets of Russian election interference such as hacking the communications of several Democratic Party officials[53] and targeting election infrastructure in numerous states of the U.S.[54]

While the activities of the Internet Research Agency were a clear example of an external security risk for elections, the corresponding internal security problems are much less clear. While many people were duped by misleading content, it seems to merely have confirmed and strengthened their views. Therefore, an appropriate course of action would have been to evaluate the role of social media in election campaigning, and to mandate relevant changes to media regulation. Instead, however, both in the United States and the European Union the solution has been to again allow social media to self-regulate itself out of the controversy.

For instance, in 2019 Facebook has announced a slate of measures, apparently influenced by the Special Counsel investigation.[55] Part of these measures are hardly controversial, aiming at better identification of suspicious patterns of activities, state-sponsored content and paid political advertisements.[56] Yet, at the same time the social media giant wowed to identify and label 'false information'.[57] In September 2020, the company clarified that it would specifically remove 'election misinformation' and prevent 'premature claims about election outcomes'.[58] A few

---

[50] Ibid, pp. 23, 27, 31.

[51] United States v. Internet Research Agency.

[52] Barberá et al. (2015), pp. 1–12.

[53] Report On The Investigation Into Russian Interference In The 2016 Presidential Election, Vol. 1, pp. 36–41.

[54] Report of the Select Committee on Intelligence, United States Senate on Russian Active Measures Campaigns and Interference in the 2016 U.S. Election, Vol. 1: Russian Efforts Against Election Infrastructure With Additional Views.

[55] Facebook Outlines New Election Security Measures In the Lead Up to the 2020 Election (2019).

[56] Ibid.

[57] Ibid.

[58] Facebook Outlines New Measures to Protect the Integrity of the US Presidential Election (2020).

weeks later a similar policy has been announced by Twitter.[59] Such policies self-assign the company the ability to determine accuracy of factual claims involving a politically fraught electoral process. Normally the requisite forum would be found in representative and judicial institution. Notably in the United States the procedure for determining the presidential election outcome is the certification of electors' votes by the houses of the U.S. Congress. Prior determinations are made by the media companies and the Administrator of the General Services Administration.[60] Nonetheless, Facebook and Twitter were quite aggressive in enforcing their new policies. For instance, they controversially relied on the updated policies to prevent sharing of a New York Post piece alleging misconduct by Hunter Biden, the son of the Democratic presidential candidate.[61] This was a clear example of collateral censorship described by Jack Balkin in his 2014 article. Furthermore, unlike the situation in the *Delfi* case, here social media companies targeted a traditional media outlet engaged in journalistic activity and therefore normally subject to heightened freedom of speech protections. Subsequently, Facebook and Twitter decisively moved to label corrective statements to posts by President Donald Trump that alleged his electoral victory or election fraud.[62] These steps occurred even though some of the alleged claims were still being litigated in state and federal courts. Although Facebook and Twitter policies were clearly impacted by circumstances specific to the United States, their policies on election-related content apply globally.[63] They are further enabled by regional actors relying on cooperation with social media companies. For example, pursuant to the Digital Services Act the European Union and major social media companies have adopted a code of practice on disinformation that includes election related aspects.[64] Ultimately election securitisation has led social media companies to designing specific sections of their policies. In case of Facebook policy, it is 'social issues', while Twitter policy relates to 'civic process'.

Election securitisation reflects a fact that elections are a sensitive procedure that invites a host of internal and external challenges. Certain legal safeguards are necessary against such threats. Yet, these safeguards must be proportionate to the threat. Otherwise, they can become a tool for suppressing very democracy they are meant to protect. Election securitisation of the social media platforms is no exception to these general principles. The platforms create an environment that does exacerbate internal and external challenges to election security. However, the response needs to remain proportionate. To assess the proportionality of measures taken by social

[59] Expanding our policies to further protect the civic conversation, Twitter (10 September 2020), l.

[60] Pursuant to the Presidential Transition Act of 1963 with subsequent amendments, the GSA Administrator issues a 'letter of ascertainment' to the 'apparent successful candidate' to facilitate acquisition of office space and communication with federal agencies.

[61] Paul (2020).

[62] Facebook, Twitter Take Action to Maintain Election Integrity as Vote Counting Continues (2020).

[63] See Election Integrity, Facebook and Civic integrity policy, Twitter.

[64] Code of Practice on Disinformation.

media companies (specifically Facebook and Twitter), I will review their policies against the existing body of international election standards. Considering the role of Internet companies highlighted by Jack Balkin, I will assume that they are regulators of speech. Therefore, they have additional obligations before end-users and societies that go beyond corporate social responsibility.[65] To the extent that social media platforms supplant 'traditional' media,[66] these obligations must ensure that the public's ability 'of discovering and forming an opinion of the ideas and attitudes of political leaders'[67] is not hampered.

## 4 Election Securitisation in Social Media Policies and Practices Judged by International Election Standards

Elections have a double role. On the one hand, they determine the identity of officeholders and allocate political power in a given community. As such, they are intimately connected with this community. In case of a nation-state there is a nexus between elections and sovereignty. The act of voting creates a symbolic connection between a citizen and decision-makers in his or her state. Thus, elections are grounded in political processes in a particular political community, which determines the relevant rules and regulations.[68] On the other, electoral rights are human rights as enshrined in global and regional instruments, including the International Covenant for Civil and Political Rights and the European Convention on Human Rights. In this regard, electoral rights are embedded in international public law.[69] At the same time, experts have actively developed 'soft law', that is advisory standards for elections and election-related regulation. One of the most prominent of those is the Code of Good Practices in Electoral Matters, developed by the Venice Commission and the Organization for Security and Cooperation in Europe (OSCE).[70] Thus, electoral regulation is both national in character and international in terms of context.

[65] Such an approach would align with Balkin's vision that social media companies have to change their self-conception. 'Ideally, they would come to understand themselves as a new kind of media company, with obligations to protect the global public good of a free Internet, and to preserve and extend the emerging global system of freedom of expression'. Balkin (2018), p. 1209.

[66] 'A widely noted and characteristic feature of the digital age is the democratization of information production, and therefore the democratization of opportunities to speak and express one's self. The 'disintermediation' often associated with the Internet does not involve the abolition of media gatekeepers but rather the substitution of one kind of infrastructure for another. Balkin (2014), p. 2304.

[67] Lingens v. Austria, Para. 42.

[68] The practice of the European Court of Human Rights, for example, recognises this by deferring to domestic decision-making in setting certain electoral rules. See Kurnosov (2021).

[69] In this regard see Boda (2005), pp. 208–29, Davis-Roberts and Carroll (2010).

[70] Golubok (2009), pp. 386–389. The membership of the OSCE and the Venice Commission includes major democracies of Eurasia and the Americas. In African context, Article 17 of the

As noted above, the Facebook Oversight Board Charter refers to human rights in the field of free speech as one of the relevant authorities.[71] In contrast, the company's policy argues that 'in most countries globally, there aren't laws or agencies that list specific social issues that are subject to regulation'.[72] Thus, while the Oversight Board is constrained by the international norms, the platform itself predicates its policies on the existence of a legal vacuum. Such an approach is hardly sustainable. One of the first decisions of the Oversight Board has underscored the tension between the human rights norms and platform policies.[73] The decision specifically recommended considering the political context when removing content.[74] If we consider Facebook and social media companies being regulators of speech (as suggested by Balkin), then their policies should primarily implement (and only rarely complement) the existing legislative frameworks for freedom of speech during elections. These should specifically include international human rights law and advisory standards concerning media in electoral environments.

Indeed, there is already some evidence that social media companies are mirroring certain aspects of the existing media regulation. For instance, in its report on 2020 elections in the United States, Facebook claims that it has 'temporary paused' social ads in the wake of the November 3 vote.[75] Such action is well-known in the regulation of traditional audio-visual media during election campaign in some countries and is usually referred to as 'period of reflection'. However, the public would have benefitted from this action being communicated in advance.[76]

The updated policies of both Facebook and Twitter place particular emphasis on certain events in the run-up and following election day. Specifically, they prohibit misleading information on requirements to vote, voter suppression and misleading information about outcomes. Twitter's policy in particular targets 'disputed claims that could undermine faith in the process itself, such as unverified information about election rigging, ballot tampering, vote tallying, or certification of election results'.[77] Such a generalised policy is problematic, given that the state of election integrity

African Union Charter on Democracy, Elections and Governance may also be pertinent to the regulation of electoral speech.

[71] Helfer and Land (2021).

[72] Facebook Election Integrity Policy. The company claims to rely on dialogue with stakeholders and its independent risk assessment.

[73] '. . .the Community Standard should clearly explain to users how bullying and harassment differ from speech that only causes offense and may be protected under international human rights law'. Case decision 2021-004-FB-UA of 26 May 2021.

[74] Ibid.

[75] A Look at Facebook and US 2020 Elections, p. 14.

[76] The ambiguity of this decision by Facebook might have been a contributing factor in operators of Telegram messenger shutting down an opposition channel before the 2021 Russian State Duma election. The messenger's administration referred to the 'period of reflection' in Russian electoral law. However, such a reading of law seems to have benefitted the country's competitive authoritarian regime.

[77] Twitter Civic Integrity Policy.

varies vastly from country to country. In states with competitive authoritarian regimes, election fraud is often one of the primary tools for retaining political power. The standard of 'unverified information' may require the level of proof beyond of reach for civic activists uncovering election fraud in a competitive authoritarian regime. Therefore, it may have a 'chilling effect' on efforts of such activists.[78] Furthermore, given the importance of election fraud for many competitive authoritarian regimes, their authorities could use these rules to put pressure on social media companies to remove content problematic for the regime. The rules could also give legitimacy to domestic regulation that would target claims of election fraud on social media. Given these concerns, the existing Twitter policy seems to reflect Western-centred approaches and ignore the multifaceted reality of contemporary election securitisation. Likewise, the stand of social media companies against 'unsubstantiated' claims of electoral victories is problematic from the standpoint of prevailing political realities in many countries. While the tradition in the United States and many other developed democracies is for the losing candidate to concede to the apparent election winner, it is not universal. Indeed, even in the United States there are cases (beyond Donald Trump's efforts to undermine the legitimacy of the 2020 presidential election) when losing candidates refused to concede to make a particular statement on the conduct of a vote.[79] Such cases are very common in circumstances where there are question marks over the legitimacy of elections. For instance, the country's electoral commission finalised the results of the 2004 Ukrainian presidential election while mass protests against suspected fraud raged on.[80] Had Facebook and Twitter policies been in place then, calls to join protests could have been removed from respective platforms. However, back in 2004, Ukrainian Supreme Court has proven protestors right, ordering the re-run of elections. This experience underscores the necessity of regulating election-related speech in a proportionate manner. Election integrity policies of social media platforms need to consider the heterogeneity of political regimes, resulting in very different standards of political behaviour. Furthermore, they need to reflect the fact that electoral fraud is a violation of internationally recognised human rights.[81]

---

[78] Facebook Oversight Board has already noted the potential risks of imprecisely worded policies for political speech on social media platforms in its decision 2021-004-FB-UA. See Helfer and Land (2021).

[79] For instance, in 2018 Democratic Party candidate Stacey Abrams refused to concede the Georgia gubernatorial election to the Republican winner citing concerns over election fairness. See The Latest: Kemp says Georgia race over, state to look ahead, Associated Press (17 November 2018).

[80] Hesli (2006).

[81] 'The state must punish any kind of electoral fraud'. Code of Good Practices in Electoral Matters, supra note 74 at 3.2. 'Free elections are to be seen as both an individual right and a positive obligation of the State, comprising a number of guarantees starting from the right of the voters to form an opinion freely, and up to careful regulation of the process in which the results of voting are ascertained, processed and recorded'. Davydov and Others, Para. 285. Moreover, empiric public opinion research suggests that appearance of electoral fraud affects public confidence in elections. See Fortin-Rittberger et al. (2017), pp. 350–368.

A possible blueprint for reforming the election-related policies of social media companies can be found in the Code of Good Practices for Electoral Matters. Specific emphasis should be placed on the general duty of neutrality in the media envisaged by the Code. The explanatory report to the Code additionally warns against the possibility of restrictions on political speech being abused by unscrupulous governments. Thus, at very minimum, election-related policies of social media platforms should be neutral towards political actors and their viewpoints and incorporate safeguards against possible abuse. However, even if these changes were to be introduced, their effects would be far from certain. The very design of social media platforms may be contrary to the idea of political neutrality if it indeed encourages political polarisation and partisan environments. Furthermore, currently the implementation of platform policies is often left to low-pay employees in poor working conditions.[82]

The policies of prominent social media companies appear to reflect the increased focus on election securitisation in response to both external and internal challenges, highlighted primarily by the 2016 and 2020 election campaigns in the United States. However, due to the market position of social media companies and the character of social media triangulation their policies apply well beyond America. Indeed, the global scope of those policies is spelled out in the document themselves. Yet, as noted in the previous Part, the state of democratic politics varies vastly from country to country. Particularly problematic are competitive authoritarian regimes, which do hold elections, but deny their participants a level playing field. Consequently, the transition of power to the political opposition would become highly unlikely. Measures, adopted due to the experience in the United States, could become highly problematic in competitive authoritarian regimes. While unsubstantiated claims of election fraud and electoral victory could undermine a consolidated democracy, in a competitive authoritarian country it will be difficult to determine their veracity. At the same time, such regimes could use the policy to attack opposition politicians and those uncovering election fraud. A possible avenue to improving election-related policies could be incorporating existing standards such as the Code of Good Practices in Electoral Matters. The emphasis could be made on equal treatment of political actors by social media platforms and preventing the misuse of restrictions on electoral speech. Yet, even with improved policies, social media companies could struggle to fulfil regulatory function due to design of their platforms and operating practices.

[82] See, for example, Newton (2019).

## 5 Conclusion

The emergence of Internet as one of the primary means of communication has drastically changed the media landscape. While initially the new space seemed to possess untapped democratising potential, the rise of social media companies and the growing awareness of governments have resulted in new avenues of control. However, as argued by Jack Balkin, these avenues as distinct from those relied upon in respect of traditional media. Regulators largely target providers of Internet infrastructure (including social media companies) to nudge them towards 'collateral censorship', in effect outsourcing regulation. Partly this process is a natural response to the demands of the public. However, the capacity of social media companies for self-regulation is constrained by design of their platforms that maximises end-user engagement. Some scholars argue that certain features of these designs may be related to undesirable social outcomes.

Election securitisation is arguably a part of the legitimate demands of the public concerning social media governance. Historically, political communities sought to secure their electoral processes from foreign interference and domestic extremists. The Special Counsel investigation in the United States has highlighted the external and internal threats to electoral process through the social media. As a response to the investigation, social media companies have enacted increasingly stringent standards for election-related speech. However, given their business model, it is questionable whether the standards alone will ensure election securitisation.

The analysis of Facebook and Twitter policies on election integrity reveals further issues. While these policies evidently reflect concerns raised by the events surrounding the 2016 and 2020 elections in the United States, they apply globally. Thus, their scope of application also includes countries with questionable commitment to election integrity. In such countries, the policies could harm opposition politicians and democracy advocates. The policies also notably fail to account for the existing media regulation in electoral environments that could have provided a workable blueprint for social media companies. Most notably, while policies do provide a degree of transparency and prevent certain types of speech, they fail to ensure equitable coverage of election participants envisaged by advisory standards in the field of elections. An additional issue is the ability of social media companies to enforce their policies, given the platform design and allegedly questionable labour practices.

Election-related aspects of social media triangulation are an evolving subject. Therefore, further research indeed, particularly in certain areas identified in this Chapter, such as the application of social media election integrity policies in competitive authoritarian states.

## References

A Look at Facebook and US 2020 Elections (2020) Facebook. https://about.fb.com/wp-content/uploads/2020/12/US-2020-Elections-Report.pdf. Accessed 16 Sept 2021

Balkin JM (2014) Old-school/new-school speech regulation. Harv Law Rev 127:2296–2342

Balkin JM (2018) Free speech in the algorithmic society: big data, private governance, and new school speech regulation. U.C. Davis Law Rev 51:1148–1210

Barberá P, Jost JT, Nagler J, Tucker JA, Bonneau R (2015) Tweeting from left to right: is online political communication more than an Echo chamber? Psychol Sci 26(10):1531–1542

Baum L (2020) Presidential General Election Ad Spending Tops $1.5 Billion. Wesleyan Media Project, https://mediaproject.wesleyan.edu/releases-102920/. Accessed 16 Sept 2021

Boda MD (2005) Judging elections by public international law: a tentative framework. Representation 41(3):208–229

Brady WJ, McLoughlin K, Doan TN, Crockett MJ (2021) How social learning amplifies moral outrage expression in online social networks. Sci Adv 7(33):5641

Code of Good Practice in Electoral Matters. Guidelines and Explanatory Report (2002) Organization for Security and Cooperation in Europe and the Venice Commission. https://rm.coe.int/090000168092af01. Accessed 19 Sept 2021

Code of Practice on Disinformation (2021) European Commission. https://digital-strategy.ec.europa.eu/en/policies/code-practice-disinformation. Accessed 16 Sept 2021

Convention on Standards of Democratic Election, Voting Rights and Freedoms in the Member States of the Commonwealth of Independent States (2002) Translation by the Venice Commission. https://www.venice.coe.int/webforms/documents/default.aspx?pdffile=CDL-EL(2006)031rev-e. Accessed 16 Sept 2021

Davis-Roberts A, Carroll DJ (2010) Using international law to assess elections. Democratization 17(3):416–441

Election Integrity at Facebook (2021) Facebook. https://www.facebook.com/business/m/election-integrity. Accessed 16 Sept 2021

Expanding Our Policies to Further Protect the Civic Conversation (2020) Twitter. https://blog.twitter.com/en_us/topics/company/2020/civic-integrity-policy-update. Accessed 16 Sept 2021

Facebook Outlines New Election Security Measures in the Lead Up to the 2020 Election (2019) Social Media Today. https://www.socialmediatoday.com/news/facebook-outlines-new-election-security-measures-in-the-lead-up-to-the-2020/565494/. Accessed 16 Sept 2021

Facebook Outlines New Measures to Protect the Integrity of the US Presidential Election (2020) Social Media Today. https://www.socialmediatoday.com/news/facebook-outlines-new-measures-to-protect-the-integrity-of-the-us-president/584768/. Accessed 16 Sept 2021

Facebook Oversight Board Charter (2019) Facebook. https://about.fb.com/wp-content/uploads/2019/09/oversight_board_charter.pdf. Accessed 16 Sept 2021

Facebook, Twitter Take Action to Maintain Election Integrity as Vote Counting Continues (2020) Social Media Today. https://www.socialmediatoday.com/news/facebook-twitter-take-action-to-maintain-election-integrity-as-vote-counti/588403/. Accessed 16 Sept 2021

Finkel EJ, Bail CA, Cikara M, Ditto PH, Iyengar S, Klar S et al (2020) Political sectarianism in America. Science 370(6516):533–536

Fortin-Rittberger J, Harfst P, Dingler SC (2017) The costs of electoral fraud: establishing the link between electoral integrity, winning an election, and satisfaction with democracy. J Elect Public Opin Part 27(3):350–368

General Comment 25(57) adopted under article 40, paragraph 4, of the International Covenant on Civil and Political Rights (1996) United Nations Human Rights Committee. https://digitallibrary.un.org/record/221930. Accessed 16 Sept 2021

Golubok S (2009) Right to free elections: emerging guarantees or two layers of protection? Neth Q Human Rights 27(3):361–390

Helfer L, Land M (2021) Is the Facebook Oversight Board an International Human Rights Tribunal? https://www.lawfareblog.com/facebook-oversight-board-international-human-rights-tribunal. Accessed 16 Sept 2021

Hesli V (2006) The Orange revolution: 2004 presidential election(s) in Ukraine. Elect Stud 25:172

Klonick K (2018) The new governors: the people, rules, and processes governing online speech. Harv Law Rev 131:1598–1670

Kommers DP (2006) The Federal Constitutional Court: Guardian of German democracy. Ann Am Acad Pol Soc Sci 603:111–128

Kreimer S (2006) Censorship by proxy: the first amendment, internet intermediaries, and the problem of the weakest link. Univ Pa Law Rev 155(1):11

Kurnosov D (2021) Pragmatic adjudication of election cases in the European court of human rights. Eur J Int Law 32(1):255–279

Levitsky S, Way LA (2010) Competitive authoritarianism: hybrid regimes after the cold war, Illustrated edn. Cambridge University Press, New York

Møller J, Skaaning S-E (2010) Beyond the radial delusion: conceptualizing and measuring democracy and non-democracy. Int Polit Sci Rev 31(3):261–283

Morozov E (2017) Digital Intermediation of Everything: At the Intersection of Politics, Technology, and Finance. https://rm.coe.int/digital-intermediation-of-everything-at-the-intersection-of-politics-t/168075baba. Accessed 16 Sept 2021

Morozov E, Barbrook R, Bria F (2016) Digital democracy and technological sovereignty. https://www.opendemocracy.net/en/digitaliberties/digital-democracy-and-technological-sovereignty/. Accessed 16 Sept 2021

Mulligan C (2016) Technological intermediaries and freedom of the press. SMU Law Rev 66(1):157

Newton C (2019) The secret lives of Facebook moderators in America. The Verge. https://www.theverge.com/2019/2/25/18229714/cognizant-facebook-content-moderator-interviews-trauma-working-conditions-arizona. Accessed 16 Sept 2021

Paul K (2020) Facebook and Twitter restrict controversial New York Post story on Joe Biden. The Guardian. https://www.theguardian.com/technology/2020/oct/14/facebook-twitter-new-york-post-hunter-biden. Accessed 16 Sept 2021

Report on Russian Active Measures Campaigns and Interference in the 2016 U.S. Election (2020) Select Committee on Intelligence, United States Senate. https://www.intelligence.senate.gov/publications/report-select-committee-intelligence-united-states-senate-russian-active-measures. Accessed 19 Sept 2021

Report On The Investigation Into Russian Interference In The 2016 Presidential Election (2019) US Department of Justice, https://www.justice.gov/archives/sco/file/1373816/download. Accessed 19 Sept 2021

Ricaurte P (2019) Data epistemologies, the coloniality of power, and resistance. Telev New Media 20(4):350–365

Richards N (2015) Intellectual privacy: rethinking civil liberties in the digital age, 1st edn. Oxford University Press, Oxford

The Latest: Kemp says Georgia race over, state to look ahead (2019) AP NEWS. https://apnews.com/article/north-america-lawsuits-us-news-ap-top-news-elections-7825dfd60aa546eda31ed26d41646a15. Accessed 16 Sept 2021

Twitter's civic integrity and election fraud policy (2021) Twitter. https://help.twitter.com/en/rules-and-policies/election-integrity-policy. Accessed 16 Sept 2021

Verkuil PR (2007) Outsourcing sovereignty: why privatization of government functions threatens democracy and what we can do about it, 1st edn. Cambridge University Press, New York

Vidmar J (2010) Multiparty democracy: international and European human rights law perspectives. Leiden J Int Law 23(1):209–240

## *Cases Cited*

### European Court of Human Rights

Bowman v. the United Kingdom, No. 24839/94, Judgment of 19 February 1998, Reports of Judgments and Decisions 1998–I

Davydov and Others v. Russia, No. 75947/11, Judgment of 30 May 2017, Reports of Judgments and Decisions 2017

Delfi AS v. Estonia, No. 64569/09, Judgment of 16 June 2015, Reports of Judgments and Decisions 2015

Democracy and Change Party and Others v. Turkey, No. 39210/98 and 39974/98, Judgment of 26 April 2005, http://hudoc.echr.coe.int/eng?i=001-68902. Accessed 16 Sept 2021

Dicle for the Democratic Party (DEP) of Turkey v. Turkey, No. 25141/94, Judgment of 12 October 2002, http://hudoc.echr.coe.int/eng?i=001-60813. Accessed 16 Sept 2021

Lingens v. Austria, No. 9815/82, Judgment of 8 July 1986, Series A, No.103

Refah Partisi (the Welfare Party) and Others v. Turkey, No. 41340/98 et seq., Judgment of 13 February 2003, Reports of Judgments and Decisions 2003–II

Socialist Party and Others v. Turkey, No. 26482/95, Judgment of 30 January 1998, Reports of Judgments and Decisions 1998–III

United Communist Party v. Turkey (GC), No. 19392/92, Judgment of 30 January 1998, Reports of Judgments and Decisions 1998–I

### Court of Justice of the European Union

Case C-131/12, Google Spain SL and Google Inc. v Agencia Española de Protección de Datos (AEPD) and Mario Costeja González, ECLI:EU:C:2014:317

### United States Supreme Court

Biden v. Knight First Amendment Institute, US_ (2021)

Reno v. American Civil Liberties Union, 521 U.S. 870 (1997)

### United States District Court for the District of Columbia

United States v. Internet Research Agency (case 1:18-cr-32-DLF)

### Facebook Oversight Board

Case decision 2021-001-FB-FBR of 5 May 2021., https://www.oversightboard.com/decision/FB-691QAMHJ. Accessed 16 Sept 2021

Case decision 2021-004-FB-UA of 26 May 2021., https://oversightboard.com/decision/FB-6YHRXHZR/. Accessed 16 Sept 2021

# Part III
# Indirect Regulation for the Protection of the Freedom of Speech

# The Marketplace of Ideas and EU Competition Law: Can Antitrust Be Used to Protect the Freedom of Speech?

**Jan Polański**

## Contents



**Abstract** The chapter discusses possible interactions between free speech and antitrust. Antitrust law is typically associated with economic phenomena and competitive market conditions. However, claims have been made during the ongoing debate over the role of Big Tech that antitrust enforcement should also be concerned with the exercise of free speech. The chapter shows that while such claims can be seen as controversial, they are not fundamentally ill-conceived as antitrust law used to interact with free speech and to be more focused on safeguarding political values, not merely efficiency. Since the free speech narrative is more present in the United States, the chapter covers the US perspective, but it ultimately aims at making a link between free speech and EU competition law, drawing a framework of possible interactions. The main conclusion of the chapter is that while more interaction between free speech and antitrust had been seen in the past in the United States,

The views expressed in this text are the author's own and do not necessarily reflect those of the Polish Office of Competition and Consumer Protection (UOKiK).

J. Polański (✉)
Polish Office of Competition and Consumer Protection (UOKiK), Warsaw, Poland



S. Hindelang, A. Moberg (eds.), *YSEC Yearbook of Socio-Economic Constitutions 2021*, YSEC Yearbook of Socio-Economic Constitutions (2022) 2021: 199–230,
https://doi.org/10.1007/16495_2021_34, Published online: 11 April 2022

EU competition law can be in fact more flexible when it comes to accommodating the interests of free speech.

## 1 Introduction

In January 2021, following events in Washington, D.C., Twitter and Facebook blocked the accounts of the then incumbent US president—a paradox of a kind as a public actor was "censored" by private companies after decades of concerns that public authorities could stifle free speech. What followed these events was a mixture of support and criticism towards the actions of the Big Tech. What preceded them, on the other hand, were long-time accusations against the Big Tech that they censor Internet speech.[1] As another paradox, the bans came as the final act of a presidential campaign, which started with concerns over private censorship being voiced at both sides of the political spectrum and with antitrust enforcement entering electoral agendas once again after a period of less publicity.[2]

Furthermore, the tensions regarding free speech led to associations being made between antitrust and free speech by, e.g., Makan Delrahim, at that time the chief antitrust enforcer in the United States, and Senator Warren, one of the early runners for the presidential office, with the latter calling for a break-up of Facebook in the context of private censorship.[3] Indeed, antirust has traditionally been seen as a remedy for the growth of private power accumulated by undertakings. Still, making connections between antitrust and free speech may seem—as yet another paradox—both counter-intuitive and natural at the same time. It's counterintuitive since most antitrust lawyers will quickly explain that antitrust is about economic efficiency and *markets for goods*, not *markets for ideas*, and free speech, which is more of a human right. It's natural since, apparently, at least some political actors and part of the public see antitrust as a check against the exercise of private power. What is also interesting is that while a heated debate over the goals of antitrust emerged currently on both sides of the Atlantic, the interaction between antitrust and free speech is less frequently discussed in Europe.

In this chapter, I explain the reasons why such discussions are not fundamentally ill-conceived. As at this point the debate is more vivid in the United States, I cover the US perspective, but the ultimate goal of the chapter is to link free speech and antitrust also from the European perspective. I approach the topic at three levels, which I call conceptual, applicatory, and pragmatic. I start the discussion with a description of two perspectives on antitrust, showing how one of them causes more

---

[1] See a review in Chilson and Mattox (2020), pp. 3–6.

[2] On that last issue see Waller and Morse (2020), p. 75.

[3] Delrahim (2019a). A few months later, Delrahim referred to free speech under antitrust in a more restrained way: Delrahim (2019b). On Warren's calls, see Lima (2019).

interest in the links between antitrust and political values, such as free speech (the conceptual level). I then turn to the United States and the interplay between antitrust and free speech there and, further, to the situation in Europe from the point of view of EU competition law (the applicatory level). Subsequently, I provide a brief outline of the practical issues arising from the debate (the pragmatic level). I conclude by observing that the relationship between antitrust and free speech is nuanced. However, taking into account the current dynamics of antitrust debates, it is not without merit that antitrust enforcement started to be seen from the point of view of not only ordinary markets but also the *marketplace of ideas*, in which free speech takes place.

## 2 The Conceptual Level: Antitrust and Political Values

### 2.1 *The Boundaries of Antitrust Enforcement: Is There Room for Free Speech in Antitrust?*

On the conceptual level, the question is what type of free speech interests are at stake and how they are generally related to antitrust. This conceptual level is abstract in the sense that it aims to answer the question: *what could be the link between antitrust and free speech?* But it is also concrete as some specific claims regarding such links are made (sometimes without much analysis of the concept of antitrust law) and have to be put into the more abstract framework of the goals of antitrust.

In that regard, the 2020 US presidential elections provide a number of clear-cut examples of concerns that have been raised in relation to the Big Tech and their bottleneck position in relation to how information circulates online.

The bans imposed on the social media accounts of the holder of the highest public office in a state can be seen as a prime example of the long-time-voiced concerns that the Big Tech are in a position to ban or manipulate the visibility of political opinions.[4] After all, if the Big Tech can ban an incumbent head of state and have their decisions largely unchallengeable, there is even less an ordinary user can do. When aggregated to large numbers, a possible pattern of the Big Tech exercising much leeway on what content is and which is not presented to social media users can be believed to influence the political process. The first link between free speech and antitrust is therefore that antitrust can in one way or another address the problem of the Big Tech exercising too much power over the speech online.

The case of Parler being "de-platformed" by Google, Apple, and Amazon (the last of which Parler sued under antitrust laws) provides another example of a typical situation in which antitrust has been hoped to provide a solution.[5] "Refusal to supply" cases are known to antitrust, but in the case of Parler, an additional circumstance was that Parler offered a forum for free speech in a time when other

[4] Chilson and Mattox (2020), pp. 3–6; Day (2020), pp. 1318–1320; Lynn (2020), pp. 56–60, 69.

[5] Alba and Nicas (2021).

platforms were less willing to do so—and blocking it removed that forum. Likewise, a few years earlier, Gab.ai encountered a similar problem with Google and engaged in antitrust litigation—and so did DataCell, a company with ties to WikiLeaks, when it was blocked by Visa and Mastercard.[6]

There are other examples too. The fact that public authorities show interest in whether the Big Tech manipulate commercial information, so that consumers are steered towards products sold by companies affiliated with the Big Tech, has led to a similar question over whether the Big Tech may manipulate political information, e.g. alter the visibility of press articles or steer voters to preferred candidates.[7] Also, long before the 2021 bans of the accounts of the then incumbent US president, the fact that the Big Tech decided to almost simultaneously ban Alex Jones, the host of controversial political channels, led to suspicions over whether the actions of the Big Tech were coordinated.[8] Finally, as there are many concerns over how the Big Tech exercise their power in relation to areas affecting free speech, an option is that no such power should exist in the first place and companies should be broken up—a sentiment outlined earlier and expressed by political actors, e.g. Senator Warren.

Those who claim that antitrust could help free speech may be inclined to do so since antitrust laws are typically broadly phrased and prohibit certain (1) multilateral actions (agreements between undertakings to restrict competition), (2) unilateral actions (activity engaged in by undertakings on their own), and (3) mergers (undertakings deciding to formally join their efforts and start operating on the market as one entity). However, none of the prohibitions, neither in the United States nor in the European Union, refers to political values such as free speech, and antitrust law itself is typically seen in action when "competition" is restricted, prices increase, and consumers are worse off.

Conceptually, the question is therefore whether there are any more meaningful reasons to look at such things as free speech under antitrust or whether such a juxtaposition of concepts is merely an empty slogan. This in fact strikes at the heart of the current debate over the role of antitrust, which re-emerged in the context of the power of the Big Tech—the discussion of whether antitrust should pursue some wider political objectives or should be limited to increasing economic welfare and thus follow purely economic goals. The discussion can be set in a broader context of what "liberty" is and whether markets (and laws that regulate them) should deliver efficiency only or be about "something more".[9] If antitrust is to serve (more significant) political goals, there is possibly more room for free speech under antitrust. If, on the other hand, antitrust should focus on economic interests, free speech considerations may be less welcome even if antitrust may still have some capacity to facilitate free speech values, e.g. as a side effect. As this issue affects why, for some, making the connection between antitrust and free speech feels

---

[6] Day (2020), pp. 1319–1320; Knox (2015).

[7] Woan (2013); Horton (2019); Lynn (2020), p. 216.

[8] Coaston (2018).

[9] Compare Burgin (2012), pp. 209, 211–212.

uncanny and, to others, more reasonable, it is useful to outline the *more political* and *more economic* approach to antitrust to see the general framework in which antitrust and free speech interact.

## 2.2 "More Political Approach"

Chronologically, the political interpretation of the goals of antitrust came first. The political perspective originally developed in the United States. As in 1890 the United States was one of the first jurisdictions to implement antitrust policy and at the same time the leading economy for the most part of the twentieth century, the US antitrust law strongly influenced the perception of the goals of antitrust around the world.

The original rationales for the introduction of antitrust in the United States are often explained by recalling the words of Senator Sherman, who during the legislative process pointed out that trusts (monopolies) are "inconsistent with our form of government (...) If we will not endure a king as a political power we should not endure a king over the production, transportation, and sale of any of the necessaries of life. If we would not submit to an emperor, we should not submit to an autocrat of trade."[10] Under this understanding, the role of antitrust was in a way "constitutional"; i.e., it defined the ground rules for economic actions.[11] As also held then by Louis Brandeis—firstly Woodrow Wilson's advisor and then a justice of the US Supreme Court (in both roles a strong supporter of antitrust laws)—the goal of antitrust was not merely economic efficiency, rather creating conditions supportive of democracy and civic development, i.e. both the personal growth of individuals and their growth as citizens.[12] The view that antitrust has a more significant political role to play became known as "Brandeisianism".[13]

While a vigorous antitrust policy ultimately became part of the New Deal, the conviction that antitrust facilitates political liberty was also shared by some of the opponents of the New Deal.[14] For instance, Henry Simons, a University of Chicago scholar, argued that *there is an intimate connection between freedom of enterprise and freedom of discussion, and that political liberty can survive only within an effectively competitive economic system. Thus, the great enemy of democracy is monopoly, in all its forms: gigantic corporations, trade associations and other*

---

[10] Quoted in Bork (1966), p. 39.

[11] Lynn (2020), p. 190; Teachout (2020); p. 203; Wu (2018a), p. 77.

[12] Berk (2009), p. 44.

[13] For more discussion, see Berk (2009); Wu (2020), pp. 59–66.

[14] Attempts were initially made under the New Deal to reshape the US economy through the National Recovery Administration (which facilitated centralised economic policy and regulation); however, this policy was eventually abandoned following a negative reaction of the judiciary, including Brandeis; see Lynn (2020), p. 162.

*agencies for price control, trade unions – or, in general, organization and concentration of power within functional classes.*[15]

In consequence, given the broad consensus about the role of antitrust, it was not uncommon to, e.g., see the justices of the US Supreme Court arguing in the late 1940s that "Power that controls the economy should be in the hands of elected representatives of the people, not in the hands of an industrial oligarchy" and that the size of undertakings may not only be an economic problem but also a social one.[16] The idea was that there are some levels of power that should not become concentrated in private hands. By the end of the 1950s, the US Supreme Court was comfortable enough with the political rationales of antitrust to declare that antitrust is a "charter of economic freedom" and to say that it *aimed at preserving free and unfettered competition as the rule of trade. It rests on the premise that the unrestrained interaction of competitive forces will yield the best allocation of our economic resources, the lowest prices, the highest quality, and the greatest material progress, while at the same time providing an environment conductive to the preservation of our democratic political and social institutions.*[17] The economic and political dimensions of antitrust were seen as two sides of the same coin.

Furthermore, the preservation of democratic political institutions was looked at not only from the point of view of unwillingness to give away too much power over the social process to an *industrial oligarchy*. The role of antitrust was also seen as a remedy against a swing into the opposite direction, i.e. a situation in which the society, dissatisfied with the growth of the power of monopolies, started developing tendencies towards nationalisation and direct regulation, leading further to a transformation of a democratic state into a non-democratic one.[18] Similar sentiments were shared in academic writing up until the 1970s, with probably the most renowned account being made by Robert Pitofsky, whose conclusion on whether antitrust should be concerned with non-economic issues was that "It is bad history, bad policy, and bad law to exclude certain political values in interpreting the antitrust laws".[19]

In Europe, antitrust was discussed and adopted at various points in time. However, looking at it from the point of view of European integration, it can roughly be said that it was adopted during the peak of the more political approach to antitrust in the United States. Ordoliberalism is typically believed to be an important source of inspiration for antitrust in Europe.[20] The ordoliberal perspective, quite similar to the antimonopoly tradition in the United States, assumes that public authorities have a role to play in preserving competition in the market and that competition law has a

[15] Simons (1948), p. 43.

[16] *Columbia Steel,* 334 U.S. 495 (1948).

[17] *Northern Pacific Railway*, 356 U.S. 1 (1958).

[18] Grunes and Stucke (2001), pp. 260–261; Pitofsky (1979), pp. 1062–1063.

[19] Pitofsky (1979), p. 1051.

[20] Amato (1997), pp. 40–43; Behrens (2018); Deutscher and Makris (2016); Gerber (1994); Gerbrandy (2019), pp. 129–130; Wu (2018a), p. 82; Wu (2020), pp. 67–73.

role in preserving a healthy political system, in which neither public nor private power remains unchecked.[21] The ordoliberal ideal was thus a competitive order deprived of political power and working in a state of competition.[22] Under ordoliberalism, competition law serves as part of the "Economic Constitution".[23] Undisturbed competition is one of the foundations of the social order, but its goal is to attain a humane, free, and democratic economic order, rather than making efficiency as the sole and ultimate goal.[24]

The political interpretation of antitrust did therefore recognise that antitrust revolves around the assessment of market activity, i.e. the sphere of economic action. Nevertheless, at the same time, antitrust enforcement had a more meaningful role to play—one in which at the end of the day antitrust was supposed to contribute to a well-functioning democratic society. This, on the other hand, provided space to take into account various political values when looking at how private power that accumulated on the market was exercised. Conceptually, under this more political approach, free speech is potentially something of interest to antitrust.

## 2.3 "More Economic Approach"

The other interpretation of antitrust is that its role should be narrowed down if it is expected to work in a consistent, reasonable, and predictable way.

There are a number of reasons for which this other approach developed. Some of them are more general and can be seen as part of a wider process of political changes, which took place in developed countries, in particular in the United States, from around the 1970s, for instance the energy crisis of the 1970s, a push towards deregulation, and a generation change in politics, which provided a stronger platform for distancing from the policies of the New Deal, of which political antitrust was a part.[25] The other type of reasons was connected to the development of antitrust itself. Part of the problem with the political interpretation of antitrust was that it preached "competition", a market and economic phenomenon, but did not always produce sound (according to the critics) economic results. For instance, being focused on the idea of eradicating certain market practices or ensuring that negative market developments will not take place, antitrust has been used to fight market conduct and

[21] In the 1960s, Oliver describing ordoliberal policies in Germany remarked: "*In general, the West Germans' program resembles Henry Simons*"', see Oliver (1960), p. 118; for more discussion about the interaction between ordoliberalism and early US neoliberalism see also Von Horn (2009), pp. 209–213.

[22] Ptak (2009), p. 123 (commenting on how the ordoliberal ideal had to be further adapted in the context of the post-war reconstruction).

[23] Gerber (1994), pp. 44–45, 49; Deutscher and Makris (2016), p. 193.

[24] Deutscher and Makris (2016), p. 189.

[25] Wu (2011), p. 242; Crane (2014), p. 835; Stoller (2019), pp. 196–223, 312–331; for other reasons, see also Amato (1997), pp. 24, 38; Orbach (2017), p. 19.

market concentration even if they did not bring a clear, immediate harm.[26] In consequence, it was pointed out that antitrust often resembled a situation in which the enforcers were like *a sheriff of a frontier town, walking down the main street and every so often pistol-whipping a few people*, and that the only consistency in some types of cases had been that "the government always wins".[27]

One of the ways of reforming antitrust was through more intensive use of economics—an approach advocated by, inter alia, the members of the Chicago School of Economics.[28] The Chicago School was primarily concerned with analysing antitrust from the point of view of price theory and neoclassical economics.[29] What was relevant was not how many market players are there or how their actions appear to look like but whether undertakings gain the ability to raise prices to the detriment of consumers. For instance, a merger between two leading undertakings does not necessarily have to cause price hikes if the third and fourth players are large enough to constrain the increase of prices. What is more, such an economic approach is "elegant" and could be argued to be "scientific".

What followed from the economic analysis was its legal conceptualisation, i.e. such an interpretation of law that provided the economic approach with legitimacy as "the correct approach". In the 1970s, this legal conceptualisation was framed as the "consumer welfare standard", with welfare being understood in economic terms.[30] From this point of view, the goal of antitrust was not to preserve unclearly defined "competition" or provide a check against concentrated market power but to maximise consumer welfare.

The Chicago interpretation led to a certain consensus, i.e. a narrative that could have and has been criticised but at the same time has shown resistance against being strongly contested.[31] The debate over the goals of antitrust was in consequence settled (at least for a time) in a similar way as the debate over how to promote market economy—the Chicago way, i.e. on purely economic grounds, without reference to values.[32] In Europe, the position of the Chicago School was historically weaker, but the more economic approach became "the approach", with ordoliberalism being

[26] Khan (2017), pp. 725–726; Hovenkamp (2019), p. 127; Teachout (2020), p. 207.

[27] Bork (1978/2021), p. 4; Stoller (2019), p. 249.

[28] The Chicago School underwent a significant evolution of its approach to antitrust and other policies from around the 1930s–1950s. The views of the early representatives of the Chicago School resembled those of Henry Simons (mentioned earlier) and ordoliberals. However, starting from the 1950s a different approach emerged under which less antitrust enforcement was advocated. For a thorough discussion of this evolution, see Mirowski and Von Horn (2009); Von Horn (2009).

[29] Posner (1978), pp. 925–926; Amato (1997), pp. 20–21; Wu (2018a), pp. 83–85.

[30] Bork (1978/2021), pp. 107–115.

[31] Khan (2020), p. 1663; Wu (2018a), pp. 107–108.

[32] For a broader context of the Chicago style of argumentation, see Burgin (2012), pp. 208–212.

marginalised.[33] Under this more economic approach, issues such as free speech are of less interest to antitrust.[34]

## 2.4 The Rediscovery of Political Antitrust

As of 2021, the debate over the role of antitrust is heated. The rapid growth of the role of the Big Tech created a natural need for a discussion whether antitrust had provided an adequate answer or failed. With the Chicago consensus being the standard and mainstream approach, a "more political approach" started to be seen as an alternative. A large part of such positions gathered around "Neobrandeisianism".[35] Neobrandeisianism is primarily a US movement, but since it promotes the political goals of antitrust, it shows some connection with the European ordoliberalism—in fact, some Neobrandeisians see the US antimonopoly tradition and ordoliberalism as close to each other.[36]

The main claim of the supporters of Neobrandeisianism is that the Chicago paradigm is ill-conceived, and so is the consumer welfare standard, which has crippled antitrust enforcement.[37] The Neobrandeisian approach assumes, once again, that antitrust should have a more meaningful role to play and that its agenda should be broader than just economic.

From the point of view of the interaction between free speech and antitrust, this creates an interesting dynamic because with the debate over the political goals of antitrust being once again opened, free speech can be seen as a type of political value under antitrust. In consequence, *at the conceptual level*, speaking about free speech under antitrust is not fundamentally ill-conceived in the sense that a stronger link between antitrust and free speech is dependent on the outcome of a broader debate over the shape of antitrust. This broader debate, on the other hand, is hard to settle as it lacks a common denominator—as long as antitrust debates took place in the framework of efficiency, there was at least a common benchmark to falsify hypotheses. Currently, however, the central issue of the discussion is whether antitrust should pursue more far-reaching goals, not merely efficiency.[38]

---

[33] Gerbrandy (2019), pp. 130–131.

[34] Hence Robert Bork argued in his seminal text: "*The same thing is even more true of other suggested values, such as free speech, the creation of leisure, and so forth. These values, if they are to be served, are better served by laws whose scope is appropriate to reach the full range of situations in which a given value is affected*", Bork (1978/2021), p. 67.

[35] Wu (2018a) and Khan (2018, 2020).

[36] Wu (2020), pp. 67–73; Wu (2018a), p. 82.

[37] Wu (2018a, b), Khan (2017) and Steinbaum and Stucke (2018).

[38] This can be seen as a part of a more philosophical problem which was left unaddressed by the Chicago School, see Burgin (2012), pp. 211–212.

# 3 The Applicatory Level: Addressing Free Speech Under Antitrust

## *3.1 Free Speech and Antitrust in the United States*

### 3.1.1 Free Speech and the Marketplace of Ideas

While conceptually there might be room for pursuing free speech values under antitrust, another issue is whether this is possible on a lower, *applicatory level*. In other words, in what way could it be possible, but from the point of view of not merely the goals of antitrust and abstract concepts but also in the existing legal framework? Interestingly, in that regard, it was not unusual to see connections being made between antitrust and free speech in the United States before the Chicago revolution.

There are two characteristics of the US law that may have contributed to this. First, the US Supreme Court, which handles antitrust cases, is also a constitutional court, interpreting the US Constitution and affording protection of constitutional rights. Free speech is one of such rights, with the First Amendment stipulating that "Congress shall make no law respecting an establishment of religion, or prohibiting the free exercise thereof; or abridging the freedom of speech, or of the press; or the right of the people peaceably to assemble, and to petition the Government for a redress of grievances", i.e. mentioning a certain political freedom (freedom of speech) but from the point of view of potential abuses of public power.

Second, from the early days of free speech jurisprudence in the United States, the language of free speech case law followed closely a rhetoric similar to that of antitrust and market advocacy. In fact, the rhetoric of free speech cases in the United States turned out to be so appealing in that regard that there was a time when the proponents of the Chicago School attempted to bolster their market advocacy by referring to free speech and arguing that the *market for goods* should be treated in a similar way as the *market for ideas*, i.e. be subject to less regulation.[39] In a similar way, in the current Neobrandeisian debate, some advocates of the movement depict the opposition against monopolies and restrictions of free speech as being a part of the same political project that started in the seventeenth-century England.[40]

The tone of the US free speech jurisprudence was set at the beginning of the twentieth century, mostly in the context of the First World War. In a streak of cases concerning *Abrams* and later on also *Schaefer*, *Pierce*, *Gitlow*, and *Whitney*, two justices, Holmes and Brandeis (the one whose name became part of the Neobrandeisian movement), delivered a number of dissents discussing the role of

[39] Director (1953); Coase (1974). A few years after Coase, Robert Bork made a similar comment in the closing remarks of his argument for antitrust focused on consumer welfare, see Bork (1978/2021), p. 442.

[40] Lynn (2020), pp. 82–83, 222–223, 252–253, where he discusses antimonopoly tradition and refers at the same time to e.g. Milton and *Areopagitica*.

free speech.[41] The dissents followed the tradition presented earlier by Milton and Mill and advocated free speech based on the idea that various viewpoints should be subject to discussion and deliberation. In *Abrams*, Holmes framed free speech in terms similar to a market interaction, stating that *when men have realized that time has upset many fighting faiths, they may come to believe even more than they believe the very foundations of their own conduct that the ultimate good desired is better reached by free trade in ideas – that the best test of truth is the power of the thought to get itself accepted in the competition of the market, and that truth is the only ground upon which their wishes safely can be carried out.*

The narrative chosen by Holmes was followed over the years and culminated in the adoption of the phrase "the marketplace of ideas".[42] For instance, in *Lamont*, Justice Brennan pointed out that *the right to receive publications is such a fundamental right. The dissemination of ideas can accomplish nothing if otherwise willing addressees are not free to receive and consider them. It would be a barren marketplace of ideas that had only sellers and no buyers*. In consequence, in a similar way as in antitrust, where there is a "market", "trade takes place", and "restrictions of trade" can be introduced, free speech gained its own "marketplace" and its own sellers and buyers.

Initially, free speech guarantees concerned primarily "political speech", i.e. speech aimed at expressing political ideas. Conversely, "commercial speech", i.e. communicating information on goods, was not protected in a similar way.[43] However, the approach changed in the 1970s, following a case concerning the advertising of pharmaceutical products, *Virginia Pharmacy Board*.[44] As it was pointed out by the court, "our pharmacist does not wish to editorialize on any subject, cultural, philosophical, or political. He does not wish to report any particularly newsworthy fact, or to make generalized observations even about commercial matters. The 'idea' he wishes to communicate is simply this: 'I will sell you the X prescription drug at the Y price.'"[45]

Another feature of free speech jurisprudence that could have added up to the perception of its interaction with antitrust is the doctrine of public forum and its application outside state-individual context. In the 1940s *Marsh* case, the US Supreme Court decided whether a corporate town could have prohibited an individual from distributing leaflets on its premises.[46] A corporate town is a town owned by a corporation (e.g. a mining town owned by a mining company), in which all "public" spaces belong to a private owner. While the town was privately owned,

[41] *Abrams*, 250 U.S. 616 (1919); *Schaefer*, 251 U.S. 466 (1920); *Pierce*, 252 U.S. 239 (1920); *Gitlow*, 268 U.S. 652 (1925); *Whitney*, 274 U.S. 357 (1927).

[42] See e.g. *Rumely*, 345 U.S. 41 (1953); *Lamont*, 381 U.S. 301 (1965).

[43] *Valentine*, 316 U.S. 52 (1942).

[44] *Virginia State Board of Pharmacy*, 425 U.S. 748 (1976). The case was preceded by another judgment—*Bigelow*, 421 U.S. 809 (1975).

[45] The approach was followed in *Central Hudson Gas*, 447 U.S. 557 (1980).

[46] *Marsh*, 326 U.S. 501 (1946).

freedom of speech had to be respected by the company in public fora. The decision of the court was motivated, inter alia, by the fact that "The more an owner, for his advantage, opens up his property for use by the public in general, the more do his rights become circumscribed by the statutory and constitutional rights of those who use it"—interestingly a logic overlapping with that of antimonopoly rhetoric and assuming that being in a position of power entails also obligations.[47] However, over time, the *Marsh* approach has been restricted, affecting also the approach to public fora in the "cyberspace".[48] In the 2020s, the result of Prager University's litigation against Google is instructive in that respect, with the court pointing out that the First Amendment did not apply to YouTube.[49]

To conclude, free speech jurisprudence created a powerful, political narrative in the United States—that of encouraging speech in a "marketplace-like" environment in which individuals can trade ideas. Moreover, speech covered both political and commercial information and, at least, initially was seen as something to be protected against any arbitrary exercise of power, public and private. At the same time, another interesting dynamic took place. On the one hand, despite an attempt to apply the public forum doctrine to private entities, the First Amendment remained to be appropriate safeguard against government actions. On the other hand, free speech protection was strengthening its links with the "market", in terms of both the language ("marketplace of ideas", "buyers and sellers") and scope (commercial speech). With antitrust legislation functioning for a long time as the "charter" of economic life and a check and balance against private power, the fact that at some point connections between free speech and antitrust started to be made can be seen as a natural development.

### 3.1.2 Antitrust as a Facilitator of Free Speech

While the first free speech precedent-setting cases were decided during and shortly after the First World War, the seminal "antitrust free speech" case took place during the Second World War. The case concerned the practices of The Associated Press and required first a district court and then the US Supreme Court to decide on restrictive agreements entered into by The Associated Press and aimed at withholding information from non-members.[50]

During the litigation, The Associated Press attempted to defend its action through a reference to the First Amendment. In other words, it tried to use free speech to shield itself from antitrust charges. Still, the district court decided against it. In

[47] Compare *Marsh* with a pre-Sherman "antitrust" reasoning in *Munn*, 94 U.S. 113 (1876) (which, however, was soon overruled, providing additional reasons for adopting statutory antitrust legislation), see also Lynn (2020), p. 140.

[48] Nunziato (2007), pp. 1130–1143.

[49] Stempel (2020).

[50] *Associated Press*, 52 F. Supp. 362 (S.D.N.Y. 1943); *Associated Press*, 326 U.S. 1 (1945).

practical terms, the court did two things. First, it refused to treat the First Amendment as a safe harbour from antitrust enforcement. Second, it opened the door for further arguments, i.e. that the values protected by the First Amendment can (should) be protected also outside its scope—free speech and freedom of the press covered by the First Amendment have at their centre the free flow of information, which can also be protected by the antitrust legislation if the restriction is a product of private parties.[51]

The Supreme Court confirmed the judgment of the district court, with Justice Frankfurter going further and saying that The Associated Press *has a relation to the public interest unlike that of any other enterprise pursued for profit. A free press is indispensable to the workings of our democratic society. The business of the press, and therefore the business of the Associated Press, is the promotion of truth regarding public matters by furnishing the basis for an understanding of them. Truth and understanding are not wares like peanuts or potatoes. And so, the incidence of restraints upon the promotion of truth through denial of access to the basis for understanding calls into play considerations very different from comparable restraints in a cooperative enterprise having merely a commercial aspect.*

In practical terms, Justice Frankfurter combined two elements: he noted that the arrangements entered into by The Associated Press were not in line with antitrust legislation. However, competition in the market was not the only interest at stake to be taken into account—The Associated Press' actions were also harmful due to the specific nature of its business and its impact on the marketplace of ideas. In his opinion, Justice Frankfurter pointed out further that the flow of information should be disturbed by neither public censorship nor private restraints. In a way then, Justice Frankfurter reached a conclusion similar to that later held in *Marsh* and currently subscribed to by the Neobrandeisians, i.e. that *power is power* and that the tools used for controlling public power can be redesigned to control its private manifestations.[52]

However, while the *Marsh* approach was put on hold, *Associated Press* reappeared in jurisprudence, e.g. in *Red Lion Broadcasting*.[53] Since *Red Lion Broadcasting* was decided in a period after the adoption of the more general term of the "marketplace of ideas", the case included a reference to this concept, too. In consequence, the court confirmed its conclusion from *Associated Press*, stating also that "it is the purpose of the First Amendment to preserve an uninhibited marketplace of ideas in which truth will ultimately prevail, rather than to countenance

[51] A few decades later, with Chicago School becoming the mainstream approach, Robert Bork commented negatively on the line of argument presented by Learned-Hand (who judged the case), see Bork (1978/2021), p. 50. According to Bork, Learned-Hand's reasoning allowed pursuing any policy desired by a judge. As Bork was an antitrust and constitutional scholar, his arguments can also be read by taking into account his views on judicial restraint and the First Amendment—Bork was critical of judicial activism and the direction of First Amendment jurisprudence, see Bork (1996/2010), pp. 200–218.

[52] Wu (2011), pp. 302–303.

[53] *Red Lion Broadcasting*, 395 U.S. 367 (1969).

monopolization of that market, whether it be by the Government itself or a private licensee", and referring also to Holmes's dissent in *Abrams*. The court further argued that "it is the right of the public to receive suitable access to social, political, esthetic, moral, and other ideas and experiences which is crucial here" and declared, referring once again to *Associated Press*, that "there is no sanctuary in the First Amendment for unlimited private censorship operating in a medium not open to all".

Both *Associated Press* and *Red Lion Broadcasting* were then invoked by the US Supreme Court in another case concerning the Federal Communication Commission, *National Citizens Committee*.[54] The case concerned the rule-making powers of the Commission. When discharging these powers, the Commission made references to the values protected by the First Amendment—taking this into account, the court commented on these references extensively. Doing so, the court held, inter alia, that the regulations imposed by the commission are similar *to the prohibitions imposed by the antitrust laws. This court has held that application of the antitrust laws to newspapers is not only consistent with, but is actually supportive of, the values underlying, the First Amendment.*

While in the 1980s the US antitrust law was already undergoing the Chicago revolution and the more political approach was fading away, free speech still made its appearance in the last, to this date, US break-up case, *AT&T*. This time it was a district court which discussing numerous other arguments for its decision, motivated its reasoning also by a reference to the *values underlying the First Amendment*.[55]

Still, in the 1980s, the "antitrust free speech" jurisprudence stopped developing in high-profile cases, leaving behind unanswered questions. For instance, the approach presented in *Associated Press* can be read as meaning that in cases with a free speech element, more caution should be exercised, which in practical terms could mean a stricter application of antitrust tests. Also, the conclusion that antitrust is "supportive of free speech values" may both mean that antitrust has its own work to do, but as a "by-product" may help free speech, or that its relationship with free speech values could be more direct. In *Red Lion Broadcasting*, on the other hand, the court mentioned that there is "a right" to receive certain information (recall also *Lamont*), but at the same time when remarking on "monopolisation", it decided to include a reference to the government or private "licensee".

### 3.1.3 Free Speech Values Under Antitrust Today

Taking into account the framework outlined above, the context of the discussions over free speech and the Big Tech in the United States is complex. On the one hand, it was the United States that became the birthplace of the Chicago revolution, creating in the United States a push towards a purely economic approach to antitrust. On the other hand, there are three elements pulling the discussion in the opposite

[54] *National Citizens Committee*, 436 U.S. 775 (1978).

[55] *American Telephone & Telegraph*, 552 F. Supp. 131 (D.D.C. 1983).

direction. First, the free speech tradition in the US law is particularly strong, making free speech arguments a socially attractive narrative. Second, there are examples of an interplay between antitrust and free speech in the US jurisprudence, providing foundations to put forward antitrust-related free speech arguments. Third, there are Neobrandeisian arguments attracting attention in the United States and a changing political mood, both aiming to swing the course of enforcement.

Taking into account cases such as the bans imposed on social media users, the de-platforming of free speech fora, and the calls for break-ups of the Big Tech, with free speech being one of the arguments, there are a number of areas in which the "old" case law might still provide inspiration on how to look at antitrust enforcement.

First of all, insofar as commercial speech is concerned, antitrust enforcement does not seem problematic as antitrust is applicable to commercial contexts.[56] In consequence, antitrust may be simply enforced, and when done so it may be indirectly "supportive" of free speech values. However, what is also possible is an approach similar to that in *Associated Press*—once a speech element is identified, a "more cautious" approach can be taken. Understandably, however, commercial speech is less of an issue than political speech and therefore also less significant in the debate over the interaction between antitrust and free speech.

When it comes to political speech, the possible role of antitrust is more complicated. The result of *DataCell/WikiLeaks* litigation in the United States is instructive in that respect.[57] DataCell was a company with ties to WikiLeaks, providing WikiLeaks with website hosting and technical support. DataCell supported its activity from donations that could have been made with credit cards. After WikiLeaks revealed classified information belonging to the US government, Visa and Mastercard ordered their licensees to stop the payment processing for DataCell. This meant that DataCell lost a source of its income. In consequence, DataCell sued Visa and Mastercard for an alleged antitrust violation. However, during the litigation, the district court expected proof of injury to some market, stating that antitrust does not simply protect *the free exchange of ideas*. As DataCell did not define any specific market, apart from mentioning broadly the "media market", the court did not see the blocking of DataCell as possibly harmful. Consequently, the court concluded that DataCell failed to establish standing and to state a plausible claim for relief.

Furthermore, insofar as unilateral practices are concerned, the US primary piece of antitrust legislation, the Sherman Act, stipulates: *Every person who shall monopolize, or attempt to monopolize, or combine or conspire with any other person or persons, to monopolize any part of the trade or commerce among the several States* is guilty of a felony. The fact that some markets should be subject to

[56] See also Day (2020), pp. 1344–1353.

[57] *DataCell*, Case No. 1:14-cv-1658 (GBL/TCB) (E.D. Va. Jul. 30, 2015). The case was litigated under Section 1 of the Sherman Act (multilateral practices). The case, however, included analysis similar to that seen in unilateral practices, as the court assessed the likelihood of an injury to a private party.

"monopolisation" may cast doubts over whether any market could be monopolised by an action such as the blocking of speech.[58] One could also speculate that under this reasoning, "monopolisation" would require obtaining the control over all carriers of free speech or at least a significant part of them. Another way of looking at this type of case would be assessing how a monopolist is using its already obtained market power, i.e. not whether it monopolises a market but whether it uses its power in a "fair" way—I return to this issue when discussing the European point of view, as EU competition law appears to be more flexible in that respect.

The limitations encountered in relation to unilateral actions may look differently in a broader perspective of a possible break-up. A break-up may follow a successful antitrust investigation. The general logic behind linking break-ups and free speech is that with the lower market power of the holder of a speech forum and with users having more options to switch between platforms, the platforms are argued to possibly be more responsive to users' needs (i.e. less arbitrary in relation to content deletion). Furthermore, moderation practices could be more diverse over a wider range of platforms, providing more safe harbours to users.

While it might be difficult to pursue a stand-alone "political speech" antitrust action, the result of *AT&T* break-up shows that things may play out differently when there is already another ground to apply antitrust remedies. In consequence, while, e.g., in *DataCell/WikiLeaks* the court found it problematic to speak about antitrust injury in relation to the "marketplace of ideas", in *AT&T* the court assessed the case in an ordinary antitrust framework and treated free speech values as an argument supporting its general conclusion. In legal terms, in such a case, the main ground for the break-up would be a more mainstream and less controversial one, while the interests associated with free speech would serve as an additional principle and value taken into account. In a way, such an approach would also be similar to *Associated Press*—there would be a general ground for action, while free speech values would serve as a reason to exercise "more caution".

The field of antitrust in which free speech interests can be as of today most easily included appears to be merger control. This is because under merger investigations, the objective is to establish in prospective terms what may be the impact of the merger on the situation on the market—the more hypothetical type of analysis leaves more room for considering possible negative effects for consumers. Also, when analysed in more hypothetical terms, consumer welfare can be more easily interpreted in broad terms. In consequence, if following a merger there is a chance that consumers would have less choice between platforms and there would be less diversity in moderation terms (as one platform would cease to exist or start to have uniform terms with its new owner), it could be argued that the quality of products on the market from the point of view of consumers would fall, providing reasons to block the merger.

---

[58] Chilson and Mattox (2020), p. 17.

This type of argument was in fact seen in the United States already in the 2000s, i.e. during a period of large media mergers.[59] The idea behind these arguments was, in the first place, like currently under Neobrandeisianism, that antitrust has a political role to play and that values such as free speech should be of interest to antitrust. Since the (traditional) media played, in the 2000s, a leading role in facilitating free speech, particular attention was attached to how they operate. Second, it was argued that if such special values as free speech are concerned, merger analysis should follow more sophisticated analysis and should focus not only on price effects (i.e. mostly the impact of a merger on advertising markets) but also on consumer welfare, seen as the availability of a plurality of views. Likewise, the significance of market power should be seen from the perspective of not only advertising but also the "marketplace of ideas", i.e. its role for free speech. In the late 2010s, i.e. during the developing antitrust debate over the Big Tech, the issue of mergers and their impact on free speech returned in a similar fashion. Arguments were presented in relation to assessing market position based on diversity of views.[60]

Last, there are multilateral practices. As pointed out earlier, in cases such as *Associated Press*, agreements between undertakings can be seen as not only simply restricting trade but also being subject to particular scrutiny as they may impact free speech. Here, what is of importance is that the Big Tech's actions in relation to controversial speech often occur in parallel, but whether they are coordinated or not can realistically be verified only by public authorities equipped with proper investigative powers. While the current antitrust debates in the United States focus primarily on monopolisation and advocating break-ups, it seems that the prohibition of anti-competitive agreements could very well also serve the purpose of preserving free speech values. This is because instances of coordination between competitors are typically most suspicious under antitrust. I return to this issue further on when discussing examples of cases in which Article 101 of the Treaty on the Functioning of the European Union (TFEU) could possibly interact with free speech.

To sum up, from the US point of view, antitrust and free speech are interrelated at the applicatory level, but the relationship between them is complex. The logic and rationales of antitrust and free speech are similar in the sense that they both introduce a preference for an exchange of goods and "ideas" that remain undistorted by artificial measures—an issue picked up in judicial reasoning. However, in the United States, the interaction between the two is also marked by possible limitations coming from the language of antitrust legislation. For the European perspective, this means that there are two possible steps of analysis: establish whether a similar general relationship could be possible and verify whether the antitrust framework itself poses similar limitations.

[59] Grunes and Stucke (2001).

[60] Stigler Committee on Digital Platforms (2019), pp. 186–187.

## 3.2 Free Speech and Antitrust in the European Union

### 3.2.1 Free Speech Values and a More Political Approach

The general relationship between free speech and antitrust in the United States was ultimately based on two elements: first, the fact that, originally, antitrust had a more significant, political role to play, which is now rediscovered under the Neobrandeisian arguments, and, second, the fact that free speech has been recognised in the United States as an important political value.

When it comes to the role of competition law, the Neobrandeisian arguments are mirrored in Europe by the ordoliberal tradition. For instance, already before the current debate over the role of the Big Tech, arguments were made that EU competition law should embrace more firmly non-economic interests such as those associated with sustainable growth.[61] Public interest considerations have also been present in case law, typically in the form of an "antitrust defence", i.e. a reason not to apply competition law.[62] The controversies associated with the Big Tech and their impact on the functioning of political systems provide a further reason to discuss the role of political values under antitrust. In consequence, when it comes to the general dynamics of the discussion on antitrust, the US and European perspectives follow a

[61] Sustainability is provided here as an example of a more contemporary claim regarding non-economic interests, see e.g. Gerbrandy (2017); Monti and Mulder (2017). In the context of more attention being given to sustainability issues, the Dutch competition authority published in 2020–2021 a draft of "Guidelines on Sustainability Agreements". Developing an approach to sustainability gained also the attention of the German and a number of other national authorities, see Bundeskartellamt (2020), pp. 28–39. However, sustainability is not the only non-economic interest claimed under EU competition law. Petit points out that various non-competition (i.e. not strictly economic) interests were argued in the past in case law, including e.g. the protection of employment, cultural diversity and media pluralism, regional development, professional ethics, see Petit (2009), pp. 6–7.

[62] The outcome of *Wouters* is often seen as an example of EU courts accepting a margin of tolerance to seemingly anti-competitive agreements provided they serve a public interest—in this case, the court accepted an industry standard banning multidisciplinary practice to ensure proper practice of the legal profession: CJEU, Case C-309/90, *Wouters*, ECLI:EU:C:2002:98. In *Meca-Medina*, on the other hand, the court saw a legitimate interest in adopting measures restricting the freedom of action as they were inherent to the organisation and proper conduct of competitive sport (CJEU, Case C-519/04 P, *Meca-Medina*, ECLI:EU:C:2006:492, para. 45). In *Ordem dos Técnicos Oficiais de Contas* the court considered guaranteeing the quality of the services offered by chartered accountants (CJEU, Case C-1/12, *Ordem dos Técnicos Oficiais de Contas*, para. ECLI:EU:C:2013:127, para. 94–95). See Monti and Mulder (2017), pp. 645–647; Witt (2012). In *Consiglio nazionale dei geologi*, the court took a more nuanced approach, holding that the rules concerning the remuneration of geologists adopted by an association of geologists may restrict competition. However, the court left to a national court the task of establishing whether a restriction of competition indeed took place and whether "*the rules of that code, in particular in so far as they apply the criterion based on the dignity of the profession, may be regarded as necessary for the implementation of the legitimate objective of providing guarantees to consumers of geologists' services*" (CJEU, Case C-136/12, *Consiglio nazionale dei geologi*, ECLI:EU:C:2013:489, para. 57).

similar pattern. Taking into account the fact that the ordoliberal perspective was discussed in Europe already before the emergence of the Big Tech debate, there are few reasons to believe that ordoliberal thinking will become less prominent.

In relation to free speech as a political value, on the other hand, there are some parallels between the US and European situations, yet there are differences too. In the United States, free speech has been constitutionally protected since the time of the adoption of the First Amendment. In addition, antitrust started as a political project, with cases being heard by the same court that ruled on the free speech issues. In Europe, the case has been different. Most of the antitrust jurisprudence shared by a large number of European states has developed at the European Union level and in the context of economic integration. In consequence, EU antitrust case law has been mostly focused on economic issues. Free speech, on the other hand, has remained either the domain of constitutional law of each European state or human rights jurisprudence developed by the European Court of Human Rights (ECHR).

However, even in this mostly economic environment, the concept of the marketplace of ideas is not unknown to EU jurisprudence. In *TED I*, the ECJ was asked to rule on the legality of the Tobacco Advertising Directive.[63] While the ECJ struck down the directive referring to its legal basis, Advocate General Fennelly provided in his opinion a more detailed overview of the case, arguing that commercial speech should be protected under EU law.[64] The Advocate General pointed to a number of reasons for which undisturbed exchange of information is of value. Firstly, the exchange of various types of information (political, aesthetic) contributes to the attainment of certain social goals, which at the same time remain at the heart of liberal democratic society's life. Secondly, while the Advocate General did not believe that the contribution of the exchange of commercial information to these goals is the same, it still serves a similar purpose. Thirdly, apart from any utilitarian arguments, there are other values that demand the protection of free communication, such as the preservation of the autonomy, dignity, and personal development of individuals—the last of which bears much resemblance to the classical Brandeisian arguments for antitrust enforcement discussed earlier.

To see how the dynamic of the US pre-Chicago jurisprudence may be closer to the logic of EU law than it may at first appear, it is interesting to also consider such judicial developments as in *Stim*. In *Stim*, the General Court was confronted with an argument that the European Commission should take into account cultural diversity when interpreting Article 101 TFEU since the Treaty itself puts such an obligation on the EU institutions.[65] The court concluded: "in the application of Article 81 EC, the Commission is required to take into consideration the objective of respecting and promoting cultural diversity, in particular where the application of that article

[63] CJEU, Case C-376/98, *Federal Republic of Germany v European Parliament and Council of the European Union*, ECLI:EU:C:2000:544; see also Krzeminska-Vamvaka (2009).

[64] Opinion of Advocate General Fennelly, Case C-376/98, *Federal Republic of Germany v European Parliament and Council of the European Union*, ECLI:EU:C:2000:324, para. 153–154.

[65] Article 167 (4) TFEU, i.e. included in the part of the Treaty concerning non-antitrust issues.

concerns an activity linked to culture".[66] Taking into account the fact that the Charter of Fundamental Rights declares in Article 11 that EU citizens have "a right" to freedom of expression, one could imagine under EU law an argument similar to that seen in *Associated Press*.

Furthermore, when making his argument in *TED I*, the Advocate General did refer to the case law of the European Court of Human Rights as a source of inspiration. The relationship between EU law and ECHR case law is complicated, taking into account the fact that all EU member states are party to the convention (and also have powers to apply Articles 101 and 102 TFEU), while the European Union is not. However, there should be no doubt that free speech constitutes a political value, being expressed in similar terms both in Article 10 of the European Convention on Human Rights and Article 11 of the Charter of Fundamental Rights.[67] With the signing of the Treaty of Lisbon and with more emphasis on fundamental rights, including the establishment of a "more political Union", the ECHR jurisprudence that enshrines the legal tradition of the EU member states might indeed serve as a source of inspiration.

From this point of view, the European case becomes even more similar to the US as the "marketplace of ideas" rhetoric known from the US jurisprudence is repeated in the ECHR jurisprudence. For instance, in *Mouvement Raëlien Suisse*, judge De Albuquerque referred in his dissenting opinion to the marketplace of ideas, saying that "If streets and parks of a city are the historical quintessential public fora, the Internet is today's global marketplace of ideas", and discussed the foundations of the concept by referring to its historic roots and *Abrams*.[68] In *Delfi*, on the other hand, judges Sajó and Tsotsoria appended their dissenting opinion with an additional statement that discussed the origins of the debate on the marketplace of ideas, i.e. the struggle between the English king and parliament, followed by Milton's *Areopagitica*.[69]

In consequence, the European perspective shares similarities with the US point of view, in relation to both the goals of antitrust and the understanding of the role of free speech. Taking into account the less frequent references to a possible interaction between antitrust and free speech in Europe, what appears to be missing is the realisation that if a more political approach to antitrust is advocated in Europe, then there might be a link between antitrust and free speech. The question then is what European antitrust could do for free speech. Interestingly, a closer look at this issue suggests that the relationship between antitrust and free speech in Europe might be easier than in the United States, where the debate is more present.

---

[66] GC, Case T-451/08, *Stim*, ECLI:EU:T:2013:189, para. 73.

[67] Cf. Article 52.3 CFR on the relationship between the ECHR and the Charter of Fundamental Rights as regards the scope of rights in the Charter that correspond to rights in the ECHR.

[68] *Mouvement Raëlien Suisse v. Switzerland*, no. 16354/06, 13 July 2012.

[69] *Delfi AS v. Estonia*, no. 64569/09, 16 June 2015.

### 3.2.2 Free Speech in the European Antitrust Framework

Same as in the United States, antitrust and free speech can interact in the European context in a number of ways. In the first place, it could be Article 101 TFEU. In consequence, if for instance a number of Big Tech companies decided to coordinate their actions in relation to certain market behaviour, e.g. blocking (censoring) speech of a given type, then possibly Article 101 TFEU could be used to counteract such activity. It can be argued that Article 101 TFEU can be used to support free speech values, in relation to both political speech and commercial speech.

What is crucial from the point of view of Article 101 TFEU is that undertakings should set their market policies independently of each other.[70] Joint actions aimed at eliminating the commercial speech of a certain kind can be seen as a collective boycott—also, as there is a commercial element involved, there should be no doubt that competition rules are applicable.[71] Coordinated actions in relation to political speech could likewise be of interest under Article 101 TFEU. This may concern both *political speech within a commercial context* (but with speech being political, not commercial) and *political speech outside such a context.*

The first situation would involve, e.g., a collective boycott of a controversial online political channel financed through platform advertising and contributions sent by viewers. Let us assume that, for instance, a group of Big Tech companies join an "alliance against fake news" and then start banning independent political channels from their platforms based on widely defined "community guidelines". From the point of view of Article 101 TFEU, the companies would act in agreement, coordinating their market conduct and refusing to provide services to a certain group of clients. As the online political channels would be engaged in their activity with a profit motive, one could argue that the scenario is not far from ordinary antitrust cases with "economic freedom" being at stake. However, there is also "political freedom" at stake as the channels are engaged in political speech, with interests being similar as in *Associated Press*, i.e. possibly requiring more caution.

[70] CJEU, Case C-199/92 P, *Hüls*, ECLI:EU:C:1999:358, para. 159.

[71] Article 101 TFEU does not distinguish "collective boycott" as a type of anticompetitive agreement. However, Article 101 TFEU provides merely a list of examples of anti-competitive agreements. "Collective boycott" generally means that a group of undertakings agrees to refuse to buy or sell goods or services from/to a selected entity. In the Commission Staff Working Document "Guidance on restrictions of competition "by object" for the purpose of defining which agreements may benefit from the De Minimis Notice" (25.06.2014), collective boycott was defined as an agreement which "*occurs when a group of competitors agree to exclude an actual or potential competitor*". This type of boycott took place in relation to e.g. *Pre-insulated pipes* cartel (case IV/35.691, para. 98–107). However, there appears to be no reason to conclude that a "collective boycott" takes place only, if it is aimed at another actual or potential competitor (and not e.g. a client or consumer). For instance, Petit (2010) argued that a (collective) boycott of a movie "Alice in Wonderland" (i.e. not obtaining it from the movie distributor) by cinemas in certain European countries could have amounted to an infringement of Article 101 TFEU, since—provided that the cinemas had jointly decided to do so—it would constitute a collective boycott.

The second situation would be similar, but instead of online political channels, the banned content would come from consumers communicating on the platform to, e.g., advocate for public gatherings in support of a controversial politician claiming that elections were "fraudulent" and "stolen". Here, there would be no economic freedom narrative involved on the part of consumers, except some room to argue that the consumers "paid" with their data for the use of social media platforms and are not getting a "fair" deal because their content is deleted.

It is also interesting to see that such cases may involve similar dilemmas as ordinary free speech cases in relation to state actions, insofar as states often see some merit in banning political speech, e.g. hate speech. For instance, the Big Tech companies pushed by stakeholders to better manage fake news (e.g. in the context of upcoming elections) may have incentives to coordinate their actions (e.g. exchange information, make sure that everyone indeed bans the content since otherwise profits and viewers may switch to competition).[72] In other words, there might be a "legitimate" interest to ensure that some speakers are not given the floor. Theoretically, under EU law, the undertakings could argue that while their actions involve coordination and a restriction of competition (for a certain group of clients, i.e. those spreading the news), they have redeeming values under Article 101 (3) TFEU.

However, the redeeming value would largely be a political one (e.g. the quality of democratic debate) rather than strictly economic (a platform free from fake news; i.e., the product becomes better for consumers—after all, the consumers may ignore the political channels or accounts with controversial content). The question under Article 101 TFEU may therefore be twofold: first, whether, e.g., some precedence ("more caution") to free speech values should be given under Article 101 (1) TFEU in a similar vein as in *Associated Press*. Second, if Article 101 (1) TFEU can be supportive of free speech under its current interpretation, should defences related to (non-economic) political values be allowed under Article 101 (3) TFEU? In this case, the question becomes similar to sustainability arguments under antitrust, which already has been subject to antitrust debates.[73]

Unilateral practices affecting free speech can be seen as more interesting in the European context than that in the United States. Section 2 of the Sherman Act puts much emphasis on "monopolisation", and it could be hard to argue that the blocking of speech leads to the "monopolisation" of the "marketplace of ideas" or some ordinary market. In the United States, unilateral conduct should ideally involve an "exclusionary" aspect in relation to competitors.[74] In comparison, at the EU level, the wording of Article 102 TFEU is more open to the inclusion of political values as

[72] See also another type of conflicting interests: Teachout (2020), pp. 5, 77, 140, 190, who, on the one hand, criticises the power of the Big Tech over the information flows, but, on the other hand, appears to see a legitimate interest in e.g. the Big Tech banning the speech of the US National Rifle Association.

[73] See e.g. Monti and Mulder (2017), pp. 644–650.

[74] See also Chilson and Mattox (2020), p. 16.

it says that "any abuse" by one or more undertakings of a dominant position is prohibited. With the emphasis being put on "any abuse", the language of Article 102 TFEU provides more room for investigating abuses that in fact have less to do with competition.

A comparison can be made between two cases. In the first case, a Big Pharma company acquires a niche drug used by a group of consumers who already use the drug and cannot easily switch to a substitute. As the price of the drug is not regulated, the undertaking sees an opportunity to raise the price. Quite likely, such a practice would draw the attention of antitrust authorities as "abusive".[75] However, it should be clear that such an action does not "restrict" competition (it might even encourage it as higher prices may theoretically lead to new market entries). In consequence, while cases of abusing market position are more difficult in the United States, in Europe acting "fair" when holding a position of power falls more easily into antitrust.[76]

In the second case, a Big Tech company operates a social media platform, and while switching to another platform is just "one click away", it may require ditching some acquaintances, making it unrealistic. At the same time, the company decides to systematically remove political content of a certain kind. In consequence, some users keep paying (with their data) the "full price" for the platform but receive less value for money (consumer welfare) and have fewer opportunities to exercise their free speech (what can be termed "citizen welfare").[77] Irrespective of the choice of the approach under Article 102 TFEU (exploitation, discrimination), it is not without sense to argue that the platform did abuse its position.

It is also interesting to see that even in such a case, there are more issues to settle. For instance, in the United States, it is not uncommon to argue that free speech requires the state not to impose speech; i.e., a possible defence against using Article 102 TFEU to support free speech could be free speech itself, i.e. the liberty of an undertaking not to host the speech of others. But then again, while in the United States such arguments could be effective, it could very well be argued that in the European context, the choice could be similar to *Associated Press*; i.e., free speech arguments cannot be used in antitrust context to stifle the free speech of others. Also, under Article 102 TFEU, undertakings can refer to objective justification for their actions; e.g., they can argue that some speech had to be deleted because of "public safety" concerns (e.g. riots following elections). Still, in such cases, the actions of dominant undertakings should be proportionate, and it could very well turn out that the "cyberspace-police" role of undertakings should be left to public authorities.[78]

---

[75] See the actions taken by the European Commission in case AT.40394 (*Aspen*). For other similar cases initiated at the level of national competition authorities, see First (2019), pp. 720–726.

[76] For the more problematic case in the United States, see First (2019).

[77] Citizen welfare standard is proposed by e.g. Stigler Committee on Digital Platforms (2019), pp. 186–187, while Van Dijck et al. (2019) propose expanding consumer welfare to include "citizen wellbeing".

[78] In case T-30/89, *Hilti*, ECLI:EU:T:1991:70, para. 182, the EU Court of First Instance dealt with a case bearing some resemblance to such a situation, i.e. an undertaking trying to justify its actions

Typically, under Article 102 TFEU, there are also various ways to prosecute cases. For instance, a typical way of framing instances of denial of contracting is investigating them under the so-called essential facilities doctrine, which revolves around the concept that only if the infrastructure (e.g. social media platform) is indispensable can its holder be expected to deliver a service.[79]

There are in fact cases of similar kind in the area of human rights. For instance, in *Appleby*, the ECHR decided on a case in which a local meeting spot had been built by a public entity but then privatised.[80] Nevertheless, the location had still been considered a popular meeting spot and a group of activists had attempted to distribute on its premises information concerning local politics. The activists had not been allowed to do so. In consequence, they had referred to the public forum doctrine (recall *Marsh*). Taking into account the fact that the case ultimately concerned horizontal relationships (the activists were a private party, and so was the owner of the meeting spot), the ECHR recognised, referring to one of its earlier judgments, *Özgür Gündem*, that in some instances the protection of fundamental rights might require positive action on the part of states (e.g. enabling speech).[81] However, the ECHR also concluded that in *Appleby*, the activists had other alternatives of informing about their cause, e.g. distributing the leaflets in public passages leading to the venue, engaging in door-to-door campaigns, or seeking exposure in the local press, radio, or television. In a way, in a non-antitrust context, the ECHR said that the meeting spot was not an "essential facility".

Still, there are also other ways of framing antitrust cases, e.g. under discrimination arguments.[82] Interestingly enough, in a dissenting opinion to *Appleby*, Judge

based on an argument that it was concerned with (product) safety. The court pointed out that it is not for a dominant undertaking to take such actions, but for public authorities. It should be stressed, however, that the case itself was an exclusionary case.

[79]The essential facilities doctrine originates from the United States but its rationales were adopted by EU courts, see e.g. CJEU, Case-7/97, *Oscar Bronner*, ECLI:EU:C:1998:569, para. 38–47; CFI, Case T-504/93, *Tiercé Ladbroke*, ECLI:EU:T:1997:84, para. 131; CJEU, Case C-418/01, *IMS Health*, ECLI:EU:C:2004:257, para. 28–30; CFI, Case T-201/04, *Microsoft*, ECLI:EU:T:2007:289, para. 331–333. The essential facilities doctrine is typically applied when a competitor is requested to provide a service or sell a good to another competitor. However, Article 102 TFEU remains flexible in application, as it can be applied when abuse takes place in relation to competitors or consumers directly (CJEU, Case 6/72, *Continental Can*, ECLI:EU:C:1973:22, para. 26). Also, the list of abuses provided in the provision is not exhaustive (CJEU, Case C-333/94 P, *Tetra* Pak, ECLI:EU:C:1996:436, para. 37; CJEU, Case C-395/96 P and C-396/96 P, *Compagnie Maritime Belge*, ECLI:EU:C:2000:132, para. 112).

[80]*Appleby and Others v. The United Kingdom*, no. 44306/98, 6 May 2003.

[81]*Özgür Gündem v. Turkey*, no. 23144/93, 16 March 2000.

[82]In antitrust, discrimination cases typically consist in price discrimination. Price discrimination means that consumers or groups of consumers are charged different prices which do not reflect differences in the costs of supply, see Bishop and Walker (2010), p. 251. While from the legal point of view "discrimination" typically bears a negative meaning, in economics it may bring positive (welfare) effects, i.e. an increased output. This is because by adjusting pricing policy (charging some consumers more and some less) an undertaking may be capable of bringing a higher volume of products to the market. Under extreme conditions (so-called first-degree price discrimination) an

Maruste pointed to an issue not taken properly into account by the majority of the judges, i.e. the fact that the activist had been treated unequally as other activists, and the local government had been allowed to make political advertising, with only the activists in question being denied to do so. In antitrust terms then, the judge argued that it was not the "essential facilities" doctrine that should be applied but that the case should be decided as a discriminatory one.

Finally, when it comes to merger regulation, the prospects of the EU merger regulation being supportive of free speech values appear to be most similar to the arguments put forward in the United States. The EU merger regulation uses a test of a significant impediment to effective competition. Still, in a similar way as in the United States, the test itself is open to interpretation, and there are no significant impediments to including in the test more broadly the problem of diversity of choice on the market insofar as products related to the exercise of free speech are involved. A type of a methodical "plurality review" was employed by the UK competition authority in 2018 under national legislation in an inquiry into 21st Century Fox's merger with Sky, which took place in parallel to an ordinary competition assessment by the European Commission.[83] In 2021, a different approach was taken by the Polish ombudsman, who decided to challenge a press merger cleared by the Polish competition authority. The ombudsman argued that a takeover of a press conglomerate by a state-owned oil company ran against constitutional free speech values—a reasoning more similar to the more abstract First Amendment arguments in the United States.[84]

To conclude, the European perspective lacks a judicial tradition similar to that present in the United States—a tradition supportive of investigating links between antitrust and free speech. However, despite no such tradition, European antitrust may be paradoxically more inclusive of free speech values than its US counterpart, in

---

undertaking may be able to charge each consumer the highest price each consumer is willing to pay (e.g. consumer A pays 10 euro, while consumer B pays 100 euro for the same product). For non-economic reasons, such a situation may be controversial and became a subject of concern for, e.g., the Neobrandeisians; see Lynn (2020), pp. 206–207, 213–215. While price discrimination is a typical subject of interest to antitrust (and exploitive prices, i.e. unfair prices, are explicitly mentioned in Article 102 TFEU), it should be remembered that from the economic point of view "price" generally denotes various characteristics of a product. For instance, increasing the price of a product has a similar effect as lowering the quality of the product, while holding its nominal market price the same. From the legal perspective, on the other hand, Article 102 TFEU mentions explicitly that an abuse of a dominant position may consist in "*applying dissimilar conditions to equivalent transactions with other trading parties, thereby placing them at a competitive disadvantage*". However, the list of examples provided in Article 102 TFEU is not exhaustive and the European Commission did enforce it also when consumers were affected (see e.g. case COMP/C-1/36.915, *Deutsche Post AG – Interception of cross-border mail*, para. 133). Furthermore, the European Court of Justice recognised that discrimination can be based on grounds other than prices, finding that e.g. discrimination based on nationality or residence within the European Union may constitute abuse; see CJEU, Case 7/82, *GVL*, ECLI:EU:C:1983:52, para. 56. Earlier, the European Commission itself had arrived at a similar conclusion in case IV/26760, *GEMA*.

[83] Competition and Markets Authority (2018).

[84] Craig (2021).

particular in relation to unilateral actions directed against the free exchange of views. This is because European antitrust is generally more inclusive towards creating checks and balances against the exploitative conduct of dominant undertakings.

## 4 The Pragmatic Level: Handling Free Speech Under Antitrust

A different problem related to antitrust being supportive of free speech values is the challenges associated with enforcement. As pointed out by Kovacic and Jones in a different context, when it comes to enforcement, the theory may often appear simple, but practical implementation is a different issue.[85] Theoretically, antitrust can be supportive of free speech in each area of enforcement, either indirectly (enforcement is still directed at economic issues, e.g. a social media platform abuses its position by discriminating the views of some users while at the same time uses their data, making a profit) or directly (e.g. stifling of free speech committed by dominant undertakings is treated in itself as "abusive"). However, antitrust authorities are mostly engaged in large cases, and it would be unrealistic to expect that they would start engaging in investigations to ensure that the free speech of individual speakers is not restricted unless the speakers are in fact the "loudspeakers" of larger groups.

On the other hand, it should be remembered that enforcement is primarily about deterrence; i.e., the possibility of enforcement taking place is expected to reduce the frequency of unwanted market behaviour taking place. There are also a number of ways to approach enforcement.

First, insofar as anti-competitive agreements are involved, public authorities are in fact well placed to investigate such cases. Anti-competitive agreements are a typical field of public enforcement, irrespective of whether they are big (large market-sharing cartels) or small (rigging of a few bids). The main problem with anti-competitive agreements is establishing that certain market conduct was coordinated. It may be easily observable for consumers that, e.g., controversial content such as that uploaded by Alex Jones was taken down at a similar time by a number of undertakings or that the accounts of a popular, but controversial, politician are suspended almost simultaneously by a number of platforms. Still, at the end of the day, these are public authorities that have powers to verify whether the actions of undertakings were coordinated. It appears there is no way around it and the possibility of investigation should not be easily discarded—the task of public authorities is sometimes to verify what cannot be verified by anyone else.

In relation to unilateral practices, individual instances of content deletion are not a proper subject of interest for public authorities. From the point of view of individual users, on the other hand, it might be illusory to litigate against a Big Tech company. However, class actions under private enforcement are an option. Also, as the actions

[85] Jones and Kovacic (2020).

of some competition authorities show, enforcement can be directed at the terms and conditions used by undertakings and may include novel interpretations of "exploitation".[86] For instance, it is hypothetically possible to conclude that terms and conditions that are wide and provide too much leeway, and no checks against misuse, may in itself be abusive—an undertaking profits from the data provided by users, but when it comes to assessing the content uploaded by the users ("the other end of the bargain"), too many advantages are provided to the undertaking at the expense of the users, in a similar way as excessive pricing ultimately leads to too many profits ending up with the undertaking.

Finally, when it comes to mergers, the role is exclusively for public authorities responsible for reviewing merger notifications.

The problem of enforcement can also be looked at from a different perspective. As pointed out earlier, some antitrust actions that are ultimately supportive of free speech values can be in fact argued under economic reasoning, but likely one that is hardly quantifiable. Still, one of the reasons for the return of the "more political approach" type of arguments is that over the years, antitrust has become less operational in the sense that the standard of evidence became too high. The other way of approaching enforcement could therefore be similar to the one argued in *Associated Press*, i.e. that once a certain type of practice or market is identified (e.g. a free speech interest or market of special interest from the point of view of free speech), "more caution is exercised". "More caution" could, e.g., mean a more "form-based" approach to prove that certain action was abusive. In fact, such approach is not uncommon in antitrust, and, for instance, under Article 101 TFEU, some agreements are considered prohibited "by object" and some "by effect", requiring less or more proof—the choice here is ultimately political and depends on the assessment of how much risk to a certain value can be tolerated.[87]

A practical challenge that, on the other hand, possibly limits what antitrust can offer to free speech, in particular in relation to unilateral practices, is that even in the European context, antitrust has boundaries. For instance, only undertakings holding a dominant position can abuse it, and the position is held in a "relevant market".[88] In practical terms, this means that even a large undertaking with much impact on how free speech is exercised can be considered not a dominant one, provided it meets

---

[86] See the antitrust case against Facebook in Germany and an exploitation theory related to data collection, Witt (2021).

[87] Compare the Opinion of Advocate-General Kokott in the CJEU, Case C-8/08, *T-Mobile Netherlands*, ECLI:EU:C:2009:110, para. 47. It can be argued that the choice between classifying an infringement as "by object" or "by effect" is not political but economic, as typically "by object" restrictions are expected to generate a higher likelihood of negative effects. However, what amounts to a high enough "likelihood" comes from a political preference. Similarly, it is ultimately a political preference which e.g. tends to lead EU institutions to exercise "more caution" in relation to market practices interfering with the free flow of goods within the internal market—for a brief discussion of a so-called "single market imperative" see Whish (2009), pp. 22–23, 120.

[88] CJEU, Case 85/76, *Hoffmann-La Roche*, ECLI:EU:C:1979:36, para. 38; CJEU, Case 6/72, *Continental Can*, ECLI:EU:C:1973:22, para. 32.

with sufficient competition. Much depends, however, on a specific market context. For instance, the German competition authority considered Facebook to be a dominant undertaking even if there is Twitter, seeing them as operating in different "relevant markets".[89]

## 5 Conclusion

Around half a century ago, Director and Coase, two prominent scholars of the Chicago School, argued for parity in the approach to "markets for goods" and "markets for ideas", having in mind that in the same way as there is much resistance to the regulation of free speech, there should also be less economic regulation. Paradoxically, 50 years later, in the context of the growing impact of the Big Tech on how free speech is exercised, arguments can be made that restrictions to free speech caused by private power should be treated the same way as restrictions in relation to ordinary goods, i.e. should be covered by antitrust. While the consideration of free speech values under antitrust is by no means a mainstream approach, there are two reasons for which a discussion in that respect should not be outrightly dismissed. First, there are areas in which free speech and antitrust intersect. Second, more interest is being given to a more political approach to antitrust, and the inclusion of other non-economic interests in enforcement, e.g. sustainability interests, also opens the doors to questions regarding different political values—free speech being one of them.

On the other hand, there were reasons for antitrust to move away from being inclusive in relation to political values. Political values bring a degree of uncertainty as conflicts between different values can be difficult to solve by a reference to clear criteria. For instance, as it was discussed, unilateral action aimed at removing some content can be argued to go against free speech values, but still, it may very well serve other political values, e.g. the quality of democratic debate. By accepting the application of antitrust to such actions, antitrust is put in a position where a wide array of complex judgments have to be made under a branch of law that turned out to be most effectively used in more clear-cut economic contexts.

A typical problem with antitrust is also that while its wording allows a broad application, specific market problems can more easily be solved through sector-specific regulation. For instance, while the setting of multilateral interchange fees has been covered by antitrust, their regulation turned out to be easier. Likewise, while ensuring the access of undertakings to infrastructure in energy and telecommunication sectors is possible under antitrust, sector regulation may be easier. On the other hand, the fact that sector-specific regulation can be applicable does not mean that antitrust cannot work as an emergency tool if other instruments fail to provide solutions or enough deterrence.

---

[89] Witt (2021).

Finally, from the point of view of antitrust itself, the issue of its interplay with free speech appears to be underrated and may justify further research in the European context. If the more political approach to antitrust gains more support, then free speech is surely a political value. Also, in such areas as merger control, the impact of mergers on the opportunities associated with free speech appears to be an interest that can be included in the interpretation of the "quality of products" and "choice of products" post-merger, i.e. as a facet of slightly tweaked mainstream consumer welfare arguments.

From the point of view of unilateral conduct, what might be interesting is possible private enforcement litigation started by, e.g., free speech non-governmental organisations (NGOs) and based on a premise that certain actions of a Big Tech company did constitute an "abuse" of a dominant position. Here, a court hearing the case would need to decide and explain what actions fall within the definition of an "abuse" and for what reasons. Taking into account the fact that in the European Union such cases are heard by member states' courts and also that national equivalents of Article 102 TFEU can be stricter than EU law, the result of such litigation could be interesting.

Lastly, when it comes to multilateral conduct, it seems that cases of this sort should not go under the radar of antitrust authorities, even if the conduct in question is aimed at purely political speech. Undertakings should decide on their market behaviour independently, and the role of public authorities in investigating possible agreements between undertakings is of particular significance since only the public authorities have the power to verify whether an agreement actually took place.

At the end of the day, however, what appears to be still needed at this point is more discussions on the possible role of antitrust from the point of view of free speech. Paradoxically, while so far more of such discussions have taken place in the United States, the framework of European antitrust can be more conducive to conceptualising such an interaction.

## References

Alba D, Nicas J (2021) Amazon, Apple and Google cut off Parler, an app that drew Trump supporters. The New York Times. https://www.nytimes.com/2021/01/09/technology/apple-google-parler.html

Amato G (1997) Antitrust and the bounds of power: the dilemma of liberal democracy in the history of the market. Hart, Oxford

Behrens P (2018) The ordoliberal concept of 'Abuse' of a dominant position and its impact on Article 102 TFEU. In: Di Porto F, Podszun R (eds) Abusive practices in competition law (ASCOLA competition law series)

Berk G (2009) Louis D. Brandeis and the making of regulated competition, 1900–1932. Cambridge University Press

Bishop S, Walker M (2010) The economics of EC competition law: concepts, application and measurement. Sweet & Maxwell

Bork R (1966) Legislative intent and the policy of the Sherman Act. J Law Econ 9:7–48

Bork R (1996/2010) Slouching towards Gomorrah: modern liberalism and American decline. HarperCollins e-books
Bork R (1978/2021) The antitrust paradox: a policy at war with itself. Bork Publishing
Bundeskartellamt (2020) Open markets and sustainable economic activity – public interest objectives as a challenge for competition law practice. https://www.bundeskartellamt.de/SharedDocs/Publikation/EN/Diskussions_Hintergrundpapiere/2020/Working_Group_on_Competition_Law_2020.pdf
Burgin A (2012) The great persuasion: reinventing free markets since the depression. Harvard University Press
Chilson N, Mattox C (2020) [The] breakup speech: can antitrust fix the relationship between platforms and free speech values? https://knightcolumbia.org/content/the-breakup-speech-can-antitrust-fix-the-relationship-between-platforms-and-free-speech-values
Coase R (1974) The market for goods and the market for ideas. Am Econ Rev 64(2):384–391
Coaston J (2018) YouTube, Facebook, and Apple's ban on Alex Jones, explained. Vox. https://www.vox.com/2018/8/6/17655658/alex-jones-facebook-youtube-conspiracy-theories
Competition and Markets Authority (2018) 21st Century Fox, Inc and Sky Plc A report on the anticipated acquisition by 21st Century Fox, Inc of Sky Plc. 1 May 2018. https://assets.publishing.service.gov.uk/government/uploads/system/uploads/attachment_data/file/713920/CMAFoxSky_report_nonconfidential.pdf
Craig E (2021) Polish Court suspends merger approval for PKN Orlen deal. Global Competition Review. https://globalcompetitionreview.com/interim-relief/polish-court-suspends-merger-approval-pkn-orlen-deal
Crane D (2014) The tempting of antitrust: Robert Bork and the goals of antitrust policy. Antitrust Law J 79(3):835–853
Day G (2020) Monopolizing free speech. Fordham Law Rev 88
Delrahim M (2019a) "…And Justice for All": antitrust enforcement and digital gatekeepers. https://www.justice.gov/opa/speech/assistant-attorney-general-makan-delrahim-delivers-remarks-antitrust-new-frontiers
Delrahim M (2019b) The future of antitrust: new challenges to the consumer welfare paradigm and legislative proposals. https://www.justice.gov/opa/speech/assistant-attorney-general-makan-delrahim-delivers-remarks-federalist-society-national
Deutscher E, Makris S (2016) Exploring the ordoliberal paradigm: the competition-democracy nexus. Compet Law Rev 11(2):181–214
Director A (1953) The parity of the economic market place. The University of Chicago Law School Record 2(3), Article 4. https://chicagounbound.uchicago.edu/cgi/viewcontent.cgi?article=1420&context=lsr
First H (2019) Excessive drug pricing as an antitrust violation. Antitrust Law J 82:701
Gerber D (1994) Constitutionalizing the economy: German neo-liberalism, competition law and the "New" Europe. Am J Comp Law 42(1):25–84
Gerbrandy A (2017) Solving a sustainability-deficit in European competition law. World Compet 40(4)
Gerbrandy A (2019) Rethinking competition law within the European Economic Constitution. J Common Mark Stud 57(1):127–142
Grunes A, Stucke M (2001) Antitrust and the marketplace of ideas. Antitrust Law J 69
Horton B (2019) Malign manipulations: can Google's shareholders save democracy? Wake Forest Law Rev 54(707)
Hovenkamp H (2019) Is antitrust's consumer welfare principle imperilled? J Corp Law 45:101
Jones A, Kovacic W (2020) Antitrust's implementation blind side: challenges to major expansion of U.S. Competition Policy. Antitrust Bull
Khan L (2017) Amazon's antitrust paradox. Yale Law J 126:710
Khan L (2018) The new Brandeis movement: America's antimonopoly debate. J Eur Compet Law Pract 9(3):131–132
Khan L (2020) The end of antitrust history revisited. Harv Law Rev 133:1655

Knox R (2015) Visa, MasterCard defeat WikiLeaks collusion complaint. Global Competition Review. https://globalcompetitionreview.com/visa-mastercard-defeat-wikileaks-collusion-complaint

Krzeminska-Vamvaka J (2009) Tobacco, market economy and market of ideas newest developments concerning freedom of commercial speech. Amsterdam Law Forum 2(1):117

Lima C (2019) Facebook backtracks after removing Warren ads calling for Facebook breakup. Politico. https://www.politico.com/story/2019/03/11/facebook-removes-elizabeth-warren-ads-1216757

Lynn B (2020) Liberty from all masters: the new American autocracy vs. the will of the people. St. Martin's Press

Mirowski P, Von Horn R (2009) The rise of the Chicago School of Economics and the birth of neoliberalism. In: Mirowski P, Plehwe D (eds) The road from Mont Pèlerin: the making of the neoliberal thought collective. Harvard University Press, pp 139–178

Monti G, Mulder J (2017) Escaping the clutches of EU competition law: pathways to assess private sustainability initiatives. Eur Law Rev 42(5):635–656

Nunziato D (2007) The death of the public forum in cyberspace. Berkeley Technol Law J 20:1115

Oliver H (1960) German neoliberalism. Q J Econ 74(1):117–149

Orbach B (2017) Antitrust populism. N Y Univ J Law Bus 14:1

Petit N (2009) The guidelines on the application of Article 81(3) EC - a critical review. IEJE working paper no. 4/2009

Petit N (2010) Windows. https://chillingcompetition.com/2010/03/08/windows

Pitofsky R (1979) The political content of antitrust. Univ Pa Law Rev 127:1051

Posner R (1978) The Chicago School of Antitrust Analysis. Univ Pa Law Rev 127(4):925

Ptak R (2009) Neoliberalism in Germany: revisiting the ordoliberal foundations of the social market economy. In: Mirowski P, Plehwe D (eds) The road from Mont Pèlerin: the making of the neoliberal thought collective. Harvard University Press, pp 98–138

Simons H (1948) Economic policy for a free society. The University of Chicago

Steinbaum M, Stucke M (2018) The effective competition standard: a new standard for antitrust. 25 September. Roosevelt Institute. https://rooseveltinstitute.org/wp-content/uploads/2020/07/RI-Effective-Competition-Standard-201809.pdf

Stempel J (2020) Google defeats conservative nonprofit's YouTube censorship appeal. Reuters. https://www.reuters.com/article/us-google-lawsuit-censorship-idUSKCN20K33L

Stigler Committee on Digital Platforms (2019) Stigler Committee on digital platforms: final report. https://www.chicagobooth.edu/-/media/research/stigler/pdfs/digital-platforms%2D%2D-committee-report%2D%2D-stigler-center.pdf

Stoller M (2019) Goliath: the 100-year war between monopoly power and democracy. Simon & Schuster, New York

Teachout Z (2020) Break 'em up: recovering our freedom from big ag, big tech, and big money. All Points Books

Van Dijck J, Nieborg D, Poell T (2019) Reframing platform power. Internet Policy Rev 8(2):2019

Von Horn R (2009) Reinventing monopoly and the role of corporations: the roots of Chicago Law and Economics. In: Mirowski P, Plehwe D (eds) The road from Mont Pèlerin: the making of the neoliberal thought collective. Harvard University Press, pp 204–237

Waller SW, Morse JE (2020) The political face of antitrust. Brooklyn J Corp Financ Commer Law 15:75

Whish R (2009) Competition law. Oxford University Press

Witt A (2012) Public policy goals under EU competition law – now is the time to set the house in order. Eur Compet J 8(3)

Witt A (2021) Excessive data collection as a form of anticompetitive conduct – The German Facebook Case. Antitrust Bull 66(2) https://doi.org/10.1177%2F0003603X21997028

Woan T (2013) Searching for an answer: can Google legally manipulate search engine results? Univ Pa J Bus Law 16:294

Wu T (2011) The master switch: the rise and fall of information empires. Vintage Books, New York
Wu T (2018a) The curse of bigness: antitrust in the new gilded age. Columbia Global Reports, New York
Wu T (2018b) After consumer welfare, now what? The "Protection of Competition" standard in practice. J Compet Policy Int
Wu T (2020) The curse of bigness: how corporate giants came to rule the world. Atlantic Books, London

**Jan Polański**, LL.M., is an antitrust policy advisor working at the Polish Competition Authority. Before working as an advisor, Jan served for over 5 years as an antitrust case handler, dealing primarily with anti-competitive agreements, dawn raids, and forensic IT. Jan graduated in Law and Economics from Utrecht University.

# Building Surveillance State in a Digital Age and What Export Control Can(Not) Do About It?

**Ondřej Svoboda**

**Contents**



**Abstract** Globalization leads to technology diffusion, which is inevitably linked to the selling of sensitive surveillance technologies. States and the private sector are close collaborators in the market for digital surveillance tools, which are a part of a new generation of disruptive technologies. As new technologies filter information, they have the potential to limit the freedom of speech or violate the right to privacy. As such, new means to mitigate their misuse and proliferation, including instruments outside of the box of traditional export control regimes, should be considered. This chapter explains the role of surveillance technologies and their effects in suppressing the right to privacy and the freedom of speech in a digital age. Next, it identifies current legal regimes of export control and its limits under the Wassenaar Arrangement. In this context, it also considers the latest EU development when it comes to

This contribution was supported by the Charles University, project UNCE—Human Rights Research Centre, UNCE/HUM/011. The opinions expressed in this article do not represent an official position of the Ministry of Foreign Affairs of the Czech Republic and are just and only the author's. I would like to thank Jan Kunstýř and Milan Lipovský for valuable comments on initial drafts.

O. Svoboda (✉)
Faculty of Law, Charles University, Prague, Czech Republic

Embassy of the Czech Republic, Tokyo, Japan

 
S. Hindelang, A. Moberg (eds.), *YSEC Yearbook of Socio-Economic Constitutions 2021*, YSEC Yearbook of Socio-Economic Constitutions (2022) 2021: 231–254,
https://doi.org/10.1007/16495_2021_35, Published online: 10 April 2022

the Dual-Use Export Regulation, as well as business due diligence. Further, it turns to private self-regulation and the need to comply with the Organisation for Economic Co-operation and Development (OECD) Guidelines on Multinational Enterprises and the UN Guiding Principles on Business and Human Rights and calls for more standard setting built on their principles.

## 1 Introduction

The digitalization of societies and economies all around the world is taking place at an unparalleled pace. The digitalization of global business has had a profound impact on corporate social responsibility (CSR) and responsible business conduct (RBC) as business may cause or contribute to human rights breaches in new ways. For instance, new technologies filter information, whereby they may limit the freedom of speech and violate the right to privacy. Such technologies are developed and used by information and communication technology (ICT) companies. These companies have become platforms for information access and sharing, expressing opinions, and debating. Additionally, to quote the Council of Europe's Committee on Legal Affairs and Human Rights, "[i]n several countries, a massive 'Surveillance-Industrial Complex' has evolved, which risks escaping democratic control and accountability and threatens the free and open character of our societies".[1] The situation is closely linked to companies' commercial interests and states' security policy goals. Indeed, such technologies may have legitimate uses, but they have also been applied by some governments as a tool for widespread human rights abuses, such as the suppression of civil society and of any criticism and the persecution of journalists, human rights defenders, or dissidents. In short, this complex technological evolution, together with inherent private commercial interests, poses serious normative challenges to existing legal rules.

The serious consequences of controlled cyberspace and the Internet are being witnessed every day. For instance, China curbed the flow of information and managed to hide the extent of the outbreak of COVID-19 in its early stages. According to certain leaks, the Cyberspace Administration of China used all available tools, including internal files and computer codes from a Chinese company, Urun Big Data Services, to monitor and manage Internet discussions.[2] Similarly,

[1] Council of Europe, Committee on Legal Affairs and Human Rights (2015), p. 1.

[2] Amnesty International (2020) and Khalil (2020).

during and after the Arab Spring,[3] mass surveillance[4] technology—which is a part of the wider ICT sector—exported by the US and EU companies was reportedly applied to monitor and suppress dissent against local autocratic regimes. Other examples can be found in the use of Ericsson in Belarus or Nokia Siemens Networks in Iran.[5] Accordingly, for some observers, the inadequacy of instruments to control the export of surveillance technology allowed "a rapid development of private industry in supplying such technology to governments all over the world, sometimes regardless of any human rights implications".[6]

Obviously, technological progress is shaping the ability of individuals to exercise their freedom of expression and other rights. Such development requires new rules at international, regional, as well as national levels. According to the United Nations (UN) Human Rights Council's Special Rapporteur on the promotion and protection of freedom of opinion and expression, the situation is so serious that he calls not only for a tighter regulation of surveillance exports and restrictions on their use but also for an immediate moratorium on the global sale and the transfer of private surveillance industry tools until "a human rights-compliant safeguards regime is in place".[7]

At this point, regulating the export of mass surveillance technologies on the state level raises questions about their overall impact on the industry. Export control compliance can be onerous in terms of the cost associated with navigating the process successfully and the time it takes to do so, particularly for smaller companies. The waiting period and the complex administrative procedures required to receive an approval for a sale can be such that opportunities are lost to foreign competitors, putting a downward pressure on employment growth. The potential direct effects of export controls on a specific subset of emerging technologies that have been identified as possible candidates for export controls are well documented.[8] Therefore, the challenge is to balance those conflicting interests brought by today's technological development.

The aim of this contribution is to discuss how to balance the difficult triangular relationship among business, economic, and social rights, on one hand, and the freedom of speech in this specific industry in the digital age, on the other.[9] The complexity raises a multifaceted question of the regulatory role of the state versus the

[3] European Parliament, Directorate-General for External Policies, Policy Department (2012), pp. 9–10.

[4] In general, surveillance can be defined as watching over someone/something, but within the context of privacy, it means interference within another person's private sphere by observance of his/her activities.

[5] Wagner (2012).

[6] Caponetti (2016), p. 70.

[7] Human Rights Council (2019), para 66a.

[8] See e.g. Ezell and Foote (2019).

[9] Or, put it differently, "export control history regarding ICT is better read against the pairs between security and commerce, foreign policy and trade policy [...]". Ruohonen and Kimppa (2019), p. 171.

commercial interests of the private sector.[10] Indeed, the conflicting interests are not new as they are to be found in the export of many other hazardous technologies, such as asbestos or chemicals, whose trading is often strictly regulated. There is an inherent conflict of interest that exists between the state as a legislator and guarantor of fundamental freedoms, on one hand, and the state as a promoter of the export of its companies and their growth in the global markets, on the other. Rapid digitalization raises new challenges. Governments are experimenting with digital identity schemes and the digitization of public records, but their policies aim at collecting personal data and other sensitive activities while applying the latest technological developments. The stringent export control of such products may limit adverse impacts on human rights. However, as one author highlighted, the export of digital technologies creates economic opportunities in destination countries, which may subsequently "give rise to a normative tension between the protection of certain civil and political rights in the short term and the development of economic and social rights in the long term".[11] To put it simply, it is not a black and white issue.

First, on a more abstract level, the contribution provides a legal analysis of the impact of ICT on the freedom of speech and related rights, such as the right to privacy, as established by the UN human rights "treaty system". The analysis will allow us to advance the global system for regulating dual-used exports—the Wassenaar Agreement. However, this multilateral export regime lacks obligatory rules to implement and enforce surveillance technology transfer control. The next section focuses on debates within the EU about updating internal export rules in this area to keep pace with technological innovation. The following part offers contours of a new regulatory framework, which should be built on a smart mix of international standards, human rights due diligence, and private self-regulation. The final section of this article argues that in order to achieve the balance between human rights, commercial interests, and technological development, lawmakers must start updating export controls, together with implementing due diligence standards.

## 2 The Impact of the ICT Industry and Its Foreign Commercial Activities on Human Rights

ICT companies have developed a wide range of tools applied in moderation processes in cyberspace. These include automated flagging, removal, and pre-publication filtering. To assess huge volumes of user-generated content, companies employ automation and, increasingly, also specific artificial intelligence (AI) algorithms, which raises new questions of possible human rights violations. Moreover, the development and application of such mechanisms lack transparency

[10] The Wall Street Journal reported in 2011 that "a retail market for surveillance tools has sprung up from nearly zero in 200 to about $5 billion a year". Valentino-DeVries et al. (2011).

[11] Kanetake (2019), p. 15.

as there is little or no information for public scrutiny and possible remedies. Accordingly, it is increasingly claimed that censorship and surveillance technology systems are so fundamentally designed to invade basic human rights that it becomes difficult to ascertain their "legitimate" or "lawful" purposes.[12]

A number of regional and international human rights instruments, including the Special Rapporteur on Freedom of Opinion and Expression, OSCE Representative on Freedom of the Media, or OAS Special Rapporteur on Freedom of Expression, have declared that the freedom of expression applies to the Internet and that the "[m] andatory blocking of entire websites, IP addresses, ports, network protocols or types of uses (such as social networking) is an extreme measure" that can "only be justified in accordance with international standards". Further, content-filtering systems "which are not end-user controlled are a form of prior censorship and are not justifiable as a restriction on freedom of expression".[13] It is consequently easily recognizable that the commercial activities of companies in this sector may impact rights to expression, opinion, privacy, and public participation, among others. In addition, the rights are interdependent. For instance, respecting privacy is a gateway to achieving freedom of expression,[14] or, in the words of the Special Rapporteur on the promotion and protection of freedom of opinion and expression, "the interference with privacy through targeted surveillance is designed to repress the exercises of the freedom of expression".[15] In accordance with this viewpoint, the present contribution focuses on the freedom of expression and also acknowledges the importance of other rights as necessary for its exercise.

In this context, Article 19 of both the Universal Declaration of Human Rights and the International Covenant on Civil and Political Rights (ICCPR) can serve as the point of reference when analyzing the current international legal framework. The respective provisions protect everyone's right to hold opinions without interference and to seek, receive, and impart information and ideas of all kinds through any media and *regardless of frontiers*. The right encompasses states' duty to ensure that the enabling environment complies with certain standards, such as media diversity and independence and access to information.[16]

Regarding state obligations towards exporters of surveillance technologies and other private actors, the UN Guiding Principles on Business and Human Rights (also "UN Guiding Principles") prescribe states to take appropriate steps to prevent, investigate, punish, and redress human rights abuses by third parties. This is also in line with the conclusions of the Human Rights Committee, which stated in General Comment No. 31 on the ICCPR that states may violate the ICCPR by "failing to take appropriate measures to exercise due diligence to prevent, punish,

[12] Wagner (2012), p. 7.

[13] Organization for Security and Co-operation in Europe (2017).

[14] Human Rights Council (2015), paras 16–18.

[15] Human Rights Council (2019), para 21.

[16] OSCE (2017), section 3. See also Human Rights Committee (2011), paras 18, 40.

investigate or redress the harm" that private entities cause.[17] To fulfil the duty, it is expected that states exercise adequate oversight of the activities of third parties under their jurisdiction or legislate by creating conditions that will lead business enterprises to respect human rights.[18] However, as in many other cases, it is easier said than done. Moreover, it is doubtful if the general conclusions on due diligence are applicable to states' export authorities, particularly if there is no direct link between the exporter's operations abroad and the violations of the ICCPR.[19]

The narrow interpretation of the ICCPR's jurisdiction may nevertheless evolve, as one recent example suggests. In 2017, the Human Rights Committee published its Concluding Observations on Italy and also made recommendations on Italy's export regime. The Committee expressed its concerns about "allegations that companies based in the State party have been providing online surveillance equipment to Governments with a record of serious human rights violations and about the absence of legal safeguards or oversight mechanisms regarding the export of such equipment" and recommended to take steps "to ensure that all corporations under its jurisdiction, in particular technology corporations, respect human rights standards when engaging in operations abroad".[20] The observation, thus, may be the first step to expanding the jurisdiction of the ICCPR and consequently to applying human rights due diligence.

In addition, the collaboration between exporters and supplier states on surveillance and censorship infrastructures often does not end by selling the product. ICT companies frequently support surveillance systems even after that point and provide their maintenance and upgrades at subsequent contract stages. For instance, in 2014, the British-German Group, also known as FinFisher company, signed "annual support contracts" with governments to provide various forms of customer support.[21] Such long-term private-public collaborations raise further doubts about whether due diligence to evaluate human rights is genuinely undertaken even in so-called vulnerabilities markets.

Authoritarian regimes worldwide take extensive measures to ensure continued control over the Internet and communication applications: "It serves not only to stifle expression and gain control over dissemination of information about protests, but also to chill freedom of speech and expand the shadow of hierarchy of state power far beyond existing expression boundaries."[22] The most developed surveillance infrastructure can likely be found in the Chinese province Xinjiang. Equipped with artificial intelligence, facial recognition, gait recognition, and infrared technology, it goes beyond virtual environments and tracks movements, monitors behaviours, and identifies individuals. According to the US government, the main systems for

[17] Human Rights Committee (2004), para 8.

[18] Human Rights Council (2011b), principle 3.

[19] Kanetake (2019), p. 12.

[20] Human Rights Committee (2017), paras 36–37.

[21] Privacy International (2014).

[22] Wagner (2012), p. 12.

mass surveillance in Xinjiang are supported also by foreign businesses and investors.[23]

The trade in surveillance technologies plays a significant role in this as the international markets provide technology that has been until recently overwhelmingly developed in North America and Europe.[24] As governments conduct "cyberattacks" on Internet activists, journalists, and bloggers, breaking into their social networks' accounts and group activities and blocking or deleting their websites and blogs, the nexus between human rights and the export of ICT equipment is undeniable. However, is export control the best and most effective response to the increasing unease in the selling of cyber-surveillance technologies to authoritarian regimes?

## 3 The Wassenaar Arrangement: Fit for Purpose?

Export regulations regulate export, re-export, and the transfer of some less sensitive military items; commercial items that have both commercial and military or proliferation applications, so-called dual-use goods; and purely commercial items without any obvious military use.[25] Government authorities are typically empowered to review, approve, and deny the exports of such goods to pursue any policy objectives. Dual-use trade controls are largely list-based instruments. As such, they cover mainly certain dual-use ("weaponizable") technologies falling within defined parameters and allowing specific applications.[26]

Initially, export control regimes were not designed as instruments for the governance of dual-use technologies. However, to keep pace with new technological developments, it was necessary to cover new technologies by adjusting control lists, as it happened with the Wassenaar Arrangement on Export Controls for Conventional Arms and Dual-Use Goods and Technologies, likely the most comprehensive international export control regime. The Wassenaar Arrangement is an

---

[23] US Department of State (2020a, b), p. 4.

[24] Sherman and Morgus (2018). However, the situation is changing as particularly China has become a major worldwide supplier of artificial intelligence surveillance technology, such as facial recognition systems, smart city platforms, and smart policing technology—a global driver of "authoritarian tech". Feldstein (2019), p. 13. Chinese companies have supplied critical technological infrastructure to countries around the world, exporting their authoritarian standards in the process. The "Freedom on the Net 2018" report identified eighteen countries out of 65 that had accessed AI surveillance technology developed by Chinese companies. Shabhaz (2018), pp. 7–8; for further details, see records and witness experts on China's digital authoritarianism. US House of Representatives, Permanent Select Committee on Intelligence (2019). In addition, trade exchange in surveillance technologies and equipment is increasingly two-way. For instance, in February 2021, it was revealed that at least half of London's 32 boroughs have bought and deployed China-made surveillance systems. Asher-Schapiro (2021).

[25] U.S. Department of Commerce, Bureau of Industry and Security (2021).

[26] Charatsis (2017), p. 53.

international arms-control agreement between 44 states. Its main aim is to promote "transparency and greater responsibility in transfers of conventional arms and dual-use goods and technologies." To fulfil this goal, the participating states are expected to apply export controls to items on the control list.

Growing concerns over a lack of export controls for technologies has led to a "cyber amendment"[27] of the control list "to curtail the proliferation of active or offensive cyber technologies [that are] used to initiate offensive cyber-attacks or actively mine and analyze protected data".[28] In December 2012, the control list was updated to encompass mobile telecommunication interception equipment.[29] Subsequently, in December 2013, further adjustments were made to cover IP network surveillance systems and intelligence-gathering software.[30] Those steps set a positive precedent by introducing cyber technologies and human rights considerations into the Wassenaar Arrangement, and they represented "the first important steps towards imposing controls on the multilateral level".[31]

However, this development has been seen as controversial from several different perspectives. Still, there is a question whether the Wassenaar Arrangement is the right forum in which to implement this kind of export control. Its founding document, the Initial Elements, says nothing about human rights. Critical voices, particularly from the United States, warned of the ambiguity of the newly incorporated definition of intrusion software. Such "pseudo-technical language" could be open to manifold possible interpretations and could even have "chilling effects on the development of anti-surveillance measures and on the discovery of existing vulnerabilities".[32] By July 2015, a group of companies in the ICT industry had formed a coalition to oppose the proposed implementation, arguing that it will lead to a negative impact on global research and development.[33]

The effectiveness of the Wassenaar Arrangement is also seriously weakened by its non-binding nature as well as the lack of any guidelines for implementation or an enforcement mechanism. This state leaves Member States free to decide whether to enact controls on listed items and whether to enforce any controls.[34] Consequently, for some observers, it is ill-suited to address the threats that digital surveillance poses to human rights.[35] In addition, implementing comprehensive export controls is difficult for licensing authorities as well as exporters because of the characteristics

[27] Pyetranker (2015), p. 162.

[28] Reiser and Hindin (2014), p. 29.

[29] Wassenaar Arrangement, List of Dual-Use Goods and Technologies and Munitions List, WA-LIST (12) 1, 12 December 2012, Category 5.A.1.f.

[30] Wassenaar Arrangement, List of Dual-Use Goods and Technologies and Munitions List, WA-LIST (13) 1, 4 December 2013, Categories 4.A.5 and 5.A1.j.

[31] Bohnenberger (2017), pp. 84–85.

[32] Dullien et al. (2016) and Sergey Bratus et al. (2014).

[33] Ruohonen and Kimppa (2019), p. 184.

[34] Pyetranker (2015), p. 168.

[35] Human Rights Council (2019), para 34.

of the ICT sector, such as high level of cross-border cooperation, increasingly multinational teams in multiple offices, delivery of customized and integrated solutions, and connectedness, dynamism, and potential volatility of the industry.[36] Others pointed out that the absence of China as a member considerably weakens the multilateral export control on mass surveillance items.[37]

The situation has become even more complex as the amending of Wassenaar Arrangement's provisions requires a unanimous decision. The difficulties inherent in the multilateral framework were evident in 2016 when the Plenary failed to rephrase several provisions despite the US government's 2-year effort and the parties' agreement in principle.[38]

Finally, conventional export controls are designed to manage tangible items. Consequently, their means cannot be the universal solution for every type of surveillance technology considered to be of dual use. The control mechanisms are designed to prevent the proliferation of the most sensitive technologies, potentially related to the development of weapons of mass destruction and certain military end uses. Accordingly, not all types of surveillance technology are eligible to be covered by the dual-use lists.[39] Despite all concerns, it is legitimate to include technology and software in the scope of export controls.[40]

## 4 The EU in the Forefront of Stricter Control

The debate on the export of surveillance technologies took prominence in the EU during and after the Arab Spring.[41] European companies are major exporters of a broad spectrum of systems for mass surveillance. For instance, in 2015, one report collected over 80 cases where cyber-surveillance systems exported from the EU have been connected with human rights abuses and threats to international or EU security.[42] In the EU, export control has been regulated by Council Regulation (EC) No 428/2009 of 5 May 2009,[43] and the amendments to the list of the Wassenaar Arrangement from 2012 and 2013 were duly reflected in the EU's control list in 2014.[44] However, for many stakeholders, the current mechanisms built in the

---

[36] Bohnenberger (2017), p. 84.

[37] Thomsen and Thomsen (2015), p. 32; Pyetranker (2015), p. 174.

[38] Thomson (2016).

[39] Charatsis (2017), p. 56.

[40] Charatsis (2017), p. 67.

[41] There were evidenced several examples when cyber-surveillance technology exported by EU companies was afterwards used by autocratic regimes to suppress dissent and resistance while massively violating human rights.

[42] Ecorys and SIPRI (2015).

[43] Council Regulation (EC) No 428/2009.

[44] European Commission (2014a).

Wassenaar Arrangement and the Regulation did not produce efficient controls. European parliamentarians, non-governmental organizations (NGOs), and human rights activists repeatedly called for the expansion of the list of dual-use items as well as the consideration of "respect for human rights in the country of final destination".[45]

Finally, a number of publicly known examples of European-exported surveillance systems prompted the European Parliament to request a revision of the Dual-Use Export Regulation in order to cover new cyber technologies violating human rights in third-party countries.[46] Correspondingly, the Council adopted a similar position in its Action Plan on Human Rights and Democracy 2015–2019, which envisaged the review of the Dual-Use Regulation to mitigate the potential risks associated with the "uncontrolled export of ICT products".[47] Clearly, the debate in the EU on the export of sensitive cyber technologies has been gaining momentum.

In response, in September 2016, the European Commission proposed the integration of human rights diligence in the process of export control, putting forward a stricter control over trade with cyber-surveillance technologies.[48] According to the proposal, export control authorities should take into account respect for human rights in the country of final destination in assessing a request for an export authorization. Furthermore, the dual-use list should include a new category specifically covering "cyber-surveillance technology", diverging from the narrower Wassenaar Arrangement list. In addition, it was also proposed to expand the scope of the Dual-Use Export Regulation by a revised "catch-all" control. Such provision, intended to strengthen human rights considerations, would enable the review of the export of items that are not specifically listed. However, invoking human rights as a normative pillar represents a significant shift from the traditional raison d'être of export control.[49]

The proposal for stricter trade control encountered resistance, particularly on the basis of a fear of losing economic competitiveness. As a leaked document showed, nine EU Member States criticized the proposed text and argued for weaker human rights protection.[50] The ICT industry raised concerns that a stricter control would hamper its legitimate commercial activities as well. For instance, the European digital industry association DIGITAL EUROPE claimed that the "existing dual-use definition should continue being based on the internationally established

---

[45] Krahulcova (2017).

[46] European Parliament (2015); European Parliament (2016), para 21.

[47] Council of the EU (2015b), para 24.

[48] European Commission (2016).

[49] Kanetake (2019), p. 7.

[50] Council of the EU (2018).

definition".[51] Similarly, the Federation of German Industries (BDI) previously claimed that companies are "not in a position to take political positions".[52]

Finally, at the end of 2020, after several years of negotiations, the European institutions reached an agreement on a revised regulation, setting out the EU regime for the control of exports. Among other elements, the new rules include provisions making the technology subject to stricter export controls in certain circumstances in order to prevent human rights violations and security threats linked to the potential misuse of cyber-surveillance technology. The new Regulation introduces a basis for EU autonomous controls, allowing the EU to make its own decisions regarding human rights controls on cyber-surveillance technologies and for the coordination of national controls on emerging technologies. According to the European Parliament's Rapporteur for dual-use export controls, this new listing mechanism allows "to go beyond Wassenaar, with its limits in scope and speed of adoption that is hopelessly behind the current technological frontier."[53] The adoption and publication of a new EU Export Control Regulation are scheduled in May 2021.

The prolonged legislative process in the EU deserves attention for two reasons. First, it shows how difficult it is to balance conflicting interests in the export control of surveillance technologies. Second, the new Regulation will significantly influence the global export control regime. It may provide a step towards overcoming the lack of clear standards for mass surveillance technology and its application in cyberspace to be effectively governed at the multilateral level. The EU's ability to shape the international regulatory environment and this policy area is known as the Brussels Effect.[54] It shows that the EU plays an important role in setting the standards for international trade as well as cyberspace.[55] Recently, with the election of US President Joe Biden, the European Union put forward a proposal to establish a new EU-US Trade and Technology Council as part of "a new transatlantic agenda for global change". The EU is proposing to develop a common approach to protecting critical technologies, including export controls, as well as cooperation on regulation and standards.[56] Indeed, the EU and the United States, as like-minded

[51] DIGITAL EUROPE (2018).

[52] Bundesverband der Deutschen Industrie (2016), p. 7. For more details see also Bohnenberger (2017), pp. 98–99.

[53] Gregorová (2020).

[54] All the EU needs to do is regulate the single market; it is the global corporations that transmit EU rules across the global marketplace, as the above examples illustrate. This dynamic allows the EU to exert a passive but deep influence on corporate behaviour, transforming global markets in the process.

[55] See e.g. recently adopted the Digital Services Act and the Digital Markets Act. There is also a broader global contest for influence over the global norms governing the digital economy. While the U.S. and the EU have their disagreements, they seem manageable when compared to their shared concern over China's or Russia's authoritarian approaches. Contesting views on cyber norms are already taking place in the United Nations. See e.g. Polyakova and Meserole (2019), p. 11; Ding (2020); Grigsby (2018).

[56] European Commission (2020), pp. 5–7.

partners, should work together on export-control restrictions for surveillance technology, coordinate respective legislative developments, and promote joint policies in international standard-setting bodies, such as the International Telecommunication Union.

## 5 Contours of New Regulatory Framework

The UN Guiding Principles on Business and Human Rights, adopted in 2012, provides a comprehensive and authoritative framework that can inform efforts by a range of actors, including governments and companies, to identify, prevent, mitigate, and remedy human rights harm related to digital technologies. In the same year, when the United Nations Human Rights Council unanimously endorsed the Guiding Principles, which have become subsequently the authoritative global standard on the subject of business and human rights, the OECD Guidelines incorporated two elements from the UN Guiding Principles: the importance of due diligence processes in companies' responsibility to respect human rights and the due diligence requirement for all subjects covered by the Guidelines.[57] Together, they create a framework establishing principles of due diligence, transparency, accountability, and remedies, which should limit interference with human rights. As a matter of principle, those international instruments and their accompanying body of soft law create an environment where businesses are increasingly expected to consider human rights implications in their all operations. As such, they provide guidance on how ICT companies should behave and mitigate the negative impact of their surveillance technologies.

However, the implementation of the standards has been slow. The reason for this lies in the fact that the UN Guiding Principles and the OECD Guidelines are not binding. An example of a weakness of the framework was provided in the case of Gamma Group company. A British Gamma Group subsidiary, FinFisher, and its German surveillance technology company partner, Trovicor, sold surveillance technologies and provided assistance to the Government of Bahrain. As a result, several civil society organizations subsequently filed complaints with the OECD National Contact Points (NCPs) in the United Kingdom and Germany against Gamma and Trovicor in 2013, arguing that the companies breached the OECD Guidelines by exporting surveillance products and services.[58] While the German NCP rejected the complaint against Trovicor on the basis of insufficient evidence of Trovicor's business operation in the given contract, the UK NCP accepted the complaint against Gamma Group. Later, the UK NCP released an initial assessment in which it stated that "while neither party has provided direct evidence about a supply by Gamma to Bahrain, the evidence provided suggests that the company's product may have been

---

[57] Ruggie and Nelson (2015), pp. 170–171; Svoboda (2018), p. 50.

[58] Privacy International (2013).

used against Bahraini activists. The NCP considers that this substantiates the issues in respect of the company's obligations to do appropriate due diligence and to address impacts."[59] In its final assessment, the UK NCP concluded that Gamma violated the OECD Guidelines and made a number of recommendations, calling for more transparency in the company's business and providing a remedy for the misuse of its products.[60] However, the follow-up report noted that "in the absence of an update from Gamma – the UK NCP can only conclude that Gamma International UK Limited has made no progress (or effort)" and "therefore sees no reason to change the view reached in its Final Statement that Gamma's behaviour is inconsistent with its obligations under the OECD Guidelines."[61]

Both case studies provide an example of the sort of challenges that NCPs face when implementing principles of responsible business conduct in the ICT industry. Importantly, they also illustrate how difficult it is under the current international soft-law framework to enforce compliance with human rights law among exporters of mass surveillance technologies. It is hardly surprising that for some NGOs, the specific instances proved NCPs' (in)ability to provide effective remedies in cases of human rights violations resulting from the sale of surveillance technologies.[62]

Despite the scepticism, a Swiss NGO, the Society for Threatened Peoples, filed in June 2020 a complaint with the Swiss NCP regarding Union Bank of Switzerland's (UBS's) relationship with the Chinese company Hikvision, the world's largest developer and manufacturer of surveillance technologies. Hikvision plays a significant role in the mass surveillance of the Uyghurs in the Chinese province of Xinjiang and has been blacklisted by the US government since Autumn 2019. However, UBS still maintains financial ties with the company. For this reason, the Society for Threatened Peoples has argued that UBS has complied neither with the OECD Guidelines nor with its own Code of Conduct.[63] As the specific instance is still pending, it will be a litmus test not only for financial involvement in human rights violations but also for the assessment of mass surveillance under the OECD Guidelines and from a due diligence perspective.

Regardless of the result and evolving nature of the NCP system,[64] states have a primary responsibility to hold companies accountable in this regard. Taking into account such complexity, a more holistic approach, including the creation of standards on due diligence and self-regulation by the industry, can provide a way forward.[65]

[59] UK National Contact Point (2013), para 25.

[60] UK National Contact Point (2014), paras 68–69.

[61] UK National Contact Point (2016), para 9.

[62] FIDH - International Federation for Human Rights (2014), pp. 26–27.

[63] Society for Threatened Peoples (2020).

[64] Svoboda (2021).

[65] See also Bromley et al. (2016), p. 48.

## 5.1 More Human Rights Due Diligence on the Horizon

Human rights due diligence has become mandatory for more and more companies. The EU and its Member States are taking the lead in this field as they introduced several initiatives.[66] To highlight probably the most important one, in April 2020, Commissioner for Justice, Didier Reynders, officially committed the EU to a legislative initiative on mandatory human rights and environmental due diligence obligations for EU companies, which should include liability, enforcement mechanisms, and access to remedy provisions for victims of corporate abuse.[67] The European Commission launched a public consultation phase in October 2020 until February 2021. As a next step, this new legislation should be presented during the second semester of 2021. In the meantime, the European Parliament adopted a resolution in March 2021 containing recommendations to the European Commission concerning corporate due diligence and corporate accountability.[68] Interestingly, the resolution requires the EU Member States to introduce rules to compel companies to "carry out due diligence with respect to potential or actual adverse impacts on human rights, the environment and good governance in their operations and business relationships".[69]

In addition to this development, in December 2020, the Council asked the European Commission to launch an EU Action Plan focusing on sustainably shaping global supply chains, promoting human rights, social and environmental due diligence standards, and transparency by 2021.[70] The drive towards the implementation of CSR and RBC standards has been recognizable in the recent past. In 2015, the Council also called on the Member States to step up their efforts to effectively implement the UN Guiding Principles on Business and Human Rights, including through new or updated national action plans containing a mix of voluntary and mandatory measures.[71] The recently adopted EU commitments on business and human rights requiring due diligence from exporters reflects common business practice "harden" soft law to when voluntary international standards are converted into binding domestic laws and regulations.[72] For instance, the EU regulation laying down mineral supply chain due diligence introduces obligations for EU importers to

---

[66] For instance, the still novel French Duty of Vigilance Law (2017) requires companies of a certain size to create and implement annual vigilance plans in order to assess and address the risks of human rights, health and safety, and environmental violations resulting from their activities, including those of their business relationships. The Finnish government announced in its official programme plans to make compulsory conduct human rights assessment for companies, while the German government proposed to establish due diligence processes within the National Action Plan on business and human rights and possibly binding legislation later.

[67] Fox (2020).

[68] European Parliament (2021).

[69] European Parliament (2021), Art. 4.1.

[70] Council of the EU (2020), para 45.

[71] Council of the EU (2015a), Objective 18.

[72] Newman and Bach (2014), p. 430.

meet international responsible sourcing standards set by the OECD in the Due Diligence Guidance for Responsible Supply Chains of Minerals from Conflict-Affected and High-Risk Areas.[73] Accordingly, the EU importers must identify, assess, audit, and address the risks in their mineral supply chain. They shall also report annually on their policies and practices in this regard. Making such commitments legally binding ensures that companies cannot state one thing in their licensing applications while making different promises in their marketing material.

To look beyond the EU, the current debates on legal and regulatory regimes in the United States and Canada mean that the consideration of human rights norms is becoming a part of legal and business planning, even specifically for the ICT industry. In September 2020, the US State Department published guidance on the implementation of the UN Guiding Principles on Business and Human Rights in connection with transactions linked to foreign government end users involving products and services with surveillance capabilities.[74] The guidance focuses on human rights due diligence and risk mitigation for a wide range of products and services, including sensors, biometric identification, data analytics, Internet surveillance tools, non-cooperative location tracking, and recording devices. Companies will need to ensure that their products are necessary, proportionate, legal, and applied in a non-discriminatory manner.[75] Similar calls were recently made in Canada with regard to the revision of the Canadian export law—the Export and Import Permits Act (EIPA).[76]

The initiatives mainly reflect a growing trend promoted by states to require companies to undertake human rights due diligence. Governments have passed issue-specific legislation, such as the US and the EU, which have enacted legislation focused on conflict minerals; the UK and Australia, concerning modern slavery and human trafficking; and the Netherlands, related to child labour. Going forward, a more comprehensive human rights diligence legal framework regulating surveillance technology exporters as well is to be expected.[77]

[73] OECD (2016); Regulation (EU) 2017/821 of the European Parliament and of the Council of 17 May 2017 laying down supply chain due diligence obligations for Union importers of tin, tantalum and tungsten, their ores, and gold originating from conflict-affected and high-risk areas. The other field concerns foreign investors' behaviour. See e.g. Svoboda (2020), pp. 462–474.

[74] US Department of State (2020a, b).

[75] More specifically, the US agencies issued the Xinjiang Supply Chain Business Advisory statement in July 2020 in which they call for "businesses and individuals should examine the end users of their products, technology, research, and services, to reduce the likelihood that their goods or services are being used to build, maintain, or support: [...] (2) the broader surveillance apparatus of the PRC government; [...]." US Department of State (2020a, b), p. 8.

[76] Anstis et al. (2020).

[77] Aryobsei and Scherb (2020).

## 5.2 International Standards and Private Self-Regulation

So far, only a few ICT companies apply human rights principles in their operations.[78] This is a reality despite guidance developed in the UN and OECD. For instance, the UN Guiding Principles establish a "global standard of expected conduct" that should apply in all companies' commercial activities.[79] It should be clear that the Guiding Principles provide a minimum baseline for assessing whether ICT companies respect human rights in the export of their products and services. The governments can be a driving force for new private standard setting, which can play a vital role in introducing responsible exports of surveillance technologies. Typically, governments can drive policies and allow involved private parties to formulate standards.

There are already examples of first steps in this direction, such as the ICT Sector Guide on Implementing the UN Guiding Principles on Business and Human Rights developed by the European Commission in cooperation with the Institute for Human Rights and Business (IHRB)[80] and Know Your Customer Standards for Sales of Surveillance Equipment produced by the Electric Frontiers Foundations[81] or a set of guidelines about risks associated with the export and use of cyber-security systems published by the UK industry association TechUK and backed by the UK government.[82]

Nevertheless, there is not much public information suggesting that human rights due diligence is a routine part of sales and after-sales support. The sentiment is further reinforced by mounting evidence of the industry's contribution to human rights violations abroad, the absence of transparency, and silence about safeguards in their operations. Unsurprisingly, some voices express their concerns that ICT companies do not provide convincing evidence of their implementation of sufficient measures on due diligence, transparency, and accountability and that their current self-regulation lacks substance.[83] Such observation does not shed a positive light on the ICT industry and its willingness to adopt responsible business policies. Therefore, it is evident that a more active and comprehensive approach from the industry is needed to provide a baseline standard that ICT exporters should follow. In particular, there is an increasing government-led emphasis on due diligence processes to identify, prevent, mitigate, and account for human rights impact and an ongoing evaluation of the effectiveness of the adopted policies, as well as the grievance mechanisms for affected right holders.[84]

---

[78] Human Rights Council (2018), para 10.

[79] Guiding Principles, principle 11.

[80] European Commission (2014b).

[81] Cohn and York (2011).

[82] TechUK (2014).

[83] Human Rights Council (2019), para 32.

[84] Human Rights Council (2011a), paras 15–25.

Much of the standard setting may be done by the industry itself in standard-setting organizations or multi-stakeholder initiatives, such as the Global Network Initiative.[85] They may provide a venue to develop and define best practices of due diligence processes in the ICT sector. In addition, it would have two important benefits. First, it allows input from other stakeholders and a broader engagement. Second, it increases rule-making and decisional transparency. This allows firms to cooperate in setting standards to reduce risks in exporting surveillance technologies while ensuring a level playing field.

The specialized use of ICT technologies is a domain in which the industry and private sectors may play a pivotal role in drafting industry-specific recommendations, taking into account the Guiding Principles, the OECD Guidelines, and the above-mentioned principles of due diligence. The need for such "smart" regulation is undisputable. The proposed approach should be flexible, effective, and comprehensive, and due diligence should be one of its main pillars.[86] To take seriously the industry-led initiatives and improve the current situation allowing the high risk of the misuse of surveillance technologies, ICT companies should undertake several steps. First of all, it's important to build on the documents and implement RBC in their export operations.

For instance, it is evident that public-private collaboration does not end at the point of sale and transfer of product. Leaked documents demonstrated that ICT companies provide after-sales support, even several years afterwards.[87] For this reason, it is important that the industry sector embraces self-regulation based on robust due diligence processes when pre-sale and post-sale scrutiny to identify potential risks and contractual options to mitigate them are part of the company's policy. For the purpose of scrutiny, past experiences and reporting should also be built into internal assessments and examinations, and their findings should be reflected in relevant operations. To prevent or mitigate risks to freedom of expression, companies should develop clear and specific criteria to identify adverse impacts.[88] And a system of effective remedy should be built into internal policies as well because of the nature of cyberspace and the increasing amount of digitized information available for misuse.[89] If safeguards are put in place to regulate exported surveillance technologies and guarantee that foreign governments use the tools in legitimate ways, it would make it possible to find the right balance between competing public and private interests.

[85] Maurer (2016).

[86] See also Global Conference on Cyberspace 2015, Chair's Statement (2015).

[87] Privacy International (2014).

[88] Human Rights Council (2019), p. 18.

[89] Lipovský (2016), p. 264.

## 6 Conclusion

Recently, the worrying development related to the strengthening of the concept of a surveillance state with new cases of censorship and advancements in surveillance technology has been witnessed. New technologies are employed in suppressing the freedom of expression or the right to privacy and are used to spy on and harm human rights activists and political dissidents. Frequently, such cyber technology originates from European and North American companies and is transferred through commercial relationships. Popular uprisings in the Middle East and North Africa provided an incentive for states in Europe and North America to reconsider how they regulate the export of surveillance technologies. However, the current developments that are taking place in China and other places due to the phenomenon of "exporting digital authoritarianism"[90] are perhaps even more serious and raise considerable human rights concerns.

Under such circumstances, this contribution delved into the complex relationship between technological advancements in the form of cyber-surveillance technologies, the regulation of their export, and human rights. At a more general level, the discussed development is a part of a broader trend to regulate cyberspace, digital critical infrastructure, and related context areas of contemporary cyber politics. The Internet and its governance are necessarily a part of the picture as well.[91]

Without a doubt, export controls are today an important and perhaps first-in-mind instrument for restricting the proliferation of cyber-surveillance technologies and software in autocratic regimes. They exercise an essential role as accountability and transparency mechanisms. Their update, such as in the case of the Wassenaar Arrangement and the EU Dual-Use Regulation, responds to the inadequacy of international trade control regimes. However, their effectiveness is limited, and it was shown that the Wassenaar Arrangement is ill-equipped to bar the export of dangerous cyber-surveillance technologies. Consequently, for some, the focus on exports is "an imperfect proxy for addressing the central problem".[92] Risks caused by the surveillance ICT industry and the repressive use of its tools are not a one-dimensional problem, and there is a need for a multifaceted response to protect an individual's ability to use online platforms as forums for free expression or access to information.

The legal framework on business and human rights in the EU has evolved significantly in recent years. The EU leads the way in terms of existing and emerging legislation on human rights due diligence, as well as reporting obligations that extend to the full range of internationally respected human rights. However, this is

[90] See, e.g., Polyakova and Meserole (2019); Khalil (2020).

[91] UN Internet Governance Forum (2014). See also the OHCHR webpage on the B-Tech Project for the full list of materials.

[92] Human Rights Council (2019), para 34.

not a panacea against various loopholes and general ineffectiveness[93] leading to the harmful export of ICT products and services to third-party countries.

Standard setting can serve as a means for states to regulate cyberspace since the growing violation of human rights emerges due to rapid technological developments. Still, the state-centric governance model for the development of new standards should shift to multi-stakeholder initiatives that are already aligning with and implementing the OECD Due Diligence Guidance. Such a step could enhance the effectiveness of existing instruments in preventing or mitigating the proliferation of surveillance technologies and intrusion software.[94] States and companies are both involved in the development of dual-use technologies; their collaboration is thus necessary for controlling the export of such technology. In addition, the industry's compliance is better achieved by adopting internal codes of conduct respecting human rights.

On one hand, one can argue that under international human rights law, the state has an obligation to enact legislation to strictly regulate or restrict the ICT industry in terms of export activities due to human rights risks. On the other hand, there is a question of whether the far-reaching regulatory role of the state would be effective and not excessive in jeopardizing the industry's innovation and commercial objectives. An alternative solution would be the governance of surveillance technology exports largely observed on the basis of binding or non-binding codes of conduct originating from the industry itself and developed in compliance with international standards. Such norms will be ideally a result of cooperation among government institutions, private sector companies, and other relevant stakeholders.

Finally, to link both developments and strengthen their synergies, approving processes for the granting of export licenses could depend on a company's evidence of how it has rigorously implemented recommendations under the OECD instruments and the UN Guiding Principles. That precondition would be an enormous incentive for exporting ICT companies to fulfil their responsibilities to respect human rights instead of the continuing commercialization of censorship and surveillance technologies facilitating systematic human rights violations. Therefore, to make it more difficult for authoritarian states to acquire such technologies, stringent restrictions are not a panacea. A balanced triangular relationship is preferable. An export licensing regime for sensitive technologies needs to be complemented by standard setting focused on due diligence in the ICT sector to achieve the right mix of hard-law and soft-law measures.

[93] Bauer and Bromley (2019).

[94] OECD (2020a, b), pp. 5–6.

## References

Amnesty International (2020) EU companies selling surveillance tools to China's human rights abusers. https://www.amnesty.org/en/latest/news/2020/09/eu-surveillance-sales-china-human-rights-abusers/. Accessed 22 Apr 2021

Anstis S, Barnett S, Deibert R, Gill L, Penney J, Reid RJ, Senft A (2020) Submission to the Government of Canada on the renewal of the responsible business conduct strategy. Citizen Lab

Aryobsei M, Scherb M (2020) Germany takes a step closer to mandatory human rights supply chain due diligence, Lexology

Asher-Schapiro A (2021) Exclusive: Half London councils found using Chinese surveillance tech linked to Uighur abuses. Reuters. https://www.reuters.com/article/us-britain-tech-china-idUSKBN2AI0QJ. Accessed 16 Feb 2021

Bauer S, Bromley M (2019) Detecting, investigating and prosecuting export control. SIPRI. https://www.sipri.org/sites/default/files/201912/1912_sipri_report_prosecuting_export_control_violations_0.pdf. Accessed 10 Feb 2021

Bohnenberger F (2017) The proliferation of cyber-surveillance technologies: challenges and prospects. Strat Trade Rev 3(4):81–102

Bratus S, Capelis DJ, Locasto M, Shubina A (2014) Why Wassenaar arrangement's definitions of intrusion software and controlled items put security research and defense at risk – and how to fix it. https://www.cs.dartmouth.edu/~sergey/wassenaar/wassenaar-public-comment.pdf. Accessed 25 Jan 2021

Bromley M, Steenhoek KS, Halink S, Wijkstra E (2016) ICT surveillance systems: trade policy and the application of human security concerns. Strat Trade Rev 2(2):37–52

Bundesverband der Deutschen Industrie (2016) EC dual-use: review of the EC dual-use regulation. https://bdi.eu/media/topics/global_issues/downloads/201601_FINAL_BDI-Assessment_Reform_EC_Dual-Use.pdf. Accessed 13 Jan 2021

Caponetti L (2016) Mass surveillance technology: trading Trojan Horse? Strat Trade Rev 2(2): 53–71

Charatsis C (2017) Dual-use research and trade controls: opportunities and controversies. Strat Trade Rev 4(4):56–72

Cohn C, York JC (2011) "Know Your Customer" standards for sales of surveillance equipment. Electric Frontiers Foundations

Council of Europe, Committee on Legal Affairs and Human Rights (2015) Mass surveillance, Report. Doc. 13734

Council of the EU (2015a) Action plan on Human Rights and Democracy (2015–2019). JOIN (2015) 16 final

Council of the EU (2015b) Council conclusion on the action plan on Human Rights and Democracy 2015–2019. 10897/15

Council of the EU (2018) Paper for discussion – for adaption of an improved EU Export Control Regulation 428/2009 and for Cyber-Surveillance Controls Promoting Human Rights and International Humanitarian Law Globally. WK 5755/2018 INIT

Council of the EU (2020) Council Conclusions on Human Rights and Decent Work in Global Supply Chains. 13512/20

Council Regulation (EC) No 428/2009 setting up a Community regime for the control of exports, transfer, brokering and transit of dual-use items

DIGITAL EUROPE (2018) Updated DIGITAL EUROPE comments on proposal for recast of export control regulation. https://www.digitaleurope.org/resources/updated-digitaleurope-comments-on-proposal-for-recast-of-export-control-regulation/. Accessed 5 Feb 2021

Ding J (2020) Balancing standards: U.S. and Chinese strategies for developing technical standards in AI. National Bureau of Asian Research

Dullien T, Iozzo, V, Tam M (2016) Surveillance, software, security, and export controls. Reflections and recommendations for the Wassenaar Arrangement Licensing and Enforcement

Officers Meeting. https://tac.bis.doc.gov/index.php/documents/pdfs/299-surveillance-software-security-and-export-controls-mara-tam/file. Accessed 14 Jan 2021
Ecorys and SIPRI (2015) Final report: data and information collection for EU dual-use export control policy review. https://www.sipri.org/publications/2015/other-publications/final-report-eu-dualuse-review. Accessed 16 Jan 2021
European Commission (2014a) Delegated Regulation (EU) No 1382/2014 of 22 October 2014
European Commission (2014b) ICT Sector Guide on Implementing the UN Guiding Principles on Business and Human Rights
European Commission (2016) Proposal for a regulation of the European Parliament and of the Council Setting up a Union Regime for the Control of Exports, Transfer, Brokering, Technical Assistance and Transit of Dual-Use Items (recast). COM(2016) 616 final
European Commission (2020) Joint communication: a new EU-US agenda for global change, Brussels, Joint Communication of the European Commission and High Representative of the Union for Foreign Affairs and Security Policy. JOIN(2020) 22 final
European Parliament (2015) Human rights and technology: the impact of intrusion and surveillance systems on human rights in third countries (2014/2232(INI))
European Parliament (2016) Resolution on the European Defence Union (2016/2052(INI))
European Parliament (2021) Resolution of 10 March 2021 with recommendations to the Commission on corporate due diligence and corporate accountability (2020/2129(INL))
European Parliament, Directorate-General for External Policies, Policy Department (2012) After the Arab Spring: new paths for Human Rights and the Internet in European Foreign Policy
Ezell S, Foote C (2019) How stringent export controls on emerging technologies would harm the U.S. Economy, Information Technology & Foundation. https://itif.org/publications/2019/05/20/how-stringent-export-controls-emerging-technologies-would-harm-us-economy. Accessed 15 Feb 2021
Feldstein S (2019) The global expansion of AI surveillance. Carnegie Endowment. https://carnegieendowment.org/files/WP-Feldstein-AISurveillance_final1.pdf. Accessed 20 Aug 2021
FIDH - International Federation for Human Rights (2014) Surveillance technologies "Made in Europe": regulation needed to prevent human rights abuses. https://www.fidh.org/en/issues/globalisation-human-rights/business-and-human-rights/16563-surveillance-technologies-made-in-europe-regulation-needed-to-prevent. Accessed 3 Feb 2021
Fox B (2020) New human rights laws in 2021, promises EU justice chief. EURACTIV
Gregorová M (2020) The European Parliament's expectations for more effective controls on cybersurveillance technologies. 2020 Export Control Forum. https://trade.ec.europa.eu/doclib/docs/2020/december/tradoc_159190.pdf. Accessed 5 Jan 2021
Grigsby A (2018) The United Nations doubles its workload on cyber norms, and not everyone is pleased. Council on Foreign Relations. https://www.cfr.org/blog/united-nations-doubles-its-workload-cyber-norms-and-not-everyone-pleased. Accessed 11 Feb 2021
Human Rights Committee (2004) General Comment No. 31: Nature of the Legal Obligation Imposed on States Parties to the Covenant. UN DOC CCPR/C/21/Rev.1/Add. 13
Human Rights Committee (2011) General Comment No. 34 on the freedoms of opinion and expression. UN DOC CCPR/C/GC/34
Human Rights Committee (2017) Concluding observations on the Sixth Periodic Report of Italy. UN DOC CCPR/C/ITA/CO/6
Human Rights Council (2011a) Report of the Special Representative of the Secretary General on the issue of human rights and transnational corporations and other business enterprises. UN DOC A/HRC/17/31
Human Rights Council (2011b) Report of the Office of the United Nations High Commissioner for Human Rights on the seminar on experiences of archives as a means to guarantee the right to the truth. UN DOC A/HRC/17/21
Human Rights Council (2015) Report of the Special Rapporteur on the promotion and protection of the right to freedom of opinion and expression. UN DOC A/HRC/29/32

Human Rights Council (2018) Report of the Special Rapporteur on the promotion and protection of the right to freedom of opinion and expression. UN DOC A/HRC/38/35

Human Rights Council (2019) Surveillance and human rights: report of the Special Rapporteur on the promotion and protection of the right to freedom of opinion and expression. A/HRC/41/35

Kanetake M (2019) The EU's dual-use export control and human rights risks: the case of cyber surveillance technology. Europe World: Law Rev 3(1):1–16

Khalil L (2020) Digital authoritarianism, China and covid. Lowy Institute. https://www.lowyinstitute.org/publications/digital-authoritarianism-china-and-covid. Accessed 2 Apr 2021

Krahulcova L (2017) The European Parliament is fighting to strengthen the rules for surveillance trade. Access Now. https://www.accessnow.org/european-parliament-fighting-strengthen-rules-surveillance-trade/. Accessed 16 Jan 2021

Lipovský M (2016) Digital aspects of the right to privacy - surveillance issues. Czech Yearb Public Private Int Law 7:253–265

Maurer T (2016) Internet freedom and export controls. Carnegie Endowment. https://carnegieendowment.org/2016/03/03/internet-freedom-and-export-controls-pub-62961. Accessed 24 Jan 2021

Newman A, Bach D (2014) The European Union as Hardening Agent: soft law and the diffusion of global financial regulation. J Eur Public Policy 21(3):430–452

OECD (2016) Due diligence guidance for responsible supply chains of minerals. OECD, Paris

OECD (2020a) 2019 Annual Report on the OECD guidelines for multinational (note by the Secretary-General). C(2020)120

OECD (2020b) Digitalisation and responsible business conduct: stocktaking of policies and initiatives

Organization for Security and Co-operation in Europe (2017) Joint declaration on freedom of expression and "Fake News, Disinformation and Propaganda". https://www.osce.org/fom/302796. Accessed 16 Jan 2021

Polyakova A, Meserole C (2019) Exporting digital authoritarianism: the Russian and Chinese models. Brookings Policy Brief. https://www.brookings.edu/research/exporting-digital-authoritarianism/. Accessed 10 Mar 2021

Privacy International (2013) OECD Complaint: Trovicor exporting surveillance technology to Bahrain

Privacy International (2014) Six things we know from the latest FinFisher documents. https://privacyinternational.org/blog/1522/six-things-we-know-latest-finfisher-documents. Accessed 15 Apr 2021

Pyetranker I (2015) An umbrella in a Hurricane: cyber technology and the December 2013 amendment to the Wassenaar Arrangement. Nw J Technol Intellect Prop 13(2):153–180

Reiser D, Hindin D (2014) Caught by surprise: Israel's export control regime and cyber technologies. World ECR. https://www.worldecr.com/archive/caught-by-surprise-israels-export-control-regime-and-cyber-technologies/. Accessed 5 Apr 2021

Ruggie JG, Nelson T (2015) Human rights and the OECD guidelines for multinational enterprises: normative innovations and implementation challenges. Brown J World Aff 22(1):99–128

Ruohonen J, Kimppa K (2019) Updating the Wassenaar debate once again: surveillance, intrusion software, and ambiguity. J Inf Technol Polit 16(2):1–26

Shabhaz A (2018) Freedom on the Net 2018: the rise of digital authoritarianism. Freedom House. https://freedomhouse.org/sites/default/files/2020-02/10192018_FOTN_2018_Final_Booklet.pdf. Accessed 22 Aug 2021

Sherman J, Morgus R (2018) Authoritarians are exporting surveillance tech, and with it their vision for the Internet. Council on Foreign Relations, BlogPost. https://www.cfr.org/blog/authoritarians-are-exporting-surveillance-tech-and-it-their-vision-internet. Accessed 2 Apr 2021

Society for Threatened Peoples (2020) Complaint submitted to National Contact Point of Switzerland

Svoboda O (2018) The OECD guidelines for multinational enterprises and the increasing relevance of the system of National Contact Points. In: Šturma P, Mozetic VA (eds) Business and human rights. rw&w Science & New Media, Waldkirchen, p 52–63
Svoboda O (2020) Investors' responsibilities beyond investment treaties: a workaround to balance the investment protection regime. Czech Yearb Public Private Int Law 11:462–474
Svoboda O (2021) Coming of age: the system of OECD National Contact Points for responsible business conduct in its twenty years. In: Bungenberg M, Krajewski M, Tams CJ, Terhechte JP, Ziegler AR (eds) European yearbook of international economic law 2020. Springer, Heidelberg, pp 1–24
TechUK (2014) Assessing cyber security export risks. https://www.computerweekly.com/news/2240235381/TechUK-publishes-guidelines-for-UK-cyber-security-exports. Accessed 17 Mar 2021
Thomsen R, Thomsen P (2015) Export controls on intrusion and surveillance items: noble sentiments meet the law of unintended consequences. J Internet Law, September 2015, pp 22–35
Thomson I (2016) Wassenaar weapons pact talks collapse leaving software exploit exports in limbo. The Register. https://www.theregister.com/2016/12/21/wassenar_negotiations_fail/. Accessed 14 Jan 2021
UK National Contact Point (2013) Initial assessment: Privacy International complaint to UK NCP about Gamma International UK Ltd
UK National Contact Point (2014) Privacy International & Gamma International UK Ltd.: final statement after examination of complaint
UK National Contact Point (2016) Follow-up statement: Privacy International complaint to UK NCP about Gamma International UK Ltd
UN Internet Governance Forum (2014) The Global Multistakeholder Forum for Dialogue on Internet Governance Issues
US Department of Commerce (2021) The Export Administration Regulations (EAR). https://www.bis.doc.gov/index.php/all-articles/25-compliance-a-training/export-administration-regulations-training/1602-export-control-basics. Accessed 16 Apr 2021
US Department of State (2020a) Guidance on implementing the "UN Guiding Principles" for transactions linked to foreign government end-users for products or services with surveillance capabilities
US Department of State (2020b) Xinjiang supply chain business advisory: risks and considerations for businesses with supply chain exposure to entities engaged in forced labor and other human rights abuses in Xinjiang
US House of Representatives, Permanent Select Committee on Intelligence (2019) Committee hearing on "China's Digital Authoritarianism: Surveillance, Influence, and Political Control". https://www.congress.gov/event/116th-congress/house-event/109462. Accessed 28 Aug 2021
Valentino-DeVries J, Angwin J, Stecklow S (2011) Document Trove exposes surveillance methods. The Wall Street Journal. https://www.wsj.com/articles/SB10001424052970203611404577044192607407780. Accessed 11 Mar 2021
Wagner B (2012) Exporting censorship and surveillance technology. Humanist Institute for Co-operation with Developing Countries

**Ondřej Svoboda** serves as a deputy head of the Political and Economic Section of the Embassy of the Czech Republic in Tokyo. Before his posting, he was a deputy head of the Unit of International Law of the Ministry of Industry and Trade of the Czech Republic, where he provided legal expertise in investment and trade law issues and led the Czech delegation at the OECD Investment Committee and the UNCITRAL Working Group III on the reform of ISDS. Furthermore, he acted as a deputy head of the Secretariat of the Czech National Contact Point for the OECD Guidelines for Multinational Enterprises and lectured public international law and international economic law at the Faculty of Law of the Charles University in Prague, where he also received his Ph.D. degree in 2020. Svoboda regularly publishes various aspects of international economic law and the EU Common Commercial Policy.

[illegible]
Stuart [illegible] (2020) [illegible]
Stephens T (2020) [illegible]
[illegible]
[illegible]
[illegible]
Thornton J (2019) [illegible]
[illegible]
[illegible]
UN [illegible]
[illegible]
[illegible]
Wouters J [illegible]
[illegible]
Wagner [illegible]
[illegible]

[illegible]

# Part IV
# Book Reviews

# Anil Yilmaz Vastardis, The Nationality of Corporate Investors Under International Investment Law

## Bloomsbury London, 2020, ISBN: 978-1-50-993360-0

**Stelios Andreadakis**

**Abstract** The issue of investor nationality has been one of the most problematic issues in investment law since its inception. Indeed, the drafters of the ICSID Convention were well aware of this and, although they finalised a Convention that does not include a definition of investment, they did include a detailed definition of 'national of a Contracting State' in Article 25(2). The nationality of the investor is in fact a crucial factor for the definition of the rules applicable to the protection of the foreign investment, as well as for the identification of the jurisdiction of any arbitral tribunal called to settle a dispute between an investor and the state hosting the investment. Furthermore, questions about investor nationality underlie problems of treaty and forum shopping in the system of investment law. For these reasons, the Nationality of Corporate Investors under International Investment Law is a timely contribution to the study of this problem.

The issue of investor nationality has been one of the most problematic issues in investment law since its inception.[1] Indeed, the drafters of the ICSID Convention were well aware of this and, although they finalised a Convention that does not include a definition of investment, they did include a detailed definition of 'national of a Contracting State' in Article 25(2). The nationality of the investor is in fact a crucial factor for the definition of the rules applicable to the protection of the foreign investment, as well as for the identification of the jurisdiction of any arbitral tribunal called to settle a dispute between an investor and the state hosting the investment.[2]

[1] See generally Romanetti (2012), pp. 231–254; Nelson (2009), pp. 451–474; Burgstaller (2006), pp. 857–881; Sinclair (2004), pp. 191–195.

[2] De Stefano (2021), pp. 59–80; García Olmedo (2017), pp. 695–727; Schokkaert and Heckscher (2009), pp. 699–722; Schreuer (2009), pp. 521–527.

S. Andreadakis (✉)
Brunel Law School, College of Business, Arts and Social Sciences, Brunel, University London, London, UK
e-mail: stelios.andreadakis@brunel.ac.uk



S. Hindelang, A. Moberg (eds.), *YSEC Yearbook of Socio-Economic Constitutions 2021*, YSEC Yearbook of Socio-Economic Constitutions (2022) 2021: 257–260,
https://doi.org/10.1007/16495_2022_41, Published online: 8 April 2022

Furthermore, questions about investor nationality underlie problems of treaty and forum shopping in the system of investment law.[3] Consequently, the matter, although it has been part of the discussions on the very formation of contemporary investment law, remains quite current and problematic.

For these reasons, *The Nationality of Corporate Investors under International Investment Law* is to be welcomed as a timely contribution to the study of the problem of investor nationality. The book analyses the problem both from the perspective of the ICSID Convention as well as the body of bilateral investment treaties and investment chapters in trade agreements. More in detail, Anil Yilmaz Vastardis' work is divided into three parts. Part I concerns the fundamental elements of corporate nationality in international investment law. This section particularly considers the problems relating to the conditions of access to the protection granted by investment treaties, the definition of nationality (both as regards that of individuals and that of objects), and the issue of corporate personality. Part I of the book is particularly interesting in its analysis of the distinguishing features of corporations for purposes of nationality. The author describes in detail, and with particular effectiveness, the nature of corporations as a legal fiction that assigns a legal personality to an intangible entity, then connected to a state through the *lex societatis*. This analysis is preparatory to the consideration of corporations in the global economy. The author particularly does not focus only on the definition of multinational enterprise, already the subject of numerous scholarly contributions, but also addresses in detail the definitions and nature of shell corporations and the role played by regulatory havens in the characterisation of corporations.

The second part of the book is dedicated to the understanding of the concept of corporate nationality. Yilmaz Vastardis proposes two fundamental case studies: one, in Chapter 4, aimed at analysing corporate nationality in the context of diplomatic protection and war-time sanctions; the other, in Chapter 5, which defines the nationality of corporate investors under the ICSID Convention and investment treaties. Chapter 4 lays the foundations of the analysis on the principles of diplomatic protection and addresses the highly interesting topic of the control criterion for domestic wartime sanctions to better identify the elements of the nationality of corporations in parallel - or, more appropriately, in contrast - with that of individuals. Chapter 5 gathers the lessons of the previous chapter to accompany the reader in the analysis of the afore-mentioned Article 25(2) of the ICSID Convention. The criticism presented by the author is particularly interesting: Article 25(2) is in fact one of the few provisions of the ICSID Convention that have an objective content, easily applicable to concrete cases, and not a harbinger of possible interpretative disputes. However, the fact that the application in arbitral practice of Article 25(2) of the ICSID Convention is rare, sporadic, and limited to a few cases in which the host state has raised the question directly has traditionally been underestimated in the scholarship. Indeed, treaty shopping has routinely been considered not as an abuse of the

[3] Böhme (2021), pp. 511–532; Dumberry (2017), pp. 1–16; Magnarelli (2016), pp. 76–87; Lee (2015), pp. 355–379.

system, but rather as one of the many advantages the system of investment law brings to the protection of foreign investors; as such, the scholarship lacked an actual critique of Article 25(2) of the ICSID Convention, and *The Nationality of Corporate Investors under International Investment Law* fills this significant gap. The key to the chapter, and the most significant contribution of this section of the book to the overall field, is the analysis of how investment treaties link corporate investors to states, which unveils the very nature of treaty shopping as simply a structural aspect of investment law;[4] this aspect may have been more or less intended when the foundations of the system of investment law were being laid, but it is certainly welcomed by investors nonetheless.

The most compelling section of Yilmaz Vastardis' book, however, is its Part III, fittingly named 'Problems and Solutions'. The author here proposes a firm critique of how the concept of nationality is traditionally used in the investment treaty system, detailing both the methodological flaws that affect the scholarship and the arbitral practice, as well as the erosion of the very concept of 'nationality'.[5] This erosion lies not only at the basis of treaty and forum shopping, but also of the progressive de facto multilateralisation of international investment law, which has made the tradition of signing bilateral treaties with reciprocal obligations almost a vacuous one, and created a sort of *à la carte* international law for the benefit of foreign investors. In the end, as the author underscores in Chapter 7, the solution to the abuses of investors' rights is 'as difficult as the problem itself', and the sole way forward seems to be the restoration of conceptual and methodological rigor in the process of analysing the actual nationality of corporate investors.

*The Nationality of Corporate Investors under International Investment Law* is a book that places itself in the critical tradition that addresses and explains the backlash against international investment law. It is not, however, a book on how investment law should be reformed, nor does it present a fascinating but utopian revolutionary solution to a concrete problem. Quite the contrary: Anil Yilmaz Vastardis concedes in her introduction that the implant of the monograph is a case against the expansionist approach to the personal scope of the protection granted by international investment law, and the reader is thus made aware of her standpoint.[6] The analysis, however, is particularly rigorous and solidly based on a positivist outlook on the rules and principles of international investment law and arbitration. Because of this, this monograph is not only a welcome contribution to the study of one of the most underestimated (but nevertheless fundamental) problems of international investment law, but also a reference point for scholars and practitioners in need of understanding the various nuances of the problem of nationality of corporate investors in a system that seems to aim at sacrificing the very concept of nationality on the altar of global economy.

[4] Yilmaz Vastardis (2020), pp. 165–173.

[5] Ibid., pp. 199–206.

[6] Ibid., pp. 4–11.

## References

Böhme B (2021) Recent efforts to curb investment treaty shopping: how effective are they? J Int Arbitr 38(4):511–532

Burgstaller M (2006) Nationality of corporate investors and international claims against the investor's own state. J World Invest Trade 7(6):857–881

De Stefano C (2021) The nationality of natural and juridical persons in international investment law. In: Gómez KF (ed) Private actors in international investment law. Springer, Heidelberg, pp 59–80

Dumberry P (2017) Shopping for a better deal: the use of MFN clauses to get 'better' fair and equitable treatment protection. Arbitr Int 33(1):1–16

García Olmedo J (2017) Claims by dual nationals under investment treaties: are investors entitled to sue their own states? J Int Disp Settlement 8(4):695–727

Lee J (2015) Resolving concerns of treaty shopping in international investment arbitration. J Int Disp Settlement 6(2):355–379

Magnarelli M (2016) The unresolved conundrum of contract-based and treaty-based claims - an extra element of contention: privity of contract and forum selection clauses in investment contracts. Eur Invest Law Arbitr Rev 1:76–87

Nelson TG (2009) Passport, s'il vous plaît? Investment treaty protection and the individual investor's citizenship. Suffolk Transnatl Law Rev 32(2):451–474

Romanetti A (2012) Defining investors: who is eligible to claim? J Int Arbitr 29(3):231–254

Schokkaert J, Heckscher Y (2009) Protected investors nationality. J World Invest Trade 10(5): 699–722

Schreuer C (2009) Nationality of investors: legitimate restrictions vs. business interests. ICSID Rev Foreign Invest Law J 24(2):521–527

Sinclair A (2004) Nationality of individual investors in ICSID arbitration. Int Arbitr Law Rev 7(6): 191–195

Yilmaz Vastardis A (2020) The nationality of corporate investors under international investment law. Bloomsbury, London, pp 165–173

# Nicolás M. Perrone, Investment Treaties and the Legal Imagination: How Foreign Investors Play by Their Own Rules

## Oxford University Press, 2021. ISBN: 978-0-19-886214-7

**Fiammetta Borgia**

**Abstract** This short essay reviews Nicolas M. Perrone's *Investment Treaties and the Legal Imagination: How Foreign Investors Play by Their Own Rules* and reflects on how this book contributes to the debate on the origins of international investment law and the role of investors in shaping such an unbalanced international legal regime.

"Imagination! who can sing thy force? Or who describe the swiftness of thy course?"[1] With these words, Phillis Wheatley sang the praises of imagination as the instrument for humans to ascend to godlike powers, and create. Philosophers, poets, playwrights, and artists use their imagination to give life to worlds unknown; lawyers, lawmakers, and scholars, in turn, use imagination to give life to world-views. James Boyd White in 1973 encouraged students and scholars to look at how the law and its language creates culture and gives life to conceptions of law and society, and to discuss the implications of realizing such conceptions;[2] more recently, Charles Taylor construed the notion of the "social imaginary" to identify ways to conceive society as a whole.[3] Ultimately, the term "imagination" tickles utopias, novelties, unrealized and perhaps unattainable ideas of society, and, in some cases, positive revolutions. Imagination, however, is a double-edged sword, and the work of Nicolás Perrone offers a rather valid (and in some ways worrying) example of this.

Despite its rather suggestive title, Nicolás Perrone's *Investment Treaties and the Legal Imagination* is a remarkably rigorous book solidly grounded in reality. The

---

[1] Wheatley (1773), pp. 65–68.

[2] Boyd White (1973).

[3] Taylor (2004).

---

F. Borgia (✉)
University of Rome "Tor Vergata", Rome, Italy
e-mail: fiammetta.borgia@uniroma2.it

 
S. Hindelang, A. Moberg (eds.), *YSEC Yearbook of Socio-Economic Constitutions 2021*, YSEC Yearbook of Socio-Economic Constitutions (2022) 2021: 261–264,
https://doi.org/10.1007/16495_2022_42, Published online: 8 April 2022

main argument of the volume revolves around the activities of entrepreneurs in the 1950s and 1960s (referred to as "norm entrepreneurs"), who managed to devise, promote and—in time, and with the cooperation of Western states and institution—impose a legal imagination about foreign investment relations between companies and host states. Such legal imagination is the by-product of the global perspective adopted by the promoters of what is now the international investment regime,[4] characterized by a plurality of rather similar bilateral treaties and widely shared dispute settlement practices. In his book, Perrone lays the foundations of his narrative by introducing the main characteristics of the three pillars of the international investment regime—namely investors' rights, investment treaties, and the system of dispute settlement—and presenting the claim that contemporary international investment law has been shaped by the imagination of the norm entrepreneurs. He then moves on to develop an analytical framework suitable to address the question of how investors' rights can define their role in relations with host states and local communities, and underscore the significance of investment arbitration in the establishment and the implications of such rights. The approach at the core of Perrone's framework is transnational and socio-legal, since "[f]oreign investment relations involve domestic and international law, and both public and private law, as much as issues that have remained silenced or actors who have been made invisible."[5] Perhaps one of the more remarkable contributions of *Investment Treaties and the Legal Imagination* is its Chapter 2, which addresses the norm entrepreneurs in the 1950s and 1960s. The chapter effectively underscores how the rules of global economy are in fact the result of the efforts of business leaders, bankers, and lawyers in the aftermath of World War II, the nationalizations of the Anglo-Iranian Oil Company and the Suez Canal, and the growing rate of state interventions in economic matters worldwide. The promotion and protection of foreign investment, fittingly embedded in the very name of virtually every bilateral investment treaty since, was thus a matter of the utmost urgency in the process of implementing a worldview, or imagination, based on free enterprise, not chained to the rules of nationality (or, for that matter, sovereignty). Here is where the term "imagination" comes to blossom. Perrone highlights how the norm entrepreneurs did not look at existing institutions or frameworks to implement their worldview, but rather imagined institutions and legal standards, rights, duties, internationalized contracts, and a new iteration of international arbitration. What the book moves on to expose in Chapter 3 is a sort of "war of imaginations": the 1970s were a time in which the legal imagination of the norm entrepreneurs had to face the demands of the countries of the Global South, looking at changing the rules of international towards the enhancement of economic sovereignty.[6] The war of imaginations, however, was put to an end in the 1990s. After a decade in which few countries had signed investment

[4]Bonnitcha et al. (2017), pp. 7 and 59–65.

[5]Perrone (2021), p. 15.

[6]Ibid. at 92. See among others Pahuja and Saunders (2019), pp. 141–174; and Flory (1990), pp. 606–613; Noudehou (1990), p. 31038.

treaties and the investment arbitral case-law was substantially insignificant, the World Bank and UNCTAD acted as the motor of a global movement to promote investment treaties and investment arbitration. The number of bilateral investment treaties increased dramatically, and gradually so did the case load of the ICSID. It was in the 1990s, moreover, that a select few practitioners gained, by means of their appointments to high profile investment arbitral tribunals, the status of *bona fide* pioneers of a new field of international law, bringing to fruition the imagination of the norm entrepreneurs of the 1950s and the 1960s.

Chapter 5, addressing the practical implications of investment arbitration as the *de facto* sole method for the settlement of investment dispute, highlights the crucial role of arbitrators not merely in shaping the development of investment law—aptly underscored in the scholarship—but also in implementing the legal imagination of the norm entrepreneurs. In particular, Perrone's chronological analysis exposes the consideration of questions of distribution,[7] recognition[8] and embeddedness[9] in the context of such imagination, stressing how the practice of investment arbitration effectively reflects the concept of foreign investment relations envisioned by the norm entrepreneurs.[10] This is, indeed, the reason why Perrone discards the analysis of investment awards as a suitable lens to understanding the legal imagination at the basis of the current international investment regime, noting that investment arbitration is primarily addressed as "a mechanism to enhance rights protection, as opposed to a system effecting a worldview."[11] The two final chapters stress the significance of investment arbitration in the implementation of such worldview. Chapter 6 shows how arbitrators often act as the long hand of investors in forcing sectoral regulation and commitments; Chapter 7 presents the particularly weak position of local communities in investment relations in contrast with that of investors, often partners with national elites and having in any case access to treaty protection and investment arbitration.

Perrone's findings are hardly comforting. Investment treaties and arbitration allow investors to predict the potential success of an economic venture abroad without considering (and often negatively affecting) the needs and interests of host states and especially local communities. In this context, arbitrators are key players in the implementation of the imagination of the norm entrepreneurs, as they often seem to exclude certain issues and actors. Perrone, however, is equally critical towards current discussions on investment reform. Indeed, such discussions appear to be led mainly by institutions and individuals that have contributed—to different extents, and at different levels of commitment—to the very implementation of that imagination the investment law regime is merely a by-product of. In essence, there can

[7] Ibid. at 30.

[8] Ibid. at 139.

[9] Ibid, e.g., pp. 137 and 145.

[10] Ibid., p. 8.

[11] Ibid. at 12, citing Koskenniemi (2017), pp. 343–353.

hardly be any reform if the discussion remains within the realm of the said imaginary.

As stated beforehand, *Investment Treaties and the Legal Imagination* is not a comforting read. Perrone's work casts a shadow on the possibility of reform of the investment law regime without sparking a revolution. Whilst this may be seen as a radical term indicating a rather drastic solution, one may question, as Perrone does, whether it would even be possible to actually reform a system that is the by-product of a certain imagination without replacing such imagination with another one. From that standpoint, Perrone's position seems quite clear. Even the most ambitious projects to revisit investment treaties and investment arbitration would fall short of actually changing the regime without a global rethinking of the imagination behind the regime itself. Obviously, as noted by Perrone, this rethinking is a more theoretical option than a practical one. Although scholars, organizations and groups have raised issues relating to the serious problems of the investment law regime in various *fora*, real reform projects are few, rare, and firmly rooted in the imagination of norm entrepreneurs. It can indeed be said that this imagination has reached its full realization over the years—to the point that projects for a radical rethinking of the system are often catalogued as utopias or, at best, as ideas of rather difficult realization. The lesson from *Investment Treaties and the Legal Imagination* is that ideas alone are almost irrelevant: the reform of the global economy cannot but pass through the imagination of a completely different, and new, system of relations between investors and states – much before investment regulation. The implementation of any reform is merely a second step: in the absence of a new legal imagination, any effort towards the reform of the regime would be in vain.

## References

Bonnitcha J, Poulsen L, Waibel M (2017) The political economy of the investment treaty regime. Oxford University Press, Oxford, p. 7 and 59–65

Boyd White J (1973) The legal imagination. University of Chicago Press, Chicago

Flory M (1990) La quatrième décennie pour le développement: la fin du nouvel ordre économique international? Annuaire français de droit international 36:606–613

Koskenniemi M (2017) It's not the cases, it's the system. J World Invest Trade 18:343–353

Noudehou J (1990) Le nouvel ordre economique international: un nouvel ordre de stabilisation interne ou un exemple de derivation? Revue de droit international, de sciences diplomatiques et politiques 68:31038

Pahuja S, Saunders A (2019) Rival worlds and the place of the corporation in international law. In: von Bernstorff J, Dann P (eds) The battle for international law: south-north perspectives on the decolonization era. Oxford University Press, Oxford, pp 141–174

Perrone N (2021) Investment treaties and the legal imagination: how foreign investors play by their own rules. Oxford University Press, Oxford, p 15

Taylor C (2004) Modern social imaginaries. Duke University Press, Durham

Wheatley P (1773) On imagination. In: Poems on various subjects, religious and moral. Bell, London, pp 65–68

The manufacturer's authorised representative in the EU is Springer Nature Customer Service Centre GmbH, Europaplatz 3, 69115 Heidelberg, Germany. If you have any concerns regarding our products, please contact ProductSafety@springernature.com

Printed and bound by CPI Group (UK) Ltd, Croydon, CR0 4YY
30/09/2026
02225490-0018